D1629991

PORTRAIT OF A GENIUS, BUT . . .

Books by Richard Aldington

NOVELS:
- Death of a Hero
- The Colonel's Daughter
- All Men Are Enemies
- Women Must Work
- Very Heaven
- Seven Against Reeves
- Rejected Guest
- The Romance of Casanova

SHORT STORIES:
- Roads to Glory
- Soft Answers

POETRY:
- A Dream in the Luxembourg
- Complete Poems

BIOGRAPHY:
- Voltaire
- Wellington
- Four English Portraits
- The Strange Life of Charles Waterton

ESSAYS:
- French Studies and Reviews
- Literary Studies and Reviews
- D. H. Lawrence

ANTHOLOGIES:
- Poetry of the English-Speaking World
- Fifty Romance Lyric Poems
- The Religion of Beauty

THE LIFE OF D. H. LAWRENCE, 1885 TO 1930

Portrait of a Genius, but . . .

BY RICHARD ALDINGTON

"*When a true Genius appears in the World, you may know him by this Sign, that the Dunces are all in Confederacy against him.*"

JONATHAN SWIFT

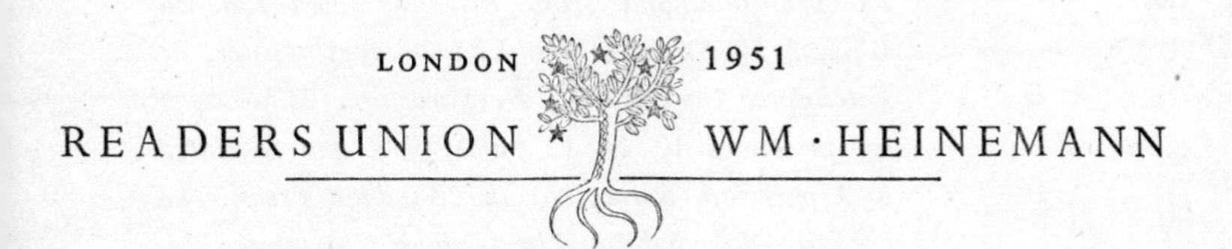

LONDON 1951

READERS UNION WM · HEINEMANN

This volume was produced in 1951 *by Readers Union for sale to its members only. Particulars of RU are obtainable from Readers Union Ltd,* 38 *William IV Street in the City of Westminster, or Letchworth Garden City, Hertfordshire. It has been set in Times* 10 *on* 12 *point type, and reprinted at Kingswood, Surrey, by the Windmill Press. The book was first published by William Heinemann Ltd.*

AUTHOR'S NOTE

USE of an odd title needs instant justification if the author is not to be suspected of affectation or some catchpenny motive or both. I call this book *Portrait Of A Genius, But . . .*, firstly because it is a portrait and not a detailed exhaustive biography, which, with all the material available, would be twice or thrice the length. Then, in going over the books and letters I noticed that somewhere or other almost everyone used the phrase: "Of course, Lawrence was a genius, but . . ." The phrase inevitably came up when people argued about him in his lifetime, usually with more emphasis on the "but" than on the "genius". Lawrence himself noticed and remembered it, for little that had reference to him escaped that intensely observant mind or faded from that almost superhuman memory. "In the early days they were always telling me I had got genius," he wrote in *Assorted Articles*, "as if to console me for not having their own incomparable advantages." Across the years one can still hear the tone of patronage; for what, after all, is it worth to be born a genius compared with having a grandfather in the D.N.B., an old school tie, or a weekly article in a weary critical journal? My title was chosen for me.

But then, what is "genius"? It is a word as out of fashion with the fastidious as with the frumps and the levellers; but why should we let them rob us of anything we want? People must have thought it meant something or they could not have been so unanimous in sticking it on him as a label, from his first critic Ford Madox Hueffer down to the yellow press guttersnipe who when he was dying called him "a sex-soaked genius". If genius is "mainly a matter of energy" then Lawrence indisputably had it, for in the mere twenty years of his manhood his experiences and his creative output were intense and continuous. He had periods of repose and change, but never of sterility. But surely by "genius" people mean much more than energy. No doubt they use the word loosely, but they mean by it someone who is born with unique perceptions, an unmistakable aptitude for some form of human excellence not mechanical or imitative. Buddha, they would say, was a religious genius; Alexander a military genius; Mozart a musical genius; Shelley a poetical genius; Edison an inventive genius. Avoiding hair-splitting and useless wrangling over terms we can all see that the popular use of the word has a meaning. D. H. Lawrence *was* a genius; but what sort of a genius? That is what this book hopes to tell, but at the outset I should say that both in living and in writing Lawrence was a genius, but . . .

CONTENTS

—

ILLUSTRATIONS

—

PART ONE

SON AND LOVER

1885–1910

1

THE mining village of Eastwood lies on the borders of two English counties, Nottinghamshire and Derbyshire, about ten miles to the north-west of the industrial town of Nottingham whose factories are served by the adjacent coal-pits, of which Eastwood's Brinsley Colliery was one. Towards the end of the 19th century the place "consisted of a drab main street and hundreds of niggardly houses . . . little grimy, brick houses with slate roofs" which taken together made up "a general effect of paltriness, smallness, meanness, fathomless ugliness, combined with a sort of chapel-going respectability." Eastwood, then, was one of the many, many haphazard communities brought recklessly into hideous reality by the Industrial Revolution, against whose squalor and degradation Ruskin had been eloquently raging through decades of futile protest and denunciation.

Yet Eastwood was not so bad as, say, Sheffield under its perpetual mushroom-shaped Vesuvius eruption of black smoke eclipsing the sun and poisoning human lungs, not so bad as the real Black Country, with its hundreds, no thousands! of square miles of coal-pits and factory chimneys and squalid streets and hundreds of thousands of pinched grey faces, resigned or resentful. Eastwood's coal-field was small and comparatively new, new enough for the miners' dwellings to be rather potential than actual slums, and small enough to permit escape to fields and farms. Some of the cottages even had wide views across open country. Neither place nor people had been quite tamed into mechanical uniformity. "There was a sense of latent wildness and unbrokenness, a weird sense of thrill and adventure in the pitch-dark Midland nights, and roaring football Saturday afternoons." Sometimes the miners went poaching in the surrounding half-wild country, and many of them every week spent on beer the "precious money" which should have gone to their families. No wonder the women bitterly hated the pubs which took away the extra five or ten shillings which would have made so much difference to their lives, and raged at the men when they came home tipsily merry. Yet who will blame the men to whom the pub meant human warmth and comradeship and conviviality and a respite from work and worry? In their way these miners and their families were religious, with strict social-moral standards and prejudices. Unconscious of the ugliness of their community, too stationary to know its comparative insignificance, they had an inflated idea of their importance in the economy of England and the scheme of things in general.

In the 1870s there came to Eastwood a coal-miner named John Arthur Lawrence and his wife, born Lydia Beardsall, who had been married on the 27th December 1875 at Sneinton Church, Nottingham. In Eastwood their children were born and reared and the parents lived out their lives.

In many ways they were a disharmonious couple. As his famous son tells us, John Arthur Lawrence belonged to the last generation of Englishmen who escaped compulsory State "education". He had never been tamed by the Board School. At the age of ten he had been sent to work in the coal-pit. He could barely sign his name and could just laboriously spell out a newspaper to his impatient wife in the evening or to himself in the early morning as he crouched before the blazing kitchen fire, toasting his breakfast bacon on a fork and catching the drips of fat on a hunk of bread. His whole life was entirely physical, made up of hard work at the coal-face, tinkering with innumerable little jobs at home, drinking and talking and sometimes going long walks with his mates. As a young man he had been a good dancer and looked "strikingly virile" with his enormously developed arm muscles, thick black hair and bushy beard. He was a "butty", which in those days meant a kind of foreman or liaison-man between the company and the other miners. At the section of the coal-face allotted to him he had "three or four men working under his direction and paid them wages from the money he received in payment for the coal hewn". Thus a butty was almost a little employer, at all events a responsible man whose earnings in good times might run as high as five pounds a week—real gold pounds. But that was in the early days of his marriage, before he had damaged his strength by drinking and had lost his chance of good places at the coal-face by offensive jeers at the overseer—an old friend who had risen above him. He was very far from being the industrialised robot, rotten with politics and journalism and radio and cinema and printed trash. He was a man who had his being centred in the coal-pit, but who loved his morning walks through the dewy fields to the pit-head, who liked and understood animals and could tell vivid stories about them. He believed that he was only part English, and that his grandfather had been a Frenchman. He worked when his mates worked, struck when they struck, without caring about the issues. For the rest, "his nature was purely sensuous", he lived out his life as fully as he could, taking the enjoyment and refusing to go sour over life's ills.

Lydia Beardsall, the girl he married, was a very different type of person both by temperament and upbringing. She believed herself to be "of a good old burgher family, famous independents, who had fought with Colonel Hutchinson, and who remained stout Congregationalists." Most families tell themselves stories of one sort or another about their illustrious origin, and so far as the influence on life goes the belief and not the fact is important. Lydia's father had been an engineer foreman at Sheerness Dockyard, and had paid for her to be educated at a small private school where later she became an assistant teacher. "She read a good deal and wrote poetry. . . . She loved ideas, and was considered very intellectual. What she liked most of all was an argument on religion or philosophy or politics with some educated man." Even when oppressed by endless housework for a husband and five children she found time to read "piles of books" from the local library. She had an unshakably good conceit of herself. "Her confidence in herself" (says Jessie Chambers, the friend of Lawrence's youth, who writes under the initials E.T.) "and her pronouncements upon people and things excited my wonder . . . she was so certain of herself and her rightness." She never used the Derbyshire dialect like her husband and the other miners and their wives, and had very little contact with her neighbours. "She was small and slight in figure," says her daughter, Ada Clarke, "with brown hair and clear blue eyes that always looked fearless and unfaltering." Her nose had been a little twisted by a childish accident, and she had small hands and feet—"beautiful hands" in the eyes of her son.

Before her meeting with Arthur Lawrence she had fallen in love with an earnest young man who wanted to be a clergyman but was trying to learn a business he hated, because his father insisted and he was afraid of his father. He was also afraid to do anything about Lydia except to talk to her and give her a copy of the Bible. Later he became a school teacher and married his landlady, but Lydia kept his Bible all her life. Four years after their separation she met Arthur Lawrence at a party in Nottingham, and each instantly had for the other all the attraction of the unfamiliar. "She was to the miner that thing of mystery and fascination, a lady" and "she thought him rather wonderful, never having met anyone like him". And very soon she married him, knowing nothing of a coal miner's ways and habits, nothing of the life conditions of a miner's wife, and apparently being deceived into thinking he was better off than he really was.

Within twelve years this ill-matched couple, in spite of constant bickering and quarrels, produced five children: George Arthur, William Ernest, Emily, David Herbert, and Ada. As these children grew up they sometimes wondered why two people apparently so unsuited to one another as their parents had ever married. The glamour of the unknown had very soon worn off. It was impossible for the illiterate miner to understand his wife's intellectual interests and for his robust hedonism to conform to her narrow pretentious idealism. After a few months of domesticity during which he became a member of the teetotal Band of Hope, the miner began to stop at a pub for a drink and a word with his mates before going home, and then for several drinks and plenty of rough friendly talk. His wife, a lifelong abstainer, condemned him bitterly, hating him for the self-indulgence and what to her was waste of money. She would wait up for him, at night, her rage seething, until on his arrival it boiled over in a torrent of biting truths which "turned him from his slightly fuddled and pleasantly apologetic mood into a brutal and coarse beast." For years these "unhappy and sordid scenes" of recrimination raged, sometimes culminating in violence, always shattering to the nerves of the young children as they lay trembling in bed. Outside their cottage in Walker Street was a great ash tree whose branches shrieked in the night gales and mingled with the angry voices of the quarrelling parents:

"Having such a great space in front of the house gave the children a feeling of night, of vastness, and of terror. This terror came in from the shrieking of the tree and the anguish of the home discord. Often he would wake up, after he had been asleep a long time, aware of thuds downstairs. Instantly he was wide awake. Then he heard the booming shouts of his father, come home nearly drunk, then the sharp replies of his mother, then the bang, bang, of his father's fist on the table, and the nasty snarling shout as the man's voice got higher. And then the whole was drowned in a piercing medley of shrieks and cries from the great, wind-swept ash-tree. The children lay silent in suspense, waiting for a lull in the wind, to hear what their father was doing. He might hit their mother again. There was a feeling of horror, a kind of bristling in the darkness, and a sense of blood. They lay with their hearts in the grip of an intense anguish."

All children over-simplify their memories of their parents, selecting what happens to impress them and forgetting all the rest. It is not possible that every night the ash tree shrieked and the parents quarrelled. Yet who that knows Lawrence can for a moment doubt the immense influence these quarrels and night terrors had on his later life? By way of extreme contrast one turns to the childhood memories of another English writer who, though in some respects so completely different from Lawrence, was nevertheless strangely akin to him both in the character of his mind and in his social views—a certain affinity and an unadmitted literary influence. In *Praeterita* Ruskin says:

"I never had heard my father's or mother's voice once raised in any question with each other; nor seen an angry, or even slightly hurt or offended, glance in the eyes of either. I had never heard a servant scolded; nor even suddenly, passionately, or in any severe manner, blamed. I had never seen a moment's trouble or disorder in any household matter; nor anything whatever done in a hurry, or undone in due time. I had no conception of such a feeling as anxiety. . . ."

Neither Ruskin nor Lawrence made an ideal husband, so evidently neither extreme is to be recommended. But Lawrence, who knew Ruskin through and through, must have read that passage and one would suppose that a man so sensitive, whose childhood had known such suffering from family discord, would have used all his influence as a man and writer to spare other children that feeling of horror, that intense anguish he records so vividly. With such an experience behind him you would suppose he would be "intensely aware" of the value of self-control, gentleness, good manners, graciousness in society and above all in intimacy. Not at all. He not only practised the raucous habits of his parents in his own childless life but furiously inculcated them upon other married people:

"If a woman's husband gets on her nerves, she should fly at him. If she thinks him too sweet and smarmy with other people, she should let him have it to his nose, straight out. She should lead him a dog's life, and never swallow her bile. With wife or husband, you should never swallow your bile. It makes you go all wrong inside. Always let fly, tooth and nail, and never repent, no matter what sort of figure you make. We have a vice of love, of softness and sweetness and smarminess and intimacy and promiscuous kindness and all that sort of thing. . . ."

So he rages on in *Fantasia of the Unconscious*, trying to justify to himself if not to others the crudities and violences he really was ashamed of. In his own childhood and when he re-lived it in his writing Lawrence felt very differently, and it would be easy enough to find passages from other parts of his work which completely contradict that snarling paragraph from *Fantasia*. But then, as we shall have only too many occasions to notice, consistency was impossible to him, just as it was to Ruskin. And after all consistency is rather a virtue of little critics than of great creators. But this habit of "always letting fly" which Lawrence praises was very much condemned by him in his father when Arthur Lawrence "let fly" at his superiors in the mine, and consequently was given less and less profitable "stalls" with smaller and smaller earnings, while to console himself he spent more and more money on beer. Forgetting his praise of the virtue of "letting fly" Lawrence thus denounced his father:

"He was usually rather rude to his little immediate bosses at the pit. He practically never had a good stall, all the time he was a butty, because he was always saying tiresome and foolish things about the men just above him in control at the mine. He offended them all, almost on purpose, so how could he expect them to favour him? Yet he grumbled when they didn't."

The cap woven for the father in after life almost exactly fitted the son.

The feeling of the mother and children in the Lawrence household was of bitter poverty, and nobody would deny that they were pinched especially when the father drank away money and left them but twenty-five shillings a week to live on. Yet these things are relative, and from the point of view of a war-wrecked, half-starved England they do not seem to have been so badly off. The different cottages in which they lived were certainly small and hideously ugly, but then most modern dwellings are either that or almost more awful tenements. The house where Lawrence was born was situated in Victoria Street, and a recent photograph shows that it had a shop window from which in her early married life his mother sold "lace caps and aprons and linen". Certainly the house was small and ugly, but does not even now justify the rhetorical phrase in his sister's book about "the rotting roof of the miner's home". Another house, where Lawrence spent the years from two to seven, was larger, with a garden, the end house of a row called The Breach. When he was seven they moved again to one of a row of six bay-windowed houses which had just been built in Walker Street, from which there was a wide view across country to High Park woods.

Clearly the Lawrence children in their childhood never thought of their home as mean and did not suffer always from the discord of their parents. "Home was home, and they loved it with a passion of love, whatever the suffering had been." They thought the Walker Street cottage "nice" and the kitchen "homelike". It had an arm-chair for the father, a rocking-chair for the mother, a sofa with "pretty red chintz" and cushions to match, a dresser, a book-case "with rows of books" and some "quite decorative oleographs". The parlour was furnished with "mahogany and horse-hair furniture and oleographs heavily framed in gilt", and of course a family portrait over the mantelpiece. It was thus similar to thousands of other respectable working-class homes, but the Lawrence children felt there was something about the house which "made it different from those of the neighbours". From the description it is a little hard to guess where the difference lay. Perhaps it was not so much the "absence of anything cheap and tawdry" but the existence of something quite impalpable, a psychological environment which was too familiar to be noticed by the inmates but instantly apparent to a sensitive visitor. Jessie Chambers says the Lawrence household had "a curious atmosphere" such as she had never known before. There was "a tightness in the air, as if something unusual might happen at any minute" which was exciting, yet made her feel "a little sick". This peculiar tension was "a constant quality", something felt always and "immediately on entering the house". The

Lawrence children felt that they were "very select", indeed all the children in their street did. They had a strong sense of importance and superiority, even that they were unique, and an equally strong wish to impress this on others.

In later life Lawrence stressed the dreadful ugliness of his childhood's surroundings and liked to harrow the feelings of his friends with tales of their grinding poverty. One can perhaps reconcile this discrepancy by the fact that the child knew nothing else and the grown man had seen the world. Yet even the details about the money of the household which have been accidentally preserved do not suggest destitution or squalor. Comparison with contemporary inflated paper currency and famine prices would be misleading; we must remember that these wages were paid in gold during a period when retail prices of necessities were extremely low.

As a schoolboy Lawrence was sent every week to collect the money due to his father and fellow workers. On one occasion we here that this amounted to seventeen pounds, eleven shillings and sevenpence with sixteen shillings and sixpence stoppages—that is nearly seventeen pounds to be shared among five men, with Arthur Lawrence presumably taking rather more than the others. On another occasion, when Lawrence was growing up and himself earning a wage, the share-out was from a smaller sum, but we hear that the butty got more than the "daymen". The miners received all the coal they burned at a very low cost, but the rent of the cottage was five shillings a week plus rates.

It was the custom for all women to be absent during the weekly share-out, but of course Lydia Lawrence could always find out what the earnings were from her son. The miner had fixed a sort of scale, whereby if he earned forty shillings he took ten shillings for himself, and so on down to sixteen shillings when he took only sixpence. Ada Lawrence does not remember her father giving her mother more than thirty-five shillings for a week's expenses. From total earnings of ten pounds eleven shillings by five men she was left with "only a measley twenty-five shillings", a decline due probably to those "tiresome and foolish things" her husband would say to his "little bosses".

The wage-earner suffered a good many mine accidents, for he was "rather a heedless man, careless of danger". When the family knew that he was not in great pain and would recover, they rather enjoyed these quiet periods, which seem to have been less poverty-stricken than when the miner was at work. They received fourteen shillings a week from the pit, ten shillings from the sick club, five shillings from the disability fund, and five to seven shillings from the other butties. This makes thirty-four to thirty-six shillings a week, and as there was no man to feed and the hospital was presumably free, they were obviously better off when he was hurt than when he was working! No wonder the children secretly rather looked forward to such accidents, and that while the miner was in hospital "the family was extraordinarily happy and peaceful". Illness, it seems, was not so highly compensated as accidents. Then, with the man in bed at home, they received only seventeen shillings plus an unspecified "portion of the stall's profits". But the neighbours helped with the housework, gave the children meals, "made broths and gave eggs and such invalid's trifles". But even at the maximum these payments were quite inadequate, and it is easy enough to understand why Lawrence even in the days of his fame still felt bitter at "the terrible indignity of such poverty".

There was no money to spend on amusements, and they had to create their own happiness. Such gifts as the children received were pathetically meagre—"a couple of postcards" for one of the girls, a fret-saw or "a bit of pretty wood" for one of the elder boys, and for Lawrence "a small tube of paints or some thick paper". At Christmas time they could not afford a tree, but only a branch of berried holly decorated with "treasures" saved over from year to year, which included "a winged angel and glistening balls". On Christmas Day they always had a pork pie for breakfast and a duck for dinner—not much among seven. But somehow or other the mother contrived that the children's stockings "were always well-filled, with a sugar pig and mince pie at the top". Sometimes, not necessarily at Christmas, the miner would buy himself such things as a canary or a fancy walking-stick—leaving his wife to pay for them out of the housekeeping money. The only time we ever hear of his wife buying something for herself it was a dish with corn-flowers for which she paid fivepence, and some roots of pansies and crimson daisies which cost fourpence. And the spending of that ninepence was the occasion for much remorse: "I'm a wicked extravagant woman. I know I s'll come to want." The mother never hid her money worries from the children, but on the contrary always made them aware of their poverty, and "never concealed the fact that she had not enough money to clothe and feed them adequately as she wished".

Perhaps it was necessary for the children to have their poverty constantly before their eyes, but there were hidden scenes of domestic quarrelling and violence which ought not to have been told to a sensitive lad. Whether he exaggerated or even invented it out of his tortured imagination Lawrence certainly believed in the reality of a quarrel which supposedly occurred only a few weeks before he was born. He believed that his father had come home drunk, had got into an altercation with his wife, had angrily pushed her out of the house into the dark little garden, and then locking the door had fallen asleep with his head on the table. Long afterwards when Lawrence and his mother and the Chambers' were on holiday at the seaside, he "broke into a storm of abuse against his father". When he had left the room, she bent her head "with a strange smile" and said: "I know why he hates his father. It happened before he was born. One night he put me out of the house. He's bound to hate his father." She seemed to think this right and natural, and even on her deathbed "she talked about her husband. Now she hated him. She did not forgive him. She could not bear him to be in the room. And a few things, the things that had been most bitter to her, came up again so strongly that they broke from her, and she told her son."

Obviously it was from his mother that Lawrence heard other stories about his early childhood. His godfather was the Congregationalist minister, who later gave the boy lessons in French and German. One day when he had called and stayed to tea the miner returned and bitterly humiliated his wife by whining to the clergyman about how terribly hard he had to work, how much he sweated, how thirsty he got in the dust, and how much he ought to be pitied. Thus she made her son writhe with anger, shame and humiliation, as she poured out her bitterness and disappointment, making permanent in him a self-conflict bred from his passionate share in the conflict of his parents.

Such was the immediate environment, with its conflicts, stresses, passions, prejudices and compensations, into which D. H. Lawrence was born and in which he grew up. If it seems a strangely unfavourable one for an artist, a poet, a man with "genius", it at least avoided middle-class mediocrity. It may have been mean, but even its drabness was not just ordinary. Perhaps it could hardly have been worse as a training ground for character, for teaching a boy and then a youth how to live easily with outsiders, happily and affectionately with intimates. It developed passions of love and hate and envy and utter lack of reticence, but not affection and consideration for others, though naturally he was extremely affectionate and could show great tenderness. But then poetry is bred from passions, not from middle-class virtues.

Even subtler and deeper injuries seem to have been inflicted on the over-sensitive child. It was not only that he seemed to inherit or to have absorbed into his own nature the bitter conflict between his spontaneous, pleasure-loving father and the prim, self-righteous puritan woman. She was a domestic tyrant and ruled her family "by a sort of divine right of motherhood. . . it seemed like sacrilege to question her authority". She used this power, particularly with her sons and above all with David Herbert, to draw the whole love of these quick passionate children to herself, withdrawing them from their father, making them priggishly despise him as a "common" working man. As the boys grew up she thwarted their relationships with girl sweethearts. In David Herbert the feeling of mistrust, of being unsure of himself, was made lifelong; yet she imposed on him her over-bearing self-confidence, so that as he perpetually wavered in beliefs and moods and whims and projects he could not help stating each ephemeral phase in terms of vehement dogmatic assertion.

Lawrence was not a strong child. He believed that he had been ill with bronchitis when he was but two weeks old. His mother remembered that as a baby there had been a "peculiar knitting" of his brows, a "peculiar heaviness of its eyes, as if it were trying to understand something that was pain." At about four he was "delicate and quiet". "A delicate pale brat with a snuffy nose," Lawrence called himself rather brutally, who "trotted after his mother like her shadow." Usually he was "active and interested" and then suddenly for no apparent reason he would be found "crying on the sofa and quite unable to explain why, and quite unable to stop. At last the exasperated mother would carry him and his chair into the garden, and 'plump' them down with the half-humorous, half-despairing order: 'Now cry there, Misery!' Lawrence himself, telling the story, seemed to think this indicated some more or less mystical nostalgia in his infant self, though materialists, such as maternity nurses, might attribute the "knitting of the brows" to indigestion, and the "misery" to wrong feeding or under-feeding. When he had these fits of crying his father is supposed to have said in a rage: "If he doesn't stop, I'll smack him till he does." That these two earliest memories were unhappy ones might be due to the fact that the stories came from his mother, who wanted him to feel that he had been forlorn and miserable and weak and she alone had understood and protected him.

Another of these early tales may very likely have been greatly exaggerated in the telling, though the fact itself is not important; it is Lawrence's belief in what his mother told him that matters. The story is that his mother was sitting one evening with him, still a baby, on her lap, weary with waiting up for his father to return from the pub. When he came in rather drunk the inevitable scene developed, from nagging and altercation to screamed insults which goaded the miner to such a frenzy of rage that he flung a drawer from the dresser at her. "One of the corners caught her brow" and cut it badly, almost stunning her, and drops of her blood dripped from her face on to the baby's white shawl. The now sobered man watched in horror as a drop of blood fell "into the baby's fragile glistening hair" and he saw "the heavy dark drop hang in the glistening cloud and pull down the gossamer."

Whether this painful episode is taken literally or merely as a symbol, it marked for young Lawrence a final break between his parents and his unqualified going over to the mother's side. In comparison he cared little or nothing when, rather as an anti-climax, she told him that his father had stolen housekeeping money from her purse to buy beer. In later life Lawrence changed—when did he not change?—and took his father's side. Considering the way the man was treated in his own home, denounced by his wife while prim children gazed at him with the appalling condemnation of their age, it is not surprising that he paraded his pit-dirt and deliberately exaggerated his "commonness" and uncouthness of table manners.

There is some reason to think that the coal-miner did not forget these insults and in due time revenged, or tried to revenge, them in his own style of humour. In 1918 Lawrence and his wife were expelled from Cornwall on suspicion of espionage and took refuge for a time in Derbyshire near where the old man was living in humble retirement. Remembering his father's skill in such jobs as cobbling Lawrence asked him to mend a pair of shoes, which in due course came back neatly soled with tin. On another occasion when his son and daughter-in-law were out on a long walk the old man just before dusk lighted a large bonfire in their garden. If they had not managed to put it out this might have resulted in their being imprisoned, since the showing of any light was forbidden and they were already under suspicion of signalling to imaginary enemies.

As the Lawrence children grew older another series of domestic battles was fought over the question of what occupation they were to follow for their living. Holding to tradition, Arthur Lawrence thundered that the boys were "to go down pit" and the girls go out as kitchen maids. His wife had very different ideas. With her virulent sense of her own unrewarded "superiority" she believed ardently in the Victorian gospel of getting on and bettering yourself, wherein (as her son himself has pointed out) she was entirely supported by the teachers in the State-paid national schools. Lydia Lawrence was bitterly determined that her children should not earn their livings by any kind of manual labour, and her whole ambition was to turn them into what are called white collar workers, in the hope that one or all of the boys might "get on and become a master man in business". She had nothing but contempt for her husband when he shouted against making the eldest son an office boy: "What dost want ter ma'e a stool-harsed Jack on 'im for?" She had the same contempt for any Eastwood lad who took on the obvious service of working in the mines, only exceeded by her contempt for any young man who joined the regular army—"A *soldier!*—a common *soldier!* —nothing but a body that makes movements when it hears a shout!" The children, having their own ambitions as well as their share of her "superiority", quite agreed with her.

According to Lawrence most of the miners' sons loathed school and longed to be done with it and get "down pit", but the elementary school was compulsory and there was no way of evading it. Having no ambitious superior mothers backing up the school teachers, these lads felt contemptuous of the "book learning" which was forced on them. In due course Lawrence was sent to the Beauvale "Board School" and at once got into trouble for scorning his Biblical name of David. The headmaster, it appears, was always contrasting him unfavourably with the go-getting materially successful elder brother, Ernest. Yet Lawrence must have been quick and intelligent in learning the curious routine stuff put before him. When he was twelve he won a scholarship to the Nottingham High School, and this after all was an essential step in his career, for without a secondary education even he could hardly have become an author. Yet at first he had hated school and its discipline, the subjecting of himself to obedience and routine: "I shall never forget the anguish with which I wept, the first day. I was captured. I was roped in." Later in life he came to think that his scholarship had been a misfortune. He believed that the daily train journey to and from Nottingham had been too great a strain on his always delicate health and that it was the real beginning of the lung disease which destroyed him.

Religion was an even more important influence on Lawrence's childhood than State education. True, he tells us that by the time he was sixteen he had "criticised and got over the Christian dogma". But theological dogma is never very important in popular religion which, as he described it, was a mixture of emotionalism and brutal ethical bullying. The family were Congregationalists, a fact in which Lawrence took a perhaps excessive pride, rather as if he believed himself called eventually to sit at the right hand of Oliver Cromwell. In the Lawrence family the children were herded to chapel three times a day every Sunday, and were compelled by their mother's teetotal zeal to join the Band of Hope abstainers. Lawrence as a child—and, never forget, a very intelligent and over-sensitive child—surrendered to this powerful, raucous religious emotionalism. However much he may have rebelled against it intellectually as a youth and man, the influence never wholly left him. Less than two years before his death he wrote that the hymns sung in the bleak ugly chapel still meant "more to me almost than the finest poetry, they have for me a more permanent value." He was equally emphatic about the lasting power over him of the Bible. "Not only was the Bible in portions poured into the childish consciousness day in, day out, year in, year out, willy nilly, whether the consciousness could assimilate it or not, but also it was day in, day out, year in, year out, expounded, dogmatically, and always morally expounded, whether it was in day-school or Sunday-school, at home or in Band of Hope or Christian Endeavour."

A comprehensive programme of crude religious propaganda.

Evidently there was no escape from this slap-bang bibliolatry, holding forth and hymn-shouting. Nor did Lawrence resent the crudity of it, however much he might in some moods jeer at it. "In Sunday School I am eternally grateful to old Mr. Remington, with his white round beard and his ferocity. He made us sing! And he loved the martial hymns." That was the great attraction, for it was all experienced as an exciting battle against the wicked, who of course were the powerful, the rich, the voluptuous, and all those mysteriously and hatefully cultured in the difficult learning of the Gentiles. At the revivalist meetings—to which he sneaked in secret since his mother disapproved of them as common—he heard ever more violent denunciations of the wickedness of all others, virulent expressions of under-dog envy, and that "special kind of religious cheek" which consists in "a religion of self-glorification and power, for ever! and of darkness".

Somehow this queer religion of intolerance and self-conceit was made to fit in with the work of the coal-mines as the miners tramped to and from work, caroused in the pubs or shouted at the football matches. Smoke and steam poured from the pit-heads, the lines of clanking trucks carried away the hard-won coal, and the fuming stinking slag-hills grew steadily. Smoke and grit settled on the dingy little town, which nevertheless was a place of romance and excitement to the boy as he played wild yelling games with other children in the deep darkness of a street faintly lighted by a single lamp.

It was surely an odd freak of Fate to throw into such an environment, with its ferocities, prejudices and conflicts, a child who in his very different way was as responsive and over-strung as Shelley himself. Each was thrown into hostile and incongruous surroundings, against which he struggled as well as he could. In Shelley's case the conflict led him into much early writing of a worthless kind and into doing numberless rash, unconventional acts which baffled and enraged people. Lawrence faced an even more difficult and complex problem, yet in his earliest writing we have to forgive him no crude horror novels or ridiculous Margaret Nicholson poems. According to Aldous Huxley, all Lawrence's decisions in life were determined by his instinctive will always to preserve the artist in him. Whether this is true or not, no one can deny that the conflict or series of inner conflicts dating from childhood gave him almost a Jekyll and Hyde personality—lover and hater, charmer and scandalmonger, artist and preacher, a Siamese twin psychology of *frères ennemis.*

Looking back on himself as a boy from his early manhood years he saw all this clearly and put it down with that peculiar honesty of his which never shrank from the truth of life. He saw his past self, the fourteen-year-old High School boy, with an "extraordinarily mobile" face already becoming "rough-featured" like his father. Usually this boy, with his vivid blue eyes, "saw things", was "full of life, and warm," while "his smile came suddenly and was very lovable." But there was another and rather disagreeable side to the lad. "When there was any clog in his soul's quick running, his face went stupid and ugly. He was the sort of boy that becomes a clown and a lout as soon as he is not understood, or feels himself held cheap; and, again, is adorable at the first touch of warmth."

As a child he had preferred girls to boys for his playmates, and at school he intensely disliked cricket and football. His eldest brother was "too far removed from him" in age to accept him as a companion. So the smaller boy "belonged at first almost entirely" to his sisters. His dislike for conventional organised games did not mean that he had no sense of fun or was wholly a prig, though he was at times very much a prig. He loved to dominate his companions and enjoyed the greater mental activity of creating games instead of following an accepted routine of competitive sport. "He had a genius for inventing games, especially indoors." Even as a boy he seems to have displayed his alert powers of noticing everything in the world about him and giving out his unique vitality to others. When he took his sisters for walks through the fields or alongside the railway track, "not a flower, tree or bird," escaped him, and he "found wonderful adventure in seeing the first celandine or early violet".

He had immense capacity for the enjoyment of simple things. His memories of the Christmas when his elder brother William came home after making his first business success in London were vivid and happy. The family was wholly self-centred and concentrated on itself for this festival of rejoicing. The children "scoured the land" for holly and mistletoe and made coloured paper-chains to hang across the living-room. "There was unheard-of extravagance in the larder." The mother "made a big and magnificent cake" and then "feeling queenly" taught the boy "how to blanche almonds", though why that should have made her feel queenly is hard to say. Then "there was a big plum-cake, and a rice-cake, jam-tarts, lemon-tarts and mince-pies, Spanish-tarts and cheese-cakes. . . . Everybody was mad with excitement."

In his fictionalised account of this undoubtedly real experience, the three children go off to meet their elder brother on the London train, which of course is very late. Lawrence was "dying for" the station-master to know "they were expecting someone by the London train: it sounded so grand," but alas, "he was much too scared of broaching any man, let alone one in a peak cap, to dare to ask." When, after a long mournful wait of more than two hours, the brother appeared, his first modest impulse was to explain to them that "this great train had stopped for *his* sake at such a small station." When they had gloated over the presents he had brought, including the gold-handled umbrella for his mother, they were all "mad with happiness", but Lawrence was not satisfied until he could boast of their opulence to his street friends. True, "home was home, and they loved it with a passion of love, whatever the sufferings had been," but it did not include the delights of bragging and rousing envy. The boy just *had* to slip out and tell the envious neighbours about the sweets he had been given, including "real pineapple, cut off in slices, and then turned into crystal—fair grand!" So grand that apparently he forgot to offer them any.

2

FROM about the age of fifteen until his early twenties the most important person in Lawrence's life after his mother was Jessie Chambers, the 'Emily' of *The White Peacock*, 'Miriam' of *Sons and Lovers*, heroine of several early stories, who has written under the initials E.T. by far the most interesting account of Lawrence in his youth. There was bitter irony in the fact that these two adolescents were first brought together through the agency of Lawrence's mother, who came to hate the girl with such blind jealousy and fought with her a long ruthless duel for the first place in Lawrence's love. The Chambers family are the 'Saxtons' of *The White Peacock*, the 'Lievers' of *Sons and Lovers*, and about the year 1900 lived at The Haggs (the Willey Farm of his novel), a solitary farm about a mile from the nearest hamlet. Mrs. Lawrence met Mrs. Chambers in chapel and after unburdening herself in talk of many troubles agreed to take her youngest boy out to the farm for tea.

Some idea of how much life was restricted by routine for the Lawrences and their kind may be imagined from the fact that this simple little excursion was a great event in the life of mother and son. He remembered it all, down to small details, with a vividness and exactness which show how much it meant to him. Before the two started out there was some almost lover's banter about her new blouse. They paused in their walk to look at the pit-head and to admire it, for in those days Lawrence had not yet discovered that it was ugly and that he hated it. Characteristic of his morbid shyness and dread of rebuff is the episode where he sheepishly hung back and left it to his mother to ask the way of a stranger. He remembered going through the fields and the little wood, the names of the wild flowers beside the path, and his first sight of the old farmhouse whose walls seemed "to embrace the sunshine". At the door he saw "a girl in a dirty apron", about fourteen years old, with "a rosy dark face, a bunch of short black curls, very fine and free, and dark eyes; shy, questioning, a little resentful of the strangers". Presently they walked and talked together in the garden, and Lawrence noted her "beautiful warm colouring and distant, rather superior manner".

The girl remembered seeing "the small vigorous woman and the slender boy" coming into the farmyard. She in her shyness took refuge in the kitchen, where he surprised her as she was boiling eggs, and "stood silently looking about him in a curious, intent way". His scrutiny was so intent that it made the girl feel uncomfortable. He was wearing the school uniform of Eton coat and collar, and she, who had been denied education, envied him. Later when she took him out to look at the wood and the distant hills he became "shy and withdrawn", as if taking in many new impressions.

The farm life, so different from the noisy street life of the mining village, fascinated Lawrence, who took to spending almost every mid-week half-holiday at The Haggs. At first it was the farmer, Mr. Chambers, who welcomed him, talking to him "almost as if he were grown up", while Jessie and her brothers were "shy of him, afraid lest he should give himself airs".

The growing friendship and intimacy were for a time interrupted by other events in Lawrence's life. His elder brother, William Ernest, was now in London, earning what seemed to them the good income of one hundred and twenty pounds a year, with even better prospects just ahead. Driven by the demon of "getting on", Mrs. Lawrence was determined that David Herbert should follow his brother, and what she determined he had no strength to resist. When his twelve-pounds-a-year scholarship ended with the summer term of 1900 she insisted that he must "look in the paper for the advertisements for a job". As a result he went through "agonies of shrinking self-consciousness". All such contacts with the outer world were torture to this over-sensitive, self-centred boy. His first day at school had been "a nightmare and a torture", and every week when he was sent by his father to the colliery office to draw the week's wages Lawrence "suffered the tortures of the damned". His "ridiculous hyper-sensitiveness" made his mother's "heart ache for him".

Now came this new torture of having to look for a job, the killing routine which would have maimed, perhaps killed, the artist he carried all unawares within him. With this threat over him "his whole being was knotted up" with the dread of it from the moment he woke, and it seemed to kill all joy and life for him. Every day he was made to go to the newspaper room of the public library, and as he crept along the street he imagined in his morbid self-consciousness that everyone he passed knew his errand and was thinking: "That boy can't get a job. I suppose he's living on his mother." No doubt that was what she had told the boy, though after all it was her husband's labour which earned what money there was. When at last he forced himself to enter the library he could not bear to be seen looking through the Situations Vacant advertisements, and so, "full of shrinking and suffering", he pretended to be going through the news, though he "knew" that the convalescent or out-of-work miners in the room wondered what a boy of his age needed with the news.

He just could not humiliate himself to look for a job in the advertisement columns while others were present, so in the hope that they would go away he would stroll to the window and "look wistfully out". He felt that "already he was a prisoner of industrialism", that "he was being taken into bondage". On one such occasion as he stood miserably by the window a brewer's dray went past with the "waggoner, throned aloft, rolling massively in his seat", a bullet-headed man with red arms and a red face "almost asleep with sunshine". Looking down at this brawny hero of the unconscious life, "I wish I was fat like him," the boy thought, "and like a dog in the sun. I wish I was a pig and a brewer's waggoner." Already then he knew and dreaded the pain and suffering of his extraordinary gifts, intuitively perhaps had a foretaste of the anger and envy and hatred such gifted persons as himself always arouse instead of the love and admiration they deserve.

Then, coming out of his bitter adolescent reverie, he saw that the room at last was empty, hastily and furtively copied out a few of the advertisements, and was able "to slip out in immense relief".

Brother William Ernest, the successful and patronising London clerk, had written out a correct "business" letter of application for this not very ardent recruit to commerce and industry. This letter, which happens to survive, mentions that the applicant was just sixteen; and as it brought him a job almost at once it must have been soon after his birthday in September 1901 that he entered the service of Messrs. Hayward of Nottingham, makers of surgical and orthopædic implements. There was an interview between the employer and mother and son, and once more Lawrence went through agonies of self-consciousness as he did on all official occasions and whenever he came face to face with people in a relationship which prevented their recognising his real quality. "He hated the little man who made such a clod of him," though in point of fact all the man had done was to ask him to read a letter written in French and then tell him that when the word "doigts" was used of stockings it did not mean "fingers" but "toes".

He was taken on as office boy at a salary of eight shillings a week, but though there is an impression that he stayed on for a wearisomely long period, in point of fact he spent only three months at this Nottingham job. He had been there only a few weeks when the family was smitten with disaster. The energetic William Ernest, pushed on by his mother's ambition and his own, wearied and weakened his strength with overwork and by fretting over an unhappy love affair. Suddenly he developed pneumonia complicated by erysipelas and died before his mother's eyes in the little bedroom of his London lodging-house. It was a dagger in the unhappy mother's heart. All her hopes in life had long dwelt on her sons, particularly on Ernest and David Herbert, and what, in spite of her intellectual pretensions, she really wanted was for them to achieve financial success in business. When they brought her son home in a coffin which seemed to fill the little parlour, it was so large, her heart and will seemed to break. After his funeral she sat day after day, lost in mournful reveries of her dead son, perhaps reproaching herself and her ambitions as the indirect cause of his death. She even cut herself off from her favourite David Herbert, who whined miserably to her for notice and was repulsed. Then suddenly she was roused from the stupor of her grief by the threat of yet another loss when one winter night, just before Christmas, Lawrence staggered in from Nottingham smitten with the fatal pneumonia which darkened his life. Then it was she realised that however much she had loved the elder son it was nothing compared with her love for the younger who "had always meant more to her than any of the others." This illness of his saved her sanity as surely as her devoted nursing saved his life, and when after weeks of danger and suffering he was convalescent the relation between mother and son was re-established more closely than ever. As they sat together in the March sunshine "they knitted together in perfect intimacy" and she felt that her life had now "rooted itself" in him permanently.

There was now no question of sending him back to read the advertisements of vacant jobs. This was not the first time Lawrence had had pneumonia, and no doubt on this occasion his parents were warned of his tubercular condition. It is characteristic of Lawrence that at no time in his life did he admit that he had tuberculosis—it was always bronchitis or my bronchials or this beastly 'flu or a vicious cold, never consumption. How near to death he was during that severe illness in the winter of 1901–2 may be guessed from his description of its crisis when he "tossed into consciousness in the ghastly sickly feeling of dissolution, when all the cells in the body seemed in intense irritability to be breaking down, and consciousness makes a last flare of struggle, like madness."

Poor as they were, his parents obeyed the medical warning and gave him six months freedom from work or school. How often in literary history, of England at any rate, genius has been given its chance owing to a severe illness and long convalescence bringing it freedom from the tyranny of routine labour and the profane meddling of "education". It certainly was the case with Lawrence, whose impulse to write was chiefly fostered by his intimacy with the family at The Haggs, above all Jessie, whom he had re-named Muriel.

As soon as he was well enough after his illness Mr. Chambers drove Lawrence up to the farm in his milk-float. "I do not know why my parents loved Lawrence as they did," Jessie Chambers wrote, "but they were as glad at his recovery as if he had been their own son." His power to evoke warm responses of friendship and love in others was exceeded only by the perverse demon in him which seemed to compel him to outrage and repel the feelings he had himself created, perhaps because he dreaded the possessive claims of those who cared for him. In that spring of 1902 Mr. Chambers welcomed Lawrence as a son and told him to come to the farm whenever he wished; and he went so often that he aroused the jealousy of his mother, who told him cattily that he ought to pack his clothes and go to live at The Haggs. In spite of this he was only happy when he was at the farm or on his way there. He never missed a Saturday at The Haggs, and though he was still only a boy his influence was felt by everybody in the family. When he entered the house he always brought "a holiday atmosphere" with him. Not only did he make them all feel kindly towards him, "he knew how to make them nicer to one another." At home he had been accustomed to do many household jobs for his mother and did them well. This was more than her own sons did for Mrs. Chambers, who felt that Lawrence was "extraordinarily kind and willing to help and most considerate" when he insisted on "bringing her water for the kitchen boiler, tidying the hearth, building the fire and even peeling onions" for her. "No task seemed dull or monotonous to him," says Jessie Chambers, "he brought such vitality to the doing that he transformed it into something creative." In those days the "dark self", which so often was really the irritated expression of his suffering lungs, was not visible, and in the happy mood of returning life and vigour he captivated them all with his warmth and vitality and the magic of his personality.

Years afterwards he was able to evoke the circumstances of his first return to The Haggs with extraordinary precision and detail. He remembered the freshness of the morning and the white clouds "crowding to the back of the hills", the distant lake "very blue against the seared meadows", the budding hedges "vivid as copper-green", the thrushes and blackbirds fluting or scolding. For the boy the world was made glamorous by the sensation of his return from the borders of death to life, and rapturous with the dawn of young love. As he met Jessie his quick eyes noted her flowering beauty, "her warm colouring, her gravity, her eyes", but in the very shyness of that awareness he startled and a little disappointed her by his first words, which were not of her but of the early daffodils. On that early spring day he thought they "looked cold" in their chill green buds. Then he went and sat in the old kitchen where he loved "the sack-bag that formed the hearthrug, and the funny little corner under the stairs, and the small window deep in the corner, through which, bending a little, he could see the plum trees in the back-garden and the lovely round hills beyond".

It was strange and a little frightening even to these people whom he loved and who loved him to realise that he possessed not only an intense appreciation of the living passing moment but an uncanny "awareness" of things and people and a habit of making intuitive guesses about the secret lives and thoughts of others. He looked at the girl less as a lover than as an artist who cannot be deceived. "She suddenly became aware of his keen blue eyes upon her, taking her all in. Instantly her broken boots and her frayed old frock hurt her. She resented his seeing everything." With a similar directness and lack of discretion he showed that he saw how the mother "exalted everything, even a bit of housework, to the plane of a religious trust", and how the boorish sons despised and resented this evangelical virtue, answering it "with brutality and also with a sneering superciliousness"—and yet in spite of themselves were influenced by her idealism and were "always restless for the something deeper".

That same afternoon Lawrence and the girl and her mother went out into the garden to look at a wren's nest. As he crouched down to look at it and spoke about it to the women with that vivid consciousness of life he possessed, "the nest seemed to start into life" for them. As they went along nothing escaped him. He saw the early celandines as "scalloped splashes of gold" an image so vivid to the girl that "the celandines ever after drew her with a little spell." Intensely appreciative of his strange, subtle gifts, perhaps almost too sensitively emotional, the girl was deeply moved, and the love between them came to live in "this atmosphere of subtle intimacy" and "their common feeling for something in Nature".

In her first; for "he was a long time before he realised her", and was bound down and pulled away from her by that unbreakable chain of mother-love.

During the summer this intimacy with the farm family and the beginning of the idyll of boy and girl love were interrupted by a month's visit to Skegness, where Lawrence stayed with an aunt who owned a boarding-house there. Strangely enough he does not seem to have left any record of his first sight of the sea, but it seems to have started him on his career of painting, for he sent back several sketches from Skegness. He painted or very often copied paintings throughout his life, but he seems to have been particularly attracted by painting during the years fifteen to twenty. Any reader can see how much his writing was inspired by the delight of the eye and the plastic sense. Yet he never attained to virtuosity or even to thorough craftsmanship as a painter. At the High School he had been repelled by the mechanical copying of plaster casts, and beyond that he seems to have received only one lesson and that from a pottery designer. He taught himself to decorate screens and to paint flowers and to copy reproductions of pictures. And in those days it seems to have been his ambition to be a painter rather than a writer.

As soon as he returned to Eastwood Lawrence's life once more became centred on the farm and his friends there. He "loved them dearly and they him". He liked to do any light work on the farm for which he had the strength, and was pleased when he learned how to milk the cows. During the hay harvest he worked daily with Mr. Chambers and his two sons in the fields rented at Greasley, four miles from the farm. They took a hamper of food and made a picnic of the long work day. "All through that epoch," says Jessie Chambers, Lawrence "seemed so happy that merely to be alive and walking about was an adventure, and his gift for creating an atmosphere of good fellowship made work a joy. One could not help being affected by his vitality and charm". Everybody who tried to put on paper the effect Lawrence had on those sensitive enough to respond to him used those words "vitality and charm" in the vain hope of expressing something that defies expression. But vitality, charm, magic, call it what you like, he certainly possessed, and they attracted not only the women and girls but the rough, uncouth, derisive young men on the farm. Mrs. Chambers went so far as to say that in Heaven she would like to sit next to Lawrence, and her farmer husband, more practical but no less appreciative, always said of him: "Work goes like fun when Bert's there, it's no trouble at all to keep them going."

Already young Lawrence was adventuring into more intellectual experiences where Jessie alone cared and was able to accompany him. Freed during these months from the burden of schoolwork he began exploring the world of books with the avidity of the born writer. For both of them this period "was a kind of orgy of reading. I think we were hardly aware of the outside world."

The influence and memories of The Haggs and those who lived there runs through much of Lawrence's early work, especially in *The White Peacock* and in *Sons and Lovers.* Some of the grimmer aspects of this remote existence are touched on in *Love Among The Haystacks.* You will find them in his early, naïve, and almost stammering poems, and in many a page of *The Rainbow.* They were a corrective to the inward-looking highly emotional life of his own home, and to that dark underground existence of the mine on which it was founded and which haunted Lawrence throughout his life. The metallurgists and mining folk were always mysterious and terrifying to those who in ancient times wandered with their herds and flocks or dwelt silently among the fields they cultivated. The daunted imaginations of the dwellers in the sun who came in contact with them brought forth weird tales of cyclopes and gnomes and kobolds. And the mining folk, in turn, told each other tales of the fairy folk who lived in the dewy fields.

Lawrence never freed himself from the dark mystery and fascination of the mine. For him it remained a symbol of the unconscious, the Unbewüsst, and in his own somewhat baffling symbolism how large a part is played by "darkness", "the dark unconscious" and all that is hidden, underground as it were, mysteriously working out of sight. It gave an added mystery to the darkness of sleep, and he identified with it, not so much the father whose life the mine had taken, as the mother who tried to monopolise his love in an ambiguous relationship to whose implications both necessarily had to be blind and dark. He "loved to sleep with his mother". And again: "Sleep is still most perfect, in spite of hygienists, when it is shared with a beloved. The warmth, the security and peace of soul, the utter comfort from the touch of the other, knits the sleep, so that it takes the body and soul completely in its healing." During the lifetime of William Ernest, Lawrence had been "unconsciously jealous of his brother". When the injured father was taken away to hospital he had said gleefully to his mother: "I'm the man in the house now." After a day spent with his mother in Nottingham he felt it had been "perfect" and "they arrived home in the mellow evening, happy and glowing and tired".

School, which he hated, and the brief disastrous experience in "business" had increased rather than diminished this spell of mysterious mine and worshipped mother, but there was something important symbolised by these escapes to the farm. They meant that he was unconsciously struggling away from the mine on which his life was founded, and forming the first fragile tender threads of a new love which in the natural course of things would wholly encompass him and draw him away from the mother to the wife. Instantly his mother was aware of what was happening and set herself to battle it. She began to dislike their whole influence, that of the parents, that of the sons (particularly the 'George' of *The White Peacock* and the 'Edgar' of *Sons and Lovers*) and of course above all Jessie. Between them, without meaning it, they were drawing the youth away from his too absorbing home life, feeding in him the love of adventure, the first thrilling start of "life on one's own".

In spite of his delicate health and of his being a mother's darling Lawrence always from childhood had possessed the sense of adventure, the boy's love of "exploring". Even when he was a very small boy and was allowed to go out with the other children in late summer to gather blackberries, they noticed that he generally managed to go farther afield than the others, quite as much apparently for the thrill of "discovery" as for the pride of getting a fuller basket. Then, not very far from Eastwood, there was a deserted quarry which is described in *The White Peacock* and in the fragment of a Utopian novel in *Phoenix*. This quarry dwelt in his memory as a place of mystery, "very old and deep", filled with "oak trees and guelder roses and a tangle of briars". The open spaces were at different seasons rich with dog-violets, daisies, honeysuckle and deadly nightshade. In its rugged walls were "little awful rocky caves" where he imagined there were adders. These caves were on the "dark side" of the quarry which so much fascinated him that he repeats it—

"the dark side . . . a fearsome place . . . it was always dark—you had to crawl under bushes".

He never took the world and his feelings about it for granted. You might say with perfect truth that he scarcely ever made his bicycle trip to and from The Haggs without seeing something that delighted him and was instantly preserved in his wonderful memory. Later, as they grew older, Lawrence organised "tramps" across country, "genuine explorations of the countryside" where he led and animated about a dozen young people who infinitely preferred these rough and tiring walks to the Matlock excursions in hired brakes organised by Lawrence's mother and The Women's Co-operative Guild. He made these walks seem so thrilling that the others never forgot them. Both Jessie Chambers and his sister Ada, writing a quarter of a century afterwards, remembered an excursion taken at Easter to Wingfield Manor, even down to the "veal sandwiches and hot cross buns" they took for their picnic. However much Lawrence might be absorbed in talking on such a walk he noticed everything, "the first to see the baby rabbit or cock-pheasant, the first primrose" as he walked "briskly along with his lithe, light step, tirelessly observant, his eager eyes taking everything in." Whatever had to be done, he originated, he led. Towards the end of this particular excursion they found themselves at a wayside station miles from Eastwood with only a few pence left after paying their railway fares. It was Lawrence who collected the remaining pennies, decided they must buy bread and butter from a cottage and astonished them all by getting so much for so little. "We were supremely happy," is Jessie Chambers' comment. When his "dark self" was in abeyance and he himself was happy he possessed a unique power of giving happiness to others.

On another of these walks there happened a little episode in connection with a broken umbrella which had a symbolical and psychological significance far beyond its actual importance. The young people had scattered and were moving in little groups of two or three or alone when Jessie, turning from some maple trees, saw Lawrence on the road bending over an umbrella. She was struck by his attitude, "his stooping figure had a look of intensity, almost of anguish." She turned back to ask him what was the matter. "It was Ern's umbrella, and mother will be wild if I take it home broken." It was of course the famous "gold-handled umbrella" which her dead son had brought her as a Christmas present and which she kept until her death. It was from that moment that the girl realised she was in love with him, from that glimpse of him when he was unaware of her presence; just as his wife, Frieda, made the discovery when, quite forgetting her, he was playing paper-boats with two children.

There was, however, another significance in the broken umbrella, for his "anguish" had nothing to do with the object itself but his vivid fear of his mother's grief and anger. His life was still centred upon her, and it was for her sake that he hated the thought of growing up, so much so that he refused to shave. The girls chaffed him about the ragged hairs on his chin, and still he obstinately refused. Partly of course he wanted to remain a child because life as an irresponsible boy was much pleasanter than working in a Nottingham office. The more powerful reason was the unconscious one of wishing to keep intact the mother-son relationship and their absorbing love.

Well, the time came when something had to be decided about the boy's future—they could not afford to keep him idle and happy any longer. Arthur Lawrence had long ago given up his efforts to get the boys "down pit" and he knew that the youngest son was not physically strong enough. Besides, in the long battle with his wife he was defeated and hardly counted in the family he supported by his labour. The real difficulty was the mother, and it was not without many pangs of regret and disappointment that she finally abandoned all hope that David Herbert might emulate the "business success" of his dead brother, William Ernest. Lawrence himself knew quite well that she never valued his art but only his achievement, the material rewards his art brought him. Unprofitable genius was of no interest to her. Therefore it was with sighs and the deflated feeling that she was agreeing to a come-down that in the autumn of 1902 she consented that Lawrence and his sister Ada should go as pupil-teachers to the British School in Eastwood. A year later they were transferred to the Ilkeston Pupil-Teacher Centre, where they were joined by Jessie Chambers. Lawrence remained there until 1906.

Intellectually Lawrence was the product of the universal national education which became compulsory for all children in England in 1870. Some have thought that the extreme vindictiveness of the

British authorities against him might have been due, at least in part, to his unparalleled impudence as one of their protégés in turning out to be a literary genius instead of an over-worked headmaster of an elementary school. Certain it is that then the life of a State-supported pupil-teacher was austere, dull and laborious, with a weekly two and a half days of education balancing two and a half days of trying to teach unruly children, and no salary to speak of. Against this might be set the camaraderie with others of the same age, the thrill of handling the otherwise forbidden keys of knowledge, even the priggish but pardonable feeling that he was qualifying for a profession which gives more than it receives.

Besides, for these children of poor parents the hierarchy of State-subsidised education was becoming on a mean and uninteresting scale something like the Catholic Church and the religious orders in the middle ages. It was virtually the only respectable means of escape from "the prison of industrialism". That it destroyed many of the virtues of the working class and created hordes of discontented parasites did not matter to them so long as it served or seemed to serve their children's purposes. Lawrence had experienced the alternative. His Nottingham employer had been a kindly man, the work light, yet he had hated it and he had broken down. Better be a schoolmaster.

Lawrence himself refers but briefly to a second experience in the world of commerce which happened at some unspecified time during his life as a pupil-teacher. It seems that an Eastwood pork-butcher offered him a weekly five shillings for two hours of work making out the Friday night bills; and though Lawrence hated the job with all his sense of superiority, he felt he ought to accept for his mother's sake. One Friday night Jessie Chambers saw Lawrence among the trotters and the chines, a weirdly incongruous figure, and turned away quickly "in shame", feeling "pained to see him there". The experiment lasted but a few weeks, yet has its ironical aspect when you reflect that totting up a pork-butcher's bills was all that prosperous commercial Eastwood could offer the only poet it will ever produce.

The transfer to Ilkeston, which happened when Lawrence was seventeen, was rather important for him. Hitherto he does not seem to have realised that he was "a genius", that he had exceptional intellectual, artistic and human gifts. He himself passes over his life as a pupil-teacher with the bleak remark that it was "three years savage teaching of collier lads". But it was at Ilkeston that he first began to realise his gifts, partly from his exceptional success as a pupil, partly from the encouragement of his headmaster, who made friends with him and often read out his essays to the other pupils with many laudatory comments. This was well-meant, but with a youth so conceited and undisciplined as Lawrence not very judicious. As we have seen, he came from a section of the community which never had the slightest doubts about its own importance and rightness, and from a family which struck even its self-righteous neighbours as remarkable for its self-confidence and self-esteem. Lawrence, who was so profoundly under his mother's influence, has recorded of her that she was "so hard and so certain . . . as if she had never had a misgiving in her life". This public flattery of boyish essays strengthened instead of checking Lawrence's attitude of overbearing self-confidence which he assumed to hide his own unsureness and vacillations. When at Nottingham University they tried to check him by roughly handling his essays he refused to take the lesson, remarking contemptuously that henceforth he would "give them the kid's stuff they want".

State and public schools cannot be, or at any rate never are, devised to foster exceptionally gifted children. They aim at turning out the type of people who can be more and more easily duped into obedience to government. If in both cases just cited the treatment was injudicious, it was probably inevitable. What is important to recognise is that even in this early obscure period his faults were more than outweighed by his gifts. Both in work and play his personality set him apart from others, and there was from adolescence something about him extraordinarily appealing to women of deep and subtle sensibility. "His own intense enjoyment", says Jessie Chambers, "gave a keener edge to our pleasure." She is speaking of the excursions which he still continued to direct, though, as his main interest at that time was in architecture, he was always shepherding his followers across country to look at churches and castles. "It was more than merely *seeing* these landmarks," she goes on, "it was a kind of immediate possession, as though to have missed seeing them would have been to lose an essential moment of life."

Looking at him across the crowded Ilkeston class-room, where he sat in the senior class, Jessie Chambers could not help noticing "his uniqueness, how totally different he was from any of the other youths". It was not that falling in love with him made her see him flatteringly but rather that love gave her eyes to see what others missed—"his finely-shaped head with small well-set ears, and his look of concentration, of being more intensely alive" than others. She, perhaps more sympathetically even than his mother, saw his "sensitiveness and delicacy of spirit" which made him "so vulnerable, so susceptible to injury." That is perfectly true, and we should never forget that if later he attacked the world savagely and venomously, the world had begun by clumsily or malevolently dealing him intolerable wounds. And after noticing his hair and skin and "clever hands" she adds: "But there was another quality of lightness about him, something that seemed to shine from within", a something one saw at times in his beautifully blue eyes.

From the first he was perplexed by his own gifts and, as it were, the induced self of his environment did not know how to behave towards the genius he was born. His consciousness of his own "uniqueness" and the headmaster's praise resulted among other things in naïve and rather priggish remarks about the duty of people with "bigger mental gifts" to "help others". How little "others" wanted to be "helped" on those terms he was to learn by bitter experience. But he was determined to help others, will they, nill they. He already contemplated very seriously achieving success on a generous financial scale. "I should like to have a big house," he confided to his friend, "and wouldn't it be fine if we could live in one of those houses, mother, and all the people we like together. Wouldn't it be fine! Wouldn't it just!"

Here is the germ of that project he clung to with such perverse obstinacy in the face of all reason and experience—the project of forming a "colony" in some part of the world inhabited by the people who liked him and hated each other. Whether he devised this misery for himself or whether it was a reminiscence of Ruskin's *Guild of St. George*, here at seventeen he had already invented what Aldous Huxley calls the "colony of escape" with which he periodically bedevilled himself and his friends. Who among those friends was not at some time or other asked, or commanded, to put down his name on some hastily drawn up list of Laurentian emigrants and followers to Sicily or Florida or the Pacific Isles or

New Mexico, there to dwell happy ever after under the rule of Lorenzo the Magniloquent?

Meanwhile, the silent almost unavowed battle went on between mother and sweetheart. True, even then many girls and young women came under his spell, and were always on some pretext or another drifting in and out of the Lawrence cottage while he worked on indifferent to the chatter, a gift which incidentally was very valuable to him in later life. True too, "all the girls loved to dance with him because his movements were so light." But it was Jessie who really mattered to him, as his mother saw so clearly and fought so bitterly. As he afterwards said himself he drew from his mother in those days "the strength to produce, the life-warmth"; but it was Jessie who "urged this warmth into intensity like a white light." He could not work without her, for he was "conscious only when stimulated". Probably what he wanted was the praise and encouragement only the loved woman can give, but he pretended, or rather really felt, that only through her response to his work was he "stimulated into knowledge of the work he had produced unconsciously."

Jessie Chambers, then, was appointed to the difficult if not impossible situation of keeper of his artistic conscience. She owed him much. He had found her a beautiful Cinderella in broken boots and a dirty apron, drudging in the kitchen for boorish insulting brothers, dreaming not of a coach and horses and dancing with a prince but of her lost hopes of learning. She was miserable because she felt that she was shut out, through lack of education, from "the feast of the human spirit". She was tortured by "desire for knowledge and a longing for beauty". And from this he had rescued her. It was his influence with her family which persuaded them to take her from the kitchen and the dairy and allow her to go back to school and to train as a teacher.

Whether intentionally or not he had begun to help her towards her ambition even before she went back to school, giving her lessons in French and algebra and other examination subjects. It does not appear that he was either a good or patient teacher, in spite of his pupil's devotion and pathetic eagerness to learn. His explanation of the mysteries of algebra was engagingly over-simplified: "It's only letters for figures. You put down 'a' instead of '2' or '6'." Clear enough to anyone who knows algebra, but how about someone who doesn't? He who many years later dumbfounded Aldous Huxley by refusing to accept the doctrine of evolution merely because he did not "feel it" in his "solar plexus" abused the hapless Jessie for trying to learn algebra with her "blessed soul". As she not unnaturally hesitated and fumbled with the symbols he had failed to explain to her, "he stormed at her, grew furious, abusing her." Even her gentle mother intervened, begging him not to be so hard on the girl. But he simply could not control himself. "He flared against her," and then one day in his rage he threw his pencil in her face.

Instead of flying at him like a wild-cat, she followed the book of the words by turning the other cheek in silence, a gesture which made him "bitterly ashamed" and perhaps was her first step towards losing him. His shame at this cad's outburst made him try to be more patient and gentle. But he could not. Whenever in her nervousness—who wouldn't be nervous with such a teacher?—she hesitated and could not learn as fast as his impatience required, "his anger burst like a bubble" and he longed to insult her again by throwing his pencil in her face. In spite of it or because of it—who knows a girl's heart?—she fell more deeply under his spell; whereupon, with that perverse spirit of contradiction he shared with his father he deliberately began to avoid her and left her ostentatiously to go off with her brothers. This she suffered for love of him and of learning, and then gradually he came back to her, not for her sake or in acknowledgement of her love but "because of the intensity to which she roused him". Thus, slowly and unintentionally, Jessie began to take the place of his furiously jealous mother, and sat in judgment on his inner life and conscience.

For help in the music and singing which he also loved, Lawrence went to his sister Ada. He learned quickly to read song music and knew a large number of songs, chiefly English and German, which he ruthlessly repeated in a shrill but true voice on every available occasion. They were always folk songs, and in later life he felt or assumed great dislike for all forms of art music. In *Point Counter Point* Aldous Huxley has given an amusing sketch of Lawrence (as Rampion) perversely refusing to admire the Sanctus music from Beethoven's Solemn Mass—obviously because Huxley had injudiciously expected him to admire it. In his pupil-teacher days he had been more catholic in his tastes, buying music for his sister to play for him, "Chopin's Waltzes, music by Tchaikovski and Brahms, Boosey's song books and opera selections." He would sit beside her, ruthlessly urging her on to practise the pieces he wanted to hear but could not play himself until she was "often on the verge of tears". Then he made her sing Mendelssohn and Rubinstein duets with him, but was always too self-conscious and fearful of criticism to attempt to sing in public.

One day, annoyed with her inability to learn as quickly as his impatience demanded, Lawrence decided that he would learn to play the piano himself. He had begun to write and to paint without any conscious study of methods or lessons or discipline, and seems to have thought he could do the same with music. For a period of about thirty minutes he was heard trying vainly to play simple exercises and "then came a loud crash of keys and an exasperated young man stalked into the kitchen. His patience was exhausted and he refused to strum his fingers off over 'beastly scales' any longer". From this moment may perhaps be dated his dislike for art music and his addiction to the folk songs which may be sung without musical training.

In much the same over-confident spirit of self-help Lawrence had taken up the arts of painting and writing. Writing of course was the art which suited his peculiar genius, however much he may have abused his gifts. He persevered much longer with painting than with music and with a certain measure of success, since his method of self-teaching included the discipline of copying the work of other artists. The photographs of eight pictures painted for his sister show that he had by his early twenties made progress, though he had not mastered the technical difficulties of accurately reproducing the human figure or the nude. But even then he had sufficiently advanced to make possible his later semi-primitive paintings and embroideries.

There is perhaps some interest in mentioning the painters he copied, work in which he always took "the greatest pleasure". For his sister he copied Corot, Brangwyn and Greiffenhagen. For his pleasure he copied a whole series of the English water-colour artists from Girtin on, and reproductions of such Italian artists as Fra Angelico, Carpaccio, Piero di Cosimo and the Lorenzetti. There were many others, as he often spent his time copying famous pictures as a relaxation from the nervous strain of writing.

For sympathy with his early love of reading, his first attempts at writing, and that passionate love of flowers which was so intimately and symbolically bound up with his genius as an artist, he went always in those days to Jessie Chambers. Every writer who interested him during those years was at once taken to her to share and to evaluate. The authors who attract and influence a young writer are an important part of his life. Since Lawrence came from a poor man's home there has been a general tendency to suppose that such literary culture as he had was scanty. This was not the fact, though of course estimates of such acquirements are purely relative—what seems little more than a smattering to specialists will look like dry tedious learning to a mere newspaper reader.

We have already seen that Lawrence's mother had a taste for books, so that from childhood he was accustomed to seeing them as an accepted part of life. She and the children belonged to the Literary Society attached to the Congregationalist Church, though whether they discussed only religious books or those of general interest we are not told. Fortunately Jessie Chambers kept a list of the authors she and Lawrence read together during the six or seven years of their intimacy.

She mentions rather more than a hundred authors, nearly all English or French and of the nineteenth century, typical students' reading of the period. Poetry, usually the favourite recreation of students with literary ambitions, was much less fully represented than one would suppose. Their chief source was Palgrave's *Golden Treasury*, which Lawrence at one time always carried in one of his pockets and enjoyed reading aloud. The rather cursory mention of Shakespeare and the "metaphysical" poets looks as if his knowledge of them came mostly from Palgrave and from school—at any rate in those days. Along with the *Treasury* they read Scott, Wordsworth, Shelley, Coleridge, Burns, Blake, Longfellow, Tennyson, Swinburne, Whitman, Rossetti, Browning and Francis Thompson. At some time during his student life he read parts of *Horace and Vergil* in the original, as well as Baudelaire and Verlaine, whom he greatly admired. In one of his *Assorted Articles* he speaks of the "lovely poems which after all give the ultimate shape to one's life—the Odes of Keats and Wordsworth, parts of Shakespeare, Goethe's lyrics, Verlaine." This is meagre indeed for a poet, but it represents the absolute known minimum of poetry that he had read by the time he reached his early twenties. Jessie Chambers warns us that he read many other books even in those days and read extensively when he was at Croydon.

All the same it is a fair inference that a list which omits practically all the greatest European poetry from Homer to André Chénier shows that this was not really his greatest interest in literature, particularly since no less than forty of the authors mentioned are novelists. They include most standard English novelists, with the exception of Defoe, Fielding, Smollett and Goldsmith, the first three of whom may have been judged "improper" for a girl in those inhibited times. For some reason he vehemently forbade her to read *Wuthering Heights*, though why, I for one cannot imagine, unless he thought Heathcliff's romantic passion was pitched too high for mortal man to emulate. The same list included the 19th century French, some of the Russians, Cooper and Alcott among Americans, and Cervantes. (Evidently no Boccaccio in those days.) George Moore, Wells, Bennett and Galsworthy were read as their books appeared.

Among philosophers, essayists and ethical writers generally, the most significant inclusions are Ruskin and Carlyle. Their dogmatic tone is akin to his, and both in temperament and opinions he had much in common with Ruskin even down to his inveterate habit of wrangling about abstract ideas in terms of a personal symbolism. You might add that both were fanatics about sex; Ruskin for purity through abstinence, Lawrence for purity through what he called "fulfilment". Although Jessie Chambers does not mention these two as being closely studied, his essays and novels, particularly *The Rainbow*, show that he did go through a "Ruskin period" of considerable intensity. Moreover, on the occasion when she and Lawrence lunched with Violet Hunt and Ford Madox Hueffer (then the editor of *The English Review*) the latter was or pretended to be greatly impressed by Lawrence's knowledge of Carlyle and Ruskin.

That he also went through what is called "a materialist phase" seems obvious, not only from the evidence of his early writings and of the man with whom he lodged in Croydon, but also because he read or tried to read Darwin, T. H. Huxley, Haeckel and J. M. Robertson. He was apparently about twenty-one when he began seriously to question the orthodoxy in which he had been brought up, another instance of his mother's deep influence over him. Clearly he would have to conceal it from her, but Jessie Chambers knew and regretted it, saying that scepticism "seared his youthful freshness". They both suffered from it, she feeling "exquisite pain, as, with an intellect like a knife, the man she loved examined her religion in which she lived and moved and had her being. But he did not spare her. He was cruel. When they were alone he was even more fierce, as if he would kill her soul". When they returned from these walks together he was "wild with torture". It is strangely unlike the dogmatically mystic Lawrence of most of his writing career to learn that he gave her "a vivid description of the nebular theory", wanted to write to their minister on the tactful topic of agnosticism, priggishly announced that he "felt himself compelled to take up a rationalist standpoint" and "coldly" but surely unfairly demanded of the poor girl that she instantly furnish him with proofs of the existence of God.

Remembering how vehemently and with what wearisome repetition he would denounce "conscious knowledge", "head knowledge", "intellect" and "talking from the top of the head", it is quite stupefying to read her notes of a dialogue such as this:

"LAWRENCE: It isn't as if you had a strong intellect.

JESSIE: I don't suppose I have. I never thought so.

LAWRENCE: No. No, you're purely emotional.

JESSIE: Well, what if I am?

LAWRENCE: Well, you see, it means that you're governed entirely by your feelings. You don't *think*, you *feel*. There's a lot of difference, you know.

JESSIE: Perhaps that's because I am more sure of my feelings than my thoughts.

LAWRENCE: Yes, but don't you see, that proves you're not intellectual. Now as for me, I trust entirely to the intellect."

As a scene of tragi-comedy that is hard to beat when you reflect that the soon-to-be-famous writer was here denouncing the girl for occupying the very position in defence of which he lavished all his eloquence and to which he owed some of his fame, while he scornfully boasted to her of an attitude for which he later repeatedly professed the greatest contempt. How often, white-faced and bitter-mouthed with unnecessary rage, did he inveigh against other people for holding exactly what he so dogmatically asserted to her was his own belief—"as for me, I trust entirely to the intellect." Even then, it seems, he had developed the habit of talking for effect and arguing for mere victory, as he later sometimes wrote purely for effect. According to his mood or the mere statement of an opinion by someone else he would swing violently from one point of view to its opposite.

Often he would assert himself with a brutal arrogance which can only have come from a fundamental unsureness, even in that love of flowers which was one of his charming traits. Jessie Chambers, who had lived all her life among them, knew and loved the English wild flowers, and could not help expressing some surprise that he, brought up in the streets, should possess or affect to possess an almost supernatural knowledge. Once she ventured to ask him how it was that he always said he knew the names of all the wild flowers they found, whereupon he turned on her furiously: "I know *because* I know. How dare you ask me how I know?" Of course his rage showed that he didn't know and was aware of it. I have been with him myself when he obstinately and vehemently maintained that viper's bugloss was borage, and when I convicted him of error by putting the two flowers side by side before him, he found the whole trifling episode supremely uninteresting and refused to discuss it further.

Their mutual love of flowers twines round their boy and girl courtship like a garland. He would have been hurt and angry if she had not loved flowers even more intensely than he, yet there were queer perverse moods in which he seemed to resent it in her, as if he were insane enough to be jealous of her touching the flowers. One evening she drew him out to look in the twilight at a magnificent bush of wild roses, and in her delight at their beauty she put out her hand to touch their petals. Instantly he turned round and made her come away. Again, next spring, when the garden was golden with daffodils she kneeled down and kissed them, exclaiming that they were "magnificent". Whereupon he said sourly: "Magnificent! it's a bit thick—they're pretty."

Humbled, she said nothing, but bent and kissed the flowers again, comforting herself. Whereupon:

"Why must you always be fondling things!" he said irritably.

"But I love to touch them," she replied, hurt.

"Can you never like things without clutching them as if you wanted to pull the heart out of them? Why don't you have a bit more restraint, or reserve, or something? You wheedle the soul out of things. I would never wheedle—at any rate, I'd go straight."

What perverse balderdash! Those were the very questions which his own critics were always asking him, and the final sentence though somehow insulting to the girl is quite meaningless. Let us note, however, that this puritanical young man objected to people who touched and kissed flowers and "wheedled the soul out of them". He wouldn't do such a thing, oh no, he would "go straight". Yet not so long afterwards when they were gathering cowslips, he describes how he knelt down, "gathering the best blossoms, talking softly all the time." The girl, he admits, plucked the flowers "lovingly and with reverence", but his bunches "had a natural beauty more than hers. He loved them, but as if they were his and he had a right to them. The flowers were very fresh and sweet. He wanted to drink them. As he gathered them, he ate the little yellow trumpets". And by way of rounding out this chapter of doing himself what he denounced in her, there is a passage where he describes going out into the garden on a moonlight night to *touch* the flowers! "He found the purple iris, touched their fleshy throats and their dark grasping hands."

Ondoyant et divers—it is four centuries since the Sieur de Montaigne found that phrase to express the waywardness of our species, and there could not be a better or more suggestive indication of the particularly wayward person whose nature we are exploring. Long after the period of Lawrence's youth the Danish painter, Gótzsche, in Mexico complained that he was "artificial and complicated". This is not nearly so good. By "artificial" Gótzsche meant that Lawrence recognised motives and aims and ways of life wholly outside his own simple-simon democrat view; and by "complicated" he was merely acknowledging a subtlety and complexity beyond his experience. But even in his early twenties Lawrence was *ondoyant et divers*, showing such divergences and contradictions both in temperament and in behaviour that he baffles description as well as analysis. Deeply as she cared for him Jessie Chambers exclaimed in exasperation that she wished she could "wring him into consistency". Consistency, being the virtue of political and literary time-servers, is a quality one is glad he managed to avoid. What angered her and what she was trying to express was his undependable quality, his curious mixture of inner unsureness with outer assertive arrogance, his wavering to and fro in feelings as well as ideas, the perversity which forced him, like his father before him, to turn friends into enemies in mere wantonness. Lawrence had brought the Chambers family the infinitely precious gifts of youthful warmth and vitality, and they had responded by treating him as son and brother. Suddenly for no apparent reason he "outraged the family feeling by some overbearing insult." Why? He did not know himself. He just couldn't help destroying in an instant the goodwill and affection he had been weeks in creating. Yet even here he could waver from a pointless malignancy to tenderness, in a moment. Having pointedly jeered at a young woman he thought was too self-centred in the "suffragette" way, he saw, or thought he saw, that the expression on her face was "misery and not scorn". Immediately "his heart grew tender for everybody, and he turned and was gentle" with Jessie.

These sudden revulsions of feeling, unmotivated or at best motivated by some subjective whim, are surely more extreme than the usual waverings of the human soul. They are not just the phases and changes most people experience. At forty Lawrence in many ways was much the same kind of person he had been at twenty. He had by then travelled himself out of home insularity and the literary parochialism of London; he was far less naïve, embittered and disillusioned, but much the same unaccountable collection of incompatible impulses and prejudices. Admirable as he was in creating his own life rhythm, in keeping his days glamorous; shrewd too in practical affairs, even in money matters; he was yet dismally incompetent in his relations with other human beings. He would begin by giving himself too recklessly, too lavishly; then abruptly turn round and take it all back, and having himself first created a false impression would bitterly accuse his "friend" of worshipping a self-created idol. He made a fetish of spontaneity and used it as an excuse for yielding to any impulse which came to him. It was impossible to argue with him because he shifted his ground and changed his principles to suit every emergency. He claimed as a right for himself the abandonment of reticence, self-control, consideration for the feelings of others, but resented with fury the most delicate criticism of himself. He unscrupulously used his great gifts to justify the unjustifiable, and when all else failed he could always fall back upon his "dark soul", or fly into a rage and throw something. How often he reminds one of Plato's myth of the human soul—the charioteer with his white and black steeds. Seldom can there have been two such restive soul-steeds as Lawrence's—the white steed so beautiful, the dark so vicious and perverse, the charioteer so completely abandoning his function in order to use his whip one someone else's soul-team.

Out of this we must not carry away too sombre an image. "The evil that men do lives after them", and it is so much easier to be offended by the failings of a "genius" than to recognise his qualities. It is true of Lawrence dead as it was of Lawrence living that he could only reveal his wonderful best self to sympathy. There will always be people who are instinctively repelled by his literary personality as many were by his living self. Here is a striking instance. All those who knew and liked him could not fail to be struck by the life and beauty of his deep blue eyes—their pure colour and strange vitality were the first things one noticed in him. After he had lunched with John Galsworthy, the successful novelist noted in his journal that he had met "the provincial genius, Lawrence", a man he could not like because of his "dead eyes". Now others have seen those eyes angry, derisive, mocking, Pan-like, devilish, laughing, inspired, serene, but never anything but most vividly alive. It was reserved for the creator of *The Forsyte Saga* to depress them for once into a temporary appearance of death.

3

THE Ilkeston headmaster may or may not have been wise in making a favourite of Lawrence and giving public praise to his essays, thus stimulating a vanity which needed no fostering; but in the academic line he had every reason to be proud of the exceptional pupil he had coached. In December of 1904 D. H. Lawrence was among the candidates in the nation-wide King's Scholarship Examination, and he came out in the First Division of the First Class. Passing examinations is of no importance in the career of a creative artist in literature, may indeed be a disadvantage by burdening him with the lumber of learning, but it is an achievement which the stupidest can recognise and the natural entry to a successful career as a pedagogue. This really was an achievement for a boy with Lawrence's handicaps. A pupil-teacher who scored that success was certain of his future provided that he went on working, showed an aptitude for the difficult science or craft of pedagogy, and avoided anything officially considered as scandalous behaviour.

Under the school regulations then in force Lawrence was compelled to remain for another six months at Ilkeston, during which his friend coached him for the London University Matriculation, which Lawrence successfully passed three months before his twentieth birthday, in June 1905. This was another triumph when you consider the interruptions to his schooling and his ill-health. If he had chosen to follow this up by working successfully for an Honours Degree—who knows?—we might have lost Lawrence the genius to gain Professor David H. Lawrence.

It is not clear to me why he failed to proceed at once to the university after these academic successes, but there may have been some regulation affecting his case which caused him to spend the next year working as an uncertificated teacher in the British School at Eastwood. Perhaps the King's Scholarship was not enough to keep him, since we learn that he "saved most of his earnings towards his college expenses", though we are not told the amount of such earnings—meagre enough, no doubt. According to *Sons and Lovers* it was one pound a week. He was just twenty-one when, in September 1906, he entered Nottingham University for a two years' training course in the Normal Department—the "normal" referring to the academic programme and not to the sexual psychology of the pupils. There he began reading for an Arts degree and received extra tuition in Latin from the Eastwood Congregational clergyman and from one of his own professors. Unfortunately—or perhaps fortunately—the over-worked professor had to discontinue the lessons, and Lawrence in his impulsive way immediately abandoned the project.

It is easy to guess how much this brilliant lad had looked forward to university life, going up with high but vague hopes of "getting something" from his teachers. As was habitual with him he hoped for far too much and allowed himself too soon to swing back into exaggerated disappointment and disgust. He made half-friends with a professor nicknamed "Botany" Smith, presumably on the ground of a common interest in wild flowers and plants; he enjoyed the classes in singing and the lectures on English poetry; and that seems to be about all. His own opinion was that the two years at the university were wasted years, and he afterwards wished that he had taken his Teacher's Certificate from outside.

Why did Lawrence pause and turn back at the very frontier of serious higher education? It was not due to any lack of mental power, for in addition to everything else he was a very "clever" man, but to a deep-seated lack of sympathy, an instinctive sense that this was not his real path. As so often what his intuition prompted was the protection of his originality as an artist, not his material advantage. Yet academically he continued successful. In his final examination he won six distinctions, including French and botany, but—pleasing irony!—not English. When after all these years of self-discipline and hard work he was at last duly qualified as a teacher, he found to his disgust that the most he could earn as a very junior teacher in his own district was thirty shillings a week. This he refused to accept, and now spent three months without working at his profession, passing the time by doing farm-labourer's work gratis at The Haggs and in writing. It was not until October of 1908 that he accepted an offer of ninety-five pounds a year as junior assistant-master at Davidson Road School, Croydon. Here his customary shrewdness deserted him, for he does not seem to have realised that this higher salary meant that the school was not liable to pay him compensation or a pension in case of a break-down in health.

Under all this commonplace routine of trying to earn a living Lawrence's bafflingly complex character developed, his talents as a writer began to claim more and more of his thoughts and energy, and he lived through the bitter suffering brought about by the implacable hostility of his mother and elder sister to his relationship with Jessie. The cruel drama of their young love—"slain like a foetus in the womb" as he wrote miserably when it was all over —dominated his life. It was his mother who encouraged him in painting, perhaps from a hope that he might earn money by making designs for textile factories, whereas it was Jessie who encouraged him in his true vocation as writer. It would be an exaggeration to say that she made him as a writer. But those who know how Lawrence always depended on a woman, how a woman always stands behind his work as the silent unknown collaborator, will realise what he owed her. The touch of her personality is unmistakable in all his early work.

It seems rather important to point out that Lawrence began writing much later than is usually the case with the born writer, whether a genius or not. Such persons usually begin writing poetry in their teens, pour out quantities of more or less imitative verse, and then on the brink of adult life have a sudden revulsion of feeling, destroy what they have written and start again, sometimes as poets, more often as writers of prose. Occasionally something survives from this period of apprenticeship—Pope and Blake each preserved a lovely poem written in boyhood—but in Lawrence's case the feverish aspirations of youth were satisfied by painting. And with the exception of some flower and fruit pieces, his paintings were all copies or unsuccessful attempts at designing commercial patterns. He was about fifteen when he began painting, but he himself dates his first attempt at writing poetry as "one Sunday afternoon, in my twentieth year". Next year we find him at work on the earliest draft of his first novel, *The White Peacock*. But apparently quite four years of his youth were devoted to painting as his method of expression, before he even thought of writing.

We can fix the year 1905, though not the month, as the time when Lawrence, walking through the fields with Jessie Chambers, suddenly asked her if she had ever thought of writing. She replied that she had thought about it all her life, and in turn asked: "Have you?" Notice his reply indicates that he thought of it from the beginning as a kind of collaboration:

"Yes, I have. Well, let's make a start. I'm sure we could do something if we tried. Lots of the things we say, the things you say, would go ever so well into a book."

It is amusing to find Lawrence starting off with the usual incompetent amateur's excuse—"I'm sure I could write something much better than half the stuff that gets published nowadays." Of course, in this case it happened to be true. Having made the suggestion he immediately recoiled in an agony of shyness, and it was not until some time later that he announced to the girl that what they were to write would be "poetry". She responded with enthusiasm, but instantly he showed that fear of ridicule, of being rebuffed, which haunted him. "But what will the others say?" he exclaimed. "That I'm a fool! A collier's son a poet!" When she urged that his father's occupation had nothing to do with his being a poet Lawrence merely "shook his head" mournfully. His feeling of class inferiority was then acute and it was a weakness he never really managed to shake off. Yet in spite of what was tiresome and "difficult" about him the girl felt intuitively that between them "some intangible thing" was taking shape. She was deeply impressed by the power in him: "An ineradicable loyalty to Lawrence grew up in me; his significance seemed to me beyond that of an ordinary man. I felt that I was in the presence of greatness, and the facts of poverty and obscurity were irrelevant."

It is my hope here to avoid literary criticism and, above all, that quasi-philosophising which now passes as criticism. I want to use Lawrence's books to illustrate and if possible to explain the history of his life and the complexities of his temperament. But then a writer's books are his life-work and without their existence we should not know of him or want to understand him. Therefore this moment of "beginning to write" is of great import and his first poems peculiarly interesting biographically. Unluckily we do not know the date of the earliest surviving poems (the two first were certainly destroyed), nor is there any certainty of the exact chronological order of those we have. When Lawrence in 1927–28 re-wrote his poems he claimed that he had re-arranged them in chronological order. To avoid boring the reader with technical arguments I shall only say that this statement can only be approximate. It is no more accurate than the division of the poems into rhymed and unrhymed—for no less than five of the first ten "unrhymed" are as a matter of fact in rhyme.

Looking over his first book of poems in the original edition one cannot help being struck by the fact that this provincial working-class young man, working entirely alone but for the encouragement of a schoolgirl, should have started producing poems which were not the echo of Victorian poets one would expect but already have a distinct originality, underivative and non-literary. Even their disregard for the craftsmanship of verse had its value, since in those days verse-craft was a fetish and to be impeccably lifeless was the ideal. Perhaps he took something from Hardy, but if he did it was mainly the lesson of building poems from his own immediate experience while dropping all those beautiful garments of æstheticism then in vogue. While he wrote some "fictional poems", his real achievement was a new sort of realism, the poetry of vivid impressionism, of truth to personal experience.

Any attentive reader of his early novels will soon notice passages which are duplicated in the poems. 'Discord in Childhood', already quoted, is a case in point. The experience embodied in 'Cherry Robbers' appears in both *The White Peacock* and in *Sons and Lovers*. It was of course written to the girl at the farm and must have pleased him since it is almost the only one of the very early poems not re-written:

"Under the long dark boughs, like jewels red
In the hair of an Eastern girl
Hang strings of crimson cherries, as if had bled
Blood-drops beneath each curl.

Under the glistening cherries, with folded wings
Three dead birds lie:
Pale-breasted throstles and a blackbird, robberlings
Stained with red dye.

Against the haystack a girl stands laughing at me,
Cherries hung round her ears.
Offers me her scarlet fruits: I will see
If she has any tears."

This is the sort of poem the school of Verlaine called an *eau-forte*, or a silhouette. Its naïveté is not really made sophisticated by the pretended cynicism of the last line, as such poets as Dowson and Symons would have made it. Nor would they have passed such clumsiness as "like jewels red", "as if had bled" and the "robberlings" invented to rhyme with "wings".

As a commentary on the poem, an explanation of the emotions it symbolised, we must look to the novels. 'Cyril', in *The White Peacock*, crowns 'Emily' not with cherries but with "ruby bunches" of guelder-rose berries and then having called up her response chills her by saying "You always have your soul in your eyes, such an earnest, troublesome soul". This of course was exactly the sort of thing with which in real life he made Jessie so self-conscious and miserable. In *Sons and Lovers* the scene is slightly different, more subtle and elaborated. This time it is Lawrence who is in the cherry tree, and as he looks down on the girl he thinks how she looks "so small, so soft, so tender, down there". He pelts her with cherries, and as she runs she snatches them up to hang over her ears like a child. He stays to watch the sunset and, climbing down in the twilight, tears his shirt. As she promises to mend the tear she touches his naked shoulder with her fingers, saying: "How warm!" Then follows one of his "dark" love scenes which so much offended contemporary readers, who were accustomed to read of such experiences in purely conventional treatment, whereas Lawrence was trying to express subtle sensations and emotions:

" 'I like the darkness,' he said, 'I wish it were thicker—good thick darkness'. "

"He seemed to be almost unaware of her as a person: she was only to him then a woman. She was afraid.

"He stood against a pine-tree trunk and took her in his arms. She relinquished herself to him, but it was a sacrifice in which she felt something of horror. This thick-voiced oblivious man was a stranger to her."

They lay down on the pine-needles, and rain began to drift in on them. Then, as seems inevitable with Lawrence, his mood suddenly changed. Now he was "very dreary at heart, very sad and very tender". They stand up and silently walk away hand in hand. "I feel so still," he says. And then: "The fir trees are like presences in the darkness: each one only a presence. A sort of hush: the whole night wondering and asleep: I suppose that's what we do in death—sleep in wonder."

The girl, who for a time had been "afraid of the brute in him", now was "afraid of the mystic". And well might she be afraid of a lover so uncertain, so complex and so enigmatic, at once charming and insulting, a life-giver who fell into moods of the dreariest misery and death-worship, a lover at once so tender and so harsh, so assertively dogmatic yet so unsure of himself, so domineering to her yet so easily swayed by her enemies. A psychological tangle of a man, clearly most attractive to women, yet with a streak of the homosexual in him, more than a streak of the sadist. Look at the poem, 'Love on the Farm'. A man has caught a live rabbit and killed it in spite of its looking back pleadingly at him "with liquid anguished eyes"; he enters the room where someone—man or woman?—is waiting, and:

> "He flings the rabbit soft on the table board
> And comes towards me: ah! the uplifted sword
> Of his hand against my bosom! and oh, the broad
> Blade of his glance that asks me to applaud
> His coming! With his hand he turns my face to him
> And caresses me with fingers that still smell grim
> Of the rabbit's fur! God, I am caught in a snare!
> I know not what fine wire is round my throat;
> I only know I let him finger there
> My pulse of life, and let him nose like a stoat
> Who sniffs with joy before he drinks the blood."

The Haggs, it may be noted, was infested with rabbits from the landlord's preserves which drove the farmer wild by their destructiveness. But the rabbit played a considerable if wholly obscure part in Lawrence's early erotic symbolism. Even as late as *Women in Love* he has a most curious chapter entitled 'Rabbit'. Two adults, a man and a woman, with a child, take a large rabbit to an enclosed court. In its struggles the rabbit scratches them both. They release it, and it bolts round and round the court, "like a shot out of a gun." Then it stops abruptly, and begins nibbling. We then find this baffling paragraph: "There was a queer, faint obscene smile over his face. She looked at him and saw him, and knew that he was initiate as she was initiate. This thwarted her, and contravened her, for the moment." I must confess I have not the faintest idea where the obscenity lies, nor in what they were "initiate", nor why she was "contravened" by it, nor why the contravention was only for a moment. Perhaps it does mean something, but what?

Jessie Chambers must have read 'Love on the Farm' since she was "his conscience" and "he always wanted to take her everything he wrote", and the poem would hardly have lessened her fear of the "mystic" in him. Again she might well have looked doubtful over such a passage as this:

"George was sitting by the fire reading. He looked up as I entered, and I loved him when he looked up at me, and as he lingered on his quiet 'Hullo!' His eyes were beautifully eloquent—as eloquent as a kiss."

George, by the way, was the fictionalised character of her brother, hero also of a bathing scene in the old mill-pond:

"He knew how I admired the noble, white fruitfulness of his form. He saw I had forgotten to continue my rubbing, and laughing he took hold of me and began to rub me briskly, as if I were a child, or rather, a woman he loved and did not fear. I left myself quite limply in his hands, and, to get a better grip of me, he put his arm round me and pressed me against him, and the sweetness of the touch of our naked bodies one against the other was superb. It satisfied in some measure the vague, indecipherable yearning of my soul; and it was the same with him. When he had rubbed me all warm, he let me go, and we looked at each other with eyes of still laughter, and our love was perfect for a moment, more perfect than any love I have known since, either for man or woman."

Well, that is a quotation from a novel, so must not be taken too literally as personal experience; yet nobody acquainted with Lawrence's methods will doubt that it was a personal experience any more than he would think it written by a man with no homosexual tendency. It should be noticed that he quite willingly forgives his fictionalised self for that "yearning of the soul" he was always denouncing in the girl. It was just like touching the flowers—what was wrong for her, was right for him if he happened to want to do it. Can we wonder that she had a habit of taking his face between her hands and looking "deeply, searchingly" into his eyes—a simple enough action from a girl with whom he was supposed to be in love, yet he could not meet her gaze, and turned away, jeering at her as "soulful" and accusing her of "trying to make him spiritual". What was he? she was asking herself as much as the Delphic oracle of him, what did he want of her? Did he know himself? Yet there were times when they were alone together when their relationship seemed blissfully perfect. "We were in a world apart," she writes, "where feeling and thought were intense, and we seemed to touch a reality that was beyond the ordinary workaday world."

Yet there were always his "dark" moods, moods of being boorish or insulting or insufferably arrogant, moods of perverse contradiction or pointless gloom or fantastic death-longing. Among the most extraordinary was his response to the influence of a full moon.

Late in life Lawrence dreamed up some half-serious symbolism about the moon not really being a planet of stone but composed of some unknown phosphorescent substance. He liked to throw out such remarks to annoy pedantic materialists, but there is plenty of evidence to show that he did sometimes experience a powerful influence from a full moon, an influence which was usually not beneficent, or, at any rate, stimulated the "dark" repellent side of him. Usually he was intensely responsive to the æsthetic appeal of soft iridescent moonlight, but there were other visitations more mysterious and disquieting which generated a peculiar and frightening violence in him. Here is his own description of such an occurrence:

"The country was black and still. From behind the sandhills came the whisper of the sea. They walked in silence. Suddenly he started. The whole of his blood seemed to burst into flame, and he could scarcely breathe. An enormous orange moon was staring at them from the rim of the sandhills. He stood staring, looking at it. . . . His blood was concentrated like a flame in his chest. . . . There were flashes in his blood. . . . He did not know himself what was the matter."

We have confirmation from Jessie Chambers that this was a real and not an imagined experience. She was with him not only on this occasion, but on two others, and from what she says it is apparent that the strange mood of frenzy evoked in him by a full moon was more frightening than he indicates. It seemed, she says, as if some "dark power" gradually took possession of him until "something seemed to explode inside him." She goes on:

"I cannot remember now what he said, but his words were wild, and he appeared to be in great distress of mind, and possibly also of body. . . . He upbraided me bitterly, and when I protested he blamed himself, and poured himself out in a torrent of passionate words."

It is true that just before the two started on this walk Lawrence's mother had showed her bitter dislike for the girl, and it is possible that this was weighing on his mind. But that does not explain why he experienced this fit of "possession" by the light of a full moon, especially since this odd half-demented behaviour was repeated before Jessie Chambers on two other occasions. One was at Robin Hood's Bay, where he "talked and behaved so wildly that it is difficult to recall what he did actually say or do", but she remembered that he "stalked some distance from me like a strange, wild creature, and kept up a stream of upbraiding". The other was at Flamborough, and was still more irrational and terrifying. There, under the white light of a full moon, he "skipped from one white boulder to another" until she "almost doubted whether he was indeed a human being". She was "really frightened", and "he created an atmosphere not of death, which after all is part of mortality, but of an utter negation of life, as though he had become dehumanised."

What was the explanation of these moon-struck frenzies? Were they in any way connected with the bad headaches from which he suffered in those days, headaches which always gave him a flushed face and hence caused heedless people to say how well he looked? The seizures as described by Jessie Chambers seem to have been exceptionally violent, but it is a fact that during most of his life he had this odd susceptibility to the light of the full moon. The physiologist or the psychologist may be able to give it a learned name, but that does not get us far unless it is known to be associated with certain types of mind and conduct.

These trials and disadvantages in her lover, even when aggravated by his domineering moods and utter disregard for other peoples' feelings, were less of a strain than the cold hostility of Lawrence's mother and his unbreakable ties with her. It was quite impossible for the girl to help him to break away from this mother clutch when he did not want to do so, when in fact he blamed her bitterly for putting him in the entirely normal position of having to choose. Which did he want, a mother or a wife? Apparently he did not want a wife then, in spite of all his subsequent propaganda when he awoke and found himself married. At that time he wanted to live with his mother and paint, on an income of thirty shillings a week, and pick up a mistress when he felt he needed one.

However that may be, Mrs. Lawrence's hostility to her son's sweetheart began very early in their friendship. On the occasion when the girl took him to see the flowering rose-tree, he was of course late in coming home, and the moment he entered his mother flew at him. "His soul, warm and exposed from contact with the girl, shrank." She made such sneers at the girl as saying that she must have been "wonderfully fascinating" for him to walk the whole way home with her. He was "hurt" by this, but instead of standing up for himself and the girl as any normal young man would do, he only felt that "he could not harden his heart to ignore his mother". He argued weakly, tried feebly to defend himself, as if there had been something wicked in his liking the girl. The mother flashed back at him contemptuously—"it is disgusting—bits of lads and girls courting." There of course she laid bare her jealousy, her sexual possessiveness. Instead of standing up to her, he weakly denied that there was any "courting", they "did nothing but talk" . . . "until goodness knows what time" the mother interjected scathingly. At last he plucked up courage to point out that she allowed his younger sister to go out with her young man, to which she could make only the lame reply that "they've more sense than you two"! When he asked why, she could only think of the typically Laurentian evasion that his sister was "not one of the deep sort". The altercation plunged him in misery, and as he went to bed he kissed her "forehead that he knew so well" and "his hand lingered on her shoulder". She had won, as obviously she would always have won against any girl with whom she disputed possession of her son.

Yet he could not or at any rate did not give up the girl. He denied even to himself that he was or had been falling in love with her, and perhaps there was some truth in this—probably he was never as deeply in love with her as she with him. But leave her alone he could not. He had to go on seeing her and receiving the inspiration of her presence, the stimulus of her personality, simply because he could not write "without a woman at my back", and no other woman was available. Always remember—his mother never valued his art but only any success it brought him, the most withering form of "encouragement".

So the battle of mother and sweetheart went on, with Lawrence playing a very equivocal part. A "number of trifling incidents" and "tiny insults" from his family decided her against coming to see him in his home any more. When she told him, instead of taking her part, he flew into a rage, refused to meet her at anyone else's house, and the Thursday evenings together which had been "so precious" to her were ruthlessly cancelled. When his mother heard of this, "she sniffed with satisfaction". The moods of hostility and harshness which he inflicted on the girl were usually the result of some prompting or nagging from his mother; but he would not admit it. At one time, for instance, he blamed the autumn, because "everyone feels like a disembodied spirit then". (Yet in his first novel he wrote: "I was born in September, and love it best of all the months.") As he continued to see and walk and talk with the girl, his mother learned of it and brooded bitterly, saying openly that Jessie was "carrying him off" from her and "exulting" in it, clamouring against the girl that "she's not like an ordinary woman who can leave me my share in him." When he met her after such a scene with his mother he was bitterly cruel to the girl; but this time blamed it on the spring.

In such unfair attacks on her he hurt himself as much as he hurt her, and walked back "wild with torture, biting his lips, torn, almost bewildered." Why did his mother suffer so much? Why was he so cruel to Jessie? Why when he thought of his mother did he hate the girl? Reaching home he made wild hysterical appeals to his mother—"Why don't you like her, mother?" Only to receive the dull meaningless reply of blind jealousy: "I don't know. I'm sure I've tried to like her. I've tried and tried, but I can't—I can't."

With the passage of time, and perhaps at his urging, Jessie once again sometimes came to see him in his home. But one evening, absorbed in their talk, he allowed a twopenny loaf to burn in the oven. Although another girl had been present the whole time, his mother on her return made a furious scene of jealousy. This time he flared up in defence of the girl and told his mother that she was not interested in books and painting as Jessie was; to which she could only make the absurd retort: "And *you* won't at my age." Yet after all the wrangling he capitulated once more, even to the extent of denying that he loved Jessie. When he submissively went to kiss his mother good night, she hit hard below the moral belt: "I can't bear it," she whimpered. "I could let another woman—but not her. She'd leave me no room. And I've never—you know—I've never had a husband—not really." At that moment—but perhaps here there is some arrangement of fact to fit the drama—the husband in question returned from the pub, and there was nearly a fight between him and his son.

Even if the details have been altered or re-arranged by him and others in the telling, there can be no doubt whatever that this is in the main the true and tragical story of Lawrence's first love. As we have already seen, he himself long afterwards spoke of it sardonically as the "slaughter of the foetus in the womb." How exasperating he must have been to the girl is hinted at in one of his own sardonic strokes at himself: "She wondered why he always claimed to be normal when he was disagreeable." When he was cruel to her he knew well enough that it was because "she loved him more than he her".

It was on Easter Sunday according to Lawrence, on the day after according to Jessie Chambers' narrative, that she fully experienced the evil power of this mother-son complication. Ironically enough his last words to her the night before had been: "I shall come up to-morrow—early." He did not come up early. There had been a bitter scene with his mother overnight, and when he arrived tardily it was not "full of warmth" for the girl, but in a mood of feeling "dissatisfied with himself and everything", and a conviction that "the deepest of his love belonged to his mother". At tea he was in "a hard, ironical mood", making fun of the people at the Primitive Methodist Chapel. He himself felt he was "too clever and cruel" and that his eyes must be "hard with mocking hate". Yet "he wanted so badly to love, to be tender," and afterwards as he played with a bull-terrier in the garden, "the rough way he bowled the dog over was really loving."

There was not much love, though, when he came to deliver the blow to her which he had promised his mother. We have two or three accounts of this painful scene. According to the girl, after beating about the bush for a time, he said "in a strained voice" and awkwardly: "This—this friendship between us—is it keeping even—is it getting out of balance, do you think?" His own version sounds more exact since it contains one of those maddeningly meaningless generalities he often used to conceal his own uncertainties and waverings: "I can give only friendship—it's all I'm capable of—it's a flaw in my make-up. The thing overbalances to one side —I hate a toppling balance. Let us have done." There was not one true statement in the whole blundering outpouring, and what can be more absurd that his "I hate a toppling balance"?

But he had promised his mother to put the girl off, to show her that they could not be lovers. With cruel clumsiness he told her that he had been in a wrangle with both his mother and his elder sister, who had put him in a dilemma—either he and Jessie must be engaged or "else not go about together". The blow was mortal, for how could they marry on his miserable salary and prospects?

Besides, that intuitive daemon which so jealously protected the artist in him would never have allowed him to bind himself at that date in marriage. "I've looked into my heart," he went on, "and I find that I cannot love you as a husband should love his wife. Perhaps I shall, in time. If ever I find I do, I'll tell you. What about you? If you think you love me, tell me, and we'll be engaged. What do you think?" Was ever woman in this humour lost? What answer did he expect to such a humiliating proposal?

When it was over he reflected cheerfully that he had come back to his mother, "she was the strongest tie in his life." Yet no sooner had he made this sacrifice of his love than he suddenly discovered he loved the whole family "so much". He loved the farm, he loved the elder Chambers son and his parents, he loved "the little poky kitchen", he loved Jessie's "long low parlour" and "the gardens"—"all this besides" her! No, simply "he could not give it up" and he continued to go to the farm just as often, but now was mostly with Jessie's brother instead of with her. He even loved Mrs. Chambers: "he could have wept with gratitude that she was deferential to him." And then after all his priggish lectures to Jessie about her feelings for him and his feelings for her, he suddenly revealed the truth: "This about not loving her physically, bodily, was a mere perversity on his part, because he knew she loved him. He was stupid like a child. He belonged to her. His soul wanted her."

So where on earth was she? No wonder the girl was hurt and bewildered and resentful. He still came to see her, but would not even walk in the garden with her alone, as no doubt he had promised his mother. No wonder she "felt scornful of a poet who needed a couple of children and a puppy circling round as unconscious chaperones!"

Lawrence was not the first young man in the world to want to eat his amorous cake and have it and put it in a book, not the only young man who has fallen in love with a girl his mother disliked, nor the first who could not make up his mind whether to defy his family or to drop the girl, and then felt miserable and shabby and furious with himself and blamed it all on her. But the intensity of his feelings, even when they were shabby, and the truth of the record lift a commonplace story into tragedy.

But what an extraordinary character! Because in this tangle of emotions he admitted humiliation and was at times abject it must not be supposed that he lacked ambition. It had been there quite early when he decided that he would "prove that his mother had been right; he was going to make a man whom nothing should shift off his feet; he was going to alter the face of the earth in some way that mattered". To be possessed by a mission of such importance and a conviction that he never could be in the wrong formed a grievous destiny for a frail penniless young man with nothing but a pen. It was an especially difficult entanglement for one whose moods swayed so uncontrollably that neither he nor anyone else knew how he would feel and behave from one day to the next. Yet every change and whim, every impulsive liking or more durable hatred was defended tooth and nail as truth—the truth of the man with a mission who was never in the wrong:

> "You tell me I am wrong.
> Who are you, who is anybody to tell me I am wrong?
> I am not wrong."

In spite of all the scenes and heart-break Lawrence had by no means come to an end with the girl, though for the time being he concentrated almost entirely on his mother. Like lovers they made ecstatically happy excursions together, one of which was to see Lincoln Cathedral. From the train they caught glimpses of the distant building, "blue and noble against the sky", and in her he guessed that the sight awoke a sense of life's fatality and disillusions while in him rose a longing "to beat against it with all the strength of his soul". His love for her was extravagant—"he wanted to get hold of her, to fasten her, almost to chain her. He felt he must keep hold of her with his hand." He buys her a lunch she thinks "wildly extravagant", buys her violets, and exhorts her: "I want people to think we're awful swells. So look ikey. Strut! Be a fantail pigeon!" How is it possible, one asks, that a man so gifted could have fallen to such levels of self-conscious conceit? If they were happy and a tenth as "superior" as they thought themselves, what did it matter what the insignificant citizens of Lincoln thought? A proud man does not show off.

Yet even this day of happiness was doomed. As they climbed a steep hill her old heart felt the strain, she could not speak and was forced to sit down to rest. "His heart was crushed in a hot grip. He wanted to cry, he wanted to smash things in fury." When she had recovered he broke out absurdly and pathetically: "Why can't a man have a *young* mother? What are you old for? *Why* can't you walk? *Why* can't you come with me to places?" It was ludicrous, but it was appalling. Could he not see he wanted the impossible and the forbidden, that he wanted his mother to be his sweetheart? And she, why did she exact this perilous and damning devotion from her son, why could she not give him to the girls of his own age he wanted?

For as he lived into his twenties there were other girls besides Jessie Chambers who attracted him, as was perfectly normal and natural. There was for instance, the girl of 'Kisses in the Train' and of 'Snapdragon', and the 'Helena' whose personality gives its special and haunting quality to his early novel, *The Trespasser.* But just as he could not break the tie with his mother to give himself wholly to Jessie, so he could not break the tie with her to give himself to these others. It was too strong. She was his "old friend, lover, and she belonged to Eastwood and home and his youth." She was his "conscience", he loved her "with his soul", though he grew warm when he thought of another girl and "the curves of her breasts and shoulders." Changing everlastingly, he now swung back to a position when he "believed himself really bound" to his Jessie. But then he decided that he was "two men inside one skin". He wanted Jessie and he didn't want her, he wanted other girls and he didn't want them. Or more exactly he wanted Jessie as his Muse, the keeper of his literary conscience, but he did not want her as wife or even as mistress. He wanted "a woman to keep him, but not in her pocket".

One actor in this drama who tends to drop entirely out of notice is Lawrence's father. Yet after all it was his daily work underground which formed the support of the whole family, even though the children now were able to make their contribution. His wife had made a chasm between him and his children which nothing seemed able to bridge, and he continued to show his resentment by abusing her, drinking and exaggerating the coarseness of his manners. He was now a man well on in the fifties and his declining physical power meant smaller earnings. Probably it was from this period that his children got the impression he never contributed more than twenty-five shillings a week. Yet the children's contribution and Mrs. Lawrence's skill in management more than made up for it. Their latest cottage, Lynn Croft, was "a comfortable house comfortably furnished" and Lawrence himself was "proud of his home", believed "it had a certain distinction". He thought the hearthrug and cushions "cosy" and that "the prints were in good taste, the china was pretty, and the table-cloth fine."

How this is to be adjusted to later complaints of "grinding poverty" which so much "humiliated" him is hard to say, except on the Laurentian grounds that when he wanted to make one sort of impression his home was "superior" and when he wanted to make another it was "squalid". His standards of destitution were high. Thus, in *The White Peacock*, he describes with obvious repugnance the squalor and poverty of the gamekeeper's cottage and family, yet his description mentions that for breakfast the children had eggs, bacon, milk and jam, and were going to have treacle pudding with their midday meal.

With all this life drama going on and the exacting task of working for examinations it seems remarkable that Lawrence continued to write and to extend his non-academic reading. He certainly continued to write poems, though few of those preserved can be certainly dated before 1908—probably not more than about eighteen. It is a curious fact that although the miner was the only person who spoke dialect in the home, Lawrence at that time handled the dialect in verse more skilfully than the standard English his mother and teachers insisted on his speaking. Here, for instance, is his memory of himself as a child on one of the occasions when a messenger came to say his father had been injured. Notice his mockery of the helpless bashful boy he was:

"Somebody's knockin' at th' door,
    Mother, come down an' see.
—I's think it's nobbut a beggar;
    Say I'm busy.

"It's not a beggar, mother; hark
    How 'ard 'e knocks!
—Eh, tha'rt a mard-arsed kid,
    'E'll gie thee socks.

"Shout an ax what 'e wants,
I canna come down.
—'E says, is it Arthur Holliday's?
—Say Yes, tha clown.

" 'E says: Tell your mother as 'er mester's
Got hurt i' th' pit—
What? Oh my Sirs, 'e never says that,
That's not it!"

Meanwhile, ever since he entered the university in 1906 he had been working on and off on drafts of a novel which eventually became *The White Peacock*. He seems to have begun this work in a rather matter-of-fact frame of mind. The usual method of constructing a novel, he told Jessie Chambers, was "to take two couples and to work out their relationship." Undoubtedly something of the kind can be traced in *The White Peacock* as we have it, for the story is almost wholly based on the relationships of Leslie, Lettie, George and Meg. He wrote that book four times and it runs to one hundred and fifty thousand words, which gives some indication of the energy and tenacity of will he put into it. However carelessly he may have spoken about the mere mechanics and skeleton of a novel, he took the task with all seriousness. When he took Jessie one of the earlier versions, he said: "I think a man puts everything he is into a book, a real book." It was his ability to do that which made his books so different from others, so living, for all their faults of taste and technique, so inexhaustible.

Yet it was in a quite matter-of-fact frame of mind that he wrote his first short stories, a form in which many of his admirers think he excels. In the autumn of 1907 a local paper offered a prize of three guineas for what they were to judge the best short story sent in. Lawrence set about winning that prize with amusing practical efficiency. He wrote three short stories, two of them genuine, one a piece of conventional sentimentality called 'A Prelude to a Happy Christmas'. He sent the two genuine stories in under his own name and that of a friend, and Jessie Chambers lent her name to the sloppy one, which won the prize. We are not told if the editor ever learned of the device practised upon him.

"A Prelude to a Happy Christmas" does not appear in Lawrence's collected works,* though it may perhaps have been a purposely sugary version of the Christmas scene later described in *Sons and Lovers*. The other two stories, when carefully re-written, became 'The White Stocking' and 'A Fragment of Stained Glass', both of them now included in his *Collected Tales*. Like every real writer he instinctively based them not on some abstract idea or emotion, but on a concrete symbol which had touched his imagination—a piece of stained glass he had picked up, a white stocking which figured in one of his mother's stories about her youth. It is probable that this prize-winning success is that described in *Sons and Lovers*, except that there it is a picture, not a story. It is characteristic that both in the novel and in real life he made no attempt to be modest about his success.

4

LAWRENCE had just passed his twenty-third birthday when he left Eastwood to teach at the Davidson Road School, Croydon, then an outer suburb of London. Except for brief excursions he had passed all his life in the Midlands. He had longed often to break free from his limited life there. "I wished that in all the wild valley where cloud shadows were travelling like pilgrims, something would call me forth from my rooted loneliness." But he had quite misjudged the extent to which he had become rooted in his valley and its people, had never guessed how his too acute sensibility would suffer from the breaking away and the subsequent loneliness. On his second day at Croydon he wrote his sweetheart a letter so dismal that it was like "a howl of terror". He could not bear the strangeness of his new surroundings, he dreaded the daylight and his work "with the anguish of a sick girl", he felt he could not live away from his old affections, and threatened that he "would grow into something black and ugly, like some loathsome bird".

Here indeed was naïveté in a man of twenty-three, and also that bitter capacity for suffering he never lost. "Battle—battle—and suffer. It's about all you do, as far as I can see," his mother had said to him in a mood of exasperation and fierce pity. It was so true, the words might always stand as the epigraph to his life. At all periods of his life he "battled" and "suffered", above all at this

* Recently published in a limited edition.

time when his future looked blank and he was "battling" with himself as well as with the world. Who shall estimate the burden and anguish of "genius"? The vulture of Prometheus, the shirt of Nessus, the fatal albatross—these are types and symbols of the pain and fortitude required by such a destiny. Something in the man struggles madly for dominion and will not be denied and rends him in endless suffering as he strives to come to terms with life and with himself. In lassitude and discouragement, death—a mere figment of rhetoric to the immortal young—seems not only desirable but the only hope. In those days Lawrence "had that poignant carelessness about himself, his own sufferings, his own life, which is a form of slow suicide."

Even when he knew the physical culmination of love he knew no respite, for to him then "life seemed a shadow, day a white shadow; night, and death, and stillness, and inaction, this seemed *being*. To be alive, to be urgent and insistent—that was *not-to-be*. The highest of all was to melt out into the darkness and stay there, identified with the great Being." There it was—youth breaking its heart in vain over all frustration and grief and futility that have been and are and will be.

It is difficult to imagine what Lawrence looked like in those early days at Croydon when he was totally unknown, his vocation as a writer quite uncertain, his loves all astray and his heart a chaos bound in bondage to his mother. Three early photographs of him have been preserved. One shows him as a mere baby, another as a small boy with a gaping pout which looks as if he had been allowed to suck a "dummy". In the third he is about seventeen, looking as he says himself somewhere "like a little prig in a high collar", an alert, perky lad with a pursed rather ugly mouth. For the next photograph we jump to 1914, at the age of twenty-eight, looking very much as he did actually look in those days, though his fine eyes are in shadow. No painting, drawing or photograph does justice to the beauty of those brilliant blue eyes which he inherited from his mother, and which contrasted so strikingly with his thick reddish hair.

The "spiritual" beauty he later developed was not visible in his twenties, though no doubt women saw it. Perhaps the nearest we can now get to him in those pre-1914 days is from David Garnett's description. At the very first glance he was struck by Lawrence's "most beautiful lively blue eyes". It is quite clear that those who saw him without noticing the beauty and life of his eyes never saw him in a friendly and lively mood—they were unique and irresistible. "Lawrence," Garnett goes on, "was slight in build, with a weak narrow chest and shoulders, but he was a fair height and very light in his movements. This lightness gave him a sort of grace. His forehead was broad but not high, his nose was too short and lumpy, his face colourless like a red-haired man's, his chin (he had not then grown a beard) altogether too large, and round like a hair-pin—rather a Philip II sort of chin*—and the lower lip rather red and moist under the scrubby moustache. Once you looked into his eyes you were completely charmed, they were so beautiful and alive, dancing with gaiety. His smile lit up all his face as he looked at you."

Contrast that impression with the gloomy picture of himself and his despair at Croydon and you will get yet another glimpse of his extreme mobility and the contradictory selves which inhabited him. True, Garnett was writing of a period four years after Lawrence arrived at Croydon, when he had escaped from England and teaching, was very happy with his new life, and knew that he was a writer—and not a Galsworthy sort of writer. Unfortunately there cannot have been many opportunities for his gaiety to show itself in those first weeks at Croydon, when he was still "battling" in a strife which brought out some of his least attractive traits. Jessie Chambers now saw him only during the holidays, there are no letters to speak of (she gives only extracts), the novels are silent. So we have to look to the poems, which fortunately are rather numerous at this time. 'Last Hours,' written just before he left home, describes him in happy mood lying on grass and flowers under an oak, watching a white cloud pile up, catching a fragrance of clover as a laden bee hums by, but then:

> "Down the valley roars a townward train.
> I hear it through the grass
> Dragging the links of my shortening chain
> Southward, alas!"

At the last moment he did not want to leave, and the next poem

* He means Philip IV. Philip II wore a beard always.

gives a dreary enough picture of what he found in Flat Suburbs, S.W. in the Morning, where:

> "The new red houses spring like plants
>   In level rows
> Of reddish herbage that bristles and slants
>   Its square shadows."

Though on the whole it must have been an improvement on the sad grimy streets he had just left.

Among the fragments of autobiography embedded in these poems perhaps the most interesting are those dealing with this new school and his life as teacher there: 'The Best of School,' 'Last Lesson of the Afternoon,' 'School on the Outskirts,' 'Discipline,' 'The Punisher'. These may be compared with the teaching experiences of Ursula in *The Rainbow*, but they were written long after the event, while the poems were noted at the time. From the testimonials given to Lawrence when he abandoned teaching we learn that he was "highly thought of" by the school authorities, and that he was particularly entrusted with classes of Nature and Art—which sounds most comprehensive and encyclopædic, but probably was not so in fact. Of course they may have overpraised him then because they knew that after he had been found to be suffering from tuberculosis he would never again be allowed to teach children in the national schools. The probability is, however, that the testimonials were genuine, as he was eventually quite successful as a teacher.

What were his own personal feelings in those days about this hard rather thankless task which, to be done conscientiously, demands such expenditure of nervous energy every day and all day? In the opening hour, when pupils and master are fresh and concentrated, he was happy and "thrilled"—always a favourite word. He felt at one with the boys:

> "I feel them cling and cleave to me
> As vines going eagerly up; they twine
> My life with other leaves, my time
> Is hidden in theirs, their thrills are mine."

but what a difference when it comes to the last lesson of the afternoon! The boys he had loved in the morning are now "a pack of unruly hounds", urchins who present "insults of blotted pages" and "scrawl of slovenly work." Lawrence is miserable and discouraged:

> "I am sick, and what on earth is the good of it all?
> What good to them or to me, I cannot see!"

He decides that he will not waste soul and strength—"for *this!*"

> "What does it matter to me, if they can write
> A description of a dog, or if they can't?"

So he ends by determining "to sit and wait for the bell"! How like him! When he felt fresh and cheerful, he loved the boys, education was a wonderful job. But when he is jaded and jangled, and they resent it, then to hell with them! What's the good of education, anyway? Looking at a situation solely from his own point of view, facing all its implications frankly, accepting them, and then turning his back on the whole thing as not his business—how characteristic! There is a desperate sort of humour about it which often comes out in his work and is often missed. Perhaps it is rather prosaic to suggest that what was really the matter with both master and boys was that the working hours were too long.

The poem, 'Discipline,' was almost certainly addressed to Jessie Chambers, and shows a great change from the earlier poems. He tells her that he had approached the boys "with love", with his heart in his hand, "like a loving-cup, like a grail," believing that love would conquer all things, achieve all things. He had been woefully mistaken, it doesn't work. Now he means to battle with the boys in discipline, they "must learn not to trespass", and so forth. Perhaps he intended a lesson for her too, she too is "to learn not to trespass" on him.

The last of these schoolmaster poems shows Lawrence as a severe judge, 'The Punisher'. We see the boys, weeping over the scolding he gives them, suffer "the harsh cold wind" of his words as he stood and expounded "the Judgment that stood in my eyes whirling a flame." However, it does not appear that stern discipline and its application achieved much more success than too much love, for he candidly admits that in a few minutes the boys have forgotten all about it and are larking and playing, while the Judge miserably complains:

> "... my head
> Is heavy, and heart beats slowly, laboriously,
> My spirit is dead."

So actually the disciplinarian chiefly punished himself. His testimonial praises him for keeping discipline "on the highest plane", but certainly he had to tussle at first, and the contest was shattering to his sensitiveness. There is a curious commentary on all this in a letter to Helen Corke, dated 21st June, 1910, in which he says:

"I was thinking to-day: how can I blame the boys for breaches of discipline? Yet I must not only blame, I must punish. Once I said to myself: 'How can I blame—why be angry?' Then there came a hideous state of affairs. Now I say: 'When anger comes with bright eyes, he may do his will. In me he will hardly shake off the hand of God. He is one of the archangels, with a fiery sword. God sent him—it is beyond my knowing'."

What magniloquence and lofty sentiments over the birching of a few small boys.

It was through some of these early poems and during his period of employment as an assistant-master in the Croydon school that Lawrence made his modest entrance to the world of letters through the pages of *The English Review*, then edited by Ford Madox Hueffer, later Ford. The launching of Lawrence was not quite so easy and effortless as he made out when writing a brief autobiography. He mentions vaguely the publication of his Christmas story and omits the fact that as early as the spring of 1908 he had discussed the publication of his work with Jessie Chambers. At that time he told her that he had sent some of his work to a writer who then wrote regularly for *The Daily News*. This consisted of "articles" which he and Jessie had discussed and thought good. Unfortunately, *The Daily News* author, whoever he was, turned out to be too busy to read the articles, and after a delay of some months his wife sent them back with this interesting information. Remembering his morbid dread of a rebuff and his exaggerated suffering when he received what he considered such even from quite unimportant people, we can understand his reaction:

"I've tried, and been turned down, and I shall try no more. And I don't care if I never have a line published."

That was mere bluff—of course he cared. No doubt, in his ignorance he had expected to be warmly welcomed by the first literary man who read his work, and he had yet to learn for himself that a hard-working author has little time and superfluous energy to spare in reading and advising beginners. However, he stuck to his resolution not to send out any more of his writings. Very nearly a year later he and Jessie began to read *The English Review*, which was at that time more alive and progressive than all the others put together. She tried to persuade him to send in some of his work, but he was still smarting from the rebuff he had received from *The Daily News* man.

"I don't care what becomes of my writing," he told her petulantly, "I'm not anxious to get into print. I shan't send anything. Besides they'd never take it."

Anybody who likes may believe those disingenuous remarks. Obviously he, like every other young author, was pining to see himself in print, but hadn't the guts to risk another refusal. Jessie pleaded with him to make the attempt, whereupon he gave himself away completely by suggesting that she might choose any of his poems she liked and send them in:

"Give me a *nom de plume*, though; I don't want folk in Croydon to know I write poetry."

Possibly dislike of the "Croydon folk" knowing he wrote poetry was a less powerful motive than his fear that "D. H. Lawrence" might again be rejected. Unfortunately, Jessie Chambers could not afterwards remember exactly which poems she copied out and sent but believed they included one of the school poems, 'Discipline,' as well as 'Dreams,' 'Old and Nascent,' and 'Baby Movements', now called 'Baby Running Barefoot'. It was good judgment on her part to put 'Discipline' first, guessing that such a title would attract attention at a time when everybody wrote poems called 'Rebellion'.

Having copied out whatever scripts she did send she enclosed them with a letter to Hueffer, explaining Lawrence's situation as a schoolmaster and asking that if the poems were published it should be under the pseudonym of Richard Greasley—a horrid name, but Greasley was the name of a village they liked; still what a beastly name for a poet! Lawrence affected complete indifference, and yet could not restrain himself sufficiently to avoid asking if she had sent them, adding immediately: "They'll never print them." Throughout his life he tried to hide feelings which were absurdly easy to wound behind a pretence, which was yet not wholly a pretence, of arrogance or truculence or satire or insult. He stabbed himself with unnecessary fears. As Jessie Chambers says, in every misunderstanding he "took refuge in an arrogance" which was nothing more than "a mask for his own wretchedness". Even in those days she noted that whenever he was upset by something going wrong in his personal relationships, which was fairly often, his misery and anger exploded in a "dehumanised vehemence that was devastating".

According to Hueffer's recollections Jessie Chambers first wrote to ask whether she should send prose or verse and he replied "both"; whereupon she sent him "three poems about a schoolmaster's life and 'Odour of Chrysanthemums'." On the strength of the opening paragraph of that short story Hueffer without reading further accepted them all and announced to "all London" that he had discovered another genius and this time a big one. Now Ford's recollections—he described himself as "an impressionist"—have a habit of being more picturesque and illustrative of Ford's pre-eminence in something or other than they are accurate. It may have been as he says, but the prosaic facts of bibliography show that Hueffer in November 1909 published five poems by Lawrence, only one of which was a "schoolmaster" poem. In February 1910 he published the short story 'Goose Fair'; in April six more poems; and it was not until June 1910—about a year after he had received the story, according to him—that he published 'Odour of Chrysanthemums'. If he admired it so much, if it was that which caused him to accept Lawrence's work and announce him as "a big genius", why did he wait a year before publishing it?

According to Hueffer he sent a letter to Jessie Chambers "next morning", but it was in June that she sent in the manuscripts, and for some reason the reply did not reach her until August, when Lawrence was away in the Isle of Wight. Hueffer's letter was a cautious one, saying the poems were interesting, the author undoubtedly had talent, but warned that luck plays a large part in a literary career and adding, that if Lawrence would come to see Hueffer "something might be done". Not perhaps as enthusiastic as old Haydn acclaiming young Mozart, but better than a frigid rejection slip. Jessie replied that Lawrence would make the call after school re-opened, but kept the letter to herself until he returned to Eastwood. This is how she describes the scene:

" 'Oh, I've got a letter for you.'

"He looked at me quickly, then his eyes narrowed.

" 'From the *English?* About the poems? Show it me.'

"I gave him the letter, and his face became tense.

" 'You are my luck,' he murmured. Then he said with suppressed excitement, 'Let me take it to show mother.' And I never saw it again."

Hueffer's account of Lawrence's first visit to him is amusing. According to him, Lawrence was so swept off his feet by this encouragement that he instantly swung from an extremity of pessimism to one of optimism, and imagined that he was already a writer of such importance that he would at once be earning two thousand pounds a year—and Jessie Chambers at a later stage confirms this. So when Lawrence visited Hueffer it was not as the beginner hoping nervously for approval but as the successful author wondering if *The English Review* was good enough to be the means of launching him on the world. According to Hueffer he looked rather disparagingly at the modest offices of *The English Review* and remarked: "This doesn't look like a place in which one could make money." "Oh," said Hueffer, "we don't make money here. We spend it." Whereupon Lawrence replied: "That's just it. The room may be all right for your private tastes, which aren't mine, though that doesn't matter. But it isn't one to inspire confidence in creditors. Or contributors."

Such is Hueffer's story, or rather the gist of it for he is inordinately prolix. Whether there is any truth in it or not is another question. There may be. Lawrence's own version of all this is very laconic:

"Hueffer was most kind. He printed the poems, and asked me to come and see him. The girl had launched me, so easily, on my literary career, like a princess cutting a thread, launching a ship."

The manuscripts which Jessie Chambers sent to Hueffer were exactly the sort of writing to please him, and he was undoubtedly the only English editor of the time who would have sponsored Lawrence. Ford Hueffer was in reaction against the romantic, idealist movements of the 19th century, having had the misfortune to spend his childhood oppressed by more or less famous relatives who gave lustre to the previous age. His father was a cultured German who came to England to spread the gospel of Wagner, became musical critic for *The Times*, and married a daughter of the pre-Raphaelite painter, Ford Madox Brown. A half-sister of Hueffer's mother married W. M. Rossetti, so that Ford with his innate modesty referred about every ten minutes to "my aunt Christina" and "my uncle Gabriel". Ford about the time Lawrence met him was very friendly with Violet Hunt, whose father was a landscape painter afflicted with what Oscar Wilde called "wonderful radicalism". With all his faults Ford was a most kind-hearted man, always most willing to help young unknown writers, though strict veracity was not his strong point. As I have mentioned he used to get over this by calling himself "an impressionist", which Yeats always insisted simply meant "a journalist". However that may be, Hueffer influenced Lawrence both by precept and example more than is usually conceded.

These defunct but illustrious relatives of his gave Hueffer a position both in literature and in what was then called Society which might not have been so readily granted to his unaided talents. At any rate he used whatever influence he had on Lawrence's behalf with kindness and zeal. In due course he was handed the much worked-over script of Lawrence's first novel, *The White Peacock*. According to Lawrence, Jessie Chambers "always admired it in all its stages", implying that she merely acted as uncritical chorus of feminine approval. He simplified too much. It was Jessie Chambers who talked him out of an early version where Lettice, "a very superior young lady", was made to marry a conventionally upright George. She also persuaded him to modify the merely "cynically brutal" first version of Annabel, the first of Lawrence's long line of symbolic gamekeepers. Nor was Hueffer's judgment of the final script wholly favourable. Riding with Lawrence in a bus he shouted, as nearly as Hueffer with his muffled utterance could shout, that it had "every fault that the English novel can have" but added: "You've got genius."

Always "genius"! and that in literary London was apparently more of a handicap than an asset. No wonder Lawrence made his rather sour comment: "In the early days they were always telling me I had genius, as if to console me for not having their own incomparable advantages." Still Hueffer backed any belief he might have in a "genius" who had not collaborated with Joseph Conrad nor studied the appalling complexities of the *mot propre*, by giving him a letter of introduction to William Heinemann, to whom he submitted the novel in December 1909. Lawrence tells us that the book was "accepted at once", but as a matter of fact its fate was still uncertain as late as April 1910, and it did not appear until January 1911.

In November 1909, the month when Lawrence's first poems appeared in *The English Review*, he was invited to a small luncheon party given by Violet Hunt at which Ezra Pound and Hueffer were present. Jessie Chambers, who shrank with extreme bashfulness from such social contacts, was more or less betrayed into attending —fortunately, for she has left a deft account of the party. As Lawrence and she journeyed to Violet Hunt's house in Kensington he grew inspired by the spectacle of London's opulence, and assured her with the utmost confidence: "I'll make two thousand a year!" The new genius and his girl friend were feasted on roast beef and brussels sprouts, plum pudding and champagne (*horresco referens*), and Violet in her rather brazen manner over-congratulated the girl on having "discovered a genius". All present took for granted that the two were engaged, which was embarrassing for her since Lawrence had just told her he intended to engage himself to a girl known to us only as 'Louie'.

After lunch Hueffer walked ponderously with them up Campden Hill, and as soon as he left them Lawrence turned eagerly to the girl and asked how she had liked having champagne for lunch; to which she replied with disconcerting simplicity that she hadn't known it was champagne. He then asked if she had noticed that, when leaving, Hueffer had murmured something about going to see Lady St. Helier. Lawrence had a great respect for titles. "Oh, how that glittering taketh me," he had muttered when the subject was under discussion.

Meanwhile, was there happiness for the genius who was so confident of making "two thousand a year" and knowing the "glittering" plutocrats who passed for an aristocracy? Hardly. If we turn to the passages in *The White Peacock* relating to his life in Croydon —which he calls Norwood—we read:

"I suffered acutely the sickness of exile in Norwood. For weeks I wandered the streets of the suburb, haunted by the spirit of some part of Nethermere. As I went along the quiet roads where the lamps in yellow loneliness stood among the leafless trees of the night I would feel the dark wet bit of path between the wood meadow and the brooks. A strange voice within me rose and called for the hill path; again I could feel the wood waiting for me, calling and calling, and I crying for the wood, yet the space of many miles was between us. Since I left the valley of home I have not much feared any other loss."

It is a fact that Lawrence never liked big towns, though in a way he was "thrilled" by London and has left some beautiful evocations of the old capital as it was before the debacle of 1914; but once the novelty had worn off he turned away from it. When he thought of Nethermere (Eastwood) it was less the people he yearned for than the place itself. The wood-meadow, the tiny brooks, the hill path to The Haggs meant to him as much as the people, perhaps even more, and had a grip on his deepest feelings.

At Croydon he was as always the strangest battleground for warring impulses and emotions. At one time, as he felt that life was opening before him and he dreamed of lucrative literary success, he seemed a happy, intensely vital young man irresistible to sensitive women. "There was about him a candour and a gentleness which made women trust him." To their peril, however, for as he wrote of himself from Croydon: "At times I am afflicted by a perversity amounting to minor insanity." By "perversity" he meant that unfortunate trait of always or nearly always wanting to contradict and browbeat the person to whom he was talking, his senseless impulse to "battle—battle". Like his father he could not help insulting anyone who could harm him, and like his mother he must self-confidently and arrogantly assert every passing whim that came to him. He admitted that he was "two men inside one skin". He contradicted himself so often and talked so wildly and at random that Jessie Chambers now "never took his assertions about people and things seriously".

The one person who knew how to deal with him and to bring him promptly off the high horse of his "perversity" was his mother, though apparently his "dark self" was more restrained with her and never deluged her with the perverse, malicious balderdash he poured over others in his bad moods. Here, fictionalised it is true but intrinsically most accurate, is his rendering of a talk between him and his mother:

" 'You know,' he said to his mother, 'I don't want to belong to the well-to-do middle class. I like my common people best. I belong to the common people.'

" 'But if anyone else said so, my son, wouldn't you be in a tear. *You* know you consider yourself equal to any gentleman.'

" 'In myself,' he answered, 'not in my class or my education or my manner. But in myself I am.'

" 'Very well, then. Then why talk about the common people?'

" 'Because—the difference between people isn't in their class, but in themselves. Only from the middle classes one gets ideas, and from the common people—life itself, warmth. You feel their hates and loves.'

" 'It's all very well, my boy. But, then, why don't you go and talk to your father's pals?'

" 'But they're rather different.'

" 'Not at all. They're the common people. After all, whom do you mix with now—among the common people? Those that exchange ideas, like the middle classes. The rest don't interest you.'

" 'But—there's the life——'

" 'I don't believe there's a jot more life from Miriam than you could get from any educated girl—say Miss Moreton. It is *you* who are snobbish about class.' "

First of all let us give Lawrence every credit for frankness and honesty in exposing his own faults so clearly, even to the habit he had picked up from his mother of making any sort of illogical or absurd retort rather than admit himself beaten in an argument. Lawrence always argued for victory, never to discover truth. Anybody who knew him must at some time or other have heard him discourse or wrangle very much on the lines of this dialogue. It enshrines prejudices which he carefully cultivated, and was liable to bring out at any moment when unfortunately his mother was not present to make her apposite and pungent comments. Only a few months before his death he published them in a London newspaper, in an article written with an air of dogmatic finality which must have impressed many people.

In addition to these class-conscious worries, he now contrived to trouble himself considerably about his lack of faith in the doctrines of Congregationalism. At one time his mother had urged him to enter the ministry, and in his usual state of uncertainty he had gone so far as to consult the Biblical lots, opening the book at random three times and jabbing his finger on a text which was supposed to offer guidance. As might have been expected, "the message was inconclusive". And in spite of his dogmatic manner, in a state of acute inconclusiveness he remained, delivering himself of such gnomic utterances as: "It's not religious to be religious; I reckon a crow is religious when it sails across the sky." On another occasion he announced: "I don't believe God knows such a lot about Himself. God doesn't *know* things, He *is* things. And I'm sure He's not soulful." But, after all, what is the use of being a thing if you don't know it?

Still, Christianity, whether he happened to be considering it as myth or metaphysics or psychology, was far too useful to the artist in him to be dropped wholly, even when he was occupied in trying to find some other synthesis. His mind thought in symbols, not in ideas, dwelt on emotions and impressions and rejected abstractions and definitions. This habit of thought is closely akin to Ruskin's, yet in both the religious impulse was sincere, and perhaps not least so when to the orthodox they seemed verging on blasphemy. Even this was an intermittent interest. "She saw again his lack of religion, his restless instability. He would destroy himself like a perverse child. He had no religion; it was all for the moment's attraction that he cared, nothing else, nothing deeper."

Having allowed the religious belief of his fathers to slip from him, Lawrence could not rest in a tranquil suspension of belief or wait patiently upon the Unknown, but must from time to time bring up some home-made substitute as a universal religion to be vehemently preached only to be as vehemently denounced later on or merely dropped. Whatever his own religious uncertainties he was perfectly ready to advise others. Thus he wrote from Croydon to his sister:

"I am sorry more than I can tell to find you going through the torment of religious unbelief: it is hard to bear, especially now. However it seems to be like this: Jehovah is the Jews' idea of God, not ours. Christ was infinitely good, but mortal as we. There still remains a God, but not a personal God: a vast, shimmering impulse which waves onward toward some end, I don't know what—taking no regard of the little individual, but taking regard for humanity.

When we die, like rain-drops falling back into the sea, we fall back into the big shimmering sea of unorganised life which we call God. . . . Whatever name one gives Him in worship we all strive towards the same God, so we be generous-hearted."

It sounds as if he had just been reading *The Light of Asia*. And this is the more probable since later in life he violently repudiated Buddhism. With him religion and philosophy were a state of mind, not a conviction of absolute truth, and changed as he changed. At this period he had not yet elected himself Saviour of Society. True, he was going to be a writer the world would listen to in some rather indeterminate way, but he was still chiefly occupied by the troubles of sex which had long afflicted him. The weary drawn-out conflict in his heart between his mother and Jessie had been complicated rather than simplified by his interest in other women.

Lawrence was the literary *enfant terrible* of his generation, saying everything that came into his mind irrespective of effects and the feelings of the audience. It was an age of encrusted humbugs and hypocritical reticences, and nowhere was it more of a humbug and more terrifiedly reticent than in all matters of physical sex. The English novel of the day seemed to be written by eunuchs for vestal virgins. But just as Lawrence unhesitatingly revealed himself in other matters, so he did here. If we take literally what he wrote of himself during the Croydon period he had worked himself into a very strange mood:

"Sex had become so complicated in him that he would have denied that he could ever want . . . any woman that he knew. Sex desire was a sort of detached thing, that did not belong to a woman."

Probably the first part of that singular statement really meant no more "complicated" thing than that the young man had not met the woman he wanted to link up with for life—it must be noted that with all his supposed frankness he had derived from his mother the sternest puritanical notions about the indissoluble nature of marriage, though needless to say he did not practise what he preached. As to the second part of his statement—what is meant by sex desire being a detached thing that does not belong to a woman? There may be a clue in the poems. 'Virgin Youth' contains these lines:

"Traveller, column of fire,
It is vain.
The glow of thy full desire
Becomes pain.

Dark, ruddy pillar, forgive me! I
Am helplessly bound
To the rock of virginity. Thy
Strange voice has no sound.

We cry in the wilderness. Forgive me, I
Would so gladly lie
In the womanly valley, and ply
Thy twofold dance."

In the longer poem, 'Manifesto', written six years later, he looked back retrospectively to the "hungers" of his youth and young manhood. He had satisfied the hunger to be sure of food and the hunger for knowledge, but there had remained the "very deep and ravening hunger . . . the very body's crying out . . . the hunger for the woman," which he likens to "a Moloch, ruthless and strong" coming upon him "like the unutterable name of the dread Lord":

"Yet there it is, the hunger which comes upon us
Which we must learn to satisfy with pure satisfaction;
or perish, there is no alternative.

I thought it was woman, indiscriminate woman,
mere female adjunct of what I was."

And further on:

"A woman fed that hunger in me at last,
What many women cannot give, one woman can;
so I have known it.

She stood before me like riches that were mine.
Even then, in the dark, I was tortured, ravening, unfree,
ashamed, and shameful, and vicious.
A man is so terrified of strong hunger;
and this terror is the root of all cruelty."

This is one of the occasions when Lawrence reveals the human soul and body, but the poem belongs to the period of his maturity, and its achievement is beyond anything of the Croydon period. It is relevant here because it looks back to that period.

A great change has come over the public attitude to sex since the beginning of this century, and to an indeterminate extent the change is due to the influence of Lawrence. In the 19th century prudery and make-believe were imposed, no doubt with the excellent motive of refining the relations between men and women and improving women's status. It was thought that the only right training for the complex, difficult and essentially sexual relation which is marriage was a state of "complete purity", which meant complete ignorance. Naturally this was seldom if ever wholly achieved, and probably large sections of the community disregarded it, but so far as the expression of sex life in literature was concerned, sex *qua* sex was held to be unmentionable, indecent, unclean. Thomas Hardy had been so much abused for *Jude the Obscure* that in protest he ceased to write novels. Havelock Ellis had been prosecuted for obscenity, and his books prohibited. It is necessary to remind ourselves of these facts when we come upon the extraordinary episode of Lawrence and Jessie Chambers seriously discussing an article by G. K. Chesterton which asserted (was it a joke?) that "any man who talks to a woman about sex is a brute". Joke or no joke the two young provincials took it seriously and felt they were being daringly rebellious when they decided that the brute was Chesterton.

Yet it was one thing for them to decide an abstract point of that sort, and quite another to rid themselves of the pressure of public opinion and the conditioning of their whole lives. It was as true of him as of the girls, and he never rid wholly himself of his mother's prudery. He was twenty-three when he first went to Croydon and lodged with a young couple who had a baby. When Lawrence's mother was told about the baby she pursed her lips and remarked primly: "I'm glad to hear it—it will keep him *pure*." Lawrence was as terrified that she might get to hear of his affairs with girls as if he were a timid husband dreading that his infidelities might come to the ears of a jealous domineering spouse. He "would have died rather than his mother should get to know of this affair. He suffered tortures of humiliation and self-consciousness. There was now a good deal of his life of which necessarily he could not speak to his mother. He had a life apart from her—his sexual life."

It appears that during their long friendship he only twice spoke to his first sweetheart about sex. No wonder when it was all over he reflected:

"Don't you think we have been too fierce in our what they call purity? Don't you think that to be so much afraid and averse is a sort of dirtiness?"

To reach that state of sanity he had been forced to go through bitter struggles, wild uncertainties and miseries. It took him a long time to find out that it was really "some sort of perversity" in people and their attitude towards sex which made them actually "not want, get away from the very thing they want". Yet at one time he is to be found asserting that only "spiritual relations" were possible between himself and Jessie, that he must go "elsewhere" for sexual satisfaction. Then, caught in some swirl of reaction or remorse he was back at her side, but still dissatisfied. Sometimes "he hated her"; and yet "he continued faithful to her". To Jessie he made such flattering statements as: "I shall go from woman to woman until I am satisfied," and on one occasion in a fit of petulance: "It doesn't matter who one marries!"

Evidently in spite of his mother's influence he had continued to see the girl for other than literary reasons, and the grave chaperonage of two children and a dog had been discarded. At this distance of time it is impossible and not necessary to follow the details and vacillations of this strange wooing. The fact is that he simply could not make up his mind whether he wanted to marry the girl or not, to take her or to leave her. The remarks quoted in the last paragraph show that for a time he had veered towards her and now was veering away again. If we may believe his fictionalised account, he suddenly told his mother that he intended to break with the girl, whereupon (naturally, as it was what she most wanted) she "was very tender with him." His account of his talk with Jessie—the breaking-off once more talk—is so extraordinary yet so characteristic and in essence probably so true that it is worth close attention. Remember that the girl really cared for him and that his recent words and actions had given her every reason to think that he (now a man of twenty-three) might at last be struggling free from his mother. He began with shattering abruptness:

"'I have been thinking,' he said, 'we ought to break off.'

" 'Why?' she cried in surprise.

" 'Because it's no good going on.'

" 'Why is it no good?'

" 'It isn't. I don't want to marry. I don't want ever to marry. And if we're not going to marry, it's no good going on.'

" 'But why do you say this now?'

" 'Because I've made up my mind.'

" 'And what about these last months, and the things you told me then?'

" 'I can't help it; I don't want to go on.'

" 'You don't want any more of me?'

" 'I want us to break off—you be free of me, I free of you.'

" 'And what about these last months?'

" 'I don't know. I've not told you anything but what I thought was true.'

" 'Then why are you different now?'

" 'I'm not—I'm the same—only I know it's no good going on.'

" 'You haven't told me why it's no good.'

" 'Because I don't want to go on—and I don't want to marry.'

" 'How many times have you offered to marry me, and I wouldn't?'

" 'I know; but I want us to break off.' "

Well, such scenes are always difficult and painful in the best circumstances, and as this is fictionalised we need not believe it happened in exactly that way. But the whole attitude of mind as well as the actual words and phrases are exactly Lawrence's own. That was how he talked, those maddeningly unsatisfactory evasions were typical. What was the use of wrangling with a man for whom the feeblest reasons or no reasons at all were valid? His principle of unvarying unhesitating truth to the feeling of the moment, however many different and contradictory feelings he experienced, was of the utmost service to him as an artist but the cause of endless difficulties to him as a thinker and in his relations with other people. Still more remarkable is that he tries to tell the truth—however unflattering—about himself as about others, he makes no attempt to gild his perversities, and very rarely defends himself. That is, of course, in the novels and stories. When he writes in the first person it is as one infallible.

Yet even after a scene so devastating he could not make a clean cut and be done with it. In one mood he struggled to get away from the girl, in another he was irresistibly swept back to her, leaving her completely bewildered. It was even useless for him to carry out his bravado about going from one woman to another until he was satisfied. Take, for instance, the episode recorded in his poem, 'Kisses in the Train,' for which he has been censured because he foolishly bragged of it and because it happened while his mother was dying:

"And still in my nostrils
 The scent of her flesh;
And still my blind face
 Sought her afresh;
And still one pulse
 Through the world did thresh.

And the world all whirling
 Round in joy
Like the dance of a dervish
 Did destroy
My sense—and reason
 Spun like a toy.

But firm at the centre
 My heart was found;
My own to her perfect
 Heartbeat bound,
Like a magnet's keeper
 Closing the round."

Parenthetically, if Milton was right in thinking that poetry is writing which is "simple, sensuous, and passionate," Lawrence there was a poet. But though he was so much carried away by the experience that he proposed to the girl and was accepted and announced the engagement, yet very soon he was writing to his old love about her: "She was here for the week-end, but it's no good. Somehow as soon as I am alone with her, I want to run away." Passionate and faithful swain! Within a few weeks we find him writing a poem to another girl:

"But since my limbs gushed full of fire,
Since from out of my blood and bone
Poured a heavy flame
To you, earth of my atmosphere, stone
Of my steel, lovely white flint of desire,
You have no name.
Earth of my swaying atmosphere,
Substance of my inconstant breath,
I cannot but cleave to you, Helen.

Since you have drunken up the drear
Death-darkened storm, and death
Is washed from the blue
Of my eyes, I see you beautiful, and dear.
Beautiful, passive and strong, as the breath
Of my yearning blows over you.
I see myself as the winds that hover
Half substanceless, and without grave worth.
But you. . . ."

It would be easy to quote others of these early poems which record his amorous experiences. The experiences are almost universal; it is the fact that they happened to him, the "genius", and were re-created in the style of that genius, which made them disturbing and somehow improper to his contemporaries. There is the 'Ballad of Another Ophelia', artistically a failure through its echo of Meredith's 'Love in the Valley', and 'Snapdragon', which has been over-quoted because of the sadism in it. If we want to see how he found in these different affairs little but dissatisfaction and frustration, we must look at 'The Hands of the Betrothed', with the sudden unexpected sting of satire at the end:

"She makes her hands take my part, the part of the man
To her; she crushes them into her bosom, deep,
Where I should be, and with her own strong span
Closes her arms, that should fold on me in sleep.

Ah, and she puts her hands upon the wall,
Presses them there, and kisses her big dark hands,
Then lets her black hair loose, the darkness fall
About her from her maiden-folded bands.

And sits in her own dark night of her bitter hair
Dreaming—God knows of what, for to me she's the same
Betrothed young lady who loves me, and takes good care
Of her maidenly virtue and of my good name."

Why was it that in the poem to Helen he tells her that she has "drunken up the drear death-darkened storm" and that through her "death is washed from" his blue eyes? It was far indeed from being the youthful poet's fanciful playing with the idea of death because death alone seems an adequate symbol for infinite desire and in youth is too remote to seem real. In the midst of his loves and his schoolmastering and his being launched as a writer death had come to strike him in his deepest and most cherished love. On the 24th August, 1910, Lawrence was at his aunt's house in Leicester. His mother, on a visit, had collapsed in such agony that she had been forced to reveal what she had long hidden—she had a cancer in her side "as large as two fists". At first Lawrence either had not realised that the disease was fatal or, as in the case of his own consumption, refused for psychological reasons to admit it. At all events, he spoke vaguely of "a tumour or something" which he hoped "wasn't serious". Two months later, writing to his publisher, he begs for an advance copy of *The White Peacock* as soon as possible: "I *do* want that book to make haste. Not that I care much myself. But I want my mother to see it while she still keeps the live consciousness. She is really horribly ill."

What he had suffered in those two months and had yet to suffer in the months to come is painful to imagine. Of course, if his hopes that it "wasn't serious" had been genuine they were doomed to speedy destruction. Probably his mother's cancer was at no time operable, but by the time she confessed to it and her son had spent two months of his meagre salary in getting a specialist's opinion, it was too late. There was nothing left for her but to die, and to alleviate her sufferings with morphia. The shock of this sudden disaster to Lawrence was overwhelming, and it is certain that no other event in his life gave him anything near as much pain and grief. This subject of the doomed and dying mother comes up again and again in his prose and his verse, but whether he wrote of it at the time or in retrospect it was never without communicating the bitter thrill of his despair. He was "terribly alone in his grief" was said of him at that time by one of those who knew him best. His suffering was on the level of tragedy:

"His grief came on like physical pain. He held tight to the gate, biting his mouth, whispering 'Mother!' It was a fierce, cutting, physical pain of grief, that came in bouts, and was so acute that he could scarcely keep erect. He did not know where it came from, the pain, nor why. It had nothing to do with his thoughts. Almost it had nothing to do with him. Only it gripped him and he must submit. The whole tide of his soul, gathering in its unknown towards its expansion into death, carried him with it helplessly, all the fritter of his thought and consciousness caught up as nothing, the heave passing on towards its breaking, taking him further than he had ever been."

He was trying to express an almost unendurable grief and despair. The key of his life changed abruptly from a jaunty, rather brassy assertiveness to tragical lamentation. Soon enough he knew that this was the end of that strange unutterably deep love which until then had ruled his whole life. Even as he entered his aunt's house, coming in gaily suit-case in hand from a holiday, and felt the tension, "a queer feeling" had gone over him, "as if all the sunshine had gone out of him, and it was all shadow." Dropping his bag, he had run to her room, where she tried to greet him with the old cheerfulness, but "he only fell on his knees at the bedside, and buried his face in the bedclothes, crying in agony, and saying: 'Mother—mother—mother!'" It seemed to him "as if his blood was melting into tears": he wept "in terror and pain" and "the tears hurt in every fibre of his body."

For a quarter of a century his life had been one with hers, they had lived in one another, and no other woman had been able to take her place; so that the inevitable parting, which for other sons is softened by transference of love, to him was the cruellest of disasters. To one so sensitive and imaginative the last touch of horror and misery came because his beloved was dying of a disease so implacable, so cruel and so slow. Had death come to her in some sudden almost painless way he might not have suffered so desperately, but through those desolate weeks of August and September and October and November he suffered with her daily and hourly. At first he tried to drug himself with hopes of cure and recovery, then even his love had to resign itself to her death:

> "And oh, my love, as I rock for you to-night
> And have not any longer any hope
> To heal the suffering, or to make requite
> For all your life of asking and despair,
> I own that some of me is dead to-night."

Every alternate week-end during that dismal autumn Lawrence was given leave of absence from school, and spent the daylight hours in his mother's room, sitting with a drawing-board on his knees working mechanically at his painting. That mere mechanical copying of another's picture distracted him from his grief, and he could even in a sort of trance attempt work of his own: "he worked away mechanically, producing good stuff without knowing it." Though the experience lacerated him, he always helped his sister as sick nurse. On one occasion he wrongly persuaded his mother to try to walk leaning on his arm, and she fainted with the pain:

"He lifted her up and carried her quickly downstairs; laid her on her couch. She was light and frail. Her face looked as if she were dead, with the blue lips shut tight. Her eyes opened—her blue unfailing eyes—and she looked at him pleadingly, almost wanting him to forgive her. He held brandy to her lips, but her mouth would not open. All the time she watched him lovingly. She was only sorry for him. The tears ran down his face without ceasing, but not a muscle moved. He was white to the lips, and their eyes as they looked at each other understood. Her eyes were so blue—such a wonderful forget-me-not blue! He felt if only they had been of a different colour he could have borne it better. His heart seemed to be ripping in his breast."

A specially bound advance copy of his novel was sent him by his publisher, and he was able to put into his mother's hands while she was still conscious this earnest of his coming world fame. Yet it meant little to her. Long ago he had perceived and bitterly recorded that she cared nothing for his art but only for his success;

and already she was so deep in the shadow of death that nothing mattered to her but her love for him, for the sake of which she still clung so desperately and sufferingly to painful life. He had her photographed—a haggard dying old woman, wrapped in shawls and rugs, sitting out in the garden with his book in her lap. It was through Jessie that he had written it, but he took it from her and gave it to his mother.

The shock and agony of this long drawn out parting brought a violent revulsion of feeling to him. Now, instead of living, he wanted her to die, to be at rest, to release his tortured heart from useless misery. He wrote a poem called 'Suspense' and another called 'Endless Anxiety', but now his anxiety was that of "waiting ever" for the news that at last she was "free". Whenever he saw a telegraph boy riding down the street on the official red bicycle his heart leaped chokingly—was he bringing the telegram to say that she was dead? And when the boy rode carelessly past the gate he did not know whether the sensation in his breast was of relief or "a deeper bruise of knowing that still she has no rest."

The longing for release became fiercer when he was with her. As he looked into her face "almost ashen with morphia" he could not bear it and longed for her to die. Did he imagine it in his pain or did he really utter the horribly cruel, utterly loving words: "Mother, if I had to die, I'd die. I'd *will* to die"? Perhaps. In his novel he is made actually to give her "rest" by making her drink an over-dose of morphia. But this was symbolical. Writing in later life he was trying to re-assure himself that at last he was free from that terrible incubus of love. By imagining that he had given her a death-draught he tried to convince himself that he had cut wholly free. Had he? In any case, when at last death released her and he stood alone by her inanimate body he was not free. To him still she was 'The Bride' and this was his farewell:

"My love looks like a girl to-night,
But she is old.
The plaits that lie along her pillow
Are not gold,
But threaded with filigree silver,
And uncanny cold.

She looks like a young maiden, since her brow
 Is smooth and fair;
Her cheeks are very smooth, her eyes are closed,
 She sleeps a rare,
Still, winsome sleep, so still, and so composed."

PART TWO

MARRIAGE AND WAR

1911–1919

1

THE death of his mother, the dominant influence and motive of his life ever since he could remember, left Lawrence shattered. During her illness he had suffered almost beyond endurance, and even when she had passed to the oblivion of the grave he could neither forget her nor resolve the crisis of his own misery and solitude:

"He stood still, rigid, with clenched fists, a flame of agony going over him. And he saw again the sick-room, his mother, her eyes. . . . He wanted everything to stand still, so that he could be with her again. The days passed, the weeks. But everything seemed to have fused, gone into a conglomerate mass. He could not tell one day from another, hardly one place from another. Nothing was distinct nor distinguishable. Often he lost himself for an hour at a time, could not remember what he had done."

After her death she seemed to hold her son back from his first sweetheart more than ever, and the two now seemed and probably were finally estranged. In her opinion he was "never the same man again" and she thought that 1911 was "perhaps the most arid year of his life". It may be so, though "arid" is hardly the right term for a year which produced the first draft of *Sons and Lovers*. There was great resilience in him, and an inner detachment which guarded the flame of life in him even when in part he longed to quench it for ever. After all, it was during the worst of his mother's illness that he had kissed the girl in the train; and it was at the time when he was supposedly meditating self-slaughter that he was creating the vivid pages of *Sons and Lovers*. He longed for death to rid himself of the incubus of this terrible love, romantically, "to cease upon the midnight with no pain", sometimes in despair, as the one means of being re-united with her.

The almost mortal wound healed at last, but all his life a touch on it pained him. Many years afterwards I was talking with him about *Sons and Lovers*—a rare event as he much disliked talking of his work—and his wife interrupted laughingly: "Do you remember, Lorenzo, how I suffered when you killed your mother?"

The jest seemed to me a perilous one, even though the Laurentian law was that you should come out plump with anything you happened to feel, and I expected him to fly at her, all teeth and claws like a wild-cat. Instead he was silent, and the silence was painful to us all.

He was lonely at Croydon, he wrote his sister, because he had "no intimate friends". But when, after leaving home, did he ever have really intimate friends? Yet he certainly was not then friendless. Even among his colleagues he found at least two who liked him and could sympathise with him. One was A. W. McLeod, of whom he must have been fond, for he continued to correspond with him long after he had left the school. The other was Helen Corke, to whom he had been showing the script of a novel he called *The Saga of Siegmund*, afterwards published as *The Trespasser*.

Not long after the publication of his poems in *The English Review* Lawrence began—through Hueffer and Violet Hunt—to meet London literary people. Now were seen some of the inconveniences of having grown up in a place so remote from such society, with the peculiar mixture of his own lack of sureness and the ideas of superiority and assertiveness derived from his mother. He expected far too much, imagining that he was about to enter the London of Byron, animated by a bohemian camaraderie in the manner of Murger, where his peculiar quality would be instantly and generously recognised. Instead he came upon people who were much absorbed in their own importance, whose interest in meeting him was of the patronising kind which amiably occupied itself in pointing out what they considered his deficiencies, and whose main recreation was malicious gossip. Clearly it would be quite untrue to say that there was no such gossip in Eastwood, but Lawrence's life had been so much absorbed in better things that his contact with it had been slight. Both in his own home and at The Haggs they had better things to talk about than the amusing—oh, so amusing! —faults and follies of their friends and rivals.

Early in life Violet Hunt had won her blue for proficiency in this essential accomplishment of the cultured metropolis. Her skill received a well-merited tribute from Lawrence in a letter where he affects a sophistication which was never his and tries vainly to conceal his astonishment:

"Do you know, I rather like her—she's such a real assassin. I evoked the memory of various friends that were her friends twelve months ago. Behold, she nicely showed me the effigies of these folk in her heart, each of their blemishes marked with a red asterisk like a dagger hole. I saluted her, she did the business so artistically: there was no loathsome gore spilt over the murdered friends."

Though she was possibly the most gifted practitioner of scandal-mongering, which had for literary ladies much the same charm and prestige that drinking in pubs and clubs had for the gentlemen, she was by no means the only one who dazzled this naïve provincial with the light of better things. There was, for instance, Katherine Mansfield, of whose influence on Lawrence, Middleton Murry writes: "She had, moreover, a lightly mocking but ruthless way of summing up various people over whom he was temporarily enthusiastic, which made him smile rather crookedly. At such a moment he was a little afraid of her." How indeed could these cultured and well-bred people help the working-class genius better than by relieving him of his positive beliefs and enthusiasms? Coming from the slums to the summit of Parnassus, almost at a step, he naturally assumed the habits of the country and in due course himself became a scandal-monger of finished malevolence. How well he learned his lesson may be judged from the account of her first meeting with him as recorded by his ardent admirer, Dorothy Brett, whose book is a kind of posthumous letter to him, which accounts for her addressing him throughout as "you":

"You sit very upright with your hands tucked under your thighs sitting on the palms. We sit drinking tea, tearing poor O. to pieces. We pull her feathers out in handfuls until I stop, aghast, and try to be merciful saying, 'We will leave her just one feather.' You laugh at that, a high, tinkling laugh, mischievous, saying, 'We will leave her just one draggled feather in her tail, the poor plucked hen!"

The "poor plucked hen" in question was their friend and patron, Ottoline Morrell, to whom just about this time Lawrence dedicated his book of poems, *Amores*, in these words: "To Ottoline Morrell in tribute to her noble and independent sympathy and her generous understanding these poems are gratefully dedicated." The "generous understanding" had, I believe, included pecuniary recognition.

At Croydon in 1911 Lawrence was still the naïve provincial, and far indeed from having learned the social graces of his superiors. I have been lucky enough to receive some recollections of him as early as 1910, from Mrs. Rachel Annand Taylor, who was invited to meet him by Ernest Rhys and occasionally saw him afterwards. She saw him at an interesting epoch, when he was still comparatively unspoiled by the influence of self-important intellectuals and before he was angered and embittered by official persecution and the indirect attempts to starve him into submission and silence. An unpublished note of his shows that he was much impressed by this learned lady and her beauty, one whose standards of culture were very different from those of *The English Review.* The first impression he made on her was "of naïveté and appeal"; he had "attained some culture the hard way," but still "there was some slum in him." She proceeds:

"Of course he told me all his story when he came to tea, stating to begin with that his mother was the person who meant most to him. Not yet had the Œdipus complex become a commonplace, so he appeared really sincere in this. By concentrating on him, flattering him, working on his emotions, she had established some organic bond of a morbid kind. He was to give her compensation for what she had endured from his father. But Emily-Miriam (I think she was also Muriel) had heartened him, helped him, and dared for him. He was restless at his debt to Miriam, who, he evidently felt, seemed a little provincial in the lofty realms of Violet Hunt. In some volume of Violet's recollections I met some rather mean allusion to L.'s slight embarrassment with the *batterie* of silver then formidably provided with a well-to-do meal.

"He was a terrific snob, he was definitely a cad, yet in this early period he was touching, he was so artlessly trying to find his way. He suddenly laughed, and said: 'Oh, I'll probably die of drink like my father.' He evidently had great emotional forces, and powers of expression. (Remember, as yet he had published no book.) What I felt was that he was possibly a genius, with all the flaws that the presence of genius usually creates in a personality; but that he was so neurotically unstable that he would collapse before he made an impression. I was wrong."

Here once more we have "the genius" with the warning: "Remember, as yet he had published no book." So much that is written and said about Lawrence ignores or takes for granted the fact that he wrote books which made some people angry, left some indifferent, and aroused enthusiasm in still others—books which have survived the changes and destructions of two wars and nearly forty years. If he had not been a great writer, these strange and painful traits of character, his sufferings and misunderstandings and adventures, his instabilities and tantrums, would be a theme for the psychologist, not for the biographer. If he had not written a word he would still have been an interesting personality, and, if known, an almost classic case for the psycho-analyst; but the world remembers him because he was a great artist in words.

Only a few weeks after the death of his mother, in January 1911, Lawrence's first novel, *The White Peacock*, was published. Towards the end of his life Lawrence wrote that he had been "tussling away for four years" on the task of "getting out *The White Peacock* in inchoate bits, from the underground of my consciousness." This lets us into the method of creation which bewildered and annoyed conventional critics who imagined that there were rules for determining the merit of a novel. For Lawrence the writing of a novel was an adventure of the mind, an exploration of his unconscious self, with his strange chaos of emotions and almost uniquely retentive memory. He did not, as his critics thought he should, set out to tell a plotted story with carefully worked-out "characters", approved "construction" and much painful attention to his "prose". When discussing with Jessie Chambers the idea of his doing a book he had merely thought that he might "try a novel" and suggested she might try too. He went on:

"The usual plan is to take two couples and develop their relationships. Most of George Eliot's are on that plan. Anyhow I don't want a plot, I should be bored with it. I shall try two couples for a start."

Thus at the very beginning of his career he had scrapped all the heavy pedantry about the art and craft of fiction, form in the novel and so forth, which were then—and for all I know still are—fashionable among self-appointed critics. In those days it was often more a matter of theory than of practice. Ford Hueffer, Lawrence's "discoverer" and one of his rather numerous would-be literary patrons and instructors, always asserted uncompromising admiration for Flaubert's methods of meticulous plotting, lavish documentation, and days of laborious "work" spent in lying on a sofa groaning because he could not find the exact word to express the precise nuance of meaning in the description of a cabbage field. As a matter of fact, Hueffer was industrious in a very different way, every morning dictating a thousand words of an improvised novel as well as writing a long weekly literary article.

In a sense, of course, Lawrence's novels also were improvisations, but the reason for the long "tussle" was not lack of matter and words—prolixity was one of his worst faults—but the difficulty of finding out what it was that his subconscious or unconscious self really wanted to say. Spontaneity was the quality he most valued and his object always was to bring into his writing his own vitality—he would sacrifice all standards to give the feeling of life. For that purpose his formula of the two couples seems extremely primitive, yet it was one he held to and even repeated. The chief merit of a novel is readability—if it is heavy or a bore, what on earth is the use of it? Whatever its faults from the viewpoint of pedants, *The White Peacock* was readable when it was published nearly forty years ago, and still is. Although first novels are generally treated leniently, this particular contribution to English literature did not receive much praise from the gentlemen of the press. Even of the very few who praised it none probably ever dreamed that it would be reprinting forty years later. It was praised of course by its sponsors, Hueffer and Violet Hunt, and by *The Morning Post;* was condescendingly noticed by *The Athenæum* and *The Saturday Review;* and attacked by the "liberal" *Daily News.*

If we must look for faults rather than enjoyment in books we might point out that a real disadvantage in *The White Peacock* is the author's snobbishness. With sure literary instinct Lawrence had chosen his characters from the people he knew best, the people nearest to him in Eastwood, but for fear lest he should be thought an inferior he takes these working-class characters and tries to make them live and talk as if they belonged to the upper middle-class. It says much for his sincerity in other respects that the book survives this falsity.

We are already familiar with some of these characters. 'The Saxtons are the Chambers family, afterwards presented in more detail in *Sons and Lovers.* Emily is a first sketch of the 'Miriam' of *Sons and Lovers.* George is obviously studied from the same original as the 'Edgar' of the later novel. Lawrence himself is 'Cyril' (rather "an old-maidish character" Jessie Chambers thought) and uses his mother's maiden name of Beardsall for a character most obviously his own mother, who is shown—and it is not very relevant to the main purport of the story—as bitterly hostile to Emily. A curious feature of the book is its fear and hatred of alcoholic drinks. In the early part of the book, by an unconscious or conscious wish-fulfilment, Lawrence kills off his father with cirrhosis of the liver, and lives with his mother in a cottage on the interest of an imaginary four thousand pounds. George, who takes to drink after marrying Meg out of pique at Lettie's rejection, is a study in the drunkard's degeneration. Those who think Lawrence "couldn't create character" might consider George Saxton. From the opening scene where the handsome powerful young farmer is introduced tearing a wasp's nest to pieces with careless brutality, down to the final scene of his habitual drunkard's repulsive late breakfast of fish and vinegar, the presentation and development of the character never falter.

A remarkable feature of the book, apparently quite unnoticed at the time, was its almost magical power of evocation of the non-human world. In this Lawrence had something in common with Ruskin among the Alps and on the roads of France; with Richard Jefferies among the little fields and woods and lanes of England; with Hudson on the pampas; but with his own originality of perception and intense feeling. The often-quoted description of the gamekeeper's funeral, that poignant lamentation where the beauty of spring contrasts so bitterly with human grief, equalled the best of Hardy. The book has tender studies of children and babies, although towards the end he has a reaction and raves against "the storms of babies". The misanthropic gamekeeper turns up so often in Lawrence's fictions that Jessie Chambers talks a little sardonically of his "obsession with gamekeepers". But as Lawrence so often wanted to write about upper-class women falling in love with working men, the gamekeeper character is rather forced on him. The upper-class girl who runs away with the chauffeur, the chiropodist, the butler, is rather an object of mirth than interest. Even a jockey might not have done, though perhaps a boxer, a cabaret performer or even a swimming guard might have been accepted; but Lawrence knew nothing about them, and preferred to stick to the gamekeeper he knew. It is odd that he should have invented this gamekeeper and his aristocratic wife long before he himself ran away with an aristocratic woman.

Undoubtedly the most entertaining review of this novel came from Lawrence's father. After Mrs. Lawrence's funeral, the miner, having nothing to do and being debarred by etiquette from the pub, "struggled through half a page" of his son's novel, which for all it gave him "might as well have been Hottentot." The puzzled reader consulted the flattered author:

" 'And what did they gi'e thee for that, lad?'

" 'Fifty pounds, father.'

" 'Fifty pounds!' He was dumbfounded, and looked at me with shrewd eyes, as if I were a swindler. 'Fifty pounds! An' tha's never done a day's work in thy life!' "

Lawrence's own feelings about this first book were, as might be expected, extreme and contradictory. Suffering probably from the nervous reaction of finishing the book he had written to his friend, Helen Corke, in 1910: "The transaction of literary business makes me sick. I have no faith in myself in the end, and I simply loathe writing. You do not know how repugnant to me was the sight of that Nethermere MSS. . . . I wish from the bottom of my heart the fates had not stigmatised me writer." For one who found writing "loathsome" Lawrence, it must be admitted, did an enormous lot in the short space of twenty years.

Soon after publication of *The White Peacock* he was faced with a situation with which he was destined to become more and more familiar as time went on. A girl in Eastwood identified herself with one of the characters, and both she and her family were much offended. When people congratulated him on this book he pretended to be annoyed, saying primly that by profession he was a schoolmaster. He even talked of suppressing *The Trespasser*! Yet when Martin Secker wrote to him in June of 1911, saying that he would like to publish a collection of Lawrence's short stories, he replied by return post that "an autumn volume" of his stories would put him "at the top of happiness".

His second novel, *The Trespasser*, was written in a fury of creative energy within the space of a few weeks in the early summer of 1910. The first draft was submitted to William Heinemann, who did not much care for it, but offered to publish it notwithstanding. Hueffer read it and reported with his usual pompous affectation: "The book is a rotten work of genius. It has no construction or form—it is execrably bad art, being all variations on a theme. Also it is erotic." Annoyed by this, Lawrence wrote to Heinemann that he had "determined not to publish the book"; he "did not want to be talked about in an *Ann Veronica* fashion." The fear of anything approaching even the mildly erotic in those days was a kind of mania, but Lawrence at least had the excuse for this prim turning up his nose at *Ann Veronica* that he was forced to maintain most unwholesome standards of total sexual abstinence in order to earn a wretched hundred a year as an usher. In spite of all which, he was already at work on the earliest draft of *Sons and Lovers*, and was pouring out poems full of poignant despair and regret for his lost mother. "I am dazed with the farewell," he says, and then:

> "You sent me a cloven fire
> Out of death, and it burns in the draught
> Of the breathing hosts. . . ."

Another opens with the unhappy words: "Since I lost you I am silence-haunted". He was haunted again and again with visions of her death-bed. In 'Brooding Grief' we find the lines:

> "I was watching the woman who bore me
> Stretched in the brindled darkness
> Of the sick-room, rigid with will
> To die. . . ."

So the bitter months dragged miserably on in his tragic feeling of loss, his estrangement from Jessie, with his time divided between routine school work and work on the new book. He was cheered by receiving kindly letters from Edward Garnett, then a reader for Duckworth, who asked for some of Lawrence's stories to send to *The Century Magazine*. But there too was frustration—the stories were rejected.

Suddenly all this drawn-out misery came to a crisis, and he had a complete break-down. It was just a year after his mother's death, in November of 1911, that Lawrence was smitten with tubercular pneumonia affecting both lungs. He was nursed in the early days by Helen Corke; and then, when she was able to get leave of absence from her own school, by his favourite sister, Ada. At the worst of his illness he came very near indeed to the death he had been longing for to join him with his mother. At the crisis of the pneumonia he said to his sister: "Ada, I could die just this minute, if I wished." Naturally the words upset her, seeing which he added quickly: "Don't worry, I shan't die yet." One curious fact about Lawrence is that however ill he was, however often the destructive power of his disease showed itself, his vitality was so great that to his friends it seemed impossible that he could die young. When Jessie Chambers was told that Lawrence was ill in Croydon, so ill that he might die, she went quietly on making notes for him about their early life together, which he had asked her to give him for a re-writing of *Sons and Lovers*. She felt confident that he had too much to do in the world to die—and such was the feeling of most who knew him at all intimately.

The illness which had brought him so near to death left him weak and with shattered health, always thereafter under the threat of tuberculosis, which sometimes suspended its attack but never left him. The doctor sent him in January for a somewhat wintry convalescence at Bournemouth and warned him that he must give up school-teaching and "live out of doors"—as if an underpaid schoolmaster could take a ticket for Egypt and hire a houseboat on the Nile for the remainder of the winter. This was merely a more or less polite way of telling him that with tuberculosis he would not be allowed again in schoolrooms; and now was seen the error of insisting on a higher scale of payment to begin with, for it seems that the higher rate was paid because the school did not accept liability for illness contracted in its service. Hueffer says he tried to get Lawrence compensation by going direct to the Minister of Education, and that this was the excuse for paying nothing.

This sudden deprivation of the only profession which gave him a living, after he had worked so long and so hard to qualify for it, might very reasonably have depressed him, coming as it did on top of so many other troubles and sufferings. Apparently he was not only "rather relieved" at getting free from the school, but "jubilant" and kept quoting happily the line: "For him no more the sitting class shall wait." Before he went to Bournemouth he was visited by Jessie Chambers, who found him "grievously thin" indeed but looking wonderfully alive, like "the naked flame of life." Strangely enough, in writing to Garnett, he complained that he felt his life burning "like a free flame floating on oil" and said he wanted it "confined and conducted again."

Free he now undoubtedly was, but a little too near the grisly freedom of the unemployed. His financial prospects were far from encouraging. Although *The White Peacock* went into a second impression in March, 1911, it had so far brought him only just enough money to pay the expenses of his illness, and he was grateful to Garnett for lending him the seven guineas which gave him his month's convalescence. With what Garnett gave him he just had enough to keep going until February, when another fifty pounds were due him. Beyond that—nothing but unsold manuscripts and "genius". His acquaintance with Garnett had led to a coolness with Hueffer, who was not pushing his work in *The English Review*—during the whole of 1911 he had but two stories and no poems issued there. All the more credit to his courage and energy, then, that he set to work to re-write *The Trespasser* before he even left for his convalescence. Lawrence at Bournemouth! For so long he was the symbol of everything anti-commonplace and non-respectable that it is very hard to imagine him in those sedate surroundings, even softened by "the torrents of rain" and "soft weather inclined to fog" of which he complained.

Nevertheless Bournemouth recruited his strength surprisingly, and he set to work on what was now his profession with the utmost zeal and industry. Writing to Garnett on the 3rd January, Lawrence mentioned that he had just re-written the first chapter of *The Trespasser*, and thought it "heaps, heaps better." By the 19th of the month he had written 135 pages, and by the 29th over 300. It is not a long novel, about 70,000 words, but in thus re-creating his book he must have written between two and three thousand words every day, which did not leave much time free. Considering how brief his writing life was, how much time he spent in travelling, that he did cooking and housework as well as writing, that whenever friends were with him—as they frequently were—he never appeared to give any time to writing, people have been puzzled to account for his large output. (In point of fact, it was far less than Balzac's, who lived only seven years longer.) But when Lawrence worked it was with an extreme concentration of attention and energy, a quite miraculous power of abstracting himself from his surroundings. He could work almost anywhere, and the conditions of his youth, when he either had to work with other people in the room or not work at all, had given him this very valuable faculty of being able to work under interruptions which would have defeated most writers. Garnett had some experience of this with him in Germany, and I recollect myself several of us talking and laughing with his wife when he was writing what I took to be a letter but turned out to be the last pages of an essay. Orioli had a story that Lawrence wrote the whole of the introduction to his translation of *The Story of Doctor Manente* in the bookshop on the Lung' Arno. He was dissatisfied by the Introduction written by someone else, turned over the galleys and produced his own, quite indifferent to the people coming in and out of the shop and all the resonant Italian voices.

This illness made the second great break between Lawrence and his past. The most obvious change was from a sedentary routine under all kinds of moral precepts to the adventurous life of the wandering writer. At the same time it did much towards loosening the tie which had held him helplessly bound in love to the memory of his dead mother, a love which, as we have seen, led him even to think of suicide. It was of that bond with his mother he was thinking when he distressed his sister by saying he could "give up and die." The will to live which triumphed in him set him on the road to freedom. Following on a number of poems to the dead mother there is one called 'Malade,' obviously referring to his illness at Croydon and written when he was beginning to recover. The poems to the dead mother do not cease, but are interspersed with others on different topics. He referred to her in a poem written in Taos in the 1920s, but I believe that the last batch of these dead mother poems must date from the time when he suffered so intensely in writing the story of his mother's illness and death. That was in the autumn of 1912. The earlier version of *Sons and Lovers* which Jessie Chambers saw stopped short of that tragical episode, because, she thought, "the whole thing was somehow tied up". But surely if it was "tied up" the reason was that he could not face the reliving of all those shattering emotions so soon after the event.

It was natural that finding himself so unexpectedly free from the ties of school he should leave Croydon, and plan, more or less vaguely at first, to go abroad for a year, as he had long wanted to do. Meanwhile, as always happened with him when he took the trouble to make himself agreeable, he rapidly became very popular with the other guests at the Bournemouth boarding-house. The charm he had for such people was undeniable and remarkable, and would have made his fortune as a fashionable doctor or politician. I have myself known a somewhat elderly landlady so captivated by his mere greetings as he passed to and fro that she burgeoned into an amber necklace, and blushed like a girl when his quick eye instantly noticed and his clever tongue praised it. But of course these devotions, although all very well in their way, were apt to become rather a nuisance; and indeed throughout his life Lawrence was "much exposed" to friendship. The Bournemouth boarding-house was an early example:

"Here I get mixed up in people's lives so—it's very interesting, sometimes a bit painful, often jolly. But I run to such close intimacy with folk, it is complicating. But I love to have myself in a bit of a tangle."

This, if true, was fortunate, for he was certainly in rather more than "a bit" of a tangle with his girls. First of all, and rather surprisingly, there was Jessie, into whose orbit he had once more swung back, perhaps for no more tender reason than that he needed her help for *Sons and Lovers*. Then there was the 'Helena' of *The Trespasser*, and 'Louie' of 'Kisses in the Train', described to Edward Garnett as: "big, and swarthy, and passionate as a gipsy—but good, awfully good, churchy." (What a "genius" Lawrence had for summing up people in one sentence beyond appeal!) But 'Helena' dropped gradually from his life after he left Croydon, and it is clear from his letters to Garnett that Louie also was leaving him rather than he leaving her.

In spite of the difference in their ages there was a genuine friendship between Edward Garnett and Lawrence, who wrote the older man chatty confidential letters which show a rather unexpected and pleasantly human young man. Now he is quizzing Violet Hunt and Hueffer (who had lost the editorship of *The English Review*); now he is drinking in pubs with the coal-miners who were on strike, and describing how the "seconds had capfuls of money" as the men "were betting like steam on skittles". Then we come upon an even more unexpected Lawrence flirting with his sister's friends at a dance:

"My sister found me kissing one of her girl friends good-bye—such a ripping little girl—and we were kissing like nuts—enter my sister—great shocks all round, and much indignation."

"Folk", "jolly", "ripping", "like nuts", "a bit", "don't you know"—Lawrence was slow to abandon these provincialisms, and clung to some of them long after they had disappeared, even in London. But after he had passed through such sufferings and deprivations he was certainly entitled to a little fun in his life. Yet this light-hearted mood of irresponsible enjoyment lasted a very short time, too short a time; for even as he was correcting the first proofs of *The Trespasser* he himself became a trespasser, and for life. But before we come to the absorbing drama of Lawrence's runaway marriage, it is worth while looking at his somewhat neglected *Trespasser*, which is rich in biographical interest.

At this distance of time it is impossible to say whether William Heinemann was influenced by Hueffer's remark that *The Trespasser* is not only "a rotten work of genius" but "erotic". We must remember that in those days "erotic" was a word of fear to publishers, for it was not so long since Vizetelly had been imprisoned and reduced to poverty for the horrible crime of publishing Zola and the Elizabethan dramatists without fig-leaves. At any rate, Heinemann's subordinate, Pawling, was indifferent if not hostile, and allowed the book to go to Garnett and Duckworth. Lawrence had yet to learn that, for a writer of his type, changing publishers is a mistake and a misfortune.

For those days the novel must be considered "daring", since its theme is the brief love affair of a girl and a married man in that British Baiae, the Isle of Wight. Siegmund, the hero, of course is Lawrence, and the book ends with Siegmund's suicide, though Lawrence survives to comment on it in the person of another character named Byrne. If we drop the machinery of Siegmund's family—and that is an obvious enough symbol of Lawrence's own disapprovingly puritanical relations—most of the rest of the book is plain autobiography. As we have seen, the first draft was written at white heat in the early summer of 1910, immediately after the events it relates. The suicide of Siegmund—a very rare if not unique example in Lawrence's large output—may be only a coincidence, but may have been added in Bournemouth from his own despair over his mother's death. Here for the first time he treated the physical passion of love realistically, and, without any kind of "propaganda" or cause-preaching, evoked it as basic, essential and laudable in the relations of man and woman. In Lawrence this was different from the scientific point of view of Havelock Ellis's *Psychology of Sex* and the social point of view of H. G. Wells's *Ann Veronica*—both important pioneer books. For Lawrence sex was a flowering of the mysterious life force, an unknown god who must be brought into the consciousness. It was he, with his disregard for reticence and passionately sensitive temperament, who merely by relating his own vivid deep experience re-expressed this forgotten truth in art.

Of course he met a public quite unprepared. For generations sex in English literature (French literature was more wholesome) had been represented by a faded symbolism. It had been spiritualised, sublimated, feebly idealised out of all reality, until the public perversity had reached a point where any statement of the truth was instantly labelled "unclean" or "unwholesome" or "unpleasant" or "unnecessary".

I have said more than once that in many ways Lawrence resembled Ruskin. Both hated industrialism because it is ugly. Both were so pictorial in imagination that they could only express abstractions in terms of symbols. They were alike in sensibility to natural beauty, though Lawrence was the closer observer and the more vivid writer. Again they shared an almost comical conviction of their power to change the world by writing a few books, from which they developed a fierce dogmatism and even hectoring style which defeat their own end. They had admirable courage in battling whatever, for the time being, they happened to think was wrong. Each had much instability of temperament and was a slave to the feelings of the moment. Need it be remarked that they both wound themselves up in endless tangles of self-contradiction and wasted much energy in vituperation and futile wrangling? Both even were fanatics about sex, but of course in utterly different ways. They differ in their attitudes to women as only such kindred spirits could differ.

Ruskin had a lamentable record as a lover, said many eloquent, many flattering and many silly things about women, but never anything to show that he had experienced and rejoiced in sexual happiness. Lawrence in his passion for reforming away this obvious cause of human misery fell into the opposite extreme of considering man and woman solely in their sexual relation. This led him to make such odd statements as calling Dante's *Commedia* "rather dishonest" because "he left out the bifurcated wife and the kids."

This criticism is surely irrelevant to a Heaven where *a priori* there is neither marriage nor giving in marriage.

Whatever else may be denied Lawrence there can be no doubt that he had a great attraction for many women, all the more so since his innate puritanism kept them at a distance. He himself noticed, deplored and even resented the fact. Without the slightest touch of fatuity but in genuine irritation, "Why do women always fall in love with me?" he asks in one of his letters. Fot the simple reason that he liked them as women. When he was not preaching that upper-class women should leave their husbands and run away with lower-class lovers, he was even more vehemently insisting that marriage is for life and inviolable. Do not ask how he reconciled such contradictions—he never bothered to try. He could seldom resist turning his charm on to a woman any more than he could resist answering the most absurd or ironical fan letter; yet he considered his own marriage inviolable, and "noli me tangere" in a snarl was about all that the others ever got.

This mystical conviction of the supreme value of physical union was one of the very few in which Lawrence never wavered, whatever hopeless contradictions it led him to. It also involved him in much misunderstanding and misrepresentation. Aldous Huxley has pointed out that Lawrence in his strange doubleness of temperament was at once both mystic and materialist. Rejecting the conventional religious views of his time he laboured in anguish of spirit to find a religion nearer to the facts. The evolutionary doctrine, which Lawrence rejected so petulantly, characteristically and amusingly merely because he did not feel it in his "solar plexus", all the same had an overwhelming influence on him. It is the evolutionary view of life which caused him to reject so indignantly the Christian notion that sex is merely a hindrance to salvation, and made him claim such importance for this essential link in the evolutionary chain. As for his other contention which caused so much anger and derision, i.e. that human consciousness is not limited to the brain, it happens to be a mere fact which can be found in any text-book on physiology or psychology. Strangely enough, the doctrine that "the Consciousness is not the Real Self" is fundamental to the Buddhism which Lawrence in Ceylon rejected with so much white man's arrogance.

In Lawrence's youth the young women he knew, in fact and not merely in fiction, approximated to the spiritualised, idealised, asexual type then fashionable in all circles which aspired. His perfectly frank, if complicated, efforts to achieve physical union were always frustrated by "virtue". His early poems and letters, *The Trespasser*, *Sons and Lovers*, abound in complaints of this frustration of normal impulse. Even Jessie Chambers's narrative has won much sympathy from Lawrence's enemies because in this respect she unconsciously showed how impossible it was for her to understand or to respond to an impulse Lawrence would neither deny nor degrade.

We may guess at the chaos of inhibitions imposed on these girls, and how much he suffered in consequence, from *The Trespasser*. Of course, his pretence that the characters are imaginary and the experiences someone else's carries no weight—only he could have lived and talked as Siegmund did. Here is an example of what happened when "the trespasser" began making love to the girl for whose sake he had gone to so much trouble and dared so much unpleasantness:

"She began to sob, dry wild sobs, feeling as if she would go mad. He tried to look her in the face, for which she hated him. And all the time he held her fast, all the time she was imprisoned in the embrace of this brute, blind creature, whose heart confessed itself in thud, thud, thud.

" 'Have you heard anything against us? Have I done anything? Have I said anything? Tell me—at any rate tell me, Helena.'

"Her sobbing was like the chattering of dry leaves. She grew frantic to be free. Stifled in that prison any longer, she would choke and go mad. His coat chafed her face: as she struggled she could see the strong working of his throat. She fought against him; she struggled in panic to be free.

" 'Let me go!' she cried. 'Let me go! Let me go!' He held her in bewilderment and terror. She thrust her hands to his chest and pushed him apart. Her face, blind to him, was very much distorted by her suffering. She thrust him furiously away with great strength.

"His heart stood still with wonder. She broke from him and dropped down, sobbing wildly, in the shelter of the tumuli. She was bunched in a small shaken heap. Siegmund could not bear it. He went on one knee beside her, trying to take her hand in his, and pleading:

" 'Only tell me, Helena, what it is. Tell me what it is. At least tell me, Helena; tell me what it is. Oh, but this is dreadful!'

"She had turned convulsively from him. She shook herself, as if beside herself, and at last covered her ears with her hands, to shut out this unreasoning pleading of his voice.

"Seeing her like this, Siegmund at last gave in. Quite still, he knelt on one knee beside her, staring at the late twilight. The intense silence was crackling with the sound of Helena's dry, hissing sobs. He remained silenced, stunned by the unnatural conflict. After waiting awhile, he put his hand on her. She winced convulsively away."

Although that is a scene from a novel, and may be slightly rearranged in consequence, there is not the least doubt that it is in the main a perfectly truthful report of an actual occurrence. What an appalling to-do about nothing! Obviously the girl was sincere in her blind revulsion from physical love, irrationally recoiling in horror because of an absurd but tyrannical conditioning. There was no clumsiness in Siegmund, no lack of preparation or charming wooing on his side, no lack of "love" in the girl, who clearly did not see herself as either contemptible or ridiculous. Before this extraordinary scene of hysteria she had of her own free will consented to go away alone with him for several days; she had made sexual advances to him, "holding his head to her bosom, with her hand among his hair," caressing his body, thrilling obviously to his kisses, even lying in his arms and "offering him herself". And then, at the decisive moment comes this insane revulsion, this anguished hysterical fear of physical consummation. She was too young? She was twenty-six.

2

ONLY after he was barred from teaching did Lawrence discover how much he had disliked it; and even then not for some time. At a later date he spoke of 'Davidson' with the sort of perverted nostalgia a man might talk of his experiences in prison. "I still dream I must teach," he wrote, "and that's the worst dream I ever have. How I loathed and raged with hate against it, and never knew." But in those early months of 1912 he was still very uncertain of his future, rather mistrustful of the intoxicating but menacing freedom which been thrust on him. In February he put an end to another of his unsatisfactory love affairs. He "met Jane and kissed her farewell at Marylebone" with a heavy heart. Who was Jane? That is all we hear of her, except that later in the year he was "sorry for her, she is so ill." He still clung to memories of his old home, and spent much of his time with his sister in Eastwood. Then suddenly he made up his mind—in May he would go to Germany.

It is a mistake to suppose that Lawrence went abroad only because of the difficulties and scandal preceding his marriage. Even as a lad he had longed to travel, though it was only through experience that he came to find that he preferred to live out of England. I don't know when it was that he first said he wanted to write a novel about each of the five continents, but he certainly did say so; and much of the inspiration of his mature work came from his travels. Possibly this longing to travel was connected with the restlessness which is said to go with consumption; and it is true that he was always discovering wonderful new places (like Shelley!) which in a few weeks or months turned out to be detestable. He blamed his own ill-health or wretched feelings on the landscape, the weather, his neighbours, local politics, an imminent revolution, or the malevolence of the Cosmos.

But why—in 1912—Germany? In those days Germany was fashionable with the British intelligentsia, for whom Italy was overdone and France decadent. Nobody but eccentrics thought of Spain or Russia, since you actually needed a passport to visit those backward despotisms. Germany, clad in shining armour, but *gemütlich* with beer and a warm heart, was the vogue. In Lawrence's case there was a practical if prosaic additional reason—he had relatives by marriage in Germany, for his Leicester aunt had married a German named Krenkow, who came from Waldbröl in the Rhineland. He had no intention of throwing himself on the hospitality of these German relatives, and he still had not sufficient faith in his vendibility as a writer to trust to his pen for a living—possibly he had not recovered from the unpleasant surprise of finding that Hueffer and *The English Review* had no money. At any rate, in spite of the doctor's warning, he was evidently trying hard to find a job as English lecturer in one of the smaller German universities. Perhaps the Disposer of Events thought this was over-doing caution even for a poet, for through a sequence of strange and unforeseeable events this attempt at safety and respectability led him to actions which separated him for ever from respectability and made safety a jest.

The staff of Nottingham University included Professor Ernest Weekley, whose articles on English philology were at one time widely popular. It was through his influence that Lawrence hoped to find his German lectureship, for the professor had useful connections in Germany. Indeed he had a German wife, who is of the utmost importance to our story, for it was at a luncheon she gave in April 1912 that the saga of Lawrence and Frieda began. Somehow, in all this drama, the German lectureship was abandoned, so may be quietly forgotten except that it accidentally served to introduce Lawrence to the professor's wife.

Frieda von Richthofen was a Silesian aristocrat, niece of that Baron Ferdinand von Richthofen whose travels in China and published books and maps of that country had made him deservedly famous. Her father, also a Baron von Richthofen, was a professional soldier, and at this time held an important military post in the garrison town of Metz—then of course within the boundaries of the Reich. How it was that this handsome, indolent but vividly alive daughter of a German aristocrat came to marry a professor at the University of Nottingham has never been made clear. Doubtless she and her family were unaware that the respect which Germans give to learning hardly existed in England, where at that time such words as "professor" and "poet" were chiefly used as terms of derision and abuse. But there it was. This magnificent creature, a sort of modern Brünhilde, went into exile, relegated to all appearances for the rest of her existence to humdrum domesticity in a neat suburb of Nottingham. She does not appear to have been actively unhappy, devoting herself to the care of her three young children, with an occasional mild flirtation with one of the less stupid students or some German visitor. With her Lawrence chose to fall passionately in love; and, despite the wranglings and crockery-smashing, for life.

Considering that for years he behaved as a kind of dictator to Cythera, issuing dogmatic if contradictory decrees ("sort of *ex-cathedra*") telling other people just how they were to order their erotic lives, there is a certain humour in the fact that our censorious perfectionist chose to elope with a married woman older than himself by several years, who spent much of their life together yearning for her children (as she says herself) "like a cat deprived of her kittens". That is not to say that there is the slightest truth in the common gossipy statement that Frieda was "the wrong woman for him". On the contrary, they were made for each other. Only a woman such as Frieda, with her health, strength, good looks, vitality and self-confidence could have endured life with a "genius" which included so much exasperation, frayed nerves, cocksure assertiveness, profound self-mistrust, and downright perversity. After his mother the only person who had any control over Lawrence was his wife, aided to some extent by her mother and her sister, Else; and she did not always succeed. They had many ups and downs, real battles of will forced on her by him, as well as wordy wrangles to the point of throwing things at each other. But anyone who thinks those two weren't in love with each other is crazy. How else could they have endured one another? Frieda, the survivor, writes in her large generosity that Lawrence gave her "a new world". Of course he did, but it was through her that he had a world to give. It was not only that, as we have seen, he could only live and work with a woman to back him, but that after he met Frieda no other woman was possible. Indeed he came to depend upon her far more than she upon him; and her influence may be seen in almost all his writing after 1912.

This does not alter the fact that such a situation was charged with misery and suffering for everyone involved. Many people would have recoiled, but it is the mean, calculating, cold-blooded, under-sexed types who hesitate in such a dilemma and are cautious and draw back. When real people like these two fall in love they brush aside all the funny little legal rules, and even such genuine human difficulties as the children in this case were. If anyone is to be blamed for starting the whole thing, on her own showing it was Frieda herself. Without her encouragement the situation would never have arisen, and if she had wanted she could at once have sent him off with a flea in his ear, as any woman in her position could have done. From her narrative of these events we can gather that she was, in Laurentian jargon, "unfulfilled"; and it was certainly she who chose him. She has described how he came for a walk with her and the children, and how she stood and watched him as he played with them, so completely absorbed in floating daisies and paper-boats down the stream that she was forgotten: "Suddenly

I knew I loved him. He had touched a new tenderness in me." Quite a number of women had that experience; Frieda was the one who found a real response. Perhaps it was the fact that he was found so lovable by women which made men hate him so much.

"After that," Frieda proceeds with inspired brevity, "things happened quickly." They certainly did. Her husband was away on a journey, and with splendid simplicity she asked Lawrence to spend the night with her. Of course he was highly scandalised at such an improper and continental suggestion, and refused. "No," he said primly, "I will not stay in your husband's house while he is away, but you must tell him the truth, and we will go away together, because I love you." Observe that it was "because I love you", not "because you love me" or even "because we love each other". Long afterwards discussing this tragical situation of leaving her children I ventured to say to her: "Why on earth did you do it, Frieda?" To which she replied: "He told me to." Well, that has a fine simplicity, but does not really answer the question. Besides, it seems to throw the whole moral responsibility on Lawrence; and, looking over Frieda's own abbreviated narrative and what little of the correspondence has survived, I hardly think it was as simple as that.

Whatever Frieda may have said to her husband in obedience to Lawrence, the break at first was far from complete, not only because she obviously wavered both in her feelings and intentions but because Lawrence, as soon as the stimulus of opposition waned, inevitably fell into his usual ambivalent attitude and could not make up his mind what he wanted to do. True, on the 4th May, 1912, they crossed the Channel in company and stayed together at the same hotel in Metz. But even this was not fatally compromising. It so happened that Frieda's soldier father was celebrating some sort of official jubilee to commemorate his long service in the German army. Consequently every room in her old home was occupied by guests, which seemed a natural explanation for her going to a hotel, just as this event in her father's military career explained her presence in Alsace. By way of contributing to the enjoyment and peaceful old age of her aristocratic father, Frieda was able to inform him that she was thinking of leaving her eminently respectable husband and her three children for a penniless almost unknown British author, an ex-schoolmaster out of a job, the son of a coal-miner.

Nobody will be surprised to learn that Baron von Richthofen advised against this course. In her narrative Frieda writes that her father backed this up by saying he "knew the world", to which she retorted that he "never knew the best". It may be so, but what she told me (long before she wrote her narrative) was that her father accused her of being an "Atavismus", by which I assume he meant that she was a throw-back to the primitive habits of her female ancestors. Later when she went traipsing through Bavaria on foot with her British Wandervôgel, the old Baron said bitterly that she was a "Kellnerin"—in those days the occupation of waitress in a German beer-hall was not considered to be a certificate of chastity.

This not very peaceful idyll in Metz was abruptly cut short by the grotesque military. Lawrence and Frieda were sitting on the grass by a large ditch and slope which turned out to be part of the obsolete fortifications of Metz, and an officious sentry insisted on arresting Lawrence under suspicion of being a British officer in disguise engaged in espionage. Oddly enough, there was something a little military in Lawrence's appearance then, perhaps because he wore a moustache and held himself very erect, but he did not look like an officer. It was this which led to the discovery of the whole situation, as Frieda had to ask her father to use his influence to have the arrest lifted. This, rather generously in the circumstances, he did; but insisted that Lawrence should leave the town at once and go to his German relatives in the Rhineland.

He had no choice but to go. However, he did not go direct to Waldbröl, but stayed for a time at Trier. The emotions generated in the two lovers and to a less extent in those about them were now rapidly rising to a climax. On the very day when Frieda's father was celebrating his jubilee Lawrence had sent a note begging her to come away from Metz with him. "I love you," he wound up, "but I always have to bite my tongue before I can say it," so hard was it for him to be gracious even to his mistress. He also told her that he wished he had the sole management of their affairs, generously conceding that "in oddments, your will is my will." Another note, merely dated "Tuesday" (he had the feminine habit of often leaving his letters undated) was also apparently written in Metz, and what he was "afraid" of was "a fit of heroics". In this he says emphatically that there were to be "no more dishonour, no more lies," and later, "no more subterfuge, lying, dirt, fear." Moreover, he had written to her husband. Of course he had everything to gain by adopting this attitude of intransigent virtue, for in fact he was presenting Frieda with an ultimatum before her passion had time to cool or she to reflect. Even then he ended a little wryly: "I love you, and Lord, I pay for it."

Events followed each other quickly. On the 8th May he wrote her in a calmer mood from Trier—which, parenthetically, he describes in the letter with a beauty only he could give—and now with some of the real sweetness that was always in him: "I love you so much. . . . I begin to feel quite a man of the world. I ought, I suppose, with this wickedness of waiting for another man's wife in my heart." Yet in the same letter he had already warned her: "Remember you are to be my wife", and had told her that she was only to receive letters from her still legal husband through him. In another letter he was particularly in love with her chin—"you've got such a nice chin"; and that letter wound up with the most sadly ironical thing he ever wrote: "We shall always have to battle with *life*, so we'll never fight with each other, always help."

He kept urging her to come to him, but put it in a form which showed that he was far from confident: "You *will* come on Saturday?" Here, as did sometimes happen, his faith in his own intuition was justified. Under pressure from her husband and her own family Frieda was beginning to waver, and Lawrence had to endure the proverbial wrongs of the absent. He saw it was useless to hang about any longer in Trier, and therefore proceeded along the Rhine by easy stages to Waldbröl. It is worth noting that all this time he made no mention of the extreme poverty which crippled him and made it seem ridiculous that he could even think of supporting a woman who all her life had been used to comfort. The only hint of it is in a letter he wrote Edward Garnett just before leaving Trier, and even then it is only to ask if his "literary affairs are shifting at all?"

These agitations and disappointments and travellings made any regular literary work impossible, but he continued to jot down poems. He wrote one which he called 'Bei Hennef', and has told us himself that this poem marked the beginning of a new epoch in his life, the real withdrawing from vain yearning for his dead mother to pivot himself on the living woman he wanted as his wife. Hennef am Rhein is a little railway junction where he had to wait for an hour on his way to Waldbrôl. There he brooded on himself and Frieda, on their "Troubles, anxieties, pains" as the twilight deepened over the river, but then he adds:

> "You are the call, and I am the answer,
> You are the wish, and I the fulfilment,
> You are the night, and I the day.
>   What else? it is perfect enough,
>   It is perfectly complete,
>   You and I,
>   What more——?"

Well, that was a moment of peace and acceptance, but did not conjure down all the legions of devils which had been raised by this unorthodox love affair. Frieda still hesitated to commit herself irrevocably to him, as well she might. He began to grow impatient, wrote her "not a nice letter" but for once had enough self-control not to send it, then wrote her instead a very Laurentian one about Waldbrôl and his German cousins, with some of his usual touches of humour: "Here, I am so good and so respectable, it is quite a rest." But his impatience breaks out in the cry, "don't leave me stranded in some unearthly German town."

Now he was hoping that Frieda would after all decide to throw away her old life and join him in Munich; wherefore he wrote again to Garnett asking rather humbly if Duckworth would advance him the great sum of ten pounds. Garnett was in his confidence, and Lawrence told him that he "felt the soles of his feet burn with impatience" as he waited for Frieda's decision. He was in such a frenzy that he was almost "driven mad" as he watched the slow-motion deliberate "buff oxen, with their immense heads that seem always asleep." Yet—see his endless vacillations and self-contradictions—on the very same day he wrote Frieda: "Do you know, like the old knights, I seem to want a certain time to prepare myself." He may have thought it was wise to conceal his extreme impatience, for he went on: "Because it's a great thing for me to marry you, not a quick passionate coming together. I know in my heart 'here's my marriage'. It feels rather terrible—because it is a great thing in my life—it is *my life*—I am a bit awe-inspired—I want to get used to it." Notice he says "my marriage" not "our marriage".

Perhaps he felt he could not say "ours" because Frieda had been married before; but even if she had been coming out of a convent to him he would almost certainly still have written "my marriage".

In a letter dated 14th May (all this had happened in ten days from leaving England) he is evidently pretty sure that she will join him. He still urges that they should "wait a bit religiously for one another", but now for the first time brings up what he calls "the money business", as a man naturally does to his wife. Their prospects as revealed were not particularly handsome. A friend in England owed him twenty-five pounds; in August—that is, three months later—he had twenty-four pounds due to him; and that seemed to be all, unless he sold some of his unpublished writings. He not unnaturally wondered if they would be able to get along on so little, but such was his state of infatuation that he actually begged Frieda to be "definite, my dear, be detailed, be business-like", when he should have known she was most happily incapable of doing anything of the sort.

One feels rather a peeping Tom in reading such intimate letters, but they are truly important to an estimate of Lawrence from their genuine sincerity and the deep devotion they reveal for Frieda. No unbiased person reading them could ever believe there was anything cheap or undignified in such a love. "When I come to you," he says touchingly in the last of them, "things shall not put us apart again." And things did not. It was on a Friday, still in the same month of May, that Lawrence made the long slow railway journey south to Munich. There he met Frieda, and the two spent a week alone together at the Gasthaus zur Post at the village of Beuerberg in the Isarthal. Probably this was all the honeymoon they could afford, for after spending a little time with Frieda's sister, they went to live in an apartment at Icking, which had been lent them.

"England, thy beauties are tame and domestic!" might have been written by Lawrence in his rapturous mood at that time. The romantic beauty of the Bavarian countryside would in itself have been intoxicating to his spirit, which had only just escaped for the first time from the tame prison of respectability; but to experience it all with such a love made him glorious with happiness. Almost literally it was true to say that he had come back to life from the grave, for it was then that at last the hold of the dead mother on his heart relaxed. Happy love made him in love with the whole world, with the chestnut blossoms, red and white, that fell on their out-of-doors breakfast table; the "pale jade green" of the river at Beuerberg, so "cold and swift"; the people who to him were so strange and to Frieda so familiar; the church and the convent which were "so peaceful"; and then the wild flowers which were always so dear to him and now "make you cry with joy"—the "pale gold great bubbles" of kingcups, the primulas "like mauve cowslips", the "queer March violets", the orchids, harebells, larkspur, lucerne, lilies of the valley, "oh, flowers, great wild mad profusion of them, everywhere."

Icking, if possible, was an even greater enchantment. There they began housekeeping in four little rooms on about fifteen shillings a week, living chiefly on rye bread, fruit, eggs and cutlets. He was truly and rapturously happy there. "I love Frieda so much," he wrote, "I don't like to talk about it." "Frieda is awfully good-looking" he says proudly to someone who evidently had shown insufficient respect, so "you needn't say things about her— she is a million times better than ever you imagine." From Frieda he could look out on the world joyously, and declare it to be "wonderful and beautiful and good beyond one's wildest imagination." Of course, even then his "dark self" was not utterly quelled, and there were some shadows. A poem written at Beuerberg contains the confession that "the first night was a failure" and "our love was a confusion." Again it was in that first week at Beuerberg that he wrote his frenziedly bitter 'Lot's wife' poem, when in an agony of jealous rage he railed against Frieda's love for her children, denouncing "the mother in you, fierce as a murderess, glaring to England" —he who later snapped at her in one of their quarrels that "mother love doesn't exist". So, in spite of his assertion that they would battle the world but never each other, they had begun to quarrel in the first week. And at her sister's house in Wolfratshausen there had fallen on him one of his recurrent moods of longing for oblivion, for "heavy, sealing darkness, silence, all immovable," that lapse into his antithetical "dark self" which was the inevitable counterpart to his vivid light self.

There was a balcony on the little house at Icking where Frieda, a comparatively uninhibited person, sat down to breakfast with bare feet and dressed in only her night-gown, to the scandal of her puritan lover. With magnificent loyalty she has accused herself at this time of being guilty of the strange Laurentian crime of "sex in the head", though one would say that is less characteristic of women who abandon all for love's sake than of men who write books about sex. There can seldom have been a more obvious case of "sex in the head" than Lawrence himself, although he was always denouncing it in others; but then he had a habit of denouncing in others what he did himself.

From this balcony they overlooked the little village, and could see far beyond the icy waters of the Isar and the dark woods to where there rose up "the great blue wall of mountains, only their tops, all snowy, glittering in far-off sunshine against a pale blue sky." There Lawrence was so happy he wrote Garnett he wanted "to live abroad for ever". Frieda went even further and pined "to clear out of Europe and get to somewhere uncivilised." Meanwhile, the poet in him was showing her the beauty of her own country and of herself:

"By the Isar, in the twilight
We were wandering and singing:
By the Isar in the evening
We climbed the huntsman's ladder and sat swinging
In the fir-tree overlooking the marshes;
While river met river, and the ringing
Of their pale-green glacier-water filled the evening.

By the Isar, in the twilight
We found our warm wild roses
Hanging red on the river; and simmering
Frogs were singing, and over the river closes
Was scent of roses, and glimmering
In the twilight, our kisses across the roses
Met, and her face, and my face, were roses."

The later version has a different and less simple ending, for it runs:

". . . and glimmering
Fear was abroad. We whispered: 'No one knows us.
Let it be as the snake disposes
Here in this simmering marsh."

Why do men grow to be ashamed of their loves? How much nicer to kiss and feel like roses than to drag in fear and a snake, and that horrible rhyme of "disposes" and "knows us"! Of course, as Lawrence wrote at the time in the sober prose of a letter, their life wasn't all "billing and cooing and nibbling grapes and white sugar." He and Frieda agree that they had "battles" in that "inner war which is waged between people who love each other", and there are echoes of that strife in such poems as 'In The Dark', 'Humiliation' and 'A Young Wife'; but to concentrate attention on those while completely ignoring the happy poems is to forget that both sets come from a book with the challenge in its title: *Look! We Have Come Through.* In every marriage there are trials and difficulties of adjustment, particularly in the case of two such passionate people, one of whom was "a genius" and well aware of the fact. True, in one of the "dark self" poems Frieda is made to say:

> "I am afraid of you, I am afraid, afraid!
> There is something in you destroys me——!"

and:

> " . . . Yes, yes, you are cruel to me. You cast
> A shadow over my breasts that will kill me at last."

But Frieda herself has written of that first summer together:

"I didn't want people, I didn't want anything, I only wanted to revel in this new world Lawrence had given me. I had found what I needed, I could now flourish like a trout in a stream or a daisy in the sun. His generosity in giving himself . . .!"

This she felt in spite of the "storms of letters from England" imploring her to return to her children and threatening that otherwise she would never be allowed to see them again! It was hard on them both, but part of the inevitable price to be paid for such a relationship. But these dreary and bitter moments only for a time blotted out their happiness in the mountains and the flowers, the singing frogs, the glow-worms, the fireflies "wafting in between and over the swaying corn-stalks", the doe they saw one day as it flashed up the hillside, the men mowing wheat with scythes, and Lawrence's joy in Frieda like a Gloire de Dijon rose in her bath or laughing across the table sprinkled with "mauve-red" roses:

"... saying
She loves me, and I blow a little boat
Rocking down the shoals between the tea-cups
And so kiss-laden it scarce can float."

Scandalous outcasts though they were, they were not without visitors. First in importance though not in time was Frieda's mother, who suddenly dropped in on Lawrence while Frieda was away with her sister. For an hour she sat there and "schimfed" (i.e. abused) him, asking him who he thought he was that a gentleman's daughter should black his boots and empty his slops, and what did he mean by eloping with the wife of a respectable man and treating her like a barmaid when he couldn't even afford to keep her in shoes? During this diatribe Lawrence was so completely taken aback that on his own confession he did nothing but "sit and gasp" and then meekly accompany the enraged lady to the railway station. True, he afterwards thought of all the replies he should have made but didn't. Instinctively she knew the right way to deal with his sort —refuse to accept him at his own valuation, hit him hard and fast with home truths, and then walk off, head in air, before he had time to recover. She was so successful that he respected her for the rest of their joint lives, and placated her constantly with letters and presents. At the time he was immensely relieved and pleased to know that after this disconcerting interview she had told Frieda's sister, Else, that she thought from his looks he was "lovable and trustworthy". However, Frieda says the remark was Else's, and Lawrence may have transferred it to the mother in his account to try and save a little face.

The second visitor was David Garnett, the son of Edward Garnett, who at his father's suggestion came over from Munich to see them. Lawrence had written that it would be easy to recognise him among the Germans as he looked "fearfully English, English to the bone", which Garnett found to be the case. I have already quoted part of Garnett's description of Lawrence's appearance, though I think he rather overdoes the plebeian aspect. Certainly it was there, both physically and mentally, but the important part of Lawrence was something quite apart from class. Garnett adds that Lawrence was "cheeky and cocky, the type who provokes the most violent class hatred", which is true enough, but Lawrence was far too proud and scrupulous and too much of an individualist to be "the man for whom trades unions exist, who lives on the dole, who hangs round the pubs, whose wife supports him, who bets on football." All absolutely untrue. Garnett's first impression of Frieda is good and accurate:

"Her head and the whole carriage of her body was (*sic*) noble. She looked one dead in the eyes, fearlessly judging one."

The young man (he was only twenty) was instantly attracted by two such obviously happy lovers, was "completely charmed by each of them", and "worshipped" them. When the couple left Icking and went to Mayrhofen in the Zillertal (Tirol), he followed them and had every opportunity to observe them. In spite of the very unwelcome letters from England, they were all kept gay by Lawrence's "courage, high spirits and mockery." Lawrence's courage rose to meet danger and difficulty, as Garnett truly says, and "at that time both their difficulties were very great."

Young as he was, Garnett noted many characteristic traits in Lawrence. There was for instance his habit, which he retained for many years, of compelling people to play at charades which he ruthlessly bossed but always made laughable. He had a great gift for mimicry, in the exercise of which he spared nobody, least of all himself. We have all of us at some time suffered from the witless and mirthless displays of people who are mistaken in thinking they possess this gift; but Lawrence's was genuine, always merciless and accurate in pouncing on pretences and affectations. When he was vindictive this might jar a little, but when he was happy and in good spirits he always kept well on the right side of cruelty and meanness. A saving grace of the whole mocking parody was that, as Garnett says, he "mimicked himself ruthlessly" and "acted ridiculous versions of a shy and gawky Lawrence being patronised by literary lions, of a winsome Lawrence charming his landlady, a sentimental Lawrence being put in his place by his landlady's daughter, of a bad-tempered, whining Lawrence picking a quarrel with Frieda over nothing."

Garnett of course noticed Lawrence's ability to work in a room where other people were talking and laughing. During those days at Mayrhofen he was writing poems and stories and sketches and apparently also working on *Sons and Lovers;* yet it never occurred to either of the others that they ought not to interrupt him. He also discovered, what everyone who knew him soon learned, that Lawrence could always break off work or talk to look after the cooking and housework. Jessie Chambers had noticed long before that with him the dullest household tasks became interesting, and he excelled at such routine jobs as cleaning, tidying and washing up. As we have seen, he had learned to do these things to help his mother, but what was unique and peculiar to him was that he never seemed bored or in a hurry to get done. Washing up, making an omelette, any piece of housework were for him a part of life and to be enjoyed as such. True, he sometimes liked a respite, but for much of his life in spite of illness and the vast energies he poured into his writing he really did enjoy these humble tasks. Here is one striking difference between him and the mass of ordinary people who want to evade at all costs the essential work of life, and thereby condemn themselves to boredom and futility.

Evidently Lawrence had quite recovered from his winter illness, for to Garnett he looked well and happy, "consistently gay and light-hearted." He was making cheerful plans for the future, and was inexhaustibly creative, pouring out new work every day. Long before he had completed his re-writing of *Sons and Lovers* he had "thought of a new novel—purely of the common people—fearfully interesting." But how little all his work then earned him may be judged from the fact that when he and Frieda set out to walk from Mayrhofen to Lake Garda they had but twenty-three pounds between them.

On the first part of this walk Garnett and a friend accompanied them, as they went over the mountains, by way of the Pfitzer Joch, to Sterzing. On the way the two writers botanised, collecting nearly two hundred species of wild flowers. They came unexpectedly upon a lonely upland chapel full of curious votive pictures, slept or tried to sleep in a hay-hut during a downpour of rain which in the night turned to snow, got wet through, and finally came to Italianised Sterzing where "grapes hung in black clusters over the lintels and a tobacco harvest stood in queer pagodas drying in a garden."

There, much to his regret in later days, Garnett left them. As soon as they were alone the two lovers "quarrelled like nuts", partly over the children problem, partly from the mere clash of strong personalities. From some accounts of Lawrence you would suppose that he and Frieda were the only couple in the world who ever had lovers' quarrels. Unfortunately, these were not the only troubles. Coming over a mountain pass above Merano they lost their way, and very nearly perished on the mountain-side in an icy wind which battered them into near exhaustion as the darkness of night "filthy and black" rolled down on them. Lawrence's energy and will at last got them over the last ridge to a rest hut. Then, still rather shaky from this trial, they trudged on to Trento, where worse befell them. Owing to their inexperience and poverty they got into a cheap and dirty hotel with sanitary arrangements dating from the Dark Ages. Frieda had "blues enough to re-pave the floors of Heaven" and Lawrence found her shedding tears of misery and self-pity at the foot of Dante's statue. They wisely made the remainder of their journey to Riva by train, for the blues and all the rest of it were mostly the result of fatigue.

In those days Riva still belonged to Austria. Even between the wars it remained clean and almost fashionable. When Lawrence and Frieda arrived in the smart little town and found themselves among Austrian officers and their well-dressed women, the couple looked at each other and realised that six weeks of carefree scrambling among the mountains had turned them into pretty good imitations of tramps. Now they went to the opposite extreme from what they had done in Trento, and rented a room which was too elegant and too dear for them. There as they ate frugal picnic meals they had to scurry to hide their food under the couch when the very superior maid-servant came in. Then came another extravagant transformation. Frieda's wealthy and fashionable sister sent her a large trunk full of Parisian models, and one of the couple suddenly became absurdly over-dressed for wandering bohemians defying the sacred conventions of England on practically nothing a year.

But now they were at their destination, for they proposed to spend the winter on the lake—with total assets of fifty pounds advance from Duckworth, a volume of *Love Poems* in the press and an incomplete novel, *Sons and Lovers*.

3

In later years both Lawrence and Frieda became very experienced travellers, though, in his frail state of health, he was not careful enough to choose the right time of the year for the places he visited. They became skilful in choosing lodgings, and within a couple of hours Frieda could transform the most ordinary room into a personal and attractive environment with the blankets and embroideries and bright coloured things they had picked up in various parts of the world. From the first of their wanderings she was of course bilingual, but in time Lawrence also learned German fairly well and they could both talk French, Italian and Spanish. They were genuine travellers, not mere ignorant tourists. But in that autumn of 1912 the inexperience which led them to choose a place as far north and as exposed as Lake Garda for the winter was matched by their total ignorance of Italian. Added to that was Lawrence's still acute shyness and fear of ridicule and rebuff which made him afraid even to ask the inhabitants about rooms and prices. Getting angry with him, Frieda went up to a man in one of the lake villages and stammered: "Prego—quartiere—d'affitare", only to have him insist on putting them in a bus which went back to Riva!

As it turned out, their inexperience served them well. Nothing could have been better for the development of his "genius" and the fighting out of their strange lovers' battles than this six months of solitude and primitive living in beautiful country, where they were forced to learn a foreign language in order to live and discover ways of living so completely unlike industrialised and suburban England. And, whatever the drawbacks, this Spartan life was much better, much less banal, than living in some English-frequented pension, gossiped about as soon as their illicit relation was discovered, with the additional horror of minor intelligentsia dropping in to teach Lawrence how to write. During the whole period they saw but two English people, and read hardly any books except the Italian they studied and a few sent out to them. During that six months Lawrence completed the final version of *Sons and Lovers*, the book which first made his reputation; wrote considerable portions of early drafts of *The Rainbow* and *The Lost Girl*, some of the *Twilight in Italy* sketches, two plays, and a number of poems. This was the most intensely creative period of his life.

It was the landlady of the over-elegant room in Riva who helped them to the kind of place they wanted, by sending them to the lakeside village of Gargnano, at that time remote and accessible only by steamer. There they found a villa in "a nice garden with peaches and bamboos" with a furnished lower floor to be let, containing kitchen, living-room, two bedrooms, "clean as a flower", and all for two pounds sixteen a month. As soon as they had secured this palace of delight the lovers "hugged each other with joy at the idea of a *ménage*" and exulted over "the gorgeous copper pans in the kitchen." Lawrence planned—"what bliss!"—to begin life there by correcting the proofs of his *Love Poems*; and scarcely had they moved in when a delayed letter arrived from Edward Marsh, asking to include 'Snapdragon' in his next 'Georgian Anthology'. What more could a mere "genius" ask?

Naturally, they were no more able to avoid the troubles of life than any other couple. First, the long summer weather they had been enjoying as if it would last for ever suddenly broke early in October—the lake was dark with "white lambs" all over it, the vines turned red and yellow and the fig trees became "a flame" of autumn leaves. Then Frieda had difficulties with her share of the cleaning and cooking. It was most fortunate for her that Lawrence was so experienced a housewife, for she seems to have been marvellously incompetent in those days. As he sat concentrated on the writing of *Sons and Lovers*—and how completely he could concentrate on a task only those who knew him can realise—he would suddenly hear a dismal wail from the kitchen: "Lorenzo, the pigeons are burning, what shall I do?" Instantly he would drop his own work and rush competently to the rescue. It will be noted that he already had the name 'Lorenzo' among intimates, for he disliked 'David', and 'Bert' was his home name.

In later days we all came to admire Frieda's gusto and skill in conducting a washing day, but at that time she evidently lacked practice. As she tells the sad event:

"The first time I washed sheets was a disaster. They were so large and wet, their wetness was overwhelming. The kitchen floor was flooded, the table drenched, I dripped from hair to feet. When Lawrence found me all misery he called: 'The One and Only is drowning, O dear!' I was rescued and dried, the kitchen wiped, and soon the sheets were hanging to dry in the garden."

It does not appear that Frieda over-worked herself at Gargnano. Every morning Lawrence got up at eight and made breakfast for her, and she often stayed in bed until noon, making him stay and talk to her. This made him feel guilty, as if he were not doing his share of work in the world. For diversion, as well as from necessity, they took Italian lessons from the village schoolmistress, a prim lady who wore black gloves and kept them both in order. Lawrence reported that they were "lisping their lessons like humble children, though of course" (of course!) *he* was much better and quicker than Frieda; in spite of which, for some unknown reason, the teacher "prefers Frieda, and constantly represses me." He was forced to get out a flask and drink some wine to show his "masculine and marital independence." In the afternoon or early evening they walked along the lake to the next village, Bogliaco, where they drank the local red wine (at sixpence the litre) sitting in the kitchen of the osteria with the family—people so uncivilised that they did not know what a tip is. And always they had the beauty of the lake and the lemon gardens, lofty slopes covered with olives and vines, and sometimes for a great treat they made a short steamer trip to one of the other villages.

During the five months which had sped past since he first landed in Metz on his runaway trip Lawrence had "scarcely seen a word of English print", so that a gift copy of a then new book by Arnold Bennett, *Anna of the Five Towns*, was eagerly and gratefully pounced on. The book impressed him, but the contrast of the life it depicted with his present surroundings made Lawrence "feel queer". He felt that Bennett ought not to have been so resigned to ugliness and dismalness, that we "all ought to take a great kick at misery". Working himself up over this he went on:

"No, I don't believe England need be so grubby. What does it matter if one is poor, and risks one's livelihood, and reputation? One *can* have the necessary things, life, and love, and clean warmth. Why is England so shabby? The Italians here sing. They are very poor, they buy two penn'orth of butter and a penn'orth of cheese. But they are healthy and they lounge about in the little square where the boats come up and nets are mended, like kings. And the women walk straight and look calm. And the men adore children—they are glad of their children even if they're poor."

The sum of living, working, thinking, seeing, enjoying achieved in that first six months of solitude for two is almost incredible. The letter just quoted shows that he was still preoccupied with the troubles and problems of the industrialised community, such as he had known for so long. It was something which was always cropping up in his life, and his attempts at solutions inspired some of his best work and also involved him in many difficulties and absurdities. This sense of responsibility to his past was one reason why he could never accept the inevitable loneliness of the writer. He always wanted to feel accepted, in some sort of relation to people who would like and esteem and respond to him. He thought the modern industrial world was shadowed by nemesis, the "stinking purpose" of more and more "complete mechanising of life" had brought into being "teeming millions" who bred cold hatred and the fearful destructiveness of modern violence and war, the cold insanity of modern politics. He wanted to stop it, and optimistically believed he could show the way out and make a newer, better world; a task about as hopeless as trying to make carnivorous ants into harmless vegetarians by reading them Keats.

In Lawrence's case the general problem was closely involved with his personal problems. In spite of his snobbery he was proud of being a working-man's son, although for other reasons he had hated his father. He had loved his home life, the contact of the streets, the quite different remote life of the Chambers family on their farm. As we have seen, however, the moment the industrial machine began to reach out for him personally, he repudiated it blindly, he was not going to let it capture him if he could help it. He saw the worshippers of the industrial machine as enemies, as the insect-men of the collectivist horror who were coldly vindictive against anyone who escaped them. Somehow he had managed to escape, and down there on the shores of ancient Lake Benacus, which owed much to nature but more to the patient life-work of generations of men, Lawrence brooded—"Why must England be grubby and shabby? Must it be so?" No doubt he reminded himself that you can't have industrial "wealth" without machines which must have fuel, and you can't win coal without making yourself and the landscape dirty, and you can't have millions of machine-minders without the frustration and shabbiness and envy he deplored. And even on Garda, where it was true the Italians sang at their work, still, most of them were only too eager to throw away the old warm way of life and emigrate to some cold-hearted land of machinery. It would be flattering him to say that he ever worked out any practical solution of a state of affairs which he was not alone in thinking a sort of mass suicide. All he could do was to avoid it himself.

It was natural that he should turn all this over in his mind as he worked daily on the story of his own life in *Sons and Lovers*. Frieda has told us how completely he was absorbed in the book and how much he suffered when he came to the point when he had to re-live his mother's illness and death. Obviously he had to get it out of himself, but for a time it was such an obsession that Frieda "got fed up" and wrote a skit of the novel which she called: 'Paul Morel, or His Mother's Darling.' She seems surprised that Lawrence received this coldly. Yet it was Frieda who had given him a clue to the situation, by telling him what she had learned about the theories of Freud from a young German who was an enthusiastic analyst. He saw at once that it was the clue, not only to himself but to many another sex-frustrated and sex-starved young man. As he wrote of his book to Edward Garnett: "It's the tragedy of thousands of young men in England. I think it was Ruskin's."

It looks as if the re-living his early life had stirred up some of the religious mysticism of his youth, which he had abandoned. Certainly long passages of this sort were rather irrelevantly introduced into *Twilight in Italy*, and he wrote a dedication of the book (afterwards cancelled) in that symbolical style he often adopted when trying to express abstract ideas which the artist in him disliked but the preacher and prophet could not resist. Unlike Blake, with whom he had not much in common, Lawrence neither invented a complete private mythology of his own nor persuaded himself that he received supernatural visitations. True, he never minded re-using old symbols, whether they were Christian or of some older religion, but it was really to give body to thought which was emotional and confused—in the manner of Ruskin. In this dedication he plays a kind of verbal fugue on the Logos, the Father, the Son, the Trinity, Woman; and concludes:

"The old son-lover was Œdipus. The name of the new one is legion. And if a son-lover take a wife, then is she not his wife, she is only his bed. And his life will be torn in twain, and his wife in her despair shall hope for sons, that she may have her lover in her hour."

It is amusing to turn from this and similar portentousness to the self-mockery in his letters written at this period. "Don't mind what I say," he wrote to one friend, "I am a great bosher, and full of fancies that interest me. My great religion is a belief in the blood, the flesh, as being wiser than the intellect. We can go wrong in our mind. But what our blood feels and believes and says, is always true." This is one of the few convictions in which Lawrence never —perhaps it would be safer to say "hardly ever"—wavered; and it is easy to see how it could be made to link up with his more or less vague theories of the role of the Unbewusst. Yet another of his beliefs was the allied though far more dangerous and dubious dogma that one should always obey one's impulses, no matter what they were. This is how he expressed it at the time:

"The real way of living is to answer to one's wants. Not 'I want to light up with my intelligence as many things as possible' but 'For the living of my full flame—I want that liberty, I want that woman, I want that pound of peaches, I want to go to sleep, I want to go to the pub and have a good time, I want to look a beastly swell to-day, I want to kiss that girl, I want to insult that man.' Instead of that, all these wants, which are there whether-or-not, are utterly ignored, and we talk about some sort of ideas."

However much he might talk about the Father and the Son and the Logos and make use of Christian symbols, it is perfectly clear from that how far he had then gone in repudiating Christian ethics and beliefs. He uses the symbolism in a merely psychological sense, and it cannot help but be misleading. But after delivering such axioms as those just quoted, comes the self-mockery: "I'm like Carlyle, who, they say, wrote fifty volumes on the value of silence"; and indeed he was more like Carlyle than he cared to admit. Did Lawrence for all his acuteness know now much he treated the world as his representation? A flower, a person, a landscape, a work of art, human relations, human history, science, religion were all perceived and interpreted solely in relation to his own needs and moods. Did he really have a perception of "mystic otherness", as Aldous Huxley assures us? I doubt it, I think the "mystic otherness" was entirely a projection of himself. He bluffed us by assuming a knowledge nobody has. For instance, none of us really has the least idea what it is like to be a tortoise or a goat or a bat; but when Lawrence, who loved playing charades, pretended for the time being that he was one and did it very amusingly and cleverly, we were all impressed. Who could contradict him?

It was exactly the same in his relations with people. If a fact displeased, hindered or contradicted him he denied the fact; and he denied the reality of other peoples' feelings to suit his own convenience. He denied, for instance, one of the most obvious and awkward facts in his own life, namely, Frieda's profound love for her children, and their need for her. "You don't care a damn about those brats really," he assured her, "and they don't care about you." What would he have said to anyone who had so brushed aside the love between him and his mother? The world was for him something plastic which could and must be altered to suit him. Thus, when Frieda unaccountably failed to accept this assurance about her "brats", he changed his ground and tried to persuade her that by writing books he would "make a new heaven and earth for them, don't cry, you see if I don't". Of course he needed her so desperately that he was ready to say and do anything to keep his hold of her. And when even she—no Rupert of debate—pointed out in one of these early battles that he was saying exactly the opposite of what he said a week before, he gave the game away completely in his necessity always to make a retort:

"And why shouldn't I? Last week I felt like that, now like this. Why shouldn't I?"

Only, she might have said, that you don't happen to be God, and that the world and its facts remain unchanged however much your feelings about them change.

This absurdity of self-contradiction as well as denying the plainest reality, so valuable to an imaginative artist, infuriated prosaic and pedantic persons into writing angry books of refutation. Those who go to Lawrence for a coherent philosophical system, or require him to state reasons and draw maps for everything he said or wrote, waste their time. What matters is not his opinions and prejudices, but himself, the life and beauty he can transmit more than anyone else of his age. As to contradiction, who does not contradict himself unless he happens to be unusually dull or a repulsively canny and crafty careerist?

Intense literary production, quarrelling and making love with Frieda, housework, learning Italian, were not the sum of his occupations at Gargnano. "I live in sunshine and happiness, in exile and poverty" he could write truly and proudly. He had few correspondents, but at one time or other he grandly invited every one of them to come and stay with them—and they would have been wise to accept for a few days since they would have learned how the fact of being alive can be made enchanting. The only one who accepted was a young man called Harold Hobson, who had been on the walk with the Lawrences and Garnett from Bavaria to Austria; and he spent Christmas with them.

Otherwise they were quite alone, and had to create their own interests and happiness. By way of rest from novel-writing Lawrence took up his painting and produced what he described as "two pictures—several". With Frieda he climbed the hill behind the little town to gather Christmas roses. Once during January he went by himself, looking for snowdrops erroneously reported by the schoolmistress, for he found only primroses and a daisy. Frieda, who responded instantly to so much in him, shared his loving passion for flowers:

"When Lawrence first found a gentian, a big single blue one, I remember feeling as if he had a strange communion with it, as if the gentian yielded up its blueness, its very essence to him. Everything he met had the newness of a creation just that moment come into being."

Even at this time he had acquired—and knew he had acquired—his habit of unblushing impudent dogmatism. "Living here one gets sort of different—sort of *ex-cathedra*," he confessed to Edward Garnett; and it was true. Why did he do it, why did he involve himself in his tangle of self-contradictions? Like Montaigne he knew that he was *ondoyant et divers*, but he could never bring himself to meet any of the endless puzzles of existence with Montaigne's shrug and "How should I know?" He was terribly at ease upon Sion. He always had to know everything and have the right answer to everything. Perhaps it is one difference between the artist and the philosopher. The philosopher can afford to doubt and to be ignorant, but the artist must live and know all his moods and experiences.

Anyway, there is no getting away from the fact of his dogmatism. It was his way of putting things which other people would have stated more cautiously and doubtfully. He knew perfectly well that his "*ex-cathedra*" habit was absurd and even warned other people to discount it, only to tumble head-over-heels into it again on the very next opportunity. He could not learn by experience to avoid it, any more than he could help hopefully trying again and again to found his "colony of friends" however often experience showed it was a disastrous idea, any more than he could help quarrelling with the only woman he loved for no real reason at all in most cases, and that in spite of the fact that he recognised he was wrong and bad-tempered and destroying his own happiness. However much the dogmatism and the quarrelling grew out of his peculiar temperament, the chief blame must be laid on bad early training and environment. In much the same way he had acquired a habit of forcing on other people unasked and usually inappropriate advice *àpropos de bottes.*

Autumn usually lasts long south of the Alps, but sooner or later the great snowy peaks send winter icily swirling down on Italy. When winter happened, Lawrence, like all inexperienced northerners, was duly surprised and hurt—and the "hurt" must be taken literally for already in mid-December he had "a cold" and felt so "seedy" that he stayed in bed "chewing Toroni". It was a dismal reminder in his happiness of the fiend at his lungs. There were rainy days which made him "amazed and indignant", and then snow descended on "a beastly wind from the Po". It was all so unexpected and disagreeable that he got "the blues", and had to cheer himself up by scrubbing the floor and making marmalade.

Unhappily there were reasons enough for "the blues" not to be driven away even by the humours and amusement of the local theatre, where their landlord gave them the key to his box. It would be untrue to say that Lawrence tried to make money in life, but he knew from much experience the bitterness of lacking it, although he was one of those who will cut down expenses to nothing to avoid debt. And he did not always manage to avoid debt. He could not help worrying about money that winter for he had taken on the responsibility of Frieda on a very small margin and doubtful prospects. He had all the more reason to worry since his book of poems was received very coldly and subscribed barely a hundred copies; and to-day you cannot buy a copy of that edition for less than four pounds!

On top of this discouragement he was much cast down by a letter from Edward Garnett about *Sons and Lovers*, making various adverse criticisms and demanding cuts in the sacred name of decency. Looking ruefully at these dismal facts he still had the courage to say that rather than give in and go back to teaching school he would be "the proverbial poor poet in the garret first", not, he hastily added, that he had "any sympathy with starvers, Gissings and Chattertons." For a little while he played with the idea of doing hack-work, and then repudiated it with the proud assertion: "I always feel as if I stood naked for the fire of Almighty God to go through me—and it's rather an awful feeling. One has to be so terribly religious."

Then there was the question of Frieda's divorce, disgust with the squalid point of view of the lawyers, not to mention the fact that he could not afford to pay for it. Still through all the strange battle he insisted on fighting with Frieda they were slowly forging their permanent unbreakable relationship, even though there were always those haunting, unforgotten, wistful children in England. "We've had a hard time, Frieda and I," he wrote to a woman friend. It hadn't been easy, he goes on—and who supposes it was?—for her to leave husband and children "like that"; nor even very easy for them to start living together in solitude in a foreign country and yet in spite of everything "dig out a love deeper and deeper." Later on he elaborated on this hard-won triumph:

"Once you've known what love *can* be, there's no disappointment any more and no despair. If the skies tumble down like a smashed saucer, it couldn't break what's between Frieda and me. I'll do my life work, sticking up for the love between man and woman."

From Christmas until early in March they remained quite alone, and then they were joined by a woman friend. Evidently Lawrence could manage to be happy sometimes without washing dishes, for he warmly welcomed her arrival because "she can do my share of the housework, thank the Lord". He complained that he felt as if he had "cooked cart-loads of food and scrubbed acres of dirty boards." Presently this friend moved to San Gaudenzio, higher up the mountain-side, and there at the completion of their tenancy the Lawrences followed, staying at the rather "illicit" inn he has described in *Twilight in Italy*.

Lawrence left Gargnano with regret. In spite of the worries and difficulties, much of their life there had been as nearly perfect as is possible. If he had ever felt any doubts about his vocation as a writer they surely should have been settled—despite Garnett's grumbles—by that masterly final version of *Sons and Lovers*. At Gargnano he had worked hard and well.

And then he was sorry to go away from the flowers which grew in such profusion, flowers which to him were always the loveliest symbol of the beautiful non-human world. They had meant much to him in his loneliness—the wild cyclamens "very cold and fragrant, real flowers of the past, as if blossoming in the landscape of Phaedra and Helen"; then the Christmas roses, "large pure cold buds, like violets, like magnolias" under the winter sunlight which was "so still and pure, like iced wine". With earliest spring had come the familiar primroses and among the olive groves "large, white, grave violets and less serious blue ones". Almonds and apricots broke into blossom "like pink puffs of smoke among the grey smoke of olive leaves"; and there were wild crocuses of pale magenta, blue hepatica, pale bee-orchids, and grape hyacinths "purple as noon, many-breasted, and full of milk, and ripe, and sun-darkened, like many-breasted Diana."

Still, much as he liked the place, he knew they had to move, and then the spring always made him restless, so that already he was thinking of Florence and Rome. After all they spent but a fortnight at San Gaudenzio, but the change enlivened him. Every day he sat in a deserted lemon-garden, high above the lake, writing a novel which he described as a pot-boiler, a novel about the Midlands suggested by his reading of Arnold Bennett's novel, afterwards re-written as *The Lost Girl.* But much of the time they were out, "up at the charcoal-burners' hut on the mountains, or away at the great scree." The people and the experiences which fill four of those sketches of *Twilight in Italy* all came to him in the course of those two weeks. Often he was at his best when able to concentrate in a book all the thronging experiences of a few days.

One morning as he sat alone looking out on the world of spring he put the novel aside and wrote a song of triumph about himself and Frieda:

"We have died, we have slain and been slain,
We are not our old selves any more.
I feel new and eager
To start again.

It is gorgeous to live and forget,
And to feel quite new.
See the bird in the flowers?—he's making
A rare to-do!

He thinks the whole blue sky
Is much less than the bit of blue egg
He's got in his nest—we'll be happy
You and I, I and you.

With nothing to fight any more—
In each other, at least.
See, how gorgeous the world is
Outside the door!"

4

SOMEHOW the move north from Lake Garda seemed rather a come-down, rather a retreat. Their baggage had been packed and labelled for Florence, when suddenly they turned north instead of south, intending to make their way back to England by way of Bavaria. Why the sudden change? Once more it was Frieda's children and her yearning to be with them—and when she really wanted something desperately, he seldom opposed it. The tragical importance of those children in their lives can hardly be exaggerated. Here was the young mother torn between them and this strange flame-like lover who had carried her off like one of Rubens's Sabine women, creating in her this insoluble conflict of loves and loyalties. It was all very well for Lawrence to promise her in his cocksure way that he would "make a new heaven and earth" for the children; all very well for him to write her sister Else such obviously specious arguments as: "if Frieda brings the children a sacrifice, that is a curse to them; whatever they may miss now, they will preserve their inner liberty, their inner pride, so we must go on, and never let go the children, but will, will and will to have them and have what we think good."

It is unnecessary to stress the absurdity and hollowness of such arguments, if arguments they can be called. But he had to do something, say something, make some pretence, for word had just come from England that Frieda might, if she insisted, be divorced, but if so then her children had no mother—she would never be allowed to see them again. Under that threat Frieda lost her head, and could think of nothing but rushing back to England to stand for hours in the street in the hope of seeing the children come out of school. To adopt Lawrence's type of symbolism, here were the lion and the unicorn fighting for the crown of Frieda, and the poor crown getting dreadfully bent and battered in the strife.

There must have been times when she was on the verge of abandoning the adventure, giving in to righteousness, going back to be horribly forgiven. Something prevented Lawrence from saying outright: "You mustn't go—I need you most—stay with me." But short of swallowing his conceit and admitting that, he used every possible device to mean that without saying it. He could never have endured another man's children, as he pretended to Else, and of course he knew there was no slightest chance of getting them. Suppose they had succeeded, how were two penniless wanderers to look after three small children? At that time Lawrence was more than ever worried about money. The utter failure of his poems had been confirmed, and he had not received even proofs of *Sons and Lovers*. At last he began to waver and to talk about teaching again—not a big school like Davidson, a small private school. With his health record would he have been accepted anywhere?

They meant to stay only a week in Bavaria, and in fact remained there chiefly from April to September, 1913. Their immediate material difficulties were solved by living in a Bauerhaus belonging to Frieda's brother-in-law, a "little wooden house, standing in a corner of a fir-wood, in a hilly meadow all primulas and gentian, and looking away at the snowy Alps." But though he had kept Frieda and there was the consolation of flowers and snow-peaks, Lawrence was not altogether happy. "It broke my heart to leave Italy," he wrote one friend, and told another "I want to go back to Italy", and until the last year or so of his life Italy was the country where he was happiest. Now, after Italy, he disliked "the tightness and domesticity" of Germany, though he admitted thankfully that even that was better than the "Sunday feeling which is so blighting in England."

At all events, though still grumbling, he settled to work again, writing alternately on early versions of *The Lost Girl* and *The Rainbow*. He worried himself with fruitless speculations as to the possible fate of *Sons and Lovers*, and chafed at the delay in publication, labelling all publishers "a damned dilatory lot". Of course, he had every reason to worry about his next novel. It was his third, and if its sales and reputation proved no higher than those of the first two, it was not a hopeful prospect. Still, whatever he felt, he kept up a front of excessive self-confidence, dismissed the mere hundred sale of his poems as irrelevant, with the boast: "I *know* I can write bigger stuff than any man in England."

In this Bavarian village of Irschenhausen he read a few new English books of the day. A novel called *The Gadfly* he dismissed as having "a sexual twist" he didn't like; and he found Wells's *The New Machiavelli* depressing and long-winded. "I like Wells," he wrote, "he is so warm, such a passionate declaimer or reasoner or whatever you like. But, ugh!—he hurts me. He always seems to be looking at life as a cold and hungry little boy stares at a shop where there is hot pork in the window." The book made him start worrying about England because he was sure that "only through a readjustment between men and women, and a making free and healthy of this sex, will she get out of her present atrophy." He picked up Bergson and found him "a little thin" and very dull. *The New Statesman*, which had then just been founded, was "measly".

Towards the end of June they made a flying visit to England, going first to Edward Garnett's house in Kent, which he lent them. That excellent friend contrived that Lawrence should find there a cheque for fifty pounds from his publisher and a selection of the favourable reviews of his novel. He had brought with him the manuscript of "the best short story I have ever done", afterwards called 'The Prussian Officer'—and there waiting for him too were letters from Austin Harrison (the new editor of *The English Review*) and from Ezra Pound, asking for stories. Finally, Edward Marsh had sent a small cheque for a poem—"manna from heaven, I call it", Lawrence commented ironically.

This was a friendly enough welcome for a couple of unrespectable outlaws, and they cheered up considerably. They even began to be known by the right people. There was Edward Marsh, editor of *Georgian Poetry*, who introduced them to Professor Walter

Raleigh and to Herbert and Cynthia Asquith. They sat in a cave near Margate and sang: "What are the wild waves saying?" with the Asquiths. In London they had met John Middleton Murry and Katherine Mansfield, editors of a periodical called *Rhythm*, "a daft paper, but the folk sound nice", and they came to see the Lawrences by the seaside. Murry has left some memories of the visit, including this one:

"Once in the early evening, in the faintly chill dusk, Lawrence darting, like a schoolboy, in and out of the waves as they slipped up the flat brown sand. Katherine Mansfield was a superb swimmer, I a good one. It is the only thing I could ever do better than Lawrence did it. There, on the deserted sand, the four of us bathed naked in the half-light, first happy, then shivering. Then we went back and ate a huge supper of fried steak and tomatoes."

So potent was Lawrence's glamour that, it appears, even the tomatoes "gleam very red" in memory's retrospect. Some if not all of these distinguished persons had felt an interest in Lawrence's early work, but the publication of *Sons and Lovers* had made his reputation. True, even such faithful admirers as Murry and Katherine Mansfield decided that the book's "approach is so purely physical" and "other parts so much a matter of memory that the final effect is a bewilderingly rich sterility"—whatever that may mean. True also, some booksellers and circulating libraries refused to handle the book ("may they fry in Hell" Lawrence hoped); but this after all was an accolade, the tribute dullness pays to "genius". Lawrence's bibliographer tells us that most existing copies of the first edition "show signs of hard use, and were evidently read, passed around, and re-read." Writing of Lawrence's reputation just before the publication of his next novel, two years later, Murry tells us: "Lawrence was, at that time, emphatically the coming man. His books were, naturally, the perquisite of the most established reviewers." This position had been won by *Sons and Lovers.*

What were the reasons for the success, which at first was a success of esteem rather than of sales? It is always easy to find reasons, but impossible to be sure they are the right ones. It is natural to point out that the book was one of the first, if not the first, of English novels to illustrate the psychological theories of Freud, then just coming into vogue in England. From the point of view of the professional critics it violated most of the canons supposedly set up for ever by such writers as Henry James, George Moore, Joseph Conrad and so forth. An unprofessional opinion may be quoted from Philip Heseltine (Peter Warlock), who about a year later wrote:

"I have just read all the novels of D. H. Lawrence—three in number. They are to my mind simply unrivalled, in depth of insight and beauty of language, by any other contemporary writer."

This was the view of a good many young people at the time. At the first reading of *Sons and Lovers* there came a sudden flash of recognition, such as came afterwards with *Ulysses* and *Du Côté de Chez Swann*—here is something really new and wonderful which will almost certainly last. In *Sons and Lovers* the writer's almost magical control of words never led him to show off—his passionate interest in the thing said caused a complete self-forgetfulness of how it was being said. The book gave a profound experience of life and at the same time revealed a new, unique personality, puzzling, irritatingly perverse, but with such rich gifts.

Enjoyment of the success of *Sons and Lovers* was not the only reason for this visit to England, for presumably "evidence" had to be manufactured for the solemn clownery of the law to provide a divorce and a large bill of costs. That accomplished, they did not linger. Though the sales of the new novel were not high, Lawrence talked no more of going back to teaching, and evidently thought he was safe for the time being. Early in August they were back in Professor Jaffe's wooden house at Irschenhausen, with the prospect of a happy year before them. Lawrence's good spirits were not even reduced by the fact that rain fell in such torrents that he sometimes took his morning bath by running round the house in a bathing dress.

Now for a time at least the contest of wills and personalities between him and Frieda came to a point of rest; and indeed might have remained there but for later events in the outer world which goaded him to irritated furies and the verge of insanity. Soon Lawrence was reporting from Bavaria that they were "settling down" and "very happy". In Bavaria Frieda was among her own people, and Lawrence, half hiding in the background, was amused to watch the ceremonies for her birthday. A procession of children arrived, including "a little niece crowned with flowers, her little nephews in white, carrying a basket of peaches, and of apricots; and sweets in boxes, and perfumes and big bunches of flowers, and other presents." She received them dressed in the beautiful Bavarian peasant costume, listened to their recital of birthday verses, and then "blew on a mouth organ."

Lawrence was glad to be out of England again, though, as he put it wistfully, "I rather love my countrymen." For some reason England had seemed to him "ravelled and dull and woolly". Among the mountains (when it wasn't raining) the world was "so living, so quick". He never wearied of looking at the distant high ranges which stood in the sunshine, fold after fold, "all varying with the changing light." There, as often, the world was his representation. In England he had been made to feel self-conscious and in the wrong by arid legalists and people who had to be apologised to for his "false position" with Frieda. It was not easy for him to be at ease with new friends of another social class, whose assumptions and prejudices differed from his, whose sense of his superiority was qualified by "criticism", who could not avoid a touch of patronage to the "genius" from the point of view of their own "incomparable advantages." Edward Marsh even kindly opened a correspondence course to teach Lawrence how to write poetry. In reply to advice about rhymes and rhythms Lawrence patiently answered: "I have always tried to get an emotion out in its own course, without altering it." To do that, of course, it was first necessary to have the emotion.

For some reason Lawrence's output of poems dropped off sharply at this time, but those he wrote are almost all about Frieda, written in moments of exultation or peace when they had fought their way:

> "Through the straight gate of passion,
> Between the bickering fire
> Where flames of fierce love tremble
> On the body of fierce desire."

Unfortunately contemporary taste was so pedantic that poetry had become—let us hope only temporarily—an almost obsolete method of expression. Lawrence was at this time using it to utter his delight in the reality of sexual love. The beautiful and unashamed 'Wedlock' is a perfect poem of wedded love. 'The Song of a Man That is Loved', was omitted through the publishers' prudery from the original edition of *Look! We Have Come Through*, and Lawrence re-wrote it for the 1928 *Collected Poems*—a doubtful improvement from the literary point of view and certainly not in the mood he wrote it. Luckily he gave Frieda a copy of the original which she has preserved for us:

"Between her breasts is my home, between her breasts,
Three sides set on me space and fear, but the fourth side rests
Warm in a city of strength, between her breasts.

All day long I am busy and happy at my work,
I need not glance over my shoulder in fear of the terrors that lurk
Behind. I am fortified, I am glad of my work.

I need not look after my soul; beguile my fear
With prayer, I need only come home each night to find the dear
Door on the latch, and shut in myself, shut out fear.

I need only come home each night and lay
My face between her breasts;
And what of good I have given the day, my peace attests.

And what I have failed in, what I have wronged
Comes up unnamed from her body and surely
Silent tongued I am ashamed.

And I hope to spend eternity
With my face down-buried between her breasts
And my still heart full of security
And my still hands full of her breasts."

I do not know how much more evidence is needed to refute the parrot-cry that "she was not the right woman for him". That poem alone should be conclusive, especially as it leads to his triumphal declaration of faith in himself and his life-work with her in the 'Song of a Man Who Has Come Through':

"Not I, not I, but the wind that blows through me!
A fine wind is blowing the new direction of Time.
If only I let it bear me, carry me, if only it carry me!
If only I am sensitive, subtle, oh, delicate, a winged gift!
If only, most lovely of all, I yield myself and am borrowed
By the fine, fine wind. . . ."

In these words he dedicated himself to love and life, with a mystical belief that he was in some way selected to express truths beyond himself; and those moments are just as true of him as the moments when he craved for darkness and destruction and the death-ritual.

5

In those days it was still not only possible but even pleasant to make walking tours in Europe, and it was still the best way to see what yet survived of a world created in days when the horseman and the man on foot set the standard of distance. Already in September the cold of the snow mountains began to fall on Irschenhausen, and the Lawrences began to talk of where they should go in the south. It was decided that Frieda for a time should visit her mother and father while Lawrence walked through Switzerland to Italy, where she would join him by train. It looks as if she did not want to risk the hardships of the year before. He, by far the more fragile in health, took the risk and was rewarded by seeing a little more of Europe before it withered under the blights of war and official *tourisme*.

He planned to go from Schaffhausen to Como by way of Zürich, Lucerne, Airolo and Bellinzona, partly by steamer but chiefly on foot with a knapsack. He found he did not care very much for the Swiss lowland country—it seemed "neutral and ordinary". Apart from the mountains he thought that in Switzerland you always get a "feeling of average, of utter soulless ordinariness, something intolerable." He felt this so acutely that he found "the only possible living sensation is the sensation of relief in going away." So without stopping for more than an hour or two at Zürich he took a steamer down the lake, and at nightfall came to a Gasthaus where he "ate boiled ham and drank beer, and tried to digest the utter cold materialism of Switzerland."

And then he made a discovery which brought him alive with vivid interest, and showed the people with whom he sympathised. He made the acquaintance of some Italian exiles, who had fled to Switzerland to escape conscription. They were rehearsing a play, and Lawrence has described them for us: Giuseppino, Alberto, Alfredo and his girl Maddelena, the play they were trying to produce, their little newspaper, *L'Anarchista*, which they wistfully believed would save the world, their warmth and humanity and home-sickness. They were only peasants who had become factory hands in "the cold mechanical world" for the sake of an unpractical ideal —and though Lawrence rather disliked and repudiated the ideal, he loved them because they were still vividly and touchingly alive.

Next morning, Sunday, he was confronted with a breakfast table of "bread and butter and a piece of cheese weighing about five pounds, and large fresh, sweet cakes." Then he set out, "quickly, over the stream" for Lucerne, only to meet very soon with church-people coming out of church "in the fat agricultural land", men "in black broadcloth and old chimney-pot silk hats, carrying their umbrellas, women in ugly dresses," all of them stiff and "reduced to a Sunday nullity." He hated them. As he sat down to attend to a blistered toe he saw two more men coming towards him, and got up hastily to pass them on foot. They were black-coated elders, and he just "could not bear the way they walked and talked, so crambling and material and mealy-mouthed." A drizzle of rain came on, so he crouched under a tree and ate the remains of the frugal meal he had bought in Zürich, and felt "so glad to be there, homeless, without place or belonging, crouching under the leaves in the copse by the road, separate as a ghost." Those are the moments when he is so lovable, when one's heart and loyalty go out unquestioningly to him in his poverty and his solitude and freedom, going south on foot, coughing his lungs out but gay and impudent and unbeatable like the Arch-Poet he was, last of the Goliards.

That day he had another adventure, somehow finding himself taking tea with two little old ladies to whom he pretended that he was an Austrian from Graz, and then had to leave hurriedly for fear he should fail in his part. He spent the night in a "detestable brutal inn" and on Monday walked over the "detestable Rigi", where he came upon a "lost young Frenchman." They liked each other and at once became close friends, so close that Lawrence promised to go and stay with him in Algiers; but soon lost the address and forgot his name, but still "he is my friend for ever." Then he met another young man, an Englishman, madly straining himself by trying to walk an insane number of mountain miles in a limited holiday, "until he was sick with fatigue and over-exertion." At first Lawrence pitied and admired him, and tried to humiliate the fat sedentary landlord by reciting the young man's exertions after he had left. And then, "suddenly I hated him, the dogged fool. What a vile nature, almost Sadish, proud, like the infamous Red Indians, of being able to stand torture."

It is less interesting to note that the Red Indians he afterwards idealised were then "infamous" than to realise how every hour and episode of life were interesting to him or made interesting by him. He still had to cross the main pass into Italy. For a whole day he plodded steadily up the Alpine road towards Andermatt, through an increasing cold which seemed to freeze his blood. The "valley beds" seemed to him like "deep graves", and the snow-peaks "breathed the very quick of cold death in the tang of snow and the noise of icy water." At last, in "the cold livid twilight" he trudged into Andermatt, but hated it so much that for all his weariness he went on until beyond he came to a poor house kept by a widow woman, "a hen-like woman" who was deaf and insisted on making him a cognac omelette which cost more than he could afford. Morning came, "blue and perfect", and now he found a young German named Emil as a companion of the road. Over the Gotthard they went, and then down the long pass into Italy, down "the sun-dried, ancient, southern slopes of the world," down from deathly winter to mellow early autumn. The first words he spoke at the first little shop were: "Quanto costa l'uva?" "How much are grapes?"

Like most walks of the kind this one ended in a railway journey, to Milan. There he met Frieda, and together they went on to Lerici. Why had they chosen Lerici? Perhaps it was the memory of Shelley; perhaps, more prosaically, they had heard it was cheap and remote. At any rate they arrived there about the end of September 1913, and immediately loved it. "I am so happy with the place we have at last discovered," Lawrence wrote, and went on to describe their pink four-roomed cottage. It was at a little place called Fiascherino, round the headland beyond Lerici, and was built on a terrace close to the Mediterranean in a large garden of vines and fig trees and olives, with vast wooded hills in the distance. It was so remote that there was not even a road leading to it, so everything had to come to them by boat or carried on their heads by the peasant women. They found the inside of the pretty cottage extremely dirty, so Lawrence tied his braces round his waist and "went for it." But then, "Lord, to see the dark floor flushing crimson, the dawn of deep red bricks rise from out this night of filth, was enough to make one burst forth into hymns and psalms."

The peasant woman, Felice, and her daughter, Elide, who came to help with the housework, had never seen a scrubbing-brush before —according to Lawrence, at any rate. He never relaxed his standards of household cleanliness; and neither Italy nor Mexico nor Australia nor rural England could provide him with sufficiently clean quarters until he had "got at it" himself. The absence of a bathroom did not trouble them much while the warm weather lasted, for they could bathe in the sea. Lawrence, brought up inland in the dread of cold water, was a very poor swimmer and would insist on bathing even when there was a dangerously rough sea. He exasperated Frieda so much by ignoring her warnings that she tried to taunt him into safety: "If you can't *be* a real poet, you'll *drown* like one."

Perhaps it was the result of breaking off work to make his walking tour, perhaps it was the languor of a Mediterranean autumn which influenced him, perhaps he was "written out" for the time being— at all events he relaxed from the intense creative activity which had been pouring out prose and verse for about eighteen months. He speaks of not "working much" and even went so far as to say that if he had even a tiny income he would be "delighted to loaf for ever". But with Lawrence "loafing" was always relative. Apparently he did not find a great deal at the moment to say in poetry, and he may have dropped for a time his work on short stories, in spite of the fact that he had already produced such good ones as 'The Prussian Officer' and 'A Thorn in the Flesh'. But if he was comparatively idle in those forms, the main reason is that he was again working on the longest and most ambitious of his novels, which had been begun at Gargnano.

Lawrence was seldom good at titles. The two short stories just mentioned have not particularly appropriate titles, and at first they were even less originally called 'Comrades in Arms' and 'Vin Ordinaire'. The suggestion is that he did not plan books or stories or even poems as more or less artificial "works of art", but allowed them to flow through his mind as "life-experiences, thought-adventures", to such an extent that he could write a large part of a novel and exclaim with exasperation that he still did not know what it was about. At all events his own titles were often so poor and vague that the existing ones were often suggested by others. His first novel had been feebly called *Nethermere* until Jessie Chambers suggested the better though quite irrelevant *White Peacock*. I believe it was his publishers who gave him *Sons and Lovers* in place of his own undistinguished *Paul Morel*. So it was with this new novel. Originally it was badly called *The Sisters*, then (much better) *The Wedding Ring*, when Frieda insisted on *The Rainbow* though the novel has not much more to do with rainbows than the first one with peacocks. If the title of *The Wedding Ring* had been retained it might have gone some way towards explaining and justifying scenes which dreary people thought indelicate.

His statement that at this time he was "not working" was far less true than what he wrote to Edward Garnett about the same time: "I am a slow writer really—I only have great outbursts of work." There is a general impression that Lawrence was a careless writer, lacking in self criticism, who re-wrote but never revised. He is himself rather to blame for this idea, though it has received some support from Aldous Huxley; but if Lawrence's manuscripts are examined it will be seen that in many cases he not only re-wrote, but corrected and re-corrected and interlined. The revisions of his script of 'Last Poems', for instance, often made it difficult to determine what was the correct reading. True, in the case of *The Rainbow*, it was rather a question of making several false starts than of detailed revision. It seems that he wrote no fewer than seven partial drafts occupying more than a thousand pages before he even found what he thought were the right tone and pace for the book. This looks as if he had started prematurely, without knowing what he wanted to say. Yet once he was satisfied that he was on the right track he wrote the whole novel in a period of less than six months of "not writing"—in scope and size the most ambitious of his books, running to at least 185,000 words.

Still, during a portion of his life at Fiascherino he evidently was either discouraged by repeated false starts on his novel or really was "not working." It troubled him, for he wrote to Marsh: "I don't write much verse now", and to McLeod: "I haven't been able to work. It is no joke to do as Frieda and I have done—and my very soul feels tired." In that rather frayed mood of exhaustion he was fretted by well-meant letters from Edward Marsh trying to teach him how to write poems of the orthodox Georgian kind. At first

Lawrence responded quite patiently, merely dropping a hint that he was bored by the advice: "Don't think that it is because your last letter offended me at all, that I don't write. In reality I quite agreed with what you said, but I've got to earn my living by prose."

The inexorably complacent and obtuse letters continued, and then in exasperation Lawrence hit out:

"It doesn't depend on the ear, particularly, but on the sensitive soul. And the ear gets a habit, and becomes master, when the ebbing and lifting motion should be master, and the ear the transmitter. If your ear has got stiff and a bit mechanical, *don't* blame my poetry. That's why you like 'Golden Journey to Samarcand'—it fits your habituated ear, and your feeling crouches subservient and a bit pathetic. 'It satisfies my ear,' you say. Well, I don't write for your ear."

It is an awfu' thing, as a Scot would say, to take on oneself the direction of "genius", for the world is apt to discover in time that the wrong road of "genius" was the right one after all; and it may be that Marsh correcting Lawrence, though much more amiable and civilised, was like Croker correcting Keats. However that may be, such rude speaking from a Georgian recruit was unprecedented and to be pardoned only on the grounds of ignorance. But pardoned Lawrence certainly was, for in the very midst of a peasant wedding party where the "wine ran very red", the Lawrences were called out to greet three Georgian poets and "a man named Waterfield", who turned out to be a painter living in a beautiful old castle near Sarzana. From a wedding feast of octopus and chicken and peasant mirth to these refined intellectuals was a startling change. "It was like suddenly going into very rare air," Lawrence reported, "one staggered and I quite lost my bearings." It might be questioned whether the staggering was due to the poets' "very rare air" or to local wine.

Strangely enough, in view of their still illicit situation, this was rather a social period with the Lawrences. In those days English people with incomes were scattered all over Europe in search of a somewhat elusive culture; and, as they were usually rather bored, and knew little of the country they were in, they welcomed English new-comers to their gatherings. So it happened to the Lawrences in spite of the fact that the divorce proceedings had been luridly reported in the yellow press. Some of their English neighbours in

Italy had either not heard this scandal or chose to ignore it; whereupon Frieda, ever courageous and straightforward, insisted that Lawrence should tell them—which thinned the visiting list. In England, Edward Marsh, among others, stood by them; and when visiting Italy that winter took the trouble to come and see them.

On the night following Marsh's departure there was a heavy and unusual fall of snow along the littoral. When the Lawrences awoke they wondered "what the queer pallor" could be, and going to the window saw that "the snow lay nearly six inches deep, and was still drifting finely, shadowily, out to the sombre-looking sea." Naturally no servant arrived, so Lawrence dressed and built a big fire and washed the dishes in "a queer, silent, muffled Fiascherino". Looking out again he saw the olive trees bowed under their burden of snow so that "whole slopes seemed peopled with despairing shades descending to the Styx", and then suddenly the weight and the cold brought tree after tree creaking and crashing to the ground, and even the cat was terrified out of its wits by the noise and the strange white world. Then into their silence there burst Elide and her brother Alessandro, clamouring against Heaven, wailing and mourning their loss: "Ma, dio, dio—senti, Signore, senti—Cristo del mondo—é una rovina—una rovina—un danno!" In the midst of this drama Lawrence was perplexed and distressed by a rumour that Marsh and his companion had been arrested. All ended well. Marsh, if ever arrested, easily escaped. The peasants staged a superb scene of tragic lamentation for an inspecting tax commissioner, and, when he had gone, "happily began chopping up the trees" remarking to one another: "Now we can get warm!"

Clearly Lawrence enjoyed all this or he would not have taken the trouble to record it in such vivid detail. Throughout he sounds thoroughly happy and amused. Yet there was always lurking and sometimes dominant even at the best of times that antithetical "dark self" which led him to do and to say such disconcerting things. He was very much the slave of his moods, and if he could express the happy ones in language of incomparable beauty, he could also set forth the dismal or vituperative ones with fantastic lack of restraint. Almost at the same time that he had been writing so gaily to Marsh to tell him about the fun of the snow-storm he was writing to someone else in the depth of gloom: "If you knew the slough of misery we've struggled and suffocated through. We are the most unfortunate, agonised, fate-harassed mortals since Orestes and that gang." Apparently "Orestes and that gang" aroused his sense of humour since he turned round and imagined that as his correspondent (Cynthia Asquith) read his letter in bed she would "stroke the counterpane with a purring motion, like an old maid having muffins for tea in the lamplight and reading Stanley in Africa."

When it was a case of real troubles, and not black brooding in more or less imaginary dumps, he met the situation sensibly. He had sent Edward Garnett a copy of one of the later versions—but not the final version we now have—of *The Rainbow*; and Garnett had been both disappointed and censorious. Even if the version he saw was as good as the existing one, Garnett had some reason for disappointment. After two exciting but not quite integrated early novels Lawrence had produced in *Sons and Lovers* a masterpiece of very high achievement. Among the qualities which had attracted readers were its mingling of precise reality with poetic imagination, its truth to ordinary life and high aspiration, its clear presentation of character and the clash of deep but completely understood emotions, its vivid writing from beginning to end. And he was still in his twenties. Naturally, Garnett's expectations of the next novel were high, especially as Lawrence had written rather boastfully of it. Imagine Garnett's disappointment when he found that Lawrence had dropped all this for a rather solemn saga of generations where character was analysed so far back to common elements that there was some difficulty in sorting out the people and remembering them. It was at once rustic and psychological, as if it were a Russian novel written by George Eliot.

Garnett wrote him frankly that he thought this book something of a betrayal of Lawrence's "genius". His real strength, Garnett thought, his real originality, lay in his instinctive gifts as an artist; and not in lengthy Freudian analyses and sermons on salvation. Lawrence admitted this in his reply, but with his unfailing obstinacy stuck to his own point of view:

"It is that which troubles me most. I have no longer the joy I had in creating vivid scenes, that I had in *Sons and Lovers*. I don't care much more about accumulating objects in the powerful light of emotion, and making a scene of them. I have to write differently."

From Garnett's point of view the book must have seemed a little pretentious, a little solemn and boring even, with not enough cheerfulness breaking in on the philosophy. Accepting his criticism that the book in its then state would not do, Lawrence set to work on yet another version. Writing at a high speed which must have averaged about 3000 words a day he had very nearly completed his task by late April. Reflection and the writer's very natural possessive feeling for his own work while it is in process of creation had now put him into a far less docile mood. From being apologetic he became aggressive:

"You know how willing I am to hear what you have to say, and to take your advice and to act on it when I have taken it. But it is no good unless you will have patience and understand what I *want* to do. I am not after all a child working erratically. All the time, underneath, there is something deep evolving itself out in me. And it is *hard* to express a new thing, in sincerity. . . . You tell me I am half a Frenchman and one-eighth a Cockney. But that isn't it. I have very often the vulgarity and disagreeableness of the common people, and as you say Cockney, and I may be a Frenchman. But primarily I am a passionately religious man, and my novels must be written from the depth of my religious experience. That I must keep to, because I can only work like that."

It depends entirely on one's estimate of this book and its immediate successors whether those lines are taken as a profound statement of convictions and ideals beyond the grasp of Garnett and his like, or whether they are read as a lame, specious and unconvincing attempt to find excuses for the fact that he could not produce another novel so vivid and fascinating as *Sons and Lovers*. The reference to his having "the vulgarity and disagreeableness of the common people" is very interesting. In other moods he would vehemently and angrily deny it, but there can be no doubt that just such defects as these jarred on his upper-class friends and estranged them, and made difficulties with many of his readers. A debate might be held as to whether he was or was not "a passionately religious man". His view was that, however unorthodoxly, he did feel "religiously" about a world which too many people merely hoped to exploit for some material gain. He would also have maintained that he felt "passionately religious" about sex, whereas these materialist-minded people who were his enemies on their own admission considered sex "dirty" and "unpleasant". The dirt and unpleasantness, he retorted, were wholly of their creating.

Meanwhile as Lawrence wrestled with his angel or demon of creation, winter faded from Lerici in spite of the great snowstorm. As early as the second week in February they were out in the ruined olive groves gathering the delicate Mediterranean flowers he loved so much—"wild narcissus and purple anemone and a few sweet violets", flowers of Theocritus. Now from dawn to dusk the sea was iridescent blue; peach trees blossomed; and there were "pink almond trees among the vapour grey of the olives". One spring day they took some food and climbed high up into the hills, from which they could see the mountains of Carrara and the wide valley and the coast "sweeping round in a curve that makes my blood run with delight." Everything seemed so lovely that he felt as if he could "jump into the air". A great longing to look at the beauty of the world came over him. He wanted to start off, at once, on foot, to "walk south, into the Apeninnes." Why didn't he? Well, he was too poor, and the vexatious novel had to be finished, and there was his puritan conscience. He had made a pact with that conscience to return to England and be legally married as soon as the divorce decree was made absolute.

That day on the mountain and his commonsense checking of his longing to wander freely in the world had a symbolical meaning beyond anything he could have known. It is true that his novels and stories to that time had almost all been the growth of the England of his youth, the English Midlands for which he cared so deeply. But it is a great error to put him forward merely as a local patriot and regionalist writer, which he certainly was not. Already he had felt intuitively that the old rigid nationalistism was breaking down, that art, like life itself, had to flow from new centres. It was from choice as much as necessity that he had turned to the wider world with his ambition to write a novel about each of the continents.

When, in June 1914, he resisted the lure of wandering adventure and returned to England from Lerici, it was with no idea of remaining there. We can tell that from the mere fact that he left behind several important note books and much of their little property. For almost two years he had been an intellectual nomad. His provincialism was broken up without his ever acquiring the more acute provincialism of literary London, which touched and harmed but did not hold him. If his strange battle with Frieda was not ended, had indeed most grievous and deadly phases yet to come, it had nevertheless been decided that they belonged irrevocably to each other. There were difficulties to face, but the world seemed opening before them, and they were confident of the future. Even before they left for London they were gaily planning a visit to Ireland and then afterwards an exploration of the Abruzzi mountains.

Within six weeks the iron tempest of war burst over Europe and spread across the world, obliterating the hopes of generations, bequeathing a hideous chaos of hatred, vengeance and confusion. Lawrence did not return to England for two or three months as he expected, but for five and a half years during which he endured strange sufferings and disasters, which left him penniless, calumniated, persecuted, an outcast, raving in almost unintelligible efforts to grapple with a world gone mad and with his own tormented, divided spirit, growing ever more embittered and unhappy until in due course he escaped into voluntary exile.

6

LAWRENCE and Frieda were legally married at a London Registry office on the 13th July, 1914. Characteristically Frieda, who in the mythology of the law was supposed to be a seduced and tainted outcast humbly yearning for security, cared not a damn about being made a comparatively honest woman again with marriage lines to show the policeman. Lawrence, on the other hand, quite failed to see the farcical side, at first took it all seriously and even with a certain amount of trepidation. He speedily recovered his sense of humour, however, and reported that he had gone through the ceremony with his heart in his boots and neuralgia in his left eye.

For some unknown reason he elected to believe that this hugger-mugger formality was "very decent and dignified", and feigned surprise that it did not make him feel "a changed man." Lawrence's discourses about fidelity and the permanence of marriage so much impressed Katherine Mansfield (one of the witnesses) that she instantly decided to abandon woman's freedom and henceforth to wear a wedding ring. Whereupon Frieda, no longer having occasion to wear the wedding ring of her first marriage, instantly presented it to her friend. There was a rich irony about this which seems to have escaped all those present. Fidelity and permanence of marriage!

Evidently the whole topic of marriage was very much in his consciousness at the time, as appears from a curious and interesting passage in one of his letters which is so important to an understanding of one at least of his more or less permanent moods that it must be read in full:

"Do you think love is an accomplished thing, the day it is recognised? It isn't. To love, you have to learn to understand the other, more than she understands herself, and submit to her understanding of you. It is damnably difficult and painful, but it is the only thing which endures. You mustn't think that your desire or your fundamental need is to make a good career, or to fill your life with activity, or even to provide for your family materially. It isn't. Your most vital necessity in this life is that you shall love your wife completely and implicitly and in entire nakedness of body and spirit. Then you will have peace and inner security, no matter how many things go wrong. And this peace and security will leave you free to act and to produce your own work, a real independent workman. You asked me once what my message was. I haven't got any general message . . . but this that I tell you is my message as far as I've got any."

At other times Lawrence conceived himself charged to deliver other messages. Only recently, as we have seen, it had been the message of "a deeply religious man", though of course he would have claimed that his view of marriage was religious, as indeed it was as here stated. Two obvious reflections come to mind. First of all, Lawrence is here writing as one who knew nothing of the realities of war, those fearful exigencies of collective violence which separate man and woman arbitrarily, without pity, perhaps for years, perhaps for ever, making this fidelity and permanence and intense domestic welding together a mere mockery. In the second place, the reader may well ask how we are to reconcile these lofty and self-imposed exigencies with the notorious fact of Lawrence's continual and bitter quarrels with his wife, degenerating into insults and personal violence and attempts on her part to leave him? Nobody can deny that this happened, and of course the most has been made of it by the malevolence of enemies. The only person who can throw any authentic light on the problem is Frieda Lawrence herself, and this is her reply:

"I certainly found him more delicately and sensitively aware of me than I ever imagined anybody would be. To be so enveloped in tenderness was a miracle in itself to me."

If she was fully satisfied, what reason have we to complain?

From such considerations he was now drawn away to attend to his literary affairs. It must be remembered that Edward Garnett was Duckworth's chief literary adviser, so that the fact that he was as dissatisfied with the latest version of *The Rainbow* as he had been with the earlier one carried serious implications for Lawrence's future. He defended the book and his ideas once more with equal warmth, though his claim that it is "a little Futuristic" seems fanciful, since the pervading flavour of George Eliot is something against which one has to struggle. But this opinion of Garnett's coming on top of the failure of *Love Poems* made Duckworth hesitant. Piqued by this, and without considering that the offer of a large advance may be rather a proof of commercial hopes in a publisher than the fundamental sympathy which is far more valuable, Lawrence instantly closed with an offer made through Pinker by Methuen to publish the book, with what seemed to him the very large advance of three hundred pounds. In describing these transactions Lawrence says that he "took Pinker's cheque" and then speaks of one hundred and fifty pounds as still due to him from Methuen; from which I infer that Pinker gave him one hundred and thirty-five pounds—i.e. one hundred and fifty pounds less ten per cent commission. Incidentally, either the publisher or Lawrence or both were dissatisfied with the form of *The Rainbow*, and he agreed to undertake the weary task of re-writing it yet again, making what appears to have been the eighth version.

Already he was looking about for the subject of another book, and, as he did not seem to have the theme for a novel ready, he decided that he would write a book on Thomas Hardy. He mentioned this idea to Edward Marsh, who at once sent him a complete set of Hardy's works, for such a book was a distinct indication of coming into the right sheepfold. It would be pleasant to be able to report that this kindness helped to produce a great book on Hardy. A comparison of Lawrence's book with the very Oxonian production of Lionel Johnson leaves one astonished that the same novels and poems could produce such totally different results. Only one chapter of Lawrence's book was published (in *The Book Collector's Quarterly*, spring 1932) before the whole work appeared in

Phoenix, in 1936. This chapter (*Containing Six novels and a Real Tragedy*) is the only one which really tackles or attempts to tackle the theme of Thomas Hardy and his books. The others deal only inferentially and at long range with Hardy, and are mostly about Lawrence. The style is in that heavily symbolical and didactic vein which Lawrence called "philosophical", and is more nearly related to Ruskin in his moods of preaching and prophecy. It is a work which is repaying to students of Lawrence's peculiar forms of thought, but is likely to repel others than such specialists. How far the book ranges from its announced theme may be guessed from such chapter headings as: 'Of Poppies and Phoenixes'; 'About Women's Suffrage' and 'Laws and the War and the Poor'; 'An Attack on Work and the Money Appetite and on the State'; 'Work and the Angel and the Unbegotten Hero'; 'The Axle and the Wheel of Eternity'; 'Of Being and Not-Being'. . . . The hands of Ruskin and of Ruskin's master, Carlyle, are heavily apparent in a series of endless digressions which come to no recognisable conclusion.

Infinitely more promising, at least from the point of view of the ordinary reader, was the first collection of his short stories now accepted by Duckworth, to which Garnett gave the then topical but misleading title of *The Prussian Officer*. By way of showing his indifference to conflicting schools of poets, he now achieved the distinction of being the only poet who contributed to both the Georgian and the Imagist Anthologies.

All through the July of that year 1914 the newspapers blared and flared with "warnings" and belligerence. A century had passed since England had been engaged in a European War, so that many people refused to believe it could happen right up till the last day. Even when war was declared it seemed like something out of a history book picked up and vulgarised by the newspapers, and hence not part of real life. There was intense excitement and much vicarious heroism, on the lines of Tartarin de Tarascon, among people who never imagined they might have to do any fighting or suffering themselves.

I do not myself believe that Lawrence took the opening of the war tragically, an impression which is supported by his letters and the evidence of both Catherine Carswell and Middleton Murry. It so happened that I dined with him and others on the evening of the 30th July, during which, as he quaintly reported, we "had some poetry", with an air of distaste as if it had been slightly corked claret. He told us, rather mockingly, that he had lunched with Edward Marsh (then Mr. Churchill's private secretary) and that he had been "very grave about the situation". My memory is that Lawrence had failed to take Marsh's hint, that he spoke of the episode lightly and rather incredulously, and passed immediately to other topics.

It seems most obvious that he cannot have had any inkling of what was coming, since he spent that fateful week-end of August 1914 walking the Westmorland moors with "three other men", one of whom, S. S. Koteliansky, became his lifelong friend and admirer. High up on the moors they came upon a pond full of water-lilies, and Lawrence twined some of them round his hat as he walked. In a little wayside inn they found a party of girls having tea in an upper room "out on a spree" and shrieking with laughter. In a storm of rain they crouched for shelter under a rough stone wall as the "rain flew by in streams"; and then Lawrence "imitated music-hall turns" and "pranked in the rain" while "Koteliansky groaned Hebrew music." Then they descended upon the industrial town of Barrow-in-Furness and learned that war had been declared. So far from their careless gaiety turning to horror and misery at this news, they "all went mad", with "soldiers kissing on Barrow station, and a woman shouting defiantly to her sweetheart." In a letter dated 10th August, he says to Pinker: "Here is a state of affairs—what is going to become of us?" He was anxious to know if Methuen had signed the agreement for *The Rainbow*, adding that as return to Italy seemed impossible he thought of taking "a tiny cottage somewhere".

Long afterwards in 'Glad Ghosts' he said of the war: "It was August, we could take it lightly." On the 5th September, 1914, he again wrote Pinker for money, this time from near Chesham in Buckinghamshire, adding: "What a miserable world. What colossal idiocy, this war. Out of sheer rage I've begun my book about Thomas Hardy. It will be about anything but Thomas Hardy I am afraid." In that book his references to the war still showed an unreal detachment: "Let there be an end then of all this welter of pity, which is only self-pity reflected onto some obvious surface. And let there be an end of this German hatred. We ought to be grateful to Germany that she still has the power to burst the bound hide of the cabbage"—whatever that may be. In October he wrote a letter to Harriet Monroe, editor of *Poetry*, who had offered a money prize for the "best" war poem. Being a neutral some thousands of miles away from the fighting she must have suggested that Lawrence should volunteer, as F. S. Flint and I had been foolish enough to do. This hint he rejected with contempt:

"I am not in the war zone. I think I am much too valuable a creature to offer myself to a German bullet gratis and for fun."

In the same vein of light persiflage he also rejects with equal contempt the idea of sending in a poem on the war, saying that all he felt inclined to do was something on the lines of 'The Owl and the Pussycat'. It is not so much surprising as inevitable with his sudden changes of mood that when he received the war number of *Poetry* he flew into a rage with what he called "the glib irreverence" of the contributors, not one of whom, it appears, had risen to the high seriousness of 'The Owl and the Pussycat'. By this time, mid-November 1914, he had written one-third of the Hardy book, had grown a beard, and had been rather ill with the usual lung trouble. His attitude then was expressed in these words: "The war is dreadful. It is the business of the artist to follow it home to the heart of the individual fighters." Excellent advice! but how was it to be followed except by going to the war? By the 5th December he has changed again. Now, as in the Hardy book, he is "glad of the war", and he was glad of it because "it kicks the pasteboard bottom in of the usual good popular novel"—which really is taking a howitzer to kill a flea.

I may seem to be labouring a number of unimportant points, but the reason is that even in the face of an appalling catastrophe like the war Lawrence had no settled attitude until it began to reach out for him personally—before that he had swerved like a weathercock in the gust of every mood. Of course other people vacillated, were uncertain, only learned from harsh experience. Even a philosopher, Bertrand Russell, tells us that until 1914 he had never thought about the subject of war. A mere artist may then be excused uncertainty, but not his censoriousness of anyone who did not happen to share his mood of the moment. Is it not true of the "artist type" that he thinks in terms of the individual experience, not the abstract public good or ill? Lawrence's phrase about the "individual fighters" indicates this; so too his more self-centred statement that he disliked the war because "it puts a damper on one's own personal movements."

We get some valuable side-lights on Lawrence at this time from notes made by Middleton Murry, who for part of the winter was his neighbour. From these it appears that during November-December they discussed anything but the war. Much attention was devoted to "the novel", to the nature of Tragedy, and to what Lawrence called his philosophy. Murry found this "very hard to understand". He could not know then or even when he wrote his *Reminiscences* that this metaphysical symbolism Lawrence poured out to him was a repetition of what he had been writing in the Hardy book. It is more than probable that Lawrence made no effort to clarify this uncertain mystical thought. He knew that Murry was an Oxford man who had been through the schools, knew the terms of philosophy and had been trained in logic. With his phobia against being worsted in an argument, his feeling that he *must* play leader and superior in every company, he may have thought that the more vaguely he talked and the more he hashed up symbolism and metaphysics the less chance Murry had to refute him. He certainly had Murry puzzled—and if a philosopher cannot understand a new philosophy, who can?

Just how temperamental, uncertain of himself and fundamentally frivolous Lawrence was on such topics may be rather neatly illustrated by his attitude towards that solemn abstraction, the Absolute. Murry has kept a note of a conversation about Dostoevsky which took place on 18th November, 1914. In the course of this Lawrence declared vehemently and dogmatically:

"Humility is death! To believe in an Absolute is death—there are no absolutes."

In January of 1915 Lawrence met the painter, Duncan Grant, and on the 27th of the month wrote of him to Ottoline Morrell as follows:

"He is after stating the Absolute—like Fra Angelico in the Last Judgment—a whole conception of the existence of man—creation, good, evil, life, death, resurrection, the separating of the stream of good and evil, and its return to the eternal source. It is an Absolute we are all after, a statement of the whole scheme—the issue, the progress through time—and the return—making unchangeable eternity."

Now, which did he mean? Did he or didn't he believe in the Absolute? Or was he not merely talking for effect, trying to impress these people with an appearance of profundity, and so completely without real conviction that he totally forgot what he had said to Murry and said the exact opposite to Ottoline Morrell? Another devoted friend of Lawrence, Catherine Carswell, has insisted on his "innocence", that mixture of naïveté and social ignorance which Rachel Taylor points out. Nowhere did it show itself more strikingly than in his apparent belief that a philosophy may be improvised and that a man can write seriously on philosophical topics without having any education in philosophy. True, every artist, particularly an artist so gifted as Lawrence, has a philosophy implicit in his work, but as a rule it is better left so for others to disengage and comment if they can and so wish. I do not deny that Lawrence thought and thought hard and sometimes profoundly, but that is not the same thing as being a philosopher. Certainly it would be a mistake to dismiss his "philosophical" writings as worthless. But his best utterances of that sort were the product of the intuition which changed almost daily, of a protean and endlessly self-contradictory personality. They are detached sayings or paragraphs, usually though not always heavily charged with symbols; quite different from the beautifully formed abstract thought, rounded and complete, of his one-time friend, Russell. Let me give at once an example of this thought of Lawrence's, taken from the Hardy book we have been discussing and hence written during this winter:

"With man it is always spring—or it may be; with him every day is a blossoming day, if he will. He is a plant eternally in flower, he is an animal eternally in rut, he is a bird eternally in song. He has his excess constantly on his hands, almost every day. It is not with him a case of seasons, spring and autumn and winter. And happy man if his excess come out in blue and gold and singing, if it be not a burden, at last a very sickness.

"The wild creatures are like fountains whose sources gather their waters until spring-time, when they leap their highest. But man is a fountain that is always playing, leaping, ebbing, sinking, and springing up. It is not for him to gather his waters till spring-time, when his fountain, rising higher, can at last flow out flower-wise in mid air, teeming awhile with excess, before it falls spent again.

"His rhythm is not so simple. A pleasant little stream of life is a bird at autumn and winter, fluttering in flocks, over the stubble, the fallow, rustling along. Till spring, when many waters rush in to the sources, and each bird is a fountain playing.

"Man, fortunate or unfortunate, is rarely like an autumn bird, to enjoy the present stream of life flowing at ease."

Is that philosophy? I call it poetry, and beautiful poetry; though what precise relation it bears to the writings, mind or life of Thomas Hardy is not easy to say. Nor as a matter of fact does that matter —it is beautiful enough in itself to justify its separate existence. If it be urged that this passage is rather too favourable a specimen of the Hardy book in particular and of Lawrence's wrestlings with the Unseen in general, the answer is that his work abounds in such poetic and symbolical writing. There are many such passages in *The Rainbow*.

Life at the Chesham cottage soon dropped into the familiar pattern, with Lawrence doing much of the housework and cooking, organising charades and the endless singing of folk songs when Murry and Katherine Mansfield came in the evening. Murry's notes contain indications that towards Christmas 1914 Lawrence was beginning to fall into moods of acute depression about the war, but they were more depressions of ill-health—which always afflicted him in a northern winter—than a true realisation of the war. Whatever he may have said to his friends, his writings at the time contain numerous references to the war so impersonal and casual that he evidently still thought of it as a moral lesson for others rather than a terrific horror which might touch him. Indeed, in one place he speaks of "this just and righteous war" as smugly as any exempted journalist.

Yet anxiety he certainly had, which showed itself in talk of plans for an escape from the world to "somewhere else" called "Rananim", a place where Lawrence imagined himself happy ever after with a select group of friends. This, as its name implies, was essentially a fantasy, but never admitted as such, like the "Gondal Land" of the Brontës. It had been a dream of Lawrence's even in Eastwood days when, as we have seen, he hoped to make two thousand pounds a year and live in a large house along with all the people he knew who disliked each other. In those days his mother had been the centre of the dream, but after her death and during the excitement and happiness of his first two years with Frieda, the dream had faded. By the end of 1914 Lawrence began to realise that the lawyers' threats to make him a bankrupt were not bluff but real earnest, while even the periodicals for which he wrote were either closing down or taking only war stuff. He saw that in the absence of demand for new books publication of *The Rainbow*, *The Prussian Officer* and his poems would be insufficient for his needs. His alleged "honest working man's" disinclination to take money for nothing is a myth. Already, at the outbreak of the war, he had accepted with alacrity a sum of fifty pounds from the Literary Fund. He would have taken money from another fund, sponsored by Mrs. Belloc Lowndes, but unhappily on meeting they did not like each other; and being liked by Mrs. Belloc Lowndes seems to have been absolutely obligatory in order to establish a claim on the fund. Rananim, the ideal "colony of escape", came to the foreground then as a most desirable alternative to financial difficulties and the distant but menacing threats of war troubles. In the early days of January Lawrence thus outlined his conception of Rananim to a selected victim, an old friend of Eastwood days:

"We will also talk of my pet scheme. I want to gather together about twenty souls and sail away from this world of war and squalor and found a little colony where there shall be no money but a sort of communism as far as necessaries of life go, and some real decency. It is to be a colony built up on the real decency which is in each member of the community. A community which is established upon the assumption of goodness in the members, instead of the assumption of badness."

Still, however good and decent, the members of the colony would first have to be transported to wherever Rananim was, and once arrived would have to be housed, fed and clothed. How was this to be achieved? Evidently this aspect was not forgotten. About two weeks after the Lawrences moved from Chesham to a cottage belonging to Viola Meynell at Greatham in Sussex, Lawrence wrote to his friend Ottoline Morrell (heroine of the feather-plucking episode), who was wife of an M.P., and daughter of the Duke of Portland, but probably not so wealthy as Lawrence imagined. What he said to her in part is as follows:

"I want you to form the nucleus of a new community which shall start a new life amongst us—a life in which the only riches is integrity of character. So that each one may fulfil his own nature and deep desires to the utmost, but wherein tho', the ultimate satisfaction and joy is in the completeness of us all as one. Let us be good altogether. It is communism based, not on poverty but on riches, not on humility but on pride, not on sacrifice but on complete fulfilment in the flesh of all strong desire, not in Heaven but on earth."

Rabelais had long before imagined such a community, less self-righteous and canting, with the motto: "Do what you please." His patron was to have been the King of France, and his Rananim the Abbaye of Thélème.

Meanwhile, the move from Chesham to Greatham had brought the advantages of a slightly milder climate, a more comfortable cottage rent-free and a share of Meynell comforts; but Lawrence was worried about money matters, and still toiling at his *Rainbow*. He wrote urgently to his agent: "Do be getting me some money, will you? I heard the wolf scratch the door to-day." And suddenly the monster of the War seemed to take an immense step nearer, as a section of the Press began a violent agitation for conscription, and the Liberal Government sought the support of the Opposition in the conduct of the war. It was in March 1915 that he wrote:

"So they are making a Coalition government. I cannot tell you how icy cold my heart is with fear. It is as if we were all going to die. Did I not tell you my revolution would come? It will come, God help us. The ghosts will bring it. Why does one feel so coldly afraid? Why does even the coalition of the Government fill me with terror? Some say it is for peace negotiations. It may be, because we are all afraid. But it is most probably for conscription. The touch of death is very cold and horrible on us all."

The functional word in that paragraph is "conscription", which provides the answer to all the rhetorical questions. As a matter of fact (as the future was to show) the state of his lungs was such that on every examination Lawrence was instantly rejected for military service; but as he always kept up to himself as well as to others the bluff that there was nothing the matter with him, he never seemed to realise this. Moreover, though his intuition was basically right, and there was conscription, it was a year later than he expected. Still, it was this conscription threat which brought him face to face with the reality of the war. In this he was not to be blamed, but was merely like everyone else. However much people may abstractedly sympathise with human woes, they only feel them profoundly when they become personal.

What was Lawrence's attitude? We have seen his waverings of mood in the uncertain early days, but at no time had he shared the public schoolboy attitude of his friend, Rupert Brooke, who on hearing that a European War had broken out felt "extraordinarily happy". Lawrence was never that sort of fool. He did use the "just and righteous war" cant phrase, but much truer to his feelings in the main was his saying (early 1915) that the war had been "a spear through the side" of all his hopes.

But why this "cold and horrible" fear of military service, this intense repulsion? Certainly, Lawrence lacked neither moral nor physical courage, he was at times almost objectionably patriotic and pro-English, and such a "battler" could not and did not have any Quaker-like scruples against fighting. True, he disliked soldiers, and evidently shared the old-fashioned English contempt for the mercenary soldier which he got from his mother. But that was not the real reason. The real fact is that all his instinctive horror and fear of the industrial machine, so acute as to be almost insane, was transferred to the military machine. Of course, like nearly everybody else, he did not feel "extraordinarily happy" at the thought of exacting military toil and hardships, with a strong possibility of mutilation or death. But they weren't uppermost and, given the need, he would have faced them with Cockney gallantry. What got hold of him was his unreasoning, almost insane horror of being caught in some human machine and crushed to its pattern—a fate which seemed to him more ghastly even than death.

We have to remember that all this came upon a man of extreme sensitiveness (perhaps a "neurotic", if the word has any valid meaning) after two years of febrile excitement and new impressions, and of great mental strain. As was said of him at a later period of crisis, in 1915 he was "physically, mentally and morally overworked." Now, Lawrence never hesitated to make a fool of himself (a "genius" never does), and he certainly grotesquely over-rated his own powers of having an immediate practical effect on the world. He had promised Frieda to make a new heaven and earth for her children, and what she actually had got was a war between her native and her adopted country. This little contretemps, however, was easily forgotten. What is more difficult to understand is that he can ever have imagined that he could have an immediate, practical and decisive effect on a world at war.

It is a problem. Of course, like many writers, Lawrence had far too sanguine a belief in the immediate power of the written word—his written word. True it is that in the long run the sage, the thinker, the religious leader, the man of science, even the poet may turn out to influence the world of men more than the wielders of power and violence who imagine themselves controllers of destiny and responsible to "History". But that is in the long run. The immediate present belongs to power and violence. But Lawrence had come to believe that words are action. He lived in the fluid, unresisting medium of ideas, forgetting or not even knowing the stubbornness of men and fact. Like his masters, Ruskin and Carlyle, Lawrence had got into the habit of cheating himself with the fairy money of ideas. Like them, he talked as if when he declared that something ought to be, then, presto! it would be.

"Let there be a parliament," he declaimed vigorously, "of men and women for the careful and gradual unmaking of laws."

All right, let there be, but how? This "Let there be . . ." type of sentence had been a great favourite with Ruskin, from whom Lawrence derived it. Like Ruskin, too, he tore his heart and spirit to tatters in order to issue dogmatic orders about things he probably did not understand and over which he certainly had no control. At this moment he fell in with Bertrand Russell, also in a state of excitement and shedding thousands of ideas at random over the "situation". The mathematical don drew up and the poet made excited comments on a detailed plan for the immediate Social Reconstruction of the world—in 1915. Russell wrote such statements as: "Why should a man be moral? Because action against the desires of others makes him disliked, which is disagreeable to him," and Lawrence commented: "No! No! No! No! No!" It all reads rather like an episode from *The House at Pooh Corner*, with Eeyore and Rabbit in action. Lawrence took it all most seriously, and as early as February 1915 was sending Russell peremptory orders:

"There must be a revolution in the state. It shall begin by the nationalising of all industries and means of communication, and of the land—in one fell blow. Then a man shall have his wages whether he is sick or well or old—if anything prevents his working, he shall have his wages just the same. So we shall not live in fear of the wolf—no man among us, and no woman, shall have any fear of the wolf at the door, for all wolves are dead. Which practically solves the whole economic problem for the present."

In pursuit of his revolution Lawrence accepted an invitation from Russell to go to Cambridge and stay the night at Trinity College. He looked forward to this with immense and fallacious hopes. When he returned, Frieda, who readily kindled to excitement, began at once to question him eagerly about what had happened.

"Well," said Lawrence, "in the evening they drank port, and they walked up and down the room and talked about the Balkan situation and things like that, and they know nothing about it."

That's Cambridge, that was.

Unfortunately all this had not the slightest effect on the course of events, and Lawrence became more and more hag-ridden with fears of nameless disasters and with frenzied longings to escape, "anywhere, anywhere".

"I wish I were going to Tibet—or Kamschatka—or Tahiti—to the ultima, ultima Thule. I feel somehow I shall go mad, because there is nowhere to go."

Indeed at this time and other occasions during the war his utterances and even his actions did verge on the insane, reminiscent of his strange "lunatick" behaviour under the influence of the full moon. From a longing to escape the war he rushed to the opposite extreme. At one moment he "almost" wanted to go to the war, not to shoot even if he were shot at, but in the ludicrous military post of a "bus-conductor". ('Ere you are, me lucky lads, tuppence all the way to Wipers.) But that did not last long. On a day-trip to Worthing he came upon some soldiers who made such a bad impression on him that he decided they must be "lice or bugs" and "will murder their officers one day". His soul and his imagination seemed sick with the horror of those murderous days. Mankind and all his works seemed to Lawrence tainted:

"London seems to me like some hoary massive underworld, a hoary ponderous inferno. The traffic flows through the rigid grey streets like the rivers of hell through the banks of rocky-ash. The fashions and the women's clothes are very ugly."

Strange! to other eyes those fashions of 1915 seemed particularly charming with their shortened flared skirts, but as Lawrence himself sadly admitted: "My eyes can see nothing human that is good nowadays: at any rate, nothing public." But he still had eyes for the beauty and wonder of the non-human world:

"I find the country very beautiful. The apple trees are leaning forwards, all white with blossom, towards the green grass. I watch, in the morning when I wake up, a thrush on the wall outside the window—not a thrush, a blackbird—and he sings, opening his beak. It is a strange thing to watch his singing, opening his beak and giving out his calls and warblings, then remaining silent. He looks so remote, so buried in primeval silence, standing there on the wall. I wish I was a blackbird, like him. I hate men."

Such moments, which in happier times made up much of his life, now became rarer and rarer and even in the non-human world of nature he began to find delirious images of his suffering and troubled spirit:

"I've got again into one of those horrible sleeps from which I can't wake. I can't brush it aside to wake up. You know those horrible sleeps when one is struggling to wake up and can't? I was like it all autumn—and now I am again like it. Everything has a touch of delirium, the blackbird on the wall is a delirium, even the apple-blossom. And when I see a snake winding rapidly in the marshy places, I think I am mad."

The fear that he was going mad or had actually gone mad haunted him intermittently during the war years. The snake which he had seen in the Sussex marsh became for him a dread symbol of some unspeakable wickedness in himself, some awful, shameful sin in him which he was loathingly forced to accept with faint hopes of getting rid of it:

"Who says that the water-lily shall rock on the still pool, but the snake shall not hiss in the festering marsh border? I must humble myself before the abhorred serpent and give him his dues as he lifts his flattened head from the secret grass of my soul. Can I exterminate what is created? Not while the condition of its creation lasts. There is no killing the serpent so long as his principle endures. And his principle moves slowly in my belly: I must disembowel myself to get rid of him. . . . Maybe the serpent of my abhorrence nests in my very heart. If so, I can but in honour say to him, 'Serpent, serpent, thou art at home.' Then I shall know that my heart is a marsh. But maybe my understanding will drain the swampy place, and the serpent will evaporate as his condition evaporates. That is as it is. While there is a marsh, the serpent has his holy ground."

These ravings come from a work he called *The Reality of Peace*, on which he worked from time to time during the war, usually when he was in these uncontrolled states of febrile excitement. A feeling of desperation, of annihilating hatred possessed him, as he raved to Ottoline Morrell:

"I cannot bear it much longer, to let the madness get stronger and stronger possession. Soon we in England shall go fully mad, with hate. I too hate the Germans so much, I could kill every one of them. Why should they goad us to this frenzy of hatred, why should we be tortured to ******** madness, when we are only grieved in our souls and heavy? They will drive our heaviness and grief away in a fury of rage. And we don't want to be worked up into this fury, this destructive madness of rage. Yet we must, we are goaded on and on. I am mad with rage myself. I would like to kill a million Germans—two millions."

At such moments his suffering becomes almost ludicrous from the absurd vehemence of its expression. But there can be no doubt that in 1915 his "dark self" had almost complete mastery of him, to the obliteration of all that was so lovely in his other self. Something that happened during this period at Greatham painfully underlines this. It is barely needful to remind the reader of Lawrence's passionate devotion to his mother and his unendurable grief over her death; and it will be remembered that Frieda had said of his love for her that she had never imagined possible "such tenderness and awareness." At Greatham she heard the news that her father, whom she had loved very deeply, was dead. After keeping the knowledge to herself for several miserable days she at last went to her husband, hoping for sympathy and comfort, and told him. All he said was: "You didn't expect to keep your father for ever, did you?"

7

THE law costs in Frieda's divorce case had amounted to the comparatively modest sum of one hundred and fifty pounds, and in May 1915 as Lawrence would not or could not pay them, they made him a bankrupt. Far from taking the philosophical view that, all said and done, Frieda was well worth the money, Lawrence became extremely angry on receiving the summons. As he happened that day to be writing to Bertrand Russell, the mathematician received the full benefit of a fine vituperation:

"I cannot tell you how this reinforces in me my utter hatred of the whole establishment—the whole constitution of England. I wish I were a criminal instead of a bankrupt. But softly—softly. I will do my best to lay a mine under their foundations. I am hostile, hostile, hostile to all that is, in our public and national life. I want to destroy it."

But how? The scheme for the instantaneous Social Reconstruction of England by giving lectures came to nothing except a breach between the joint sponsors of the scheme. Then Lawrence discovered that the "philosophy" which he had been writing was all wrong, and needed to be re-written. It is impossible to say whether or not this change of mind was due to his reading Burnet's *Early Greek Philosophy*, a book which Russell had given him. Lawrence delighted in this work, and was influenced by it considerably; so much so that when in later years he was asked to furnish captions for an illustrated edition of his *Birds, Beasts and Flowers*, he took several of them from Burnet, and they now figure in *Phoenix* as the original work of Lawrence himself. Certain it is that the "philosophy" was judged defective soon after he read Burnet.

Throughout that summer of 1915 he continued to pour out preachings, exhortations and prophesyings of dire things to come, chiefly to Cynthia Asquith and Ottoline Morrell. He several times visited the latter's beautiful and ancient home, Garsington Manor, which, strange to say, produced from him almost the only piece of stilted conventional prose he ever wrote. But in spite of occasional relapses he had now temporarily passed through that terrible dark mood of near insanity, and was returning to himself. Perhaps it is worth noting that he seems to have written little or no poetry during this period of "philosophy". Just before this turning away from creative art he had written yet another poem about Frieda called 'One Woman to All Women':

"If you knew how I swerve in peace, in the equipoise
With the man, if you knew how my flesh enjoys
The swinging bliss no shattering ever destroys,
You other women:

You would envy me, you would think me wonderful
Beyond compare;
You would weep to be lapsing on such harmony
As carries me, you would wonder aloud that he
Who is so strange should correspond with me
Everywhere.

You see he is different, he is dangerous
Without pity or love.
And yet how his separate being liberates me
And gives me peace. . . ."

It is of course meant to be spoken by Frieda, and what might be called its "argument" is a piece of Laurentian special pleading. "Frieda ought to keep other women from coming too near me," was his colloquial prose rendering of the same mood. The fact that so large a proportion of his chief correspondents and warmest admirers were women has given the impression that he had a Svengali influence over them. But most of them were fastidious upper-class women remarkable for their intelligence and sensitive qualities. What interested them was his "genius", the fine qualities which went to his making as a great artist. They were interested in him, attracted by him, not because he was "a lurid sexual specialist", but because he wasn't. It is curious that he should then have issued a poem so uncompromisingly "don't touch me", but the reason may have been that men friends had chaffed him about his female admirers.

Lawrence's stay in Greatham came to an end in August 1915, when the cottage was required by its owner. What determined their next place of residence is impossible to say, but Lawrence may have felt that if he were in London he would be more occupied and see more people, and hence save himself the agonies of brooding he had lately endured. At all events, they rented and furnished a small flat in Byron Villas, Hampstead, a northern suburb of London. Another motive for this choice may have been a wish to be nearer Katherine Mansfield and Murry, with whom Lawrence was planning to collaborate.

We first hear from him on this topic in a letter to Cynthia Asquith (5th September, 1915) in which he speaks of "issuing a little paper" which would be read by "people who care about the real living truth of things." On Murry's suggestion the periodical was called *The Signature*, but as it was a complete failure only three numbers were issued. Lawrence's contribution was part of a work called *The Crown*, published in book form ten years later with other essays, the whole entitled *Reflections on the Death of a Porcupine*. It should be mentioned that in his Introduction to this book Lawrence, writing from memory, gave a rather inaccurate account of *The Signature*, which is contradicted by his own letters of the period —Murry's account is much closer to the real facts. *The Crown* itself is a fascinating little book, written in a style so symbolical and fantastic as to suggest the wildest rhetoric of Ruskin, de Quincey's dream-fugues and even poor Gérard's mad Aurélia. If it can be said to have a main theme it is that of mental death and resurrection in this life, an experience which to Lawrence was a reality from his periodic attacks of tuberculosis followed by recovery. At such times it must really have seemed to him that he had gone through death to life, and the psychological experience finds imaginative expression in *The Crown*. Much later in life, after several other attempts, Lawrence gave it final form in *The Man Who Died*.

But just as he was busying himself with the salvation of the world by *The Signature* Lawrence was recalled to hideous reality by a half-successful attempt to vilify, suppress and ruin him. It seems inevitable that every outstanding personality should arouse opposition and hatred, and Lawrence's peculiar personality seemed designed to make him enemies. He offended people by his sharp tongue, his arrogance, his perverse contradictoriness. He had an unhappy faculty of attracting people greatly by his charm and then wantonly repelling or even insulting them into dislike and resentment. His writings, so powerful in their implications, were a repudiation of conventional life and morals which were struggling to survive the shocks of war.

As we have seen, *The Rainbow* was the product of a long patience —three years of concentrated writing and re-writing. No man, merely wishing to write a pornographic book, would dream of wasting so much time and energy. What Lawrence had done through his story of three generations of Brangwens was to build up an exposition of his belief in marriage as the consummation of life in Man and Woman. In "real" marriage after the desperate clash and battle and agony of the sexes, a mystical unity and peace are supposedly attained. It is a serious book, almost too serious, verging at times towards heaviness. As I have said, the title *The Wedding Ring* would have explained and defended it much better than *The Rainbow*. Nearly all Lawrence's varied gifts as a writer are seen in the book, and, in spite of its seriousness, it has long passages of genuine old English humour such as the chapter called 'Wedding at the Marsh'. Sometimes under his analysis his characters seem to dissolve out of life as individuals into elemental states of passion or ecstasy or rage or misery. Among exceptions is the long scene where Tom Brangwen tries to comfort his little step-daughter in her hysterical grief when she thinks she has lost her mother. It has deep pathos and tenderness, almost unbearable as the storm of the child's unreasoning grief slowly subsides into long quivering sobs. It is a mystery—or perhaps it isn't—how the reviewers of the time failed to record that those pages alone showed Lawrence was a master of pathos.

The Rainbow was published on the 30th September, and reviewed in *The Daily News* for the 5th October. The reviewer began by admitting that Lawrence had a high reputation but—with the wedding and step-daughter scenes before him!—had the impudence to deny that *The Rainbow* possessed "humanity, imaginative intensity or humour". To him it was "like Strindberg trying to write a novel in the manner at once of Pierre Louys and of Miss Victoria Cross." Then he thought Lawrence wrote like a veterinary surgeon —"his men and women are cattle who chronically suffer from the staggers." He thought most of the book "windy, tedious and nauseating." He thought it "largely a monotonous wilderness of phallicism" and the kind of book "an artistic schoolboy wants to write." He warned "ordinary readers" to leave the book alone because they "would be sure to dislike it intensely, especially those pages which are reminiscent of Diderot's *La Religieuse*." This was headed 'The Downfall', and signed by Robert Lynd.

The tip-off was enough to rouse the slumbering energies of the smut-hounds, and this intellectual notice was followed by more broadly sensational squawks from James Douglas and Clement Shorter. By a singular irony, an Irishman, a Scotchman and a Jew combined to vilify the most original English writer of his generation. Who the "common informer" was I have not been able to discover, though Lawrence believed it was "Mr. Horton and the Purity League", whoever they may have been. Unfortunately, when the case came on for hearing, no defence was presented, and no attempt made to appeal to a higher court. The publisher had only been interested in the book as a commercial speculation, and hastened to cut his loss by apologising abjectly, withdrawing the book and agreeing to its destruction. Lawrence only heard of what was going on through a friend who had noticed the sudden cessation of the advertisements.

The police-court proceedings were reported by *The Daily Express* under the headlines: Obscene Novel to be Destroyed—Worse than Zola. According to *The Times* a person called Muskett said in court that *The Rainbow* was "a mass of obscenity of thought, idea and action throughout, wrapped up in a language which he supposed would be regarded in some quarters as an artistic and intellectual effort." The magistrate, by name Dickinson, ordered the book to be destroyed, fined Methuen the enormous sum of ten guineas for this obviously disgusting offence, but regretted that high-souled personage (Methuen) had been "soiled by the publication of this work".

Those who do not form part of the tiny literary world (that is to say, practically the whole human race), if they do happen to hear of something so trifling as the suppression of a book, cannot realise what a disaster it is for the author. The average attitude—fanatics apart—is: "Well, it's silly, and bad luck on the fellow, but he must have asked for it—should have been more careful. Anyway, nobody thinks any the less of him for it." "There is something in the misfortunes of our best friends which is not altogether disagreeable to us"—otherwise, where would the newspapers be? But consider. The book was condemned to destruction without the author even being told, let alone heard. No attempt at a proper investigation was made by the magistrate. Though in all other cases what the soldier said is not evidence, here what journalists said was so accepted. In this kind of case the hair-splitting law, so pedantic in its lucrative jesuitical distinctions, makes no attempt to distinguish between the crudely ithyphallic and vulgar productions of the clandestine press and a serious work which happens to enrage the Chadbands of Slobocracy. Lawrence was left owing his publishers the advance; he lost all chance of earning anything for three years of work; he lost his copyright; he was publicly stigmatised as "obscene"; and his name was made so notorious that publishers and periodicals for a long time avoided using his work. When he did a book on European history for the Oxford University Press it was published under a pseudonym.

These "iniquitous" legal proceedings, as Murry moderately calls them, gave Lawrence a shock it would be hard to over-estimate. No man could have been more remote than he from the Victoria Cross of Lynd's review. He was no cynical exploiter of public prudery, but an "intensely religious man"; and what he proclaimed as a pioneer in 1915 most civilised people take for granted to-day. Lawrence's comment on the situation was highly characteristic:

"I am not very much moved; am beyond that by now. I only curse them all, body and soul, root, branch and leaf, to eternal damnation."

There is something very engaging about that "only".

It would be quite untrue to say that Lawrence was indifferent to the money loss involved. Nobody knew better than he by harsh experience what penury means. What he resented was the public insult.

Soon arose a faint seagull-like clamour of plaintive intellectuals, but naturally they did nothing effective. In the circumstances nothing could be done. Philip Morrell and Donald Carswell (the barrister husband of Catherine Carswell) advised appeal to a higher court and the bringing of libel actions against the journalists. If Lawrence had been related to persons of wealth and public influence, these actions might have succeeded; but then, had he been such a person, neither journalists nor magistrate would have dared to act as they did. They knew all along that he was a poor man with nothing but "genius". How could Lawrence engage in expensive and protracted legal action?

Philip Morrell asked a question in Parliament, and received the usual evasive put-off. Arnold Bennett and May Sinclair wrote personal protests, but there was no organised action, and it does not appear that anything was done by the Authors' Society. Henry James, the then reigning American dictator of English literature, was appealed to, but as no prestige was to be gained in this unpopular cause, without result. Indeed, the Great Stylist had already put on record a not too favourable opinion of Lawrence in the columns of that infallible journal, *The Times Literary Supplement.* Writing on what the cognoscenti boldly asserted was "the contemporary novel", the then American dictator had "lucidly" declared that Bennett and Wells had "practically launched the boat in which we admire the fresh play of oar of the author of *The Duchess of Wrexe* and the documented aspect exhibited successfully by *Carnival* and *Sinister Street* and even by *Sons and Lovers*, however much we may find Mr. Lawrence, we confess, hang in the dusty rear."

It is hard to decide which one admires more—the critical judgment which preferred Hugh Walpole to Lawrence, or the classic style which provided a rowing-boat with a dusty rear.

If Lawrence ever had any hopes that anything effective would be undertaken in his defence, he was soon disabused; and in his despair turned once more to thoughts of escape, emigration to America. His immediate financial needs had been met by friendly loans or gifts—Edward Marsh gave him twenty pounds, Philip Morrell and his wife gave thirty, Pinker the agent advanced forty, and Bernard Shaw gave five. I do not think Lawrence was grateful—why should he be for such paltry compensation for so gross an outrage? In any case he was now possessed with the idea of emigration, for, as he wrote Marsh: "I am so sick, in body and soul, that if I don't go away I shall die." And indeed in his state of health every winter in a northern climate was a dire threat to his life.

For some reason Lawrence had now fixed his utopian Rananim in Fort Myers, Florida. This may have been because Philip Heseltine's friend, Delius, owned an abandoned plantation in Florida; but one of Lawrence's letters refers to an unnamed American who would give letters of introduction to friends at Fort Myers. Perhaps both operated. At one time the plan was to take a boat to "Barbadoes" (like most Englishmen he misspells the name of this ancient colony) and thence to Florida—a very complicated undertaking. The choice of Fort Myers as a refuge for a penniless exile once more displays Lawrence's "innocence" of the world. Fort Myers is indeed a very charming town laid out in excellent taste, but is mainly frequented by millionaires who come for the Gulf fishing—and arranges its prices accordingly. Besides, the great heat of a Florida summer would have been as hard on his damaged lungs as a northern winter.

The whole scheme was fantastic, for Lawrence as usual proposed to take along his friends of the moment, who at that time included such rough-and-ready pioneers as Aldous Huxley and Philip Heseltine. Moreover, he failed to grasp the fact that, in war-time, travel permits are only issued to people in the national service. It was characteristic of him that he always wanted to leave "for ever" any place which had unpleasant associations. In this case, of course, it was Hampstead; and without waiting for any certainty in the future he hastily gave up his lease and sold his furniture. The act restored him to sanity and to his nomadic freedom. He was "Vogelfrei, thank God," and free too (for the time being) from struggles to save a hostile world from itself:

"Enough grizzling—I'm not going to grizzle any more, while I live. I'm not going to lament and fret over the world any more. I'm not responsible for the world, as it is."

Thus, as early as December 1915, he was making resolutions which of course he did not keep—to abandon his self-imposed task as one of mankind's saviours. But of course he could never prevent himself from laying down the law about any public question which happened to come before him. He spent that Christmas with his family in the Midlands, partly to keep up old custom, partly to show his old associates that he was not hanging his head and accepting the legal insult to himself and his book. He had not been there forty-eight hours when he found himself "differing violently" on the subject of the coal-miners from his elder brother, who was "a radical nonconformist". Lawrence recoiled in horror and disgust from the radical nonconformist:

"These men, whom I love so much—and the life has such a power over me—they *understand* mentally so horribly: only industrialism, only wages and money and machinery. They can't *think* anything else. All their collective thinking is in these terms only. That is why we are *bound* to get something like Guild Socialism in the long run, which is a reduction to the lowest terms—nothing higher than that which now is, only lower. But I suppose things have got to be reduced to their lowest terms. Only, oh God, I don't want to be implicated in it."

The thought of that inevitable future, which he foresaw so clearly, filled him with sorrow and despair. So, it was with intense relief that he left the implacably industrial Midlands and their parasitic London, for Cornwall. The novelist, J. D. Beresford, offered the Lawrences, free, the cottage at St. Merryn which he occupied only in the summer. As always with Lawrence a successful move to some new and interesting place, especially if it was an escape from towns, uplifted his heart and spirits in thanksgiving: "Already, here in Cornwall, it is better. Here one is outside England, the England of London—thank God."

Instantly he began writing cheerful letters to his friends, full of appreciation and hope. To Cynthia Asquith he wrote praising Beresford's house:

". . . a nice old house with large clear rooms, and such wonderful silence—only a faint sound of sea and wind. It is like being at the window and looking out of England to the beyond. This is my first move outwards, to a new life. One must be free to love, only to love and create, and to be happy."

To Katherine Mansfield he wrote more belligerently, stressing his dislike of London and its literary inhabitants, once more repudiating any further effort at saving the world. The "Jack" referred to is of course John Middleton Murry:

"I've done bothering about the world and people. I've finished. There now remains to find a nice place where one can be happy. And you and Jack will come if you like—when you feel like it; and we'll all be happy together—no more questioning and quibbling and trying to do anything with the world. The world is gone, extinguished, like the lights of last night's Café Royal—gone for ever. There is a new world with a new thin unsullied air and no people in it but new-born people: *moi-même et* Frieda. No return to London and the world, my dear Katherine—it has disappeared, like the lights of last night's Café Royal."

Eloquent and just, but easier to write than achieve. The letter had scarcely been sent off when the Lawrences were joined by two Café Royal habitués—first Philip Heseltine and then, for a much shorter period, Michael Arlen. It was, as we have seen, a habit of Lawrence's, as soon as he reached a new place where he and Frieda were quite happy together, to send out urgent invitations to people to come and join him. When these were accepted, Lawrence's peculiarities of habit and temperament invariably resulted in a quarrel and in turning friends into enemies. He never realised that this was a deplorable waste of goodwill and a failure in himself.

How much Philip Heseltine admired his books is clear from the quotation from one of his letters already given here. But it was a gross error in Lawrence to suppose from this literary admiration that Heseltine, so different in education, point of view and temperament, with a talent so different in kind from Lawrence's, could possibly live cheerfully and amicably in the same house with the most irritable of the irritable race of poets.

It is to Heseltine's credit that so young a man (he was barely of age) realised more fully than other friends of Lawrence how fatally he was infected with tuberculosis, but Heseltine does not seem to have realised how the excitement of his company and the inevitable wrangles might harm a man so over-sensitive, especially one still suffering from the shock of prosecution. Certainly Lawrence was very ill during Heseltine's visit. Dr. Maitland Radford, son of Lawrence's poet-friends, Ernest and Dollie Radford, came down to Cornwall in February 1916 to examine him medically. In reporting to others what doctors said to him Lawrence invariably concealed the fact that his lungs were infected with tubercles and invented vague euphemisms to avoid admitting it. His account of Dr. Radford's diagnosis and advice runs as follows:

"He says the stress on the nerves sets up a deferred inflammation in all the internal linings, and that I must keep very quiet and still and warm and peaceful. There was a sort of numbness all down the left side, very funny—I could hardly hold anything in my left hand."

The reference to "numbness all down the left side" would seem to indicate some sort of nervous shock following the sufferings caused him by *The Rainbow* prosecution. The doctor's advice is that normally given a tubercular patient, the advice Lawrence invariably received from doctors, and invariably neglected. Whether Maitland Radford warned Heseltine about Lawrence's precarious health and the danger of upsetting him cannot now be known. What is certain is that Heseltine went down to Cornwall with the best intentions, prepared to issue at his own expense (provided he received enough subscriptions) a new private edition of *The Rainbow*. Only thirty favourable answers were received after Heseltine had sent out six hundred circulars to carefully selected people supposedly interested in literature and freedom. In view of this indifference to both, the publishing project was dropped, including that of Lawrence's strangely-titled essay on homosexuality, 'The

Goat and Compasses', which Heseltine unpardonably destroyed.

For all his intuitive quickness Lawrence was often unaware how much he had offended others or that their private judgments of him were more severe than good-breeding permitted them to express. His habit of saying domineering or flatly insulting things to all and sundry seemed to belong to a more primitive state of society than that which he actually lived in, while he never realised that those who let such things pass uncommented had noticed, had judged and did not forgive. Thus Lawrence wrote quite affectionately of Heseltine long after Heseltine had ceased to think of him as a friend. Even as early as January 1916, Lawrence wrote placidly: "So far Heseltine has been here with us all along. We get on very well with him." But almost on the same day Heseltine wrote to Delius about Lawrence:

"He is a very great artist, but hard and autocratic in his views and outlook, and his artistic canons I find utterly and entirely unsympathetic to my nature. He seems to be too metaphysical, too anxious to be comprehensive in a detached way and to care too little for purely personal, analytical and introspective art. His views are somewhat at variance with his own achievements. But he is, never-the-less, a great and attractive personality, and his passion for a new, clean, untrammelled life is very splendid."

Unfortunately, in spite of the fact that Lawrence had urged them to join his "colony" and that both Heseltine and Arlen greatly respected him, he contrived to alienate both and to send them away from Cornwall in a very different mood from that in which they had arrived. Michael Arlen worked off his annoyance by a squib in *The New Age* about an author who was too good to be published. Heseltine's feelings were evidently more deeply outraged, since in April 1916 he wrote to Delius:

"Lawrence is a fine artist and a hard, though horribly distorted thinker. But personal relationship with him is impossible—he acts as a subtle and deadly poison. The affair by which I found him out is far too long to enter upon here. . . . The man must really be a bit mad, though his behaviour nearly landed me in a fearful fix—indeed it was calculated to do so. However, when I wrote and denounced him to his face, all he could say was 'I request that you do not talk about me in London'—so he evidently had a very bad attack of guilty conscience."

The "fearful fix" to which Heseltine refers is believed to have been matrimonial, the Lawrences having the bad habit of trying arbitrarily to marry off their young friends to unsuitable spouses.

Meanwhile, as ever, Lawrence continued his heroic labours in literature in spite of all difficulties and misunderstandings. At St. Merryn, where there were "terrifying rocks like solid lumps of the original darkness" with the "ponderous cold light of the sea foaming up", he worked to put together his book of poems, *Amores* from note-books which had been rescued for him from Fiascherino by the British consul. He also worked on the proofs of *Twilight in Italy*, that book so full of sensitive beauty, which at the time of publication was so stupidly and arrogantly treated by *The Times Literary Supplement*.

The germ of another book, the essays on American literature, may be traced at least as far back as this period. Among Beresford's books was a copy of Herman Melville's *Moby Dick*, then out of fashion and almost forgotten. The other members of the party saw nothing in it, but Lawrence found it "very odd, interesting". The book stimulated his interest in America, and set him reading or re-reading American books. Melville moved Lawrence deeply and seemed to reveal him to himself. There are passages in his essay on *Moby Dick* which are truly more applicable to Lawrence than to Melville. Take this for example:

"Nobody can be more clownish, more clumsy and sententiously in bad taste. He preaches and holds forth because he is not sure of himself. And he holds forth, often, so amateurishly. The artist was so *much* greater than the man. The man is rather a tiresome New Englander of the ethical mystical-transcendentalist sort. But he was a deep, great artist, even if he was rather a sententious man . . .when he forgets his audience, and gives us his sheer appreciation of the world, then he is wonderful, his book commands a stillness in the soul, an awe."

Truly, if one did not know who had written that or on whom, it could easily be taken as a penetrating summary of Lawrence—but for the "New Englander", and after all there was so much of the New England conscience in him, one could easily take that as a figure of speech. Proceeding with his analysis of Melville, Lawrence suddenly grows angry about his preaching and accuses him of being an ass who "brays, brays, brays." Inevitably one remembers Lawrence's dictum that criticism always reveals the critic; was not "holding forth" among his own regrettable lapses?

In spite of the estrangement of Arlen and Heseltine, he continued to risk losing his friends by seeing too much of them at close quarters. Hardly had they left when Lawrence wrote to Gertler announcing that he hated mankind thoroughly, and then inconsistently begs that Gertler and Koteliansky will come to live with him. At a later date he cherished the happy thought of inviting together Ottoline Morrell, the daughter of a Duke, and Ivy Low, who subsequently married the Soviet Commissar, Litvinoff. In March 1916, when he had left St. Merryn for an even more remote place in North Cornwall, called Higher Tregethern, Zennor, he urged Murry and Katherine Mansfield to join him, holding out as an inducement the fact that he had also asked Heseltine. Setting aside Heseltine's own angry feelings, this was peculiarly tactful since Murry had been hurt by Lawrence's abandonment of *The Signature* publishing scheme for Heseltine's plan. Thus was he for ever weaving schemes for the destruction of his own tranquillity, and disregarding the doctor's urging him to "keep very quiet and still and warm and peaceful". It was without a suspicion of self-ridicule that he gravely wrote Murry: "I have no business genius". But there are pathetic self-pity and need for tenderness in the cry: "I begin to tremble and feel sick at the slightest upset. Do be mild with me for a bit."

This new resting place, Higher Tregethern, Zennor, was very sympathetic to Lawrence. He remained there eighteen months and would probably have stayed on until the end of the war but for the interference of Destiny, and Intelligence, Military. It was a tiny group of cottages, facing north, "under high shaggy moorlands, and a big sweep of sea beyond", seven miles from Penzance, with "great enormous boulders and gorse . . . only the gorse, and the fields, the lambs skipping and hopping like everything, and sea-gulls fighting with the ravens, and sometimes a fox, and a ship on the sea". The Lawrences had a two-room cottage, for which they paid five pounds a year. It was a "granite hole" which had to be made into a "livable place". Dropping all thoughts of "philosophy", the Lawrences set to work eagerly. First they cleaned the place thoroughly and then covered the walls with a very pale pink wash. The handyman and artist in Lawrence produced a dresser and cupboard, which he painted a royal blue. The bedroom upstairs had "a large deep

D. H. LAWRENCE IN 1914

FRIEDA VON RICHTHOFEN
By permission of Mrs D. H. Lawrence

window looking at the sea and another window opposite looking at the hill-slope of gorse and granite"; and there they hung a piece of embroidery on the wall and covered the bed with a "brilliant and gay counterpane"—both gifts of Ottoline Morrell. For reading he took to *Thucydides* (also a gift from Ottoline Morrell), and very surprisingly was filled with admiration for the text-book of statesmen—"a very splendid and noble writer, with the simplicity and the directness of the most complete culture and the widest consciousness. More and more I admire the true classic dignity and self-responsibility".

All this looked like a recovery of physical and mental health. The rasp of the northern winter on his lungs relaxed, he temporarily abandoned the literature of soul-malady, and seemed almost to have forgotten the wrongs and insults he had suffered from venal hacks and petty officials. It is all the more disconcerting, then, to find that the *fata morgana* of Rananim was still with him, that he pined for extraneous companionship and would take no denial. Undeterred by recent failures, he sent letter upon urgent letter to the Murrys, who were then staying at Bandol on the south coast of France. He drew them plans of the cottages, urging "you must come, and we will live there a long, long time, very cheaply." Murry and Katherine Mansfield got the impression that he was very lonely and needed them badly, and it was almost more from a sense of obligation than from choice that they left Bandol, where they were perfectly happy. On hearing their decision Lawrence wrote:

"Good, all is well between us all. No more quarrels and quibbles. Let it be agreed for ever. I am *Blutbruder;* a *Blutbrüderschaft* between us all. Tell K. not to be so queasy."

Thus, in accordance with their promise, the Murrys arrived one "cold slatey-grey day in early April", with Katherine Mansfield sitting disconsolately in a farm cart, "high up on all the goods and chattels". The omens were not auspicious; indeed, how was it humanly possible that four such persons could live in such close intimacy of solitude without clashes? Candidates for Rananim who took it seriously overlooked the fact that it would not be a free and easy republic of letters but an arbitrary autocracy under the rule of King David the First and Only.

There can be little doubt that in these years Lawrence liked Murry more than any other of his not very numerous men friends. The very violence of his later reaction against Murry indicates the depth of his former affection. But there was a twist to this affection which Murry could not accept. Lawrence had at this time got into his obstinate head the notion of *Blutbrüderschaft* (blood-brotherhood) reinforced perhaps by reading Melville's description of the relationship between Ishmael and Queequeg. Be that as it may, he began as was his wont—"hammer, hammer, hammer"—at this idea of blood-brotherhood, expounded at length in the scenes between Gerald and Birkin of *Women in Love*. In all this Lawrence did not once apparently stop to consider his friend's feelings. At that time Murry was making his reputation as a literary critic, and Lawrence never seemed to consider that while Cornish solitude might be excellent for a creative writer like himself it was quite the wrong thing for someone with his hand on the intellectual pulse of the time. Similarly, he never stopped to ask whether this barbaric whimsy of blood-brotherhood had any charm for his friend.

And what of Katherine Mansfield? It is the fact that among his contemporaries Lawrence chiefly admired insignificant writers, and had poor literary judgment. He seems to have been greatly surprised at the willingness of editors to publish Murry, and I find very little evidence that he appreciated Katherine Mansfield. *Women in Love* shows that he was annoyed by what he considered faults in her—her summary disposal of persons and things with a flippant epigram, her tendency to whimsy-whamsy, her infantilism; but there is small acknowledgement of her literary talent. This Cornish escapade was not altogether in her line. That wuthering heights of strange emotions with Lawrence's "genius" tearing him to pieces and reacting powerfully on all near him must surely have been distasteful, a sacrifice of her gifts to his. Hear what she says in a letter written in May of 1916 from Zennor:

"To-day I can't see a yard, thick mist and rain and a tearing wind with it. Everything is faintly damp. The floor of the tower is studded with Cornish pitchers catching the drops. Except for my little Cornish maid . . . I am alone, for Murry and Lawrence have plunged off to St. Ives with rucksacks on their backs and Frieda is in her cottage. It's very quiet in the house except for the wind and the rain and the fire that roars very hoarse and fierce."

She goes on to say that when her letter is done she will lie down and smoke and think of a story about Marseille. Now, merely to think of Marseille, in that dismal damp isolation, might have filled her with nostalgia for the Mediterranean in May with the sun and the nightingales and the vines coming into flower. Murry says she "was very unhappy, and conceived a hatred of Cornwall that lasted the rest of her life". This, however, is to some extent contradicted by a letter of hers to Virginia Woolf written in April 1919, in which she admits the Cornish place has "many imperfections" but "there is a . . . something . . . which makes one long for it." And she winds up, ". . . the house is like a ship. I mustn't talk about it. It bewitched me." Clearly, then, apart from the dismalness of wet days, it was not so much the place as Lawrence that drove them away.

With unconscious symbolism Murry had shown his sense of dissatisfaction by painting all his chairs a funereal black. Unwarned by these forebodings and ignoring Murry's evasions Lawrence persisted—"hammer, hammer, hammer"—in trying to force on his friend his mystical-sensual notions of blood-brotherhood. Lawrence instantly perceived Murry's instinctive hesitation and feeling of repulsion, and the frustration revived in him all those nervous symptoms which at Greatham had fringed insanity. He had terrible nightmares, during which he frightened them all by calling out: "Jack is killing me!" Sometimes "a paroxysm of black rage would sweep down upon him" and leave them "trembling and aghast". What made these outbursts even more uncanny and disturbing was that Lawrence appeared to forget all about them, and next day "would be kinder and more affectionate than ever". This was his habitual way of trying to apologise for such hideous outbursts—being too conceited to do so frankly—which he never made any effort to suppress or divert, as he "did not believe in self-control".

Which of these two antithetical selves was the real one? How could so sensitive a man, so resentful of any criticism or intrusion from others, expect others to treat such outbursts of hatred and violence as "nothing"? It may sometimes be possible to forgive a friend for behaving crudely and hatefully, but how forgive oneself? The discordance never seemed to trouble him for a moment.

The crisis came when Lawrence tried to force Murry into some kind of blood-shedding sacrament of the Teutonic sort. His refusal goaded Lawrence in to a frenzy of rage and repulsion: "I hate your love. *I hate it.* You're an obscene bug, sucking my life away."

There was a certain truth in this, unpleasantly and violently as it was put. Other people, particularly intellectuals, *were* apt to drain Lawrence of his vitality, quite unaware themselves how much they were living upon him. But after such a scene there was nothing the Murrys could do, except leave; which they did, while the Cornish rain slanted down on the spiritual ruins of yet another shattered Rananim.

8

So once more they were left alone, with Lawrence in a misery of baffled rage and spiritual exhaustion. Yet in the summer of 1916 he still had before him three years of penury, moral suffering and that endless "battle—battle" with the world his mother had long ago lamented in him. At the moment when he felt instinctively the Murrys' withdrawal from him was coming he had written to Catherine Carswell: "It is queer, how almost everything has gone out of me, all the world I have known, and the people, gone out like candles." Yet he claimed that he felt "fundamentally happy and free".

Suddenly he was disturbed by the news that married men of his age-group must be medically examined for military service, and instantly wrote to Cynthia Asquith asking her advice on how to avoid it. But his mood was now quite different from the exceeding horror with which he had considered such a prospect a year or so earlier. Then he had gone into frenzies of protest and near insanity. Now he was gaily, almost cynically, fatalistic. " 'Carpe diem' is the motto now, pure gay fatalism." And again, not altogether sensitively and tactfully to a woman whose husband was at the front and whose father-in-law was still head of the War Cabinet:

"Life mustn't be taken seriously any more, at least, the outer social life. The social being I am has become a spectator at a knockabout dangerous farce. The individual particular me remains self-contained and grins. But I should be mortally indignant if I lost my life or even too much of my liberty, by being dragged into the knockabout farce of this social life."

When one thinks of the shortness of the time, the knockdown blow of the prosecution, of his illnesses and of all these various occupations and emotional troubles, it seems quite miraculous that by the date of his calling up (28th June, 1916) he had almost completed a new long novel, *Women in Love*. It was already under way when the Murrys arrived, for he reported: "I am doing another novel—that really occupies me. The world crackles and busts, but that is another matter, external, in chaos. One has a certain order inviolable in one's soul." In the middle of May he told Pinker that he was "half-way through a novel, which is a sequel to *The Rainbow*, though quite unlike it." So, since the book was "almost ended" in late June it was obviously then in existence in its first version, though it was entirely re-written, and not published in England until 1921.

Novelists are apt to prefer those of their books which are most harshly treated, and the fact that Lawrence preferred or said he preferred *The Rainbow* and *Women in Love* to all his other books throws more light on him than on literary criticism. Since *The Rainbow* both Lawrence and the outer world had gone through sensational and painful experiences, yet this new novel is burdened with a left-over from the old pre-war Brangwen saga. Much of the book is occupied with the working out of Lawrence's favourite formula of two couples, Birkin-Ursula and Gerald-Gudrun. Birkin and Ursula are most obviously Lawrence and Frieda, and whatever changes were made for purposes of fiction, he intended the other two for Murry and Katherine Mansfield. They are involved, but not deeply, in a malicious satirical comedy where all the people are caricatures of his 1915 vintage of "friends".

One might call it a book of retaliation, almost of revenge. Thus Gudrun abandons Gerald for a garrulous German Jew, and Gerald dies of despair and cold on an Alpine glacier. As for the book being about women in love, it is more truly about everybody in hate with the possible exception of Birkin and Ursula, and even they have tremendous squabbles of a most authentic realism. It was perhaps fortunate that this novel was not published in England until after the Lawrences had gone abroad. Imagine the delight of Ottoline Morrell when she read of herself as Hermione:

"Ursula resented Hermione's long, grave, downward-looking face. There was something of the stupidity and unenlightened self-esteem of a horse in it."

The curious may compare this suggestion with her portrait by Augustus John. Whether true or not in this particular case the image is certainly true of a not uncommon type of English woman.

Still, true or not, anyone can see how much the victim would be offended, especially since she regarded Lawrence as a protégé whom she had tried to help. Another victim was her friend, Bertrand Russell, presented as "a learned, dry baronet of fifty, who was always making witticisms and laughing at them heartily in a harsh horse-laugh". Philip Morrell was depicted as he entered the garden, "striding romantically like a Meredith hero who remembers Disraeli" bringing with him "the atmosphere of the House of Commons . . . the Home Secretary had said such and such a thing, and he, Roddice, on the other hand, thought such and such a thing, and had said so-and-so to the P.M." Why did they all deny that Lawrence had a sense of humour? Could it have been because it was turned so disconcertingly on themselves?

The most stringent of these caricatures was of Philip Heseltine and his associates, forming altogether a merciless satire of the Bloomsbury-Café Royal sets. Lawrence's bitterness against Heseltine was partly the usual reaction against ex-friends, but chiefly because Heseltine had sat in the Café with friends reading, parodying and jeering at the poems in *Amores.* Katherine Mansfield got up from her table, asked to see the book, which Heseltine sheepishly gave her, and walked out with it. The episode has been denied by Heseltine's friends. Middleton Murry assures me of its truth and that he still has the copy of *Amores.* Michael Arlen, who was sitting at Heseltine's table, permits me to quote from his letter in answer to my query:

"It was Heseltine, most mockingly, but alas with malice more than mockery, who read from D. H's 'Amores'. In 1915–16 Lawrence thought—I was too young to know for certain—very highly of Heseltine. But Philip later, despising himself, decided to goad Lawrence into despising him, Heseltine, too. You must remember Heseltine's background—son of fairly rich parents, misunderstood chap."

So much for that, to which there needs only to be added that when *Women in Love* was published Heseltine, alone among the victims, threatened libel proceedings, which he settled for fifty pounds, after absurdly trying to get the book suppressed by the Purity League.

Personally satirical novels usually contain one character (male or female according to the sex of the author) who is miraculously exempt from the vices, failings and humorous appearance of the others. *Women in Love* is a conspicuous exception, for none of the characters is more satirised, ridiculed with greater insight, than Birkin-Lawrence. The author sees how maddening Birkin is. Thus there is a scene where Hermione in exasperation hits Birkin on the head with a large piece of lapis-lazuli which he parries with a quarto of Thucydides. After Birkin has restored his serenity by undressing in a wood and rolling naked among the primroses, he addresses this note to Hermione:

"I will go to town—I don't want to come back to Breadalby for the present. But it is quite all right—I don't want you to mind having biffed me, in the least. Tell the others it is just one of my moods. You were quite right to biff me—because I know you wanted to. So there's the end of it."

All this is delightfully characteristic, and shows how far he was really prepared to go in his belief that truth to the impulse of the moment is the essence of life and must not be thwarted. In a way it sounds an admirable doctrine and a release from the social tyranny of all democracies, but had its risky side. Suppose Hermione in her "impulse" had "biffed" him so hard that she cracked his skull? The whole episode is instructive. It shows that once his moods of malice or frenzied rage had evaporated Lawrence was quite prepared to forget and even forgive all the insults and upsets he inflicted on his friends. He bore his victims absolutely no ill-will —or at least not until he came to write about them.

It appears that his relations with Frieda were often conducted on this plan. One reason that he found Frieda indispensable, could not live without her, was that she was the only person beside his mother who took the trouble to stand up to him, gave him back abuse for abuse, let him rage and boil and employ every device of dishonest casuistry in argument, and afterwards bore him no ill-will but on the contrary loved him as much as ever. He might have advertised for a decade in dubious periodicals without ever finding a woman to take her place.

The satire of himself in this novel is ruthless. Thus, in a chapter called 'An Island', there is a long wrangle between him and Frieda, in which he quite intentionally exposes his wearisome habit of holding forth and his pig-headed perversity. Birkin, he tells us, had "a wonderful, desirable life-rapidity" but . . . "there was at the same time this ridiculous mean effacement into a Salvator Mundi and a

Sunday-school teacher, a prig of the stiffest type." Again he reveals his social awkwardness—at Hermione's oppressively intellectual party Birkin is "ignominious in the eyes of everyone, completely insignificant."

It was a habit of women, especially when they first met the Lawrences, to lecture Frieda on her shortcomings as the wife of genius, with implications that the kind friend advising would do the job very much better. Evidently Ottoline Morrell was among them, but the speech Lawrence puts into her mouth shows an acute awareness of his own character:

"He is frail in health and body, he needs great, great care. Then he is so changeable and unsure of himself—it requires the greatest patience and understanding to help him. I can't tell you how much suffering it would take to make him happy. He lives an *intensely* spiritual life at times. And then comes the reaction. He is so uncertain, so unstable—he wearies, and then reacts. I couldn't *tell* you what his reactions are. I couldn't *tell* the agony of them. That which he affirms and loves one day—a little later he turns on it in a fury of destruction. He is never constant, always this awful, dreadful reaction."

Perfectly true, and confirmed by all that we have been gradually discovering about him here. Only, we must always be careful not to pay too much attention to his irritating defects and thereby forget his "wonderful vitality" and "intense spiritual life".

In another chapter, 'Excurse', there is another wrangle with Frieda, who turns and rends him. Yet as he battles her with unscrupulous wits, he admits to himself the truth of her denunciations:

"He knew she was in the main right. He knew he was perverse, so spiritual on the one hand, and in some strange way degraded, on the other. He knew that his spirituality was concomitant of a process of depravity, a sort of pleasure in self-destruction."

Then comes the reconciliation. Ursula walks away in tears, Birkin picks out of the mud the rings he had offered her as a present and she had flung in his face. How characteristic that he does not pick them up for any human sentiment, but because he could not bear to see "tokens of the reality of beauty" lying in the mud. Presently Ursula drifts back:

" 'See what a flower I found for you,' she said wistfully holding a piece of purple-red bell-heather under his face. He saw the clump of coloured bells, and the tree-like, tiny branch: also her hands, with their over-fine, over-sensitive skin. 'Pretty!' he said, looking up at her with a smile, taking the flower. Everything had become simple again, quite simple."

"Pretty!" It was the word his mother had always used to him when as a boy he brought her some little gift and she wanted to fold him in love. For him it had overtones of meaning even Frieda could not know, a boundless tenderness she could feel but not wholly understand. It was a transference of that unforgotten mother-love to her.

It was this book, with all its intimate self-revelations and—from a worldly point of view—imprudent caricatures on which he was completing work when the military summons reached him. He met this with yet another surprising change of front, writing of it jauntily to Catherine Carswell with a music-hall bravado:

"I shall go, and take my chance of being accepted. If I must be a soldier, then I must—ta-rattata-ta! It's no use trying to dodge one's fate. It doesn't trouble me any more. I'd rather be a soldier than a school-teacher, anyhow."

The reality, however, turned out to be not quite so simple and sprightly. On the train journey to Bodmin (the chief town of Cornwall), the other recruits "sang all the time, or howled like dogs in the night" the sentimental inharmonious "songs" which expressed the emotions of that heroic epoch. As Lawrence saw them, these recruits were "bitterly, desperately miserable, but still manly: mostly very quiet, yet neither sloppy nor frightened". It is evidence of his quick observation that he noticed one man on the train was quite different from the others, "the only blatherer, a loose fellow" who jeered at Lawrence's beard and boasted that he had come all the way from Canada to enlist—as if that were necessary! He was, of course, a Canadian deserter re-joining before the police got him; though Lawrence could not know that.

At Bodmin he found the barracks "prison-like", the food "disgusting", but the sergeant "not a bad chap". The place seemed so like a prison that it made him think of Oscar Wilde in Reading Gaol. When he undressed he was ashamed for the other men to see his old darned underclothes, for he had been made too poor to buy new ones. He spent a restless night on the hard bed, kept awake by the moans and groans of the other men in their sleep and by one man's "hysterical cough". After reveille and the push to get a cold-water wash on a piece of borrowed soap, there came a "sickening breakfast" and the sergeant's order to tidy up. Like every other man who came up with a beard, Lawrence was of course called "dad", and on account of his supposed age was exempted from the broom fatigue. He was medically rejected for military service, but told he ought to volunteer for civilian service; which he refused to do. The other men then looked at him "grudgingly", since they thought (as he supposed) he had been unfairly favoured because "he was not a working man".

As he sat before the fire with Frieda that night after returning home, looking at his knees in their old grey flannel trousers, he said: "If ever I see my legs in khaki I shall die. But they shall never put my legs in khaki." It was his emphatic way of saying he hoped he would never be found fit for active service. And of course at the same time he hated being rejected as a crock, a man infected with consumption. He was not blind to the necessity for conscription, and though he might say he would disobey orders because of his horror of being crushed to the military pattern, he would never have pleaded conscientious objection. Sometimes he was tempted by the idea of taking work "of national importance", realising that it would ease the situation for him and for "his influential friends in London" to whom "in his remoteness, writing occasionally an essay that bothered them, he was a thorn in the flesh." He realised perfectly that for them with relatives at the front "it was small pleasure" to read such assertions of his as: "this trench and machine warfare is a blasphemy against life itself." He knew everybody couldn't be rejected and sit far off in Cornwall in condemnation of it all. He even "felt a dreary misery" at the thought of the men who were in it. But the Bodmin experience, trifling as it was, disturbed him greatly:

"It is the annulling of all one stands for, this militarism, the nipping of the very germ of one's being. I was very much upset. The sense of spiritual disaster everywhere was quite terrifying."

And to another correspondent he wrote:

"You are quite right, I do esteem individual liberty above everything. What is a nation for, but to secure the maximum of liberty to every individual?"

Apparently he never stopped to ask himself what happens to

individual liberty when a nation loses its liberty. But only a few days after his rejection he was shaken by hearing that a man, to whose family Lawrence was under some obligation, had been killed in action. In October 1915, *The English Review* had published his story *England, My England*, which was not so much a satire as a cruel jeer at this man and his family, who had been both annoyed and hurt by the publication. Now, just as his too prophetic story had announced, this husband and father had been killed. Lawrence's first feelings were of acute and conscience-stricken misery:

"It upsets me very much to hear of X——. I did not know he was dead. I wish that story at the bottom of the sea, before ever it had been printed. Perhaps Y—— won't be hurt by that wretched story—that is all that matters."

Unfortunately, he could not let it go at that, but his antithetical self would not be silenced by shame. He would not lower the Jolly Roger fluttering from his literary craft, if only because it would be condemning beforehand so much of his work, including most of his last novel. He had had to bite his tongue to be able to tell Frieda he loved her; but not even this man's death could keep him remorseful and contrite. He just *had* to put a postscript:

"No, I *don't* wish I had never written that story. It should do good, at the long run?"

9

THAT summer and autumn the visitors to Rananim were a few peaceful women: Catherine Carswell, Ivy Low, Dollie Radford, who sincerely admired and liked him without the slightest wish to take over Frieda's job; friends who came for limited visits and not "for ever", and were content to enjoy the vitality he could give out so joyously without wrangling with him about his prejudices. Catherine Carswell was quite right in saying that an important factor in getting on easily and peacefully with him was the very simple one of doing a share in the normal housework without fuss.

But if there were no wars with indiscreet or unlucky visitors, there were still flares-up of the battle with Frieda, and those often on the old unhappy theme of her children. Still she was officially not supposed to see them—just imagine a law that orders such separations!—and had to lurk miserably in London streets just to get a glimpse of them. Now, once again, she wanted to see them; and not only was money very short, but Lawrence was abominably jealous. He felt it was sheer perversity on her part that, after living with him for four years, she should still love her children and want them. He was more important to her than children; and having children was a blunder anyway. As he wrote to Catherine Carswell:

"Having children is a clutching at the past, the back origins, for fulfilment, and fulfilment *does not lie in the past.* You should be glad you have no children: they are a stumbling-block now. There are plenty of children, and no hope. If women can bring forth hope, they are mothers indeed. It is not in children the future lies. It is the truth, the new perceived hope, that makes spring."

Whether it was his usual "hammer, hammer, hammer" on the lines of this perverse balderdash or something else, the fact is that he exasperated Frieda to such an extent that, like Hermione in *Women in Love*, she "biffed" him on the head—with a soup plate, not an elegant piece of lapis. Then after war there was peace, and the long wrangle ended (as was to be foreseen) in Frieda getting her way—she went to see her children.

Unluckily, while she was absent, the beginnings of winter as usual brought him illness. Already in October he was complaining that his health was miserable, "damnable". Two weeks later he told his agent: "I am tired to death of being always pinched and penniless and in bad health." With his novels suppressed or out of print, his stories unwanted, his "philosophy" unsaleable, he had little indeed to live on during those harsh war years. He had a few sporadic periodical publications, he got out a book of his old poems and his Italian sketches, but mostly he lived on what he called "precarious borrowing", from Pinker, from his sister Ada, from Amy Lowell in America, and friends in England. Once more he began to long for the America of which he knew nothing, to go "to the far western mountains" from which he imagined "one can see the distant Pacific Ocean."

Even as he wrote, another and wholly unexpected persecution was descending on him. By the end of 1916 the length of the war and the success of the enemy's submarine campaign had made the British authorities more willing to listen to the repeated warnings of the French that much enemy espionage was in fact based on

England. Incredulity gave way to something like over-credulity, and the delicate task of tracing the real spies and quietly picking them up seems to have been entrusted to people without sense or experience. It is a most extraordinary fact that Lawrence, who knew absolutely nothing about military and naval matters and cared less, was first arrested by the Germans as an English spy and then suspected by the English of being a German spy.

It began by an apologetic policeman, acting under military orders, coming to the cottage for identification. Consider the situation. Frieda's father had been a German regular officer; her uncle Ferdinand was in all the reference books as one who had extended German influence in China; her airman cousin had his famous "flying circus". Why on earth was this German aristocrat living with a penniless ex-schoolmaster of dubious literary reputation, in a remote cottage overlooking the Atlantic shipping routes to and from Bristol? And had he not stayed in Germany, had he not German relatives? Were they not still sending letters to Germany through Switzerland, and receiving replies?

All quite true, though it was of course not true that he was German, as they seemed to think. However, Lawrence was exceedingly indignant at this suspicion and made no attempt to soften it, either in the authorities or in his Cornish neighbours. He went in fact to the opposite extreme, talking openly against the war, jeering at newspaper propaganda, and defiantly singing German folk songs. On one occasion, as they returned from shopping, the Lawrences were stopped by a couple of men in khaki who examined their basket. One of them insisted that a square parcel in the bag must be a camera, whereas it was merely a pound block of salt. But before the men were out of hearing Frieda laughed jeeringly: "The poor innocent salt!" and Lawrence had looked "black with rage". On another occasion Frieda started running along the cliffs with her white scarf flying in the wind, and Lawrence had to shout to her: "Stop it, stop it, you fool! Can't you see they'll think you're signalling to the enemy?" Notice, by the way, that he instinctively said "the enemy", which a German or even a spy would not have done.

At Christmas 1916 came another shock. The Lawrences had two American guests, one of them Robert Mountsier, who was afterwards Lawrence's agent in America. On a night of pouring rain a policeman was sent to examine their papers. When Mountsier returned to London he was (according to Lawrence) "arrested, and conveyed to Scotland Yard: there examined, stripped naked, his clothes taken away." When he was liberated, he was advised to return to America; and thus the astute Intelligence turned a very anti-German American into someone not exactly pro-English. All Mountsier had done that was suspicious was to stay with the Lawrences. The episode exasperated and rattled Lawrence. In writing to Catherine Carswell soon after he did not mention it but betrays his mood:

"We seem all to be pretty down, floored. I feel myself awfully like a fox that is cornered by a pack of hounds and boors who don't perhaps know he's there, but are closing in unconsciously. I am applying for re-indorsement of my passports to New York."

This was a foolish thing to do. Was it likely that a suspected spy would be allowed to escape to America (then still neutral), where he was evidently supposed to have confederates? The sensible thing surely would have been to go to London with Frieda and to ask Marsh or Morrell what he should do to show his innocence. But Lawrence was in a mood both of depression and defiance, and felt all his former friends were dropping away. *Women in Love* was refused everywhere; he knew that his "philosophy" was virtually unsaleable; and after his former experience he could not have hoped much from the new volume of poems, *Look! We Have Come Through.* During 1916 nothing of his appeared in periodicals except one poem, and it was some way into 1917 before *Poetry* (Chicago) issued poems and *The English Review* resumed publication of his prose. Indeed, in those days he had little heart for writing, so acute was his feeling of oppression and of persecution. It was a very bitter moment for him, in January 1917, when he carried the packet containing the passports to "the tiny post-office in the hamlet" through fields where "there was a thin film of snow, like silver," among the huge boulders on the moor.

As he walked through that sad winter landscape he felt "like a ghost walking in a strange land of death", and "as if he *had* left his country: and that was like death". And of course all this emotional suffering had been quite useless. He went through all the agony of parting, of forcibly tearing himself away from the England he loved so much. And it was all quite useless. The Foreign Office simply kept the passports, and contemptuously returned no answer to his application.

The situation at Tregethern became worse. Official suspicion strengthened, and in turn was strengthened by the suspicions of the neighbours. The Lawrences were supposed to be signalling to German submarines if they tarred the chimney against a leak, or when Frieda hung out the washing. Hints and warnings were dropped to him by the more friendly neighbours, but he refused to listen to them, standing on what in his naïveté he imagined were his civic rights. That spring was "a curious interval" for him. Outwardly he busied himself with planting and working on his garden, and by writing his *Reality of Peace.* Inwardly he felt as if "the skies had *really* fallen", and persuaded himself that therefore the war would soon be over. At one time he thought that "if we have to stay here, I too shall become a farmer". Sometimes he longed to preach, to hold forth, like the people at "the peace demonstrations every Sunday in Victoria Park." Or he lapsed into other moods:

"I lay on the cliffs and watched the gulls and hawks in the perfect sky. Already the pigeons were cooing and it was warm as summer. I feel I don't know where I am, nor what I am. This is somnambulism or a trance."

When, in April, Frieda went to see her children, he remained behind, "sick to death of struggling in a cauldron of foul feelings with no mind, no thought, no understanding, no clarity of being." Unable to endure Frieda's absence and his own unhappy state of mind he went to the Midlands to see his family. On the way back through London he "suddenly collapsed with sickness", which he quaintly attributed to "the evil influence of aggregate London." Koteliansky rescued him and nursed him for two days, and when he returned to Zennor in a very "shaky" condition he found Frieda already there "laid up quite ill."

This was a miserable time for them both, with poverty and failure and suspicion seething all round them and the seemingly everlasting misery of the war. In his despair Lawrence began to slip back, almost to the condition of a farm labourer. He made friends with a farmer named William Henry, in *Kangaroo* infelicitously given the fictitious name of 'John Thomas' (Freudians, avaunt!), who helped him to plough and plant a whole field with vegetables. He liked the man's family, which doubtless reminded him of lost happy days at The Haggs, and he seemed more and more sinking into a mere farm labourer as he worked and talked with William Henry and his friends. Night after night he left Frieda all alone, to be with William Henry, for whom he had evidently developed one of his mystical-sensual *Bludbrüderschaft* relations. "In those days," writes Frieda blithely, "Lawrence seemed to turn against me, perhaps on account of the bit of German in me." The bit of German! But of course it wasn't that at all; it was the temporarily superior attraction of William Henry.

In the midst of all this he still kept in touch with public affairs. In view of his friendship with younger members of the family, Asquith's fall was naturally a great blow to him; and perhaps because he was beginning to dislike the Cornish, he was enraged at England being ruled by Lloyd George, a Celt. He even passionately asserted that "all Jews, and all Celts, even whilst they espoused the cause of England, subtly lived to bring about the last humiliation of the great old England."

Yet through all this he never lost sight of or failed to find delight in the wheel and change of the seasons. As the summer of 1917 drew nearer he watched the gorse as it "blazed in sheets of yellow flame", while the blackthorn was "like white smoke" filling the valley. As the sun seemed to roll down the sky towards its setting "in a flood of gold" he was rapt in ecstasy, feeling that he "would not be astounded to see the cherubim flashing their wings and coming towards us." Yet the practical work of his gardens was done and well done, and he boasted to Murry of his pansies and fuchsias as much as of his long lines of spinach and peas and beans. After an interval they had resumed correspondence, though on Lawrence's side the intimacy was not renewed as it had been nor the trust. He told Murry that "philosophy interests me most now —not novels or stories. I find people ultimately boring." But Murry's efforts at conciliation and renewal of affection were rejected: "You shouldn't say you love me. You disliked me intensely when you were here, and also at Mylor."

He was quite aware that the "philosophy" would bring him little or no money, but he was prepared to shift that responsibility to higher quarters—"I can't be bothered, the Lord will have to provide." More than ever as he brooded over strange symbols and emotions he became influenced by the ancient Cornish landscape and the "subtle, furtive Celts". Sometimes they seemed to carry him beyond the realms of sanity. Curiously enough it was again his *Reality of Peace* which (as with the snake episode at Greatham) seemed for a time to unbalance his mind. He had been re-casting this "philosophy" as he retyped it, he wrote Catherine Carswell, when "suddenly I felt as if I was going dotty, straight out of my mind, so I left off." The experience impressed him so unpleasantly that after talking of other things he added a postscript: "I'm sure the war will end soon. I wonder if I *am* a bit dotty?"

Dotty or not, he continued to be imprudent in parading his "irritable opposition" to war. When Edward Marsh in the midst of official duties found time to send him a 'Georgian Poetry' cheque and a hope that he was "flourishing", Lawrence retorted that he "would like to flourish a pistol under the nose of the fools who govern us" with some pointed references to "time-keepers and time-servers". He talked in the same strain to the labourers, urging them on in their loathing for military service. A ship was torpedoed off the coast, and sly questions showed that he was supposed to have something to do with it. Irritated by the absurdity he became more instead of less reckless, ostentatiously singing German songs after dark, though he knew or thought he knew "coast watchers" were lying outside hoping to hear treason.

Obviously if he sometimes sat at home singing German songs with Frieda, he cannot have spent every evening with William Henry. Yet when William Henry made a remark which showed he had noticed that Lawrence was reverting to a labourer, he was half pleased but half "rebuked". For he had not abandoned intellectual pursuits. While he worked in the fields he also worked at home on his essays which became *Studies in Classic American Literature.* He perpetually buoyed himself with hopes that the war was just about to end, whereupon he would go to America and give them as lectures. As for books—"there seems to be nothing but futility in writing nowadays."

They were not wholly out of touch with the great world. There arrived a number of "herb-eating occultists who fast or eat nettles" and also apparently the Lawrences' food, while they "made most dreadful fools of themselves at St. Ives". Possibly it was from them that Lawrence learned of *Isis Unveiled* and similar books of an occult kind which he certainly read though he did not think them "*very* good". Later there came to live not far away a musical friend of Heseltine's, Cecil Gray, who introduced them to the songs of the Hebrides, about which he was enthusiastic. Gray lived at some distance, and the advantage of this instantly struck Lawrence, so that in a contemporary revival of Rananim he placed even such close friends as the Carswells at a distance of "one and a half miles". After a brief but unhappy marriage Heseltine had returned to Cornwall and for a time "re-established friendly relations with Lawrence", being of course then unaware of the caricature of himself in *Women in Love*, though at some time before publication Gray read the manuscript and told him. Curiously enough, it was Gray who unintentionally brought to a head all the suspicion and hatred which Lawrence had unconsciously created around himself.

The Lawrences were invited to spend a week-end with Gray at his house, "Bosigran". After dinner (according to Lawrence) there was "something wrong with the mood" and he "sang to himself, in an irritating way, one German folk song after another, not in a songful, but in a defiant manner." At last this got on Gray's nerves and he asked Lawrence to stop. In "the tense and irritable silence" which followed, there was a banging on the door, and "a lieutenant with three sordid men" came in announcing that a light had been shown at one of the upper windows. It seems that there was an uncurtained window on the upper landing which the housekeeper had passed with a lighted candle on her way to bed. The explanation was not accepted. the trifling episode was reported as a breach of wartime lighting regulations, and Gray was insulted and fined twenty pounds.

Here at last was the concrete evidence against Lawrence which had been lacking. Apparently only a few days later their cottage was searched in their absence, and next morning the Lawrences were visited by an army officer, two detectives and a policeman. Notebooks and papers were confiscated, and he was handed an official order from the "competent" military authority ordering them both to leave Cornwall within three days, forbidding them to remain in any part of Cornwall, with peremptory instructions to report to the police within twenty-four hours of reaching any new destination.

Before leaving Cornwall, Lawrence "made a great fire of all his old manuscripts." What was then lost we shall probably never know, but it is a natural inference that in this fire perished his own copy of 'The

Goat and Compasses', the lost chapters of *The Reality of Peace* and possibly a number of poems. This destruction of his work was the natural reaction to the shock of this expulsion order, which, as Frieda tells us, "changed something in Lawrence for ever." The mere memory of it five years later was so painful that he "trembled helplessly under the shock".

They travelled to London by a night train, full of soldiers and sailors on leave howling the same dismal "war songs" he had heard on the Bodmin journey, though he now thought "a bitter irony" had taken the place of sentimentality. As for Lawrence, he sat in the train "feeling that he had been killed: perfectly still, and pale, in a kind of after death. He had always *believed* so in everything—society, love, friends. This was one of his serious deaths in belief." Even the "iniquitous" and unjust prosecution of *The Rainbow* had failed to teach him, as this event did, how much he was hated in his own country, how implacably enemies sought to crush him.

They had far too little money to be able to afford hotels and restaurants, above all in a crowded war-time London of rising prices. A telegram had brought them a temporary refuge with Dollie Radford, who knew something of English liberty, having seen William Morris arrested for making a speech. But for Lawrence it was "prison and misery to be in other peoples' houses", and he grasped eagerly at the opportunity of somewhere on their own:

"The American wife of an English friend, a poet serving in the army, offered her rooms in Mecklenburg Square—very grateful indeed to the American girl. They had no money. But the young woman tossed the rooms to them, and food and fuel, with a wild free hand."

The Lawrences had the rooms to themselves for a number of weeks, and then the "poet serving in the army" most inconsiderately turned up on long leave. This caused a move first to a flat owned by some relatives of Gray's at Earl's Court, and then, after Christmas with his sister, to Dollie Radford's cottage in Berkshire. Possibly Lawrence did some writing during these troubles—he still had his wonderful power of detachment—but it is impossible to say what. At first Lawrence greatly disliked London, finding it a city of mere "factors, really ghastly, like lemures, evil spirits of the dead." But, much to his surprise, he also found he still had admirers and friends ready to help him in any way they could, though powerless to check the spy hunt. Then he began to feel himself "in some queer way, vitally active" and even London people seemed "to give back a strange new response."

Now he was no longer at all anxious to return to Cornwall but (apparently under the influence of his friend, Dr. Eder) formed a plan for transporting Rananim to the slopes of the Andes with a splendidly grotesque group of incompatibles, "Frieda and I, and Eder and Mrs. Eder, and William Henry and Gray, and probably Hilda Aldington, and maybe Kot and Dorothy Yorke." Gray must have been enchanted to hear (if he ever did hear) that he was contributing a thousand pounds to the expenses of the expedition. The "poet serving in the army" was rightly left to carry on his dirty work without hope of salvation.

Indeed, Lawrence had little liking for the military and no interest in their peculiar ways. I recollect that on one occasion in London during the war when he was shifting quarters he would not afford a taxi to carry his bags nor allow me to pay for it. I was in the delicate situation of a cadet just about to be gazetted, when the smallest breach of military insanity would have been fatal. Carrying bags in the street was at that time considered "unbefitting an officer and a gentleman . . ." altogether, what with fears of meeting an assistant-provost-marshal it was an agitating little trip for me, but Lawrence never noticed.

For some reason he was most indignant at being followed by the C.I.D., but who else would follow up a person suspected of espionage in war time? He was rather lucky not to be interned without further investigation. Some have thought that this C.I.D. investigation was a mere "story" due only to Lawrence's "hysteria"—Robert Nichols said so in print without apparently making any attempt at verification. I am positive this did happen because I met and had a long talk with one of these detectives. As I was in uniform we got on very well (he was in mufti but for his boots) and I had almost convinced him that the whole thing was a mistake when most unhappily we blundered into literary criticism and disagreed. Gray also saw one or more of these "followers" and unthinkingly mentioned the fact to Lawrence, who at once discovered "an atmosphere of terror all through London, as under the Czar when no man dared open his lips."

It is easy for us at this distance of time to treat this spy charge lightly and to realise that it was only the kind of injustice to the individual that inevitably must happen in the enormous upheaval of a great war. Lawrence could not see it that way. He was far too important to himself to realise that to the military he was just a routine case, informed against by the petty malice of petty enemies. He was outraged and rose to the height of indignant invective:

"I refuse their imputations. I despise them. They are *canaille*, carrion-eating, filthy-mouthed *canaille*, like dead-men-devouring jackals. I wish to God I could kill them. I wish I had power to blight them, to slay them with a blight, slay them in thousands and thousands." In another mood he merely remarked on the same situation, "this is getting a bit too thick." The comment depended upon which of the many Lawrences was holding the pen.

The early chapters of *Aaron's Rod*, though not published until April of 1922, contain a fictionalised account of the lighter side of these months in London wherein everyone who did anything to help him is mercilessly satirised. After Christmas, the Lawrences spent four months at Hermitage, Berkshire, in great poverty. They were so poor that, it seems, they were reduced almost wholly to a diet of oatmeal porridge. Certainly Lawrence gladly accepted a gift of ten pounds sent through a barrister friend, Monty Sherman, and would have accepted help from the Royal Literary Fund, if it had been available. He tried to raise a little money by putting together a small volume of his "war" poems, which after many delays appeared after the war. What was the novel "as blameless as Cranford", of which he had written one hundred and fifty pages by the middle of March 1918? It can only have been a first draft of *Aaron's Rod*, thrown together anyhow "under the dark cloud of penury" which also overshadowed the later American essays.

For some reason Rananim had already been transferred from the "slopes of the Andes" to the more accessible Italy, but already it was a much reduced and rather different party, for after the obligatory "Frieda and me" there were left only "you and Gertler and Kot and Campbell and anybody else you like." (The you was Sherman.) They were to have a house by the sea and "row and bathe and talk and be as happy as birds for a bit." It was, he thought, "owing to us". Sometimes he felt that the war would last "for ever"; sometimes he announced that "this particular war" was about to end at once. The thought gave him little encouragement—

"people won't alter and they won't die in sufficient quantities to matter." So the only thing to do was "to lapse along pleasantly with the days."

As usual, spring brought an immediate alleviation to the darkness of his moods. I observe in his *Letters* that when I sent him word that I was returning to the front he received the news with serene equanimity. Indeed he assured his correspondent (another totally exempted man) that "it is harder to bear the pressure of the vacuum over here than the stress of congestion over there" and felt sure I was "glad to go." He was reading Gibbon with much satisfaction because "the emperors are all so indiscriminately bad" (which is far from being the case), and another book on occultism which interested him but was "very antipathetic". But this good humour was all of the surface. Underneath he felt very different:

"My soul, or whatever it is, feels charged and surcharged with the blackest and most monstrous 'temper', a sort of hellish electricity."

10

THE Radfords needed their Berkshire cottage in May of 1918, so once more there was the problem of where to go. Perhaps in part because it was still militarily-forbidden fruit Lawrence now rather pined to go back to Cornwall, but his sister Ada—who through all these troubles and pseudo-disgraces stood nobly by him—found a bungalow at Middleton, in Derbyshire, and offered it to him rent-free. He had come to like the appropriately named Hermitage in spite of the fact that Army lumberers were fast destroying its woods for duck-boards and pit-props, and felt regretful at the thought of leaving. On the evening of the Sunday before they left he took a long walk, gathering large cowslips "whose scent is really a communication direct from the source of creation—like the breath of God breathed into Adam", and in the woods came on the body of a dead owl, "a lovely soft warm-brown thing" which seemed to have a symbolical meaning for him too elusive for expression.

When they reached Middleton he found the bungalow stood "in the darkish Midlands" on "the rim of a steep deep valley, looking over darkish, folded hills." He fancied the place was the very navel of England, and though it was so near his own old home he felt like Ovid in Thrace, "very lost and queer and exiled." In reality he was marking time, hoping the war would suddenly end, and trying to recover from his indignant rage at being expelled from Cornwall and shadowed by detectives. While the war lasted there was little hope for his work, and he still existed chiefly by "precarious borrowing" eked out by the sale of a few pieces to periodicals. At no time was there much hope for the "philosophy" on which he had spent so much time and energy, and indeed much of it was not published until after his death. He knew perfectly well that it missed both the general public and the specialist public of people with a philosophical education; and there is a wistful naïveté in his appeal to Donald Carswell:

"I wish you would read the essays I left with Catherine. You will say I repeat myself—that I don't know the terms of real philosophy —and that my terms are empty—the empty self—so don't *write* these things to me, I know them beforehand, and they make me cross. None the less, read the essays and see if you find anything in them."

Part of August 1918 was spent with the Carswells in the Forest of Dean, and on Donald Carswell's suggestion Lawrence wrote some rather *ex-cathedra* articles on Education (they will be found in *Phoenix*) for *The Times Educational Supplement*, which prudently declined them. He worked on his unhappily-titled *Movements in European History*, and wrote some "bits of poems" which were published in *Poetry*. More hopeful even was the fact that he had finished his American essays, which began appearing in *The English Review*, and turned back at last from essays and "philosophy" to the short story. About this time he developed his preference for the novelette or short novel or long short-story, for he then began work on 'The Fox'. Another story, a real short story, of that year was 'Wintry Peacock', suggested to him partly by a dream and partly by a heavy snowfall later on, in the winter. He dreamed he saw a bird falling to earth, "a young peacock, blue all over like a peacock's neck, very lovely", and it kept calling out, and suddenly a woman came running from a cottage and took the bird from him, saying it would be all right. Such was the dream out of which he built his story.

Another story, 'The Blind Man', had come to him during his visit to the Forest of Dean. Mrs. Carswell, to whom we owe this piece of information, does not say if it was suggested by any real episode. Her description of the Lawrences on their arrival gives a startling image of the poverty to which they had been reduced by the war and the malice of his enemies. Frieda was dressed in a bright-patterned but very cheap cotton frock. Lawrence was wearing rope-soled shoes without socks, an old panama hat, an old green and red striped blazer and his old grey flannel trousers. Both main garments were so shrunk with age and repeated washing that his wrists and ankles stuck out, and he cheerfully volunteered the information that as this was his only pair of trousers he had to wash them at night when he went to bed and hope they would be dry in the morning. It was like Lawrence to feel much aristocratic displeasure when the country copulatives showed their amazement at his appearance.

He was happy on this holiday and the change and companionship did him good. The Carswells, who of course at that time knew only of his outward troubles and little of the extremities of emotion he had gone through during the war, must have felt very hopeful when they bade him good-bye. But a new blow awaited him only a very short time after his return to Middleton. On his birthday, 11th September, he received a fresh notice to report for medical examination, and found his "own Midlands" a good deal harsher and more intolerably "official" than Cornwall or London. The moral atmosphere of the medical-board room was "full of an indescribable tone of jeering, gibing shamelessness." Lawrence watched them secretly amusing themselves with the clumsy antics of a heavily-built coal-miner who did not understand what he was told to do. After Lawrence had reported having pneumonia and consumption he was sent to an examiner who first turned his back for several minutes, and then snapped: "Yes. What have you to say?" Lawrence told him and gave the dates of his pneumonia; and then, "in a tone of sneering scepticism", the man said: "What doctor said you were threatened with consumption? Give his name." He was then sent to another, "a chemist-assistant puppy" who made him bend forward with his legs apart and kept him so while various jokes were passed among the gentlemen. "They had exposed all his nakedness to gibes. . . . So he cursed them in his blood, with an unremitting curse."

They marked him "Fit for non-military service", a grade which he "knew" would have permitted them "to seize him and compel him to empty latrines in some camp." As he wrote to Cynthia Asquith about them: "It kills me with speechless fury to be pawed by them. They shall *not* touch me again—such filth." In his anger he determined that he would not remain in the Derby Military Area, "neither would he report, nor give any sign" of himself. So, in desperation they packed and made their way once more to the Hermitage cottage.

Fortunately, this happened but a few weeks before the end of the war, but those autumn weeks of late 1918 were hard. "There was hardly any food," but they did not mind. He and Frieda, alone together, were "wonderfully happy again", going out into the autumn woods "gathering the little chestnuts and the last few bilberries."

At twilight, when the lumbermen had gone, Lawrence "went with a sack to pick up the unburnt faggots and the great chips of wood the axes had left golden against the felled logs. Flakes of sweet, pale gold oak. He gathered them in the dusk, along with the other poor villagers. For he was poorer even than they. Still, it made him very happy to do these things—to see a big glowing pile of wood-flakes in his shed—and to dig in the garden, and set the rubbish burning in the late, wistful autumn—or to wander through the hazel copses, away to the real old English hamlets, that are still like Shakespeare—and like Hardy's Woodlanders."

Still his income was so very precarious that through Cynthia Asquith he tried to get a job under the Board of Education, hoping that the Minister, H. A. L. Fisher, might know something of letters and wish to help even a "genius"; but nothing came of it save a fruitless journey to London—not quite fruitless, for he saw Katherine Mansfield, with whom he was his old self:

"Lawrence and Frieda have been in town," she wrote Dorothy Brett in October 1918. "Frieda was ill and in bed but I saw a very great deal of Lawrence—for me, at least, the dove brooded over him too. I loved him. He was just his old, merry, rich self, laughing, describing things, giving you pictures, full of enthusiasm and joy in a future where we become all 'vagabonds'—we simply did not talk about people. We kept to things like nuts and cowslips, and fires in woods and his black self *was* not. Oh, there is something so lovable about him and his eagerness, his passionate eagerness for life—that is what one loves so."

A fortnight later came the Armistice. In the evening he and Frieda sat alone together and sang German folk songs, and Frieda wept. They felt as if they had been living Poe's pit and the pendulum for years, and had escaped just in time. But was it "in time"? "How strange peace is," he wrote, adding sadly, "Is it peace?"

Now, against Frieda's protests, he insisted on leaving the sheltered and fairly comfortable Berkshire cottage for bleak and wind-swept Derbyshire. But bitterly trained by necessity to avoid "the wickedness of waste", he could not bear to have rent paid in two places, and insisted on going back. It was so obviously foolish, when he was rested and easy at Hermitage, that it broke the peace with Frieda, who turned obstinate and would not go beyond London.

In those strange revolutions of his feelings which made him move in cycles of attraction and repulsion for those few people who remained in touch with him he had now, for one cause or another, satirised and dismissed all or almost all, including of course Murry and Katherine Mansfield. Even in late 1917 he had written: "I'm afraid I can't believe any more in Murry", but now he had come to a point when he wished to renew the intimacy. Possibly this explains why he had been so charming to Katherine Mansfield, using her as a means of linking up again with Murry, as this extract from a letter to her indicates:

"I believe tremendously in friendship between man and man, a pledging of men to each other inviolably. But I have not ever met or formed such friendship. Also I believe the same way in friendship between men and women, and between women and women, sworn, pledged, eternal, as eternal as the marriage bond, and as deep. Excuse this sudden burst into dogma. Please give the letter to Jack. I say it to him particularly."

And transparently, for obviously here he was with his "mulish obstinacy" and "hammer, hammer, hammer" once more leading up to *Bludbrüderschaft* and his unquenched longing for at least one disciple who would give unquestioning obedience. So much was Lawrence caught up by this revival of a perennial hankering that he added several postscripts, one of which read: "Don't you think you and Jack might come here for Christmas?" Either Katherine Mansfield was too ill or they had both grown wary of these winsome invitations, which resulted in oppressive proximities in small country cottages. In spite of a refusal he continued to write charmingly to her and sent her a yellow bowl, to which she responded with an inventive Christmas parcel.

"The barber cut my hair," he reported in one letter, "and shaved me bald and made me look like a convict, clipping my beard: also gave me an ensuing cold.—Courage, mon ami, le diable vit encore." It was far worse than a cold, being one of his recurrent lung inflammations, which he made very much worse by going out into the snow when it was "terribly cold and windy". Now, however, he could congratulate himself that he had failed to tie himself to a job, though he fretted at the delays in getting away from the England he felt had insulted him and at his inability, at thirty-three, to earn even a modest living by writing.

That winter of 1918–19 was very cold and snowy, and he should not have been compelled to spend it so far north, "laid up with a putrid disease—I have never felt so down in the mud in all my life." So much did the illness bring him down that Frieda grew alarmed and took him to his sister's home, where he was warmer and more comfortable and could be better nursed. Yet no sooner was he well than he insisted on getting out and about, in spite of the snow. Here once more is an example of how he never missed the beauty of the world:

"Yesterday I went out for a real walk—I've had a cold and been in bed. I climbed with my niece to the bare top of the hills. Wonderful it is to see the footmarks on the snow—beautiful ropes of rabbit prints, trailing away over the brows; heavy hare marks; a fox, so sharp and dainty, going over the wall; birds with two feet that hop; very splendid straight advance of a pheasant; wood-pigeons that are clumsy and move in flocks; splendid little leaping marks of weasels, coming along like a necklace chain of berries; odd little filigree of the field-mice; the trail of a mole—it is astonishing what a world of wild creatures one feels round one, on the hills in the snow."

That is from a letter (February 1919) to Katherine Mansfield, who, as he well knew, would be charmed with its lovely precise observation and delicate poetic touch. This was just about the time when Murry was appointed editor of *The Athenæum*, and one of his first acts as editor was to write to Lawrence to ask for contributions. Lawrence was quite childishly elated by this news, while the request from "the editor" made him feel self-important. He wrote back at once an almost deferential, certainly most conciliatory letter. He begged to be told exactly what was required, promised he would "try to be pleasant and a bit old-fashioned", and even offered to write over a pseudonym or anonymously if his name was considered too wicked and unpopular.

The first and only article published under this dispensation was signed "Grantorto" and was evidently written in Derbyshire just as a belated thaw melted the snow and showed the bodies of many birds dead of thirst and hunger and cold, while the first hesitating pipings came from the weakened survivors. The parallel with the war, the half-veiled symbolism gave him a chance he would not miss. It was a beautiful piece of writing, with such paragraphs as this:

"Such a long, long winter, and the frost only broke yesterday. Yet it seems, already, we cannot remember it. It is strangely remote, like a far-off darkness. It is as unreal as a dream in the night. This is the morning of reality, when we are ourselves. This is natural and real, the glimmering of a new creation that stirs in us and about us. We know there was winter, long, fearful. We know the earth was strangled and mortified, we know the body of life was torn and scattered broadcast. But what we are and what, it seems we have always been, is this quickening lovely silver plasm of pure creativity. All the mortification and tearing, ah yes, it was upon us, encompassing us. It was like a storm or a mist or a falling from a height. It was entangled with* us, like bats in our hair, driving us mad. But it was never really our innermost self. Within, we were always apart, we were this, this limpid fountain of silver, then quiescent, rising and breaking now into the flowering."

Probably the full meaning of this would not have been apparent to the casual reader at the time. Ostensibly it is a praise of spring after winter, a poetic thanksgiving for the thaw after the long hard frost; but it was really a declaration that Lawrence dissociated himself from the destruction and killing of War and identified himself with the new flowering of Life, "this limpid fountain of silver." It was a challenge, in spite of the promise to be "pleasant and a bit old-fashioned!" The next article sent in did not even have a mask of symbolism, and was rejected by both Murry and Katherine Mansfield as "embittered and angry". And this rejection led to

* In place of the meaningless "estrangled upon" of Phœnix text.

what Frieda called a "rumpus", which Katherine Mansfield tried to brush off as a joke when writing about it to Koteliansky.

Lawrence had been reading the *Fioretti of St. Francis* when he wrote that "pleasant and old-fashioned" essay-sermon about the birds; but his real mood in those days was as if he had "a child of black fury curled up inside his bowels", and it was beyond his strength to dissimulate further. Besides there was the irresistible pleasure of putting Murry in a dilemma, especially as we can now see from *Aaron's Rod* that Murry had been re-chosen in Lawrence's mind as the disciple who was to "submit" to the master.

It is possible that Lawrence had not expected this rejection, though of course his article broke the compact he had himself suggested; but when Murry went down to see him in the Berkshire cottage in the hope of putting things right Lawrence refused to be placated. Murry found him still (May 1919) looking "ill and weary" after his bad winter; and he talked very gloomily of industrial England "slowly and greasily melting like a dead thaw" and declared that the only hope was "a new life in a new country." Now this was certainly true for Lawrence, who felt so hopeless about his life in England that he had determined to leave permanently as soon as he could get a passport. But it was hardly likely to appeal to an editor of a literary journal which depended almost wholly on England for support. The breach was serious, and Murry virtually disappears from our story until the founding of the Adelphi in 1923.

The last words of Lawrence's last letter to Katherine Mansfield were: "I wish it was spring for us all." As each northern winter corroded his lungs, an annual disaster, he longed for spring. But "spring" now had a new symbolical meaning, it meant getting away from England and its cold unsmiling bureaucrats. What had he to stay for? They said his writings were obscene; had suppressed them and insulted him. He was a sick man, a consumptive; and because he did not flatter the ruling clique they conscripted him and bullied him. They said he was a spy and expelled him from his home; and yet forbade him to leave their jurisdiction. His so-called best friend had rejected his work for a feeble little literary paper. Why on earth stay with such people?

"It was a great mistake that we did not clear out in 1915 when we had those other passports. One must keep one's flag flying, and sail off for new scenes. Over here it really isn't any good hanging on or trying afresh. I'm sure I can make enough to live on in America, fairly easily."

Robert Nichols—much spoken of in those days as a poet—had then just returned from a lecture tour in America, and Lawrence wrote to him for advice about America. But then Frieda wanted to see her family before leaving for the ends of the earth; and anyway passports were still refused them. It was indeed Frieda who loathed the tyrannies of Europe and longed to go far away—Australia, America—but insisted she must see her mother and sisters first. And still the bureaucrats withheld their kind permission for Lawrence to move about the world into which he, like them, had been born. To pass the time, as he waited on their gracious pleasure, he busied himself with such literary jobs as producing a Foreword to a book translated by S. S. Koteliansky and corresponding with Douglas Goldring about the proposed production of his play, *Touch and Go*.

They received their passports after a brief delay of about a year, and then Frieda left first to see her family in Baden-Baden. Although Lawrence had been a German spy in England, it was thought well that as an Englishman he should not show himself in Germany; so, after selling his books and anything else he had, to buy his ticket, he started off for Italy, planning to live in a cottage of the Abruzzi in a place called Picinisco, in the province of Caserta.

By chance I was among the last persons who saw him just before he left. He had written to me from Hermitage offering to hand over the tenancy of his cottage, a valuable gift in that particular post-war scramble; and asked me to meet him in Red Lion Square at the flat of some friends to whom also he wished to say good-bye. I did not of course realise that he was expatriating himself, and nothing in his manner indicated that he was leaving for anything but a long trip abroad. He sat in his favourite position close up to the fire on one side, warm and hunched up, and talked gaily. He jeered at me, very properly, because I was writing for *The Times*; and much more acidly for going to the Poetry Bookshop—I did not know then that for some Laurentian reason he disliked Harold Monro. But in the main he was his friendly and unaffected self, without any bitterness or bravado about going away.

We left the flat together about ten, and I walked with him to his station on the Underground. It was only a short distance, but I had an opportunity to see for myself what hostility was created in a street mob merely by his appearance. I suppose it was the red beard, but then he had the look of being someone "different", with the innate superiority which is so much resented. Insulting remarks, to which he paid not the slightest attention, were called after him; and it was a relief to watch his tall slim figure with the firm quick tread descend into the lighted white-tiled entrance.

Much of what he was really feeling during those last days in England was incorporated in the chapter of *The Lost Girl* called 'The Wedded Wife'. In the next, 'The Journey Across', he has transferred to Alvina Houghton the emotion which swept over him when he looked back from the Channel steamer at the vanishing snow-covered cliffs of England:

"So they turned to walk to the stern of the boat. And Alvina's heart suddenly contracted. She caught Cicio's arm, as the boat rolled gently. For there behind, behind all the sunshine, was England. England beyond the water, rising with ash-grey, corpse-grey cliffs, and streaks of snow on the downs above. England, like a long, ash-grey coffin slowly submerging. She watched it, fascinated and terrified. It seemed to repudiate the sunshine, to remain unilluminated, long and ash-grey and dead, with streaks of snow like cerements. That was England!"

Photo: Edward Weston

D. H. LAWRENCE IN 1923

From photograph in possession of Mrs T. Luhan

THE LAWRENCES AT OAXACA POTTERY MARKET
The Indian is Rosalino in "Mornings in Mexico"
From photograph in possession of the Hon[ble] Dorothy Brett

PART THREE

THE WORLD'S REJECTED GUEST

1920–1930

Villa Mirenda Scandicci Florenz

4 May 1928

Dear Else

I simply can't write biographical facts about myself. Will you answer this Britton man if you feel like it: & if you think it is worth while. I have never heard of him. I must ask Curtis Brown if they have arranged with him about Islands.

You have heard by now that we are keeping on the Mirenda. I took down the pictures & we began to pack: but Frieda became so gloomy, that I hung the pictures up again & paid six months' rent. Not worth while getting into a state about. So here we are, just the same. And probably we shall stay till the end of the month, as the proofs

SPECIMEN OF LAWRENCE'S HANDWRITING
Letter to his sister-in-law Else.

1

THAT vision of his country, which he loved with so much bitterness, sinking over the horizon like a grey coffin, held many symbolical meanings for Lawrence. It was like those experiences of spiritual death and resurrection which he went through several times as illness gripped him and then he gradually returned to life. The symbol became a fearful reality to him. After his illness at Greatham in 1915, when on the one hand he seemed to be touching death and on the other insanity, he had written:

> "When I am trodden quite out, quite out,
> every vestige gone, then I am here
> risen, and setting foot on another world
> risen, accomplishing a resurrection
> risen, not born again, but risen, body the same as before,
> new beyond knowledge of newness, alive beyond life . . ."

And as he stood on the boat that cold winter day looking back he suffered in his heart that sensation of psychological death in life. He had always such courage in abandoning a worn phase of life, cutting free from a dead past, letting his old life drop away like a loosed burden, and turning to the new life with zest and curiosity. Those past five years in England had been a time of much suffering. It was not merely the endless battle of Blake's "mental strife" to which he was doomed, not even the humiliation of living so long on "precarious borrowing". There was no need to tell him that he gave far more than he ever received. What had hurt and insulted him beyond forgetting was the treatment given *The Rainbow*, and his various brushes with underlings in authority.

So he was leaving the England which he felt had insulted him, not then in anger, which flared up much later, but in grief, bewilderment and humiliation. To be conscious of great powers and to have them brutally ignored or denied must cause suffering; and at this time they had ceased even to admit that he was "a genius, but . . ." On the other hand we must recognise that he was himself confused about where his power really lay. He was too eager to under-value himself as a great artist, one whose influence on his fellow-men is gradual, indirect and enduring, in order to play the part of a sort of messiah, a leader imposing his will dogmatically on selected disciples. The fact that they almost invariably rebelled and had to be punished by pitiless caricaturing of themselves in print never seemed to warn him. There were certainly times also when he imagined himself as directing the destinies of nations in a practical way, for I do not think he was joking when he wrote that he wished he had been in Lloyd George's place at the Peace Conference—cocksure that he could know and do better. The reality was less splendid, and for the last ten years of his life he was destined to be an intellectual nomad who was always trying to fit in somewhere and never quite succeeded.

It is quite true that for some years after the war he was primarily an American writer, in the sense that for him publication in England was of much less importance. But he could no more cease to be English than he could cease to be a white man. Whatever he did and wherever he went he remained "fearfully English", defiantly so, "English in the teeth of all the world, even in the teeth of England." He exaggerated both the frustration of his "societal self" and the hardships of what he absurdly called his "savage enough pilgrimage". But it was true that he struck root nowhere, and did deserve Shelley's "the world's rejected guest" as a kind of epigraph.

In that November of 1919 England had gone sour and stagnant for him, and it was the sure instinct of the artist in him which took him away, though materially it seemed madness on so little money. Yet within a few weeks he had passed through experiences enough to fill two or three books. His plan of going to Picinisco was modest enough, but he had forgotten in five years that a hamlet in the mountains of the old kingdom of Naples would not be as placid and comfortable as a Berkshire village. Meanwhile he decided to wait in Florence or Rome, while Frieda made her way through a tangle of restrictions and frontiers to rejoin him.

For some reason he found Paris "a nasty city" and the French "unsympathetic". In northern Italy an introduction brought him the acquaintance of some wealthy English at Turin with whom he stayed two nights—"great luxury—rather nice people really—but . . ." He reproduced in his satirical way some of his experiences there in *Aaron's Rod*, to the great annoyance of his hosts, who talked about "a breach of hospitality" instead of being honoured at sitting as models for an artist in words.

What is interesting is that this brief experience fills close on fifty pages, and fascinating pages, of *Aaron's Rod.* Lawrence always wrote well when he was on the move and interested by new experiences. It is characteristic that the end of *The Lost Girl* and a large part of *Aaron's Rod* are staged in Italy, rather because Lawrence had just returned there than that the action of either of the books imperiously demands it. If he had gone to Liberia or Iceland, instead of Italy, he would have taken his characters there just as readily and, no doubt, just as entertainingly. The only reason given for Aaron's so suddenly leaving London is that it "got on his nerves"! In such a plight a penniless musician out of a job with a family to support naturally would go to Italy, and be entertained by "fearfully wealthy" British.

Norman Douglas, in his pamphlet on Lawrence and Magnus, made efforts to pump up moral indignation at this breach of hospitality. Of course we all know how sensitive Douglas is to fine moral points and how much his sensibility must have suffered at Lawrence's outrageous behaviour to people who were, I believe, unknown to Douglas until he began collecting "evidence" for his disinterested little work. I must say I rather enjoy the thought of the penniless but cocky poet refusing to be impressed by "security and bank-balance and power" and standing up "for naked liberty". Lawrence blames himself even for his mild concession of deferring to his hostess and not retorting her patronising reproofs, which were "like vitriol in his ears" when he stood alone in the middle of his "blue silk bedroom . . . grimacing to himself". At that moment he felt as if:

". . . he had dropped his mask on the floor, and broken it. His authentic self-describing passport, his complete and satisfactory idea of himself suddenly became a rag of paper, ridiculous. What on earth did it matter if he was nice or not, if his chin was normal or abnormal?"

From Turin Lawrence moved on to Lerici, staying for a night at the same hotel where he had been with Frieda in September 1913. He would of course have found some of his friends among the peasants of Fiascherino, though Elide had died; and probably picked up any remaining note-books and other small property. From there he took the train again, and landed in Florence "on a dark, wet, wintry evening in November." At Cook's he found a note from Douglas directing him to a cheap pension looking over the Arno. Installed in the same pension and on terms of close intimacy with Douglas was another man of about forty, "very pink-faced and very clean, very natty, very alert, like a sparrow painted to resemble a tom-tit." This was Maurice Magnus.

While Frieda was struggling to make her way through the post-war chaos from Baden-Baden to Florence, her husband lived in this pension and amused himself with the comedy of his acquaintances. After years of penurious rustication Lawrence found a great stimulus in the company of Douglas, with whom "he could not help being charmed. The other man had a certain wicked whimsicality that was very attractive, when levelled against someone else, and not against oneself. He must have been very handsome in his day, with his natural dignity, and his clean-shaven strong square face." Nobody was better equipped than Douglas to knock on the head Lawrence's pruderies and puritanisms and habit of holding forth. After the bloodless abstractionism of Russell and Murry, a course of Douglas —whose sole object was to live and to enjoy life—was most salutary.

Magnus was another matter, an entertaining little adventurer in his way, but a rather dangerous threat to other people's pockets. But he supported by opposing Douglas's pungently witty cynicism, excellent discipline for the school-master in Lawrence, who was thus forced to listen to a discourse of unabashed hedonism in a *trattoria* over a jugged hare and Chianti. During the dismal war years the adventurer and artist in Lawrence had gone astray in a theological wilderness. Now he came through Douglas in touch with life again.

Florence itself, outwardly untouched by war, was itself a stimulus of beauty after drab repression and ugliness. Arriving just as the rain was breaking a long drought, Lawrence had the good fortune to see the Arno for the first time a rare jade-green as it slipped silently under the arches of the old bridge. He liked the market-town side of its modern existence, the hand-carts rattling over the beautifully laid stony streets, the great white Tuscan oxen in the farm-carts "shouldering one another affectionately" as they slowly hauled, and the horses "in great brilliant scarlet cloths, like vivid palls".

He delighted in it so much that when at last Frieda arrived at four o'clock in the morning he insisted on taking her at once for a drive to see Florence by moonlight. He liked Florence, he told her, because you could still see it had been a capital of true culture, because of its "native sombreness and intensity" and because it was "a town of men". Of course it is true that most of the statues in the piazza are male nudes; but might they not have been put up for the women, as in Paris statues of naked women are put up for the men? Not in Lawrence's view. They were male nudes put up by men for men. So he, who at one time or another totally rejected off-hand Assisi, Rome and Paris, took Florence to his heart because his first morning there happened to be market-day ("all, all men", as farmers usually are) and its naked statues were male.

Why then did he not stay? Probably it was lack of money which sent them south, through Rome which was summarily dismissed as "vile", to the "farm" which had been lent them. Just how remote Picinisco then was can be known only from Lawrence's narrative. From the railway station of Caserta a shabby rickety bus took them interminably up and down mountain ridges in chilly darkness. They had to get out at "an old unfinished market-town" where the buildings were "nipped between high rock faces". There they bought a few provisions, piled the baggage on a donkey, stumbled through the vast stony bed of a dry torrent, crossed a stream on a single plank, and "climbed unfootable paths".

There at last was Picinisco, "staggeringly primitive". The farm was a fair size, but one room was occupied by a wine-press, and others were used for storing wine and maize in piles of orange-coloured cobs. The kitchen was huge, bare, barrel-vaulted, with ice-cold stone floor and iron-barred windows. Chickens in the day-time strolled in and out, and the donkey left his droppings on the door-step. Cooking had to be done over a wood-fire in a "great, dark open hearth", where Lawrence blew up the flame through an old iron tube "with a winged foot to stand in the ashes". There were only two cups, two glasses, one saucer, one teaspoon. Meals had to be eaten from their knees, "gipsy-fashion".

But the cold! Up there in the Abruzzi they were surrounded with snow-peaks "glittering like hell". The river was icy cold and rushed by "pale and fizzy with ice". The air itself "had a tang of ice". They were fifteen miles from a railway station, a mile and a half from the nearest shop, and even to get letters Lawrence had to scramble up "an accursed goat's climb of about eighty minutes, to the god-lost village of Picinisco." Yet Frieda found the courage to say that she thought it was "fun", and for a day or two Lawrence seriously thought of buying a few of the missing needments and trying "to settle in". The place itself was marvellously beautiful, even to the local costume, with the men in sandals and "white swathed strapped legs", and the women "in sort of Swiss bodices", white skirts, full sleeves, and in one village with head-dresses of goffered linen "with an odd shell-pattern". All in a setting of savage unspoiled mountains.

Alas, it was really too primitive, too "icy-mountainous", and after a few days of hesitation they fled to Naples and to Capri. They had experienced only the beginning of winter, and if they had persisted in remaining at Picinisco, Lawrence would probably have been seriously ill. Even so, an effort was needed to escape. On the Saturday before Christmas it had snowed all day long, and when they left on Monday they had to rise at half-past five, and walk five miles to catch the bus to take them to Cassino. They caught the afternoon boat from Naples to Capri, but a storm blew up, and it was long after dark when they reached the Marina Grande of Capri, where in those days passengers had to be taken off the ship in rowing-boats. In the heavy sea the small boat "almost hopped" on to the deck and then "fell back into an abysmal gulf of darkness, amid yells unparalleled even in Italy." They had to spend the night rolling at anchor off Sorrento—"the Italians *were* sick: oh dear!"—until in the red sunrise they returned to Capri and were thrown "like sacks into the curvetting boats."

Probably through the good offices of Compton Mackenzie the Lawrences found a furnished flat with two rooms and a kitchen at the top of an old house, looking on to the tiled dome of the church. Capri, Lawrence reported, was "one of the most wonderful places in the world", from the point of view of natural beauty and its vistas across the sea to the mainland and the island of Ischia. Unhappily the place was "covered with cosmopolitans" and "the utmost limit for spiteful scandal", so virulent that "Suetonius would blush to his heels if he heard it."

For some unexplained reason Lawrence wrote to Magnus as soon as he got to Capri; and of course got a reply by return. The letter made no direct appeal for funds, Magnus was too experienced a borrower for that, but he wrote in such a wistful tone that Lawrence could not help feeling, as he was intended to feel, that the man "was in trouble, in monetary difficulty." Now, in the two months since he had left England there had been a great improvement in his own finances and prospects, and he was by no means so poor as he asserted. Probably he did leave England with only nine pounds; and his pocket was certainly picked in Florence. But by early February 1920, he had sold the American rights of *The Rainbow* and was making arrangements with Martin Secker for several books in England. Already he had been able to pay back money advanced by Pinker (including, I believe, some which had come from Bennett) and still had one hundred and five pounds to his credit. At Christmas Amy Lowell had sent him a hundred dollars. Catherine Carswell had insisted on handing him fifty pounds from a literary prize of two hundred and fifty pounds she had won. Lawrence held this as a reserve, but burned the cheque on the 31st May. In his Magnus narrative Lawrence asserts that at that very date he had "only sixty pounds" in the world. His own diary shows that he had in fact a credit of one hundred and seventy-one pounds, with money still to come to him from Secker, with whom he had just signed agreements.

Such were the facts. But if Lawrence had been worth ten or twenty times as much there was no reason why he should give any of his hard-earned money to a mere acquaintance like Magnus, a scribbler of no literary merit who would have been utterly forgotten by now but for his association with Lawrence and Douglas. Now Douglas has himself told us that he made the acquaintance of Magnus in 1909 owing to the fact that Magnus came and begged some money from him, a total stranger, which suggests already both a plausible manner and practice. He had certainly not dropped the habit of "borrowing" in the ensuing decade. In his whimsical way Douglas was in the habit of describing people poorer than Lawrence as "rich as Croesus", while he pathetically wished he had "their income as his capital." He may unintentionally have led Magnus to think that Lawrence was fairly well off, but frugal from avarice; and it was a fact that Lawrence was then on friendly terms with Mackenzie, one of the most successful writers of the day. What I cannot understand is how Lawrence, so frugal and careful and unwasteful, could have fallen to the wiles of a begging letter from Magnus; still less why he visited Magnus a little later at the monastery of Monte Cassino. Magnus must have had some special attraction for him.

At all events Lawrence at once responded by sending Magnus five pounds—remember he had only just emerged from the "precarious borrowing" stage himself—and after a delay due to illness started for the Benedictine monastery on the 19th February, 1920. His description of his stay there is now famous, and evidently the then undestroyed age-old religious site made a very deep impression on him:

"I looked down on the farm cluster and the brown fields and the sere oak woods of the hill-crown, and the rocks and bushes savagely bordering it round. Beyond, the mountains with their snow were blue-glistery with sunshine, and seemed quite near, across a sort of gulf. All was still and sunny. And the poignant grip of the past, the grandiose violent past of the Middle Ages, when blood was strong and unquenched and life was flamboyant with splendours and horrible miseries, took hold of me till I could hardly bear it. It was real agony to me to be in the monastery and to see the old farm and the bullocks slowly working in the fields below, and the black pigs rooting among weeds, and to see a monk sitting on a parapet in the sun, and an old, old man in skin sandals and white bunched swathed legs come driving an ass slowly to the monastery gate, slowly, with all that lingering nonchalance and wildness of the Middle Ages, and yet to know that I was myself, child of the present. . . . To see all this from the monastery, where the Middle Ages live on in a sort of agony, like Tithonus, and cannot die, this was almost a violation to my soul, made almost a wound."

Well, that Tithonus-agony of the Middle Ages at Monte Cassino had not so much longer to endure, and was soon ended by the culture and humanitarian science of to-day. What is so difficult is to associate Magnus and his money troubles with these mystical experiences of Lawrence in the old monastery. He was haunted by the people he saw in and about the place:

"They were the old-world peasants still about the monastery, with the hard, small bony heads and deep-lined faces and utterly blank minds, crying their speech as crows cry, and living their lives as lizards among the rocks, blindly going on with the little job in hand, the present moment, shut off from all past and future, and having no idea and no sustained emotion, only that eternal will-to-live which makes a tortoise wake up once more in spring, and makes a grasshopper whistle on in the moonlight nights even of November."

That gives the quality of Lawrence's musings and feelings during his two days at the monastery, and it is a grotesque drop from those poetic heights to the thought that Magnus was there all along hoping to "touch" him for a little more money. Lawrence had foreseen this and rather cleverly provided against it by leaving his cheque-book at home and bringing only just enough Italian money to cover his own expenses. When he offered Magnus the beggarly sum of twenty lire, it was of course refused.

In Lawrence's diary jottings the note: "Returned from Monte Cassino" is under date the 21st February, so that his dates in the 'Introduction' to the *Memoirs of M.M.* are a little out, as his sums of money are. But two years passed before Lawrence wrote his account, and the marvel is not that he should have made trifling errors of this sort but that he should have remembered so much, so accurately and so vividly.

Even before he made the journey to Monte Cassino Lawrence had decided to leave Capri, that "stew-pot of semi-literary cats", and had been making enquiries about living conditions in Sicily. Before the end of the month the Lawrences left Naples by ship for Palermo, whence they travelled slowly by train along the north coast to Mount Etna and Taormina. On the lower and eastern slope of the mountain, outside the town, they found and rented an old farm-house called Fontana Vecchia, which became their head-quarters for the next two years.

2

THIS period in Italy, like the first, was one of artistic renewal and intense production, including the beginnings of his very original book of poems, *Birds, Beasts and Flowers*. When, after innumerable delays, Lawrence at last received from Germany the unfinished first draft of *The Lost Girl*, he was directly linking up with the creative period at Gargnano. That novel is a curious mixture of a book. Started deliberately in imitation of Arnold Bennett while *The Rainbow* was in a very early stage, *The Lost Girl* began as a pot-boiler which didn't boil. Lawrence re-wrote the whole book in Sicily with much more serious intent, but he was not able to obliterate that defect from the work. The last newest part is by far the best.

He worked fairly rapidly; for the final version was completed by July. *Aaron's Rod*, which had been started in 1918 and announced by its author as quite innocuous, was taken up and re-written by the spring of 1921. It is the most carelessly improvised of all his novels and is made up, like *The Lost Girl*, of two quite unrelated parts. The former is a satirical account of the people who had helped him in London after his expulsion from Cornwall; and Murry is introduced as 'Aaron' the flute-player. The scene where Lawrence-Lilley fusses over a sick Murry-Aaron is no doubt a reminiscence of an episode at Greatham, when Murry had arrived ill and Lawrence had insisted on nursing him. The scene where Jim Bricknall gets so angry with Lilley's taunts that he hits him in the chest did actually happen to Lawrence at the Hermitage cottage. But as soon as Aaron leaves England his adventures are Lawrence's adventures, and his rather vaguely drawn character becomes much more closely identified with Lawrence. When Lilley and Aaron are together, they sort themselves out a little, like a Doppelgänger. The end of the book is biographically interesting because it shows Lawrence once more returning to his dreams of "leadership", and making a determined bid to influence Murry into "submissive" discipleship. The plea and hint in these words cannot be mistaken:

"All men say they want a leader," Lilley says to Aaron. 'Then let them in their souls *submit* to some greater soul than theirs. . . . You, Aaron, you too have the need to submit. You, too, have the need livingly to yield to a more heroic soul, to give yourself. You know you have. And you know it isn't love. It is life-submission. And you know it. But you kick against the pricks. And perhaps you'd rather die than yield. And so, die you must. It is your affair.'

"There was a long pause. Then Aaron looked up into Lilley's face. It was dark and remote-seeming. It was like a Byzantine eikon at the moment.

" 'And whom shall I submit to?' he said.

" 'Your soul will tell you,' replied the other."

In addition to these novels he completed during this Italian period (December 1919 to February 1922), Lawrence wrote *Sea and Sardinia*, 'Mr. Noon' (posthumously published), *Fantasia of the Unconscious* (mostly in Bavaria), completed his 'Oxford Press' history, wrote the long Magnus 'Introduction', 'The Fox', 'The Captain's Doll', *The Ladybird*, short stories and poems, and began translating the Sicilian author, Giovanni Verga.

That would be a very considerable output for an author who was giving his whole time to work and nothing else, but during this period the Lawrences were often away on journeys and excursions. No doubt he could write as easily in a ship's cabin or a hotel bedroom as in his own cottage, while he gave no time to elaborate "plotting" and "construction". With him a story or a novel blossomed as spontaneously as a poem. In his case inspiration was a fact, and the moment it failed he stopped writing, as we have seen he did at some point with most of his novels. Then he would continue or finish off in a white heat of creative energy. The method obviously had its defects as well as advantages, losing in balance, finish, solidity what it gained in spontaneity, energy and zest.

Not all of this work was up to his best level, but it was, taken as a whole, a far finer blossoming of his genius than what had been produced during the unhappy war years. During those years he had said and written more than once that satire was the only possible form of literary expression. In February 1920 he wrote to a friend: "No, I don't want to do a satire. It all just dries up one's bowels." As a matter of fact *Aaron's Rod* is a very satirical book, and in his later work the satire becomes more and more venomous and destructive. On the whole this Sicilian epoch was happy, not perhaps as happy as pre-war, but as good as could be hoped. True, towards the end he felt very anxious to get away from Europe, but that was when he began to realise what offence he had given in England with *Women in Love.* When Heseltine began threatening a libel action, he noted characteristically: "Have a month of loathing everybody, particularly the *canaglia* of England. *Canaille!*"

The situation of Fontana Vecchia was one of very great beauty, and the house itself a great improvement on those the Lawrences had been forced to occupy in England. It was "a nice big house" with fine rooms and "a handy kitchen", standing on a steep slope in a large garden of almond trees and vegetables. During that spring of 1920, his first out of England for six years, the world seemed lovely to Lawrence as he looked out on it from "our own house above the almond trees, and the sea in the cove below." They looked towards the Ionian Sea, to the great mountains of Magna Graecia, "Scylla and Charybdis" and the straits to the north "glimmering like a changing opal" and "all the great blueness of the lovely dawn-sea in front, where the sun rose with a splendour like trumpets" and Lawrence rejoiced in it "like a madness". Below the garden there were pools of green water for irrigating the scented groves of lemon and orange trees; and as spring came on they found wild flowers, narcissus and anemones and cyclamens, "dawn-rose cyclamens, pricking their ears like delicate very-young greyhound bitches."

In April they accompanied their friends the Jutas to Syracuse for a few days, and again Lawrence was deeply happy in "the lovely, lovely days", when he found large purple anemones and blood-of-Adonis anemones and from the moving train saw the wheat "rising strong and green in the magical, malarial places". He delighted in Syracuse, "the round harbour where the Athenian ships came", the little fishing port where the boats still have eyes painted on the bows to see their path over the waves as you can see them on Greek vases, the painted carts which were famous long before Athenaeus wrote of them in the 3rd century, the modern Sicilian crowd where he saw Arabs in white burnouses mixed in with the Italians and Turks "in red fezzes and black alpaca coats" strolling under the hibiscus and the pomegranates, and the cathedral with "the grand Greek columns embedded there in the walls."

In the happiness of that spring, the first real after-the-war spring, he too was flowering with new poems:

> "Fig trees, weird fig-trees,
> Made of thick smooth silver,
> Made of sweet untarnished silver in the sea-southern air—
> I say untarnished, but I mean opaque—
> Thick, smooth-fleshed silver, dull only as human
> limbs are dull,
> With the life-lustre,
> Nude with the dim light of full, healthy life
> That is always half-dark,
> And suave like passion-flower petals. . . ."

"Well," says Lawrence, joking a little at his own expense, "into this lyricism crept the serpent." Of course it was Magnus again, an awful blot of pathos on the bright Syracusan spring—Magnus pleading for sympathy and help and protection and money, a good deal more money than Lawrence cared to give. According to Magnus it was all a tragical mistake. . . . Before meeting Lawrence at the monastery, Magnus had been staying in a hotel at Anzio—the best hotel, of course—and had given a cheque on his bank in America. Most unfortunately, the foolish and negligent people who should have paid money into his account had omitted to do so, and the cheque had been returned. Nor had he any other means of paying the bill. Of course Magnus meant to pay and would pay—as soon as he could sell some of his articles to American papers. Meanwhile the Anzio hotel people had grown impatient and had informed the police—in short, Magnus had only just had time to escape by a side path from Monte Cassino, leaving his bags and effects behind.

He had gone to Rome first, and then doubled back on his tracks making direct for Lawrence at Taormina, only to find him absent. For days Magnus had been waiting for him at Taormina, without a penny, but living of course at one of the most expensive hotels. All he asked was that Lawrence would pay his hotel bill and take him into his own home until Magnus could sell enough articles to pay his fare to Alexandria; or, alternatively, advance him thirty-five pounds on the valuable security of Magnus's manuscripts. Meanwhile—another little request—would Lawrence mind running up to Monte Cassino to collect Magnus's baggage? Apart from the expense and time involved, this meant either going to Palermo for the Naples boat (and back) or making that dreadful crawling train journey from Reggio.

It seems very curious that in so serious a plight Magnus applied to a comparative stranger and not to some of his real friends such as Norman Douglas, who in his panegyric of Magnus admits he had received much material kindness from the fugitive, whereas Lawrence had only been touched for a fiver. Now if Lawrence had cared to spend fifty pounds of the one hundred and seventy he had (of very hard-earned money) he could probably have paid for Magnus's stay in Sicily and have sent him to Alexandria—to start doing exactly the same sort of thing over again there. If Lawrence's net income that year exceeded three hundred pounds it would be surprising, and it was the first time he had been able to earn money since the war. He had at once paid off debts, and was sending money and presents to his father and sisters (who had helped him) and to Frieda's mother. Why on earth should he give a sixth of his year's earnings to a comparative stranger who was wanted by the police?

Lawrence himself realised on reflection, as soon as Magnus's plausible tongue was out of the way, that he would be a fool to make such a sacrifice. What he did do was to pay Magnus's hotel bill, give him a hundred lire, and Italian money for a seven-guinea English cheque Magnus had earned through Lawrence's recommendation. Magnus thereupon departed for Malta, wafting a gracefully worded note of thanks on his way, and Lawrence once more "breathed free", hoping to be rid of him. "But no!"

It so happened that Mary Cannan, wife of the novelist Gilbert Cannan, was at Taormina and very anxious to visit Malta. Apparently she could not go unaccompanied and begged the Lawrences to come, offering to pay their expenses; and Lawrence felt he could not refuse. Lawrence calculated that as Magnus had a week's start he would by then be established in the best hotel in Malta, to which needless to say the Lawrences and Mary Cannan did not aspire. But when they reached Syracuse, the port of departure, they found the ship had been held up by a strike of seamen, and Magnus was still there begging with tears for another loan to pay his bill in the best hotel in Syracuse!

Well, Lawrence paid again. And lo! on board ship they in the second-class beheld Magnus in the first talking with an officer of the Royal Navy, much to the annoyance and indignation of Frieda and Mary Cannan. When Magnus left the ship he bestowed "condescending nods" on the naval officer and Lawrence. And this was the end? By no means. Strikes held them longer in Malta than they had meant to stay, and Lawrence very unwisely allowed Magnus to give him lunch, and drove with him in a car belonging to one of two Maltese citizens Magnus had picked up through the Monte Cassino monks. These Maltese found Magnus a house, lent him furniture and advanced him fifty or sixty pounds.

Meanwhile, Lawrence was back in Taormina, hoping whenever he thought of Magnus that he had seen and heard the last of him. Suddenly one November day he received a Maltese newspaper with a marked paragraph:

"Yesterday the American Maurice Magnus, a well-built man in the prime of life, was found dead in his bed in his house at Rabato. By the bedside was a bottle containing poison."

The police had come for him about the Anzio cheque, and he had managed by a trick to get back into the house and take poison, leaving a note that he should be "buried first class". Magnus had bequeathed his manuscripts to Norman Douglas, but they were impounded by his creditors, who refused to trust them to Douglas, and instead begged Lawrence to try to sell them in order to pay off Magnus's debts. This, with Douglas's written permission, Lawrence did; producing the brilliant *Introduction* which is most unfortunately buried in Magnus's book. Such was the story which, cleverly re-edited, was published by Norman Douglas with the implication that through sordid avarice Lawrence had sent a wronged and pathetic Magnus to his doom. But as Lawrence said when replying to this pamphlet in a letter to *The New Statesman:* "As for Mr. Douglas, he must gather himself haloes where he may."

3

It was necessary to follow this curious story of Magnus to its unhappy end, and thus we have pushed on several months ahead. When the Lawrences returned from Malta to Taormina on the 28th May, the English visitors were fast dropping away, but Lawrence decided to stay on, enjoying "the lovely hot bright sun and sea" and "the cool breeze" which came off the straits of Messina. In the hot Sicilian summer he went often barefoot and in his pyjamas, stripping naked when he washed his clothes or when floors had to be cleaned.

On one of the hottest days he went out to get water and saw a snake glide into the stone trough, and it:

> ". . . sipped with his straight mouth,
> Softly drank through his straight gums, into his slack
> long body."

Lawrence had a great feeling for the beauty of snakes and almost, one might say, some of the antique reverence for their mysterious life. He thought the snake was poisonous, but still he felt "honoured" that it should drink of his water, though he was also a little afraid of it. But always the two selves in him, their split and endless debate! At the very same time he was feeling "honoured" he was telling himself that if he were not a coward he would kill the poisonous reptile. Meanwhile the snake, having drunk, "looked around like a god, unseeing, into the air" and slowly began to disappear into a hole. This released Lawrence from his bemused trance. He dropped his pitcher and threw "a clumsy log" at the snake, which was "convulsed in undignified haste . . . writhed like lightning" and was gone. Whereupon his mood instantly changed once more:

> "And immediately I regretted it.
> I thought how paltry, how vulgar, what a mean act.
> I despised myself and the voices of my accursed
> human education!"

It is not necessary to labour the point of that poem's self-revelation, even down to the repudiation of his "accursed human education". There is even an unconscious symbolism about it, for this was exactly how Lawrence behaved to people—"honoured" at first for them to drink at his life-fountain, and then suddenly flying into a moral rage and throwing "clumsy logs" at them.

That summer as Lawrence wandered alone about Italy he went on adding to the poems in this new style he had developed. The Lawrences had decided that Frieda should again go by herself to Germany since it was "still inhospitable to foreigners". Accordingly on the 2nd August they left Sicily "for Anticoli" (now Fiuggi) and remained away until the 20th October. Lawrence spent a little time in Rome and in Florence, where (or rather at Fiesole) he wrote his 'Turkey-Cock' and the 'Tortoise' poems which caused so much flurry when they were first published and now seem so simple and harmless.

He evidently intended to use the money he had to see more of Italy, for he certainly stayed also at Argegno on Lake Como, where it was "such fun having excursions into the hills and then on the lake". Either before or after he went to Venice:

"Abhorrent green, slippery city
Whose Doges were old, and had ancient eyes,
In the dense foliage of the inner garden
Pomegranates like bright green stone,
And barbed, barbed with a crown."

That sounds as if he had found Venice "repulsive", but the impression cannot have been permanent, for barely a year later he was writing to his friends there saying that he thought it so beautiful he would like to write a story or a book about it. He also must have visited friends at San Gervasio in Tuscany, for there he dates some of his mysterious, lovely and crudely perverse poems—'Pomegranate', 'Peach', 'Medlars' and 'Sorb-Apples', 'Figs', 'Grapes'.

Then in October Frieda rejoined him and they returned to Sicily, where the late autumn turned out very wet. Sicily, he wrote, was "like a land inside an aquarium—all water—and people like crabs and black-grey shrimps creeping on the bottom." His description makes one think of one of those very rainy wet Japanese prints with everyone huddled in straw coats. Lawrence consoled himself for the continued wet days by painting, copying an old Italian picture, and by "swotting Italian history" for an extra chapter to that apparently endless history book of his. Still the rain poured down on Sicily and Lawrence looked from his picture of Lorenzetti's monks on to the twisted almond trees in his drenched garden:

"Wet almond-trees, in the rain,
Like iron sticking grimly out of earth;
Black almond trunks in the rain,
Like iron implements twisted, hideous, out of the earth,
Out of the deep soft fledge of Sicilian winter-green,
Earth-grass uneatable,
Almond trunks, curving blackly, iron-dark, climbing
the slopes."

He could see the weird beauty of them, and again it is strangely like Hiroshige or Hokusai, but he fretted at his imprisonment in the house. Escape, escape! To move away became "an absolute necessity", but where to go? And he was still debating the point when suddenly the rain ceased, the sun came out, and Sicily was "so pleasant, magical." What point could there be in going away from "the sunny Ionian sea, the changing jewel of Calabria like a fire-opal moved in light; Italy and the panorama of Christmas clouds. . . . Etna, that wicked witch, resting her thick white snow under heaven, and slowly, slowly rolling her orange-coloured smoke." It was all beautiful, but "charged with terrible vibrations of wicked and beautiful electricity", and inhabited by "impossible Sicilians, a sort of sulphureous demons"—but so vastly preferable to "our sanctified humanity".

It was all so exactly what he had longed for in "sanctified" England, so of course the absolute necessity to go away became ever more absolute. He thought of Africa. He had been reading a book by a learned German, one of those convincing German books which conclusively prove an obviously false thesis, and had grown excited about Africa's "dark culture", far-off, dim, with plenty of space for the imagination. Tunis lies invitingly near to Sicily, and as he was pining for Africa the obvious thing was to go in the opposite direction. Not back to Naples or Rome or Florence, which had become "no good at all", but to the West, to Sardinia, which he asserted had never been caught "in the net of European civilisation."

Thus it was that he came to write that magical little book he called —or someone else called for him—*Sea and Sardinia.* Only he could have experienced so much in such a very short time, and certainly nobody else could have recorded the experiences in language so vivid and beautiful that they become part of one's own life. A book of about three hundred pages, written in six weeks, containing the experiences of two poor people—and it is magical. Really and truly, at this point the whole book ought to be quoted, for here is an exactly true account of ten days of Lawrence's life as he lived it with Frieda. Of course it is his life as a traveller, and not his home-life, and so is much fuller of extraneous experiences and the impact of the outer world.

It would be an impertinence to try to condense *Sea and Sardinia* into a concise narrative of the journey, and taking out passages is rather like chipping off a finger or an ear of a statue to show its quality. The book is full of him, as if still alive. At one moment an experience makes him predict, in 1921, that "as sure as fate we are on the brink of American empire"; and on the next page he is telling of a night spent in a stone-cold primitive inn high up in the wintry mountains, when their uneasy sleep was broken by the crowing of a cock; "throughout the night—yea, through all the black and frosty hours this demoniac bird screams its demon griefs"! Then they are travelling by bus in the lonely highlands of Sicily, and it stops to allow a religious procession to pass:

"The high morning was still. We stood on all this ridge above the world, with the deeps of silence below on the right. And in a strange brief, staccato monody chanted the men, and in quick, light rustle of women's voices came the responses. Again the men's voices! The white was mostly men, not women. The priest in his robes, his boys near him, was leading the chanting. Immediately behind him came a small cluster of bare-headed, tall sunburnt men all in golden-velveteen corduroy, mountain peasants, bowing beneath a great life-size seated image of Saint Anthony of Padua. After these a number of men in the costume, but with the white linen breeches hanging wide and loose almost to the ankles, instead of being tucked into the black gaiters. So they seemed very white beneath the black kilt frill. The black frieze body-vest was cut low, like an evening suit, and the stocking-caps were variously perched.

"After the men was a little gap—and then the brilliant wedge of the women. They were packed two by two, close on each other's heels, chanting inadvertently* when their turn came and all in brilliant, beautiful costume. In front were the little girl-children, two by two, immediately following the tall men in peasant black-and-white. Children demure and conventional, in vermilion, white and green—little girl-children with long skirts of scarlet cloth down to their feet, green-banded near the bottom: with white aprons bordered with vivid green and mingled colour: having little scarlet, purple-bound open boleros over the full white skirts, and black head-cloths folded across their little chins, just leaving the lips clear, the face framed in black. Wonderful little girl-children, perfect and demure in the stiffish, brilliant costume, with black head-dress! Stiff as Velasquez princesses! The bigger girls followed, and then the mature women, a close procession. The long vermilion skirts with their green bands at the bottom flashed a solid moving mass of colour, softly swinging, and the white aprons with their bands of

* A mistake, surely, for "negligently"?

brilliant mingled green seemed to gleam. At the throat the full-bosomed white shirts were fastened with big studs of gold filigree, two linked filigree globes: and the great white sleeves billowed from the scarlet, purplish-and-green edged boleros. The faces came nearer to us, framed all round in the dark cloths. All the lips still sang responses, but all the eyes watched us."

How long had he to take all that in? Five minutes? Surely not ten, for even a slowly-moving religious procession is soon past and gone. In that short time he took in and remembered not only the general effect of gorgeous moving colour, but exact details and shades of the brilliant clothes of children, women and men. He never made notes of such things, like Douglas with his tiresomely obsolete erudition, but trusted to the living imaginative memory. It is that which gives Lawrence his unique quality as a writer, this bringing a life experience to the reader not as a mere piece of fine writing but as a moment of heightened life shared. And underlying the purely æsthetic emotion is a poignant nostalgia, such as comes out in the Monte Cassino passages, for a way of life designed by artists down to the smallest detail giving dignity and meaning and beauty to even the humblest lives.

How many experiences might be given from this book alone—the landscapes, the dawns, the streets of old villages, the starry night skies at sea—there are scores of them. I pass them all over in favour of a totally different experience, enjoyed and transmitted just as vividly, which I recommend to those who believe or at any rate say in print that Lawrence had no sense of humour. It is the scene of the three socialists eating their soup in the village inn of Mandas:

"And they fell on their soup. And never, from among the steam, have I heard a more joyful trio of soup-swilkering. They sucked it from their spoons with long gusto-rich sucks. The *maialino* was the treble—he trilled his soup into his mouth with a swift sucking vibration, interrupted by bits of cabbage, which made the lamp start to dither again. Black-cap was the baritone, good, rolling spoon-sucks. And the one in spectacles was the bass: he gave sudden deep gulps. All was led by the long trilling of the *maialino*. Then suddenly, to vary matters, he cocked up his spoon in one hand, chewed a huge mouthful of bread, and swallowed it down with a smack-smack-smack! of his tongue against his palate."

It is not as anthology pieces that those and the scores of others in *Sea and Sardinia* should be read—they should be enjoyed as part of the living world, as moments from Lawrence's own abundant life. Long ago I wrote that being with him was like moving from an ordinary atmosphere into one of oxygen. Everything became more exciting and vivid. But he—and we—paid for this unique self of his by the existence of his antithetical self, perverse, destructive, hating, hateful, conceited as a gutter Lucifer. At the very time when he was writing all that lovely *Sea and Sardinia* prose he was brooding over his ever-disappointed ever-renewed longings for people, even one person, "to submit" to him as a leader, a messiah, a boss. In Taormina he met Mr. Nelson-Hood, who in Sicily was Duke of Bronte, and instantly despised him—"if I was Duca di Bronte in Sicily, I'd be tyrant of Sicily. High time there was another Hiero."

Only a few months later his power-longings were taking another and opposite line:

"If I knew how to, I'd really join myself to the revolutionary socialists now. I think the time has come for a real struggle. That's the only thing I care for: the death struggle. I don't care for politics. But I know there *must* and *should* be a deadly revolution very soon, and I would take part in it if I knew how."

A year or so later he was in Ceylon and promptly despised the Prince of Wales, whom he saw at a great night torch-lighted ceremony called a "pera-hera"—a "pale little wisp" looking the "pale fragment of a Prince" whose motto was "I serve" when it ought to be: "Serve me!"

> "I wish they had given the three feathers to me;
> That I had been he in the pavilion, as in a pepper-box aloft and alone,
> To stand and hold feathers, three feathers above the world
> And say to them: *Dient Ihr! Dient!*
> *Omnes, vos omnes, servite.*
> *Serve me, I am meet to be served,*
> *Being royal of the gods.*"

So Bonaparte is said to have felt when he looked at Louis XVI; but he was a man of action. Was it not Lawrence's worst error in life to think that because he had unique and very real power as an artist and a personality he was also entitled to the very different power of the man of action, the ruler, the messiah? Certainly the hope haunted him for years, and the inevitable frustration maddened and embittered him. As a matter of fact he mistook the very nature of power. An exceptional man longs passionately to change something, to achieve something, and power comes to him; but Lawrence wanted power for the sake of the sensation, being far too unstable to have any dominating steady purpose. To be Lawrence and want to sit on an elephant holding three feathers was a strange derogation —*il aspire à descendre.*

4

Lawrence's plans seem always to have been in a state of chronic uncertainty. Take, for instance, the first months of 1921. On the 14th January he made a private memorandum that he had decided to keep on Fontana Vecchia for another year. On the 22nd February he wrote to Robert Mountsier to ask him to investigate an available farm in America and to cable his opinion about it. And on the 2nd March Lawrence wrote another friend: "I have been planning to go to America", obviously not intending to go.

Whether these plans were serious or not they were suddenly swept away by a telegram from Germany to say that Frieda's mother was very ill and needed her at once. Now, Lawrence never liked being separated from Frieda, even in his worst tantrums, and so tried to persuade her that this telegram was "a trap". However, Frieda quietly made her preparations to leave, and Lawrence journeyed with her to Palermo and put her on the boat for Naples. The day after his return he was very disconsolate: "I sit in Fontana Vecchia, and feel the house very empty without Frieda. Don't like it at all."

What was to be done? Obviously emigration to America was temporarily out of the question, and he sat on gloomily in the empty house working to finish *Sea and Sardinia.* Then, as it was posted to his agent, he decided he could stand the solitude no longer and must go to Frieda in Germany. But not direct, she must not be allowed to score too obvious a victory. So he went to "the stewpot of semi-literary cats", Capri, and there made friends with two

American painters, Achsah and Earl Brewster. It was through them that the Lawrences eventually went to Ceylon, for Brewster was greatly interested in Buddhism and wished to study it at first hand. Lawrence did not altogether approve of this, and said to him:

"Can't you rest in the actuality of your own being? Look deep into the centre—to your solar plexus."

It was an inveterate habit with him at parting to bestow, unasked, some such disconcerting mandate or gnomic advice. Having puzzled Earl with this, Lawrence left ostensibly for Rome and Florence, but after a few days, as he afterwards admitted, he "went direct to Baden-Baden", which of course meant to Frieda. He found his Schwiegermutter, as he insisted on calling her, "much better, but shaky". Since her husband's death she had lived at the Ludwig-Wilhelmstift, an official residence for impoverished widows of high-ranking officers. Lawrence always behaved very politely to these old military ladies, who insisted on calling him Herr Doktor, and the Schwiegermutter lived in terror lest they should find and read one of his books.

She liked to spoil him a little, giving him tea with the delicacies he liked. Curiously enough at a time when Germany was supposed to be starving, Lawrence was writing to tell how cheaply and sumptuously they fared at their little Ebersteinburg inn, which was "so different from Taormina. Cheap too—thirty-five marks a day each—seventy marks for us two—about six shillings. Good food—good German sausages and beer, *good* Rhine wine, *good* whipped cream, and the first strawberries. No sausageless Nirvana: no! no!"

This was written to tease the Brewsters, vegetarians and budding Buddhists, to whom he added a lusciously provoking postscript: "Ah, the flesh-pots! We had asparagus (German, the best in the world), *strawberries*, and *Rhine wine* and *Roast Pork* for dinner! WHAT did you have?"

In those days he was finishing off *Aaron's Rod*, and at the very antipodes to the "serenity" and "happiness" and "way to security" and "profound and lasting friendship" with which Murry credited him when reviewing the book. Exactly at the time when Lawrence was ending that book he was vehemently declaring that "love doesn't exist, save as a word," and vowing "finally and for ever" that he intended to leave off "loving anything or everything or everybody." Warming up, he went on to assert that you can't kill the tiger-soul even if you kill all the tigers, for the slayer always takes on the nature of the slain, as "white America has taken on the nature of the red American". Far from being either "serene" or "profoundly friendly" Lawrence goes on in his vehement way:

"But the point is I don't *want* the tiger superseded. Oh, may each she-tigress have seventy-seven whelps. And may they all grow in strength, and shine in stripes like day and night, and may each one eat at least seventy miserable featherless human birds, and lick red chops of gusto after it. Leave me my tigers, leave me spangled leopards, leave me bright cobra snakes and I wish I had poison fangs and talons as good. I *believe* in wrath and gnashing of teeth and crunching of coward's bones. I believe in fear and pain and in oh, such a lot of sorrow."

It was just about this time (May 1921) that Selzer in New York published the first edition of *Psychoanalysis and the Unconscious*, which was naturally much disliked there. But these genial reflections on tigers were not provoked by the reviews of his book (they had not in fact reached him) but by Earl Brewster's praise of Buddha. Evidently Lawrence's verve was functioning well in those days. When, a little later, he wrote his so-called defence, *Fantasia of the Unconscious*, he indulged fully in his satirical vein. Nothing could be better than his humorous scorn of the social-scientific utopias so dear to the innumerable sentimentalists of Germany and England. He imagines a new German twilight sleep, "perfect and serene", and "into the sleeper are inculcated the most useful and instructive dreams, calculated to perfect the character of the young citizen at this crucial period, and to enlighten permanently the mind of the happy mother, with regard to her new duties towards her child and towards our great Fatherland." Thirty years ago that was a joke; now it is no joke, but the regulation twaddle of official clowns in clover.

For July and August of that year the Lawrences went to Austria and stayed at Zell-am-See, where they bathed and rowed on the lake, and also went for excursions to the mountains. Anyone who wishes to experience one of those excursions, in all its pleasant and unpleasant details, should read section XIV to the end of 'The Captain's Doll'. Of course, the autobiography is woven into a story, but at the point I mention Hepburn and Hannele evolve out of themselves and into Lawrence and Frieda with uncanny speed. He is displayed in a mood of uncommon cussedness and perversity, even for him, boiling up into a first-class rage with Frieda and a seething bubble of conceit, as he is the first to recognise—on paper:

"'You came to see the glacier and the mountain with me,' he replied.

"'Did I? Then I made a mistake. You can do nothing but find fault even with God's mountains.'

"A dark flame suddenly went over his face.

"'Yes,' he said. 'I hate them, I hate them. I hate their snow and their *affectations*.'

"'*Affectations!*' she laughed. "Oh! Even the mountains are affected for you, are they?'

"'Yes,' he said. 'Their loftiness and their uplift. I hate their uplift. I hate people prancing on mountain tops and feeling exalted. I'd like to make them all stop up there, on their mountain-tops, and chew ice to fill their stomachs. I wouldn't let them down again, I wouldn't. I hate it all, I tell you; I hate it'."

And, strange to say, for that moment he really did hate it, although almost at the same moment he was on his knees to the splendour and savage beauty of the mountains with their "great fangs and slashes of ice and snow" down to the "wonderful hare-bells, some big and cold and blue, like purple-dark ice" and others which had "little tufts of tiny pale-blue bells, as if some fairy frog had been blowing spume-bubbles out of the ice", and then the "many stars of pale-lavender gentian" and the yellow monkshood and the other monkshood which was "dark-blue, black-blue." Probably all the hating of the affected mountains came from the fact that Frieda was being too happy and carefree with her German friends, and he was almost chauvinistically jealous. He wrote a friend about Zell: "Everything is free and perfectly easy. And still I feel I can't breathe. Frieda loves it and is quite bitter when I say I want to go away. But there it is—I do."

So in a jealous rage he went fishing in the lake and addressed them in free verse:

"Fish oh Fish,
So little matters. . . ."

Which is profoundly true, but why make the important discovery known to senseless fish when it should be hammered into young people who still have time to enjoy life? Then, it seems, he caught a fish. I am told that there is a very considerable literature of angling, and that it is mostly from the point of view of the predatory and self-gratulating angler. Lawrence, awkwardly catching a lake fish like a schoolboy, is instantly aware of the fishy mystery of fish and muses thereon:

"I have waited with a long rod
And suddenly pulled a gold-and-greenish, lucent fish
from below,
And had him fly a halo round my head,
Lunging in the air on the line.

Unhooked his gorping, water-horny mouth,
And seen his horror-tilted eye,
His red-gold, water-precious, mirror-flat bright eye;
And felt him beat in my hand, with his mucous, leaping
life-throb.

And my heart accused itself
Thinking: *I am not the measure of creation.*
This is beyond me, this fish.
His God stands outside my God."

Once more "the sense of wonder", but how much greater to find the wonder of the living world in a fish than in wearisome Celtic legends and Valleys of Black Pigs and the elaborate hoaxes of the occult.

That summer of 1921 was the longest and hottest that had been experienced for a long time, some said for a century. At any rate it was very hot and very long. Now, considering the state of Lawrences's lungs, when excessive cold or heat or strain was almost certain to bring an attack of tubercles, you would think that having been surprised by the prolonged heat-wave on the side of a cool lake with snow mountains at hand, he would have stayed there, however much Frieda might have been enjoying herself. "But, no!" As he often boasted, he believed in self-discipline but not in self-control, and he could not control his jealousy of handsome young men with blue eyes, gold hair, hob-nailed boots and leather shorts.

Go he would, and go he did. At the very hottest part of the hottest year of this century he dragged Frieda and himself through the gehenna of the interminable railroad journey from Zell to Florence, second-class, in over-crowded trains, infinitely ill-organised. Self-pityingly he announced that he felt "battered by all the summer travel", and in August came to a temporary halt in a flat of sun-drenched Florence looking over the sun-shrunken Arno, with his bedroom "a crash-box over that great stone rattle the Via de'Bardi." In Florence he met the Carswells, who found him "restless, remote and even impatient". Once more he had begun to talk of leaving Europe.

Then they went south, to Capri, after "a rather lovely day in Rome". They found the Brewsters in Capri, packing up to leave for the East, and Lawrence talked of joining them in Ceylon. There was more in this than mere longing for adventure. During that summer Lawrence had been growing more and more perversely irritable, as comes out in that piece of dialogue from 'The Captain's Doll'; and the main reason was that the publication of *Women in Love* in England, in May 1921, had raised an amount of cold dislike and disapproval for which he was unprepared. The satirical portraits of the people who had been his closest friends in the war years had aroused anger and consternation. See how people drop off from his correspondence! Another group was due for dismissal in *Aaron's Rod*, and Murry especially had yet to experience the art of the short story in Lawrence's hands. Murry had attacked *Women in Love* with the rage of the caricatured. He said of the characters that "we remain utterly indifferent to their destinies"; and he said of Lawrence: "He would, if he could, put us all on the rack to make us confess his protozoic god; he is deliberately, incessantly, and passionately obscene in the exact sense of the word."

This was only a beginning. Lawrence and Frieda reached Fontana on the 23rd September, 1921, in "a whirlwind and rain", and found an accumulation of letters. That night, in addition to Murry's compliments, he read in a periodical called *John Bull* that *Women in Love* was "A Book the Police should Ban" and a "Loathsome Study of Sex Depravity Leading Youth to Unspeakable Disaster." Luckily, the editor of that paper, a creature called Horatio Bottomley, had already involved himself in a series of legal actions which eventually resulted in his serving a sentence of penal servitude.

There was more to come. The next letter was from Martin Secker, a little worried about these reviews, and telling him that Philip Heseltine was threatening an action for libel.* Since at least half a dozen other people could have done so with equal justification, Secker had some reason to feel uneasy. Then came a very cold letter from Lawrence's literary agent, saying that *Aaron's Rod* could "not be accepted", it was full of libellous matter. Small wonder that Lawrence felt "seedy and hateful". The post arrived and brought him "nothing nice; not one single word since I am back." Then he had "a month of hating everybody" and got into "such a hell of a temper" and wrote "such spiteful letters to everybody that now the postman never comes". He was even "so disagreeable" to a poor old Sicilian woman who came to help in the house that she "crept about as if a dagger was at her neck". Even the goat, he reported titteringly, "refuses to have her belated kid for fear I pounce on her." Of course none of this was due to his making enemies, but to the disagreeable constituents of the world:

"It is a world of *Canaille;* absolutely. Canaille, canaglia, Schweinhunderei, stinkpots. Pfui!—pish, pshaw, prrr! They all stink in my nostrils."

He was out-doing Carlyle in atrabilious vehemencies of disgust with his fellow creatures. Nothing would have induced him then to admit that he was in the slightest to blame. No, no; he was the injured one. All his life he maintained that *Women in Love* was his best, his favourite book, the one which contained the quintessence of his message to Mankind. And then, all of sudden, he would have a mood of abandoning this ferocious hatred of the *canaille*, and would feel very wistful and injured: "my heart and soul are broken, in Europe. It's no use, the threads are broken."

Almost all his old friends had gone; even Edward Garnett, to whom Lawrence owed so much, was dismissed in a peculiarly offensive letter. So he clung all the harder to his newer friends. He announced that "before March" he would accompany the Brewsters to Ceylon. He exhorted and held forth to the Brewsters by letter: "Let us pitch our tents side by side in the howling wilderness of these christian countries. Let us go from this Sodom of angels like Lot and Abraham, before the fire falls." Realising that this was a

* He was paid £50.

trifle vehement even for him, he added: "But seriously, let us agree to take a way together into the future."

At this moment there arrived a letter with a proposal which fitted in well with these projects of leaving Europe. A wealthy American woman, Mabel Dodge Sterne (now Luhan) had read parts of *Sea and Sardinia*, which had begun to appear as a serial in *The Dial* for October, 1921. She herself had grown weary of expensive fashionable life and had moved to what was then the remote little town of Taos, New Mexico, where she amused herself by studying the life of the Indians, defending their cause, and in building an artist's colony. Recognising the unique quality of Lawrence's writing in *Sea and Sardinia*, she saw at once that if he could be attracted to Taos he could and most probably would write about it as no one else was able to do. She therefore wrote to invite him to come and live there, and with American lavishness offered him, furnished, one of the new adobe houses and studios she was building.

This letter reached Lawrence on the 5th November, 1921. On the 2nd he had written to Earl Brewster that he didn't care where he lived; that people everywhere are "bloody swine—or bloodless swine", and consoled himself with the thought that at Taormina "at least I have a fair space of land and sea to myself." Still, he did not consider himself attached there, and if tempted could easily "splash my way to Ceylon." His diary jottings under date 5th November record: "Had a letter from Mabel Dodge Sterne asking us to go to New Mexico—to Taos. Want to go." That same day he wrote to her in his enthusiastic vein, almost promising—but not quite—that he would accept her offer and go to Taos. Oddly enough, in his various projects for removing himself he had already thought of New Mexico. In October he had written Brewster:

"My plan is, ultimately, to get a little farm somewhere by myself, in Mexico, New Mexico, Rocky Mountains or British Columbia. The desire to be away from the body of mankind—to be a bit of a hermit—is paramount."

But Lawrence would not have been Lawrence if he had come at once to a clear decision and had acted upon it without hesitation. He had scarcely posted his letter to Mabel Luhan when his inner uncertainty asserted itself, and a seemingly endless debate began. Should he go to Taos by way of New Orleans to avoid "that awful New York"? Or should he go to the Brewsters in Ceylon?

Or—happy thought!—why not stay on in Sicily? There was some difficulty about raising money for a long move. He had spent most of his English royalties on the various summer wanderings of Frieda and himself; and he did not at that moment know what money, if any, was due him from the United States. That difficulty was soon cleared. Within a few weeks he heard that in America he had upwards of $1500.00 and from England received the James Tait Black Memorial Prize of one hundred pounds for the best novel of the year—*The Lost Girl*, the worst he ever wrote. Another fifty pounds came from other earnings in England.

There was really nothing to prevent his making his long talked-of exit from Europe except his own chronic indecision and almost pathological self-mistrust. As a writer he had come to a natural pause after a prolonged burst of intense creative energy. He busied himself with finishing off 'The Captain's Doll' and *The Ladybird*, and began putting together the short stories which appeared in book-form in America in October 1922 under the title *England, My England*; wondering as he worked what he should do. At Christmas he went down with one of his usual lung illnesses, but recovery still found him uncertain and at last conscious of the absurdity of his indecision. On the 18th January, 1922, he wrote:

"We have made all arrangements to go to Taos, New Mexico. But we have booked no passage. Shall I come to Ceylon? Dio mio, I am so ridiculous, wavering between east and west."

Wavering he certainly was, for on the 21st November he had written Mabel Luhan: "I am persisting in my intention to come to Taos in January." On the 4th December he had written again to her: "We are persisting in the Taos intention." After the letter to Brewster of 18th January, he wrote on the 24th to Catherine Carswell:

"I have once more gone back on my plan. I shrink as yet from the States. Ultimately I shall go there, no doubt. But I want to go east before I go west: go west via the east."

He goes on to tell her about the Brewsters, and pities himself very much—he is "tired of the world" and "wants peace like a river." It is noteworthy that after the publication of *Women in Love* he seemed to give up hope of being on terms of intimacy with anyone from England, and turned to Americans as friends. But at last the wavering compass of his will settled in the direction of Ceylon and the Brewsters. On the 26th January Frieda was made to write a letter tactfully breaking the news to Mabel Luhan, which she did in these terms: "We were coming *straight* to you at Taos, but now we are not." The next day Lawrence wrote more apologetically and explicitly:

"It is vile of us to put off Taos for the moment. But I have a Balaam's Ass in my belly which won't budge, when I turn my face west. I can't help it. It just stubbornly swerves away in me. I *will* come. But I detour. I am writing to book berths on the *Osterley* from Naples, February 26th, for Colombo, Ceylon."

5

HOWEVER ludicrous his indecision, it was a tremendously important step for a poor man whose literary earnings were not large. No sooner had he made the decision and sent the ticket-money than he began to suffer the inevitable revulsion of feeling. He sat mournfully among the packed bags and wrote:

"My heart is trembling now, mostly with pain—the going away from home and the people and Sicily. We can always return quickly when we've had enough. I don't say no: I don't say anything for certain. To-day I go, to-morrow I return."

Was there ever such a weathercock of a man, or one more helplessly given over to self-torment? There he was on the eve of an adventure which he had longed for during years, would have envied as the height of luck and felicity if it had happened to someone he knew during his Eastwood or Croydon or war days, and all he can think about is coming back at once, and all he feels is the pain of departure! But the moment he was safe on board the *Osterley* he instantly shed all evil nightmares and indecisions and bilious humours, and became perfectly happy. "He was," as Norman Douglas truly says, "a man of naturally blithe disposition, full of childlike curiosity." That this nature was constantly frustrated or self-frustrated is one of the strangest things about him.

The moment he felt free from the tangle of disagreeables he had manufactured for himself in England and found himself in novel and interesting surroundings, he was instantly happy and charming. This was his first experience of ocean travel, and he instantly appreciated the order and quiet, the luxury and service of an English liner of that epoch. With his frailty, his over-sensitive reaction to impressions, his weakened lungs, he ought to have had much more of such tranquil luxury, and far less of the strenuous charlady's life to which he insisted on disciplining himself. He praised the *Osterley* with enthusiasm, it was "splendid, so comfortable, so much room", and though he did not say so he undoubtedly thrilled at the thought that it was all English. With sea air and abundant food he even developed the appetite which is so often lacking to consumptives. "One eats all the time," he reported, with the inevitable touch of puritanism; and then returns once more to his praise of the ship, "so still, so quiet, so civilised, and such a cleanliness."

Everything was so soothing, so delightful. He made friends with the passengers, he danced, he even flirted. "We have not had one single bad moment", he reported cheerfully. And Lawrence would not have been Lawrence if he had failed to see and to record the beauty and interest of the new scenes opening before him. He loved the eastern Mediterranean and was moved by a distant glimpse of Crete, but the sense of romance in him was really quickened when he came to Port Said, and saw the women, "little black waddling heaps of black crepe and two houri eyes", the beggars, the water-carriers, "the scribe who sits with the little table and writes letters", an old man reading from the Koran, grave bearded men smoking "chibouks" in open cafés.

The ship slowly made its way through the Suez canal, and from the deck Lawrence watched the long vistas of desert and the sun setting "like a sword burning green and pink". When he woke next morning they were in the Red Sea:

"There stands Mount Sinai, red like old dried blood, naked like a knife and so sharp, so unnaturally sharp, like a dagger that has been dipped in blood and has dried long ago and is a bit rusty and is always there like something dreadful between man and his lost paradise. All is Semitic and cruel, naked, sharp. No tree, no leaf, no life: the murderous will and iron of the idea and ideal—iron will and ideal. So they stand, these dreadful shores of this Red Sea that is hot like an oven without air. It is a strange exit, bitter. Behind finally lie Jerusalem, Greece, Rome and Europe, fulfilled and past —a great dreadful dream."

Then he would turn from such sights and his musings over them to the passengers, many of whom were Australians. On the strength of this rather brief acquaintance he set up as an authority on Australia, and wrote to a friend in Italy: "Australia is a good country, full of life and energy," and adding the advice, "it is the country for you if you had anything specific in mind." Always this mania for inviting people to join him at some immense distance when he knew perfectly well he would detest them in forty-eight hours!

His phrase "if you had anything specific in mind" is striking, especially if you realise that he was really thinking of himself. In making this break with the past, undertaking this long voyage which already had cost a large fraction of his money, had he "anything specific in mind"? Well, yes, he wanted "to get out of Europe", but that was vague and negative enough. Really he was only going *away* from Europe, and not *to* anything, not even to Taos. No doubt he hoped he might find somewhere to settle, some society into which he could fit, though even he must have known that the "frustration of my societal self" on which he came to pity himself so much was entirely due to his own faults. No society is going to adapt itself to an individual, especially such a porcupine of prejudices as Lawrence. If he wanted to be matey with "folk" he could have done it almost anywhere by adapting himself to local prejudices and customs. He had no intention whatever of doing this, even in Taos. He had written to Mabel Luhan on the topic of the Indians these most significant and ominous words:

"I too believe in Taos, without having seeing it. I also believe in Indians. But they must do *half* the believing: in me as well as in the sun. Vediamo."

You could hardly call that a "fair warning", for Mabel Luhan knew nothing of Rananim or of his dream of the community which was to submit to him without reserve and to obey him. The Indians were to believe in him as well as in the sun-god. Possibly he intended to take the place of the sun-god.

Meanwhile the *Osterley* sailed on, and one morning there was a smell of cinnamon in the air, and it was Colombo, where they found Brewster waiting to welcome them. Soon he took them to his own temporary home, "a nice spacious bungalow on the hill above Candy in a sort of half jungle of a cocoanut-palm estate." Almost at once there came the excitement of the Prince of Wales's visit and the great torchlight ceremony, and Lawrence wishing he was in the Prince's place to make everybody serve him. But Ceylon soon palled. The climate was very damp and hot, which naturally had a bad effect on Lawrence's health and nervous system. Brewster's studies in Pali and researches into the mysteries of Buddhism were treated with derision. Lawrence, without taking the faintest trouble to study the question, instantly decided that he "shrewdly suspected that high-flowness of Buddhism exists mostly on paper." When he was asked to meet some of the native scholars of Ceylon who were instructing Brewster, Lawrence suddenly became a typical British imperialist. He would not allow anyone except himself to make the slightest criticism of British rule in the East. Before he had been three weeks in Ceylon he wrote to an Englishman he had chanced to meet and whom he evidently hoped to bring into his orbit:

"I am making up my mind to return to England during the course of the summer. I really think that the most living clue of life is in us Englishmen in England, and the great mistake we make is in not uniting together in the strength of this real living clue—religious in the most vital sense—uniting together in England and so carrying the vital spark through."

The Ceylon jungle made a great impression on Lawrence with "its noisy, scraping and squeaking tropical creatures" which make themselves heard at night. Years later he once asked me if I had heard the night noises of a tropical jungle, and then instantly emitted a frightening series of yells, squawks, trills, howls and animal "help-murder" shrieks. Only when living in the tropics myself did I realise that he had accomplished the seemingly impossible task of remembering and being able to imitate all that medley of fantastic noises.

It was the heat of Ceylon which put Lawrence against the place. Unfortunately that was a particularly hot year there, and the whole party suffered more or less in health—Lawrence of course more than any of them. Ill-health always was blamed on the place where it developed. From a practical point of view he was undoubtedly right in his decision to move to somewhere drier and cooler at once. Had he ever been seriously interested in Buddhism? During his numerous wibble-wobbles at Taormina he had written to Brewster saying that he had decided not to go to America, and elaborated:

"What is the good after all of going to where everything is just *unlearnt* and confused to the utmost? Perhaps it is true, Buddhism is true realism, *things as they are*. And America is utterly *things as they are not*. But the future—where is that?"

I cannot find any other record except an early letter that Lawrence was ever seriously interested in Buddhism, and this reads like one of his innumerable passing whims. How far from Lawrence were Buddhism's serenity and blind acceptance and the fivefold way even to letting yourself be eaten by a starving tiger in order to advance a step towards Nirvana! And then the fact that the *Blutbruder* of the moment, Brewster, was seriously and conscientiously studying something Lawrence didn't know was quite enough to make him deride it.

So on to Australia! The Lawrences had reached Colombo in the middle of March, and had already left for Fremantle before the end of April. Had the life in common with the Brewsters been as easy and amiable as their urbane memoirs suggest? At all events about four years passed before they met again and there was a considerable gap in their correspondence in 1923. Brewster has misdated a letter, so not four months elapsed, as he says, but seven, without a letter.

Again Lawrence recovered all his good spirits as soon as he was at sea, this time on a ship called the *Orsova*. Unluckily there are very few notes on this voyage, and it was not until the 30th April, when they were within four days of Fremantle, that he wrote of them being "somewhere in a very big blue choppy sea with flying fishes sprinting out of the waves like winged drops, and a Catholic Spanish priest playing Chopin at the piano—very well—and the boat gently rolling." He went on to say that he didn't know why he was going to Australia, nor what he would do there, nor did he particularly care, though he hoped it would be cooler than Ceylon. He admitted that he had seen little of the East but predicted that the British Empire there was fast ending, "now we're going to fall." Still, that dismal prospect only made him feel "English in the teeth of all the world," and he winds up with the very odd statement that crossing the Indian Ocean on a luxury liner made him feel "like Virgil in the shades".

From Fremantle, where they disembarked, the Lawrences went to stay with friends near Perth, where they travelled "a long way into that strange vague bush"—as much as sixteen miles, in fact.

It was here that Lawrence met Molly Skinner, with whom he afterwards collaborated in the writing of a novel of Australia, *The Boy in the Bush.* Of course Lawrence never went far enough into either Western Australia or New South Wales to catch even a glimpse of the real wild bush. But with his uncannily quick intuition he instantly perceived "the strange and empty and pre-primeval" quality of Australia. It was very beautiful, he thought, but it rather scared him. He went a mile or two into the bush under the bright Australian moonlight, and the silence and mystery of the night turned to terror for him.

In fact he saw the bush that night under the influence of that moon-madness which had come upon him in youth in far-off England. Yet he could have wept with joy and ecstasy at the beauty of it all. "The sky was pure, crystal pure and blue, of a lovely pale blue colour: the air was wonderful, new and unbreathed; and there were great distances." As he walked under "the huge electric moon" he came upon "a clump of tall, nude, dead trees, shining almost phosphorescent," and suddenly he was possessed by a weird moon- and bush-terror, he felt "a presence", and "the hair on his scalp stirred and went icy cold with terror". He did not give way to panic, but he felt this "presence" as something "provoked by the moon, the roused spirit of the bush", and as he walked back he could feel it "watching and waiting" with the gruesome conviction that if "it" wanted, "it" could have "reached out a long black arm and gripped him".

The unexpectedness of those vast Australian solitudes gave him this weird sensation of terror, very much as the unexpected apparation of a fear-maddened wild cat in the Rockies gave him a sense of supernatural terror—not funk, but awe. In crowded Europe he had pined to be "a bit of a hermit" (which bit?), but in Western Australia, where there was room enough for a multitude of hermitages, he forgot all about it. There was what he had so often said he wanted—beautiful untouched country, where he could have lived cheaply and no one would ever have bothered him, nobody would have interrupted his communing with primeval Nature. After two weeks, he had had enough and went away. It is noticeable that the places where he chose to stay and be "a bit of a hermit" were mostly Florence or Taormina or Taos, centres of champagne-bohemia where there were plenty of gossips.

So he fled on, three thousand miles more, to Sydney, and before he ever reached it he wished he had never left Western Australia. And as he walked the streets of Sydney, in solitude, for he presented none of his letters of introduction, he was filled with a "bitter burning nostalgia for Europe, for Sicily, for old civilisation and real human understanding"—the Europe and the oldness and the people he had longed to escape. What *did* he want? Not Australia at that moment, for he found it "crude, raw and self-satisfied." It was "a weird place, in the established sense it is socially nil, happy-go-lucky, don't-you-bother, we're-in-Australia." Still, he did not leave. His motive in staying may have been nothing more than the need to wait for more royalties before taking the last and biggest stride of his round-the-world route to Taos. The Lawrences simply took a train south from Sydney, looking out of the window, and dropped down in the first place that seemed possible, where they rented a bungalow. It was called Thirroul and was a small coal-mining town —how curious to come thirteen thousand miles and reject the bush in order to settle into an Australian Eastwood!

He realised this himself, for in writing to thank his friends near Perth he says: "Remember me nicely to Mrs. Gawler, tell her I agree with her; I am a fool." And certainly it was an odd whim to cut himself off so completely from all society and yet to stick in one ordinary little community without troubling to see anything much of Australia but a suburb. And yet seeing so little, by sheer intuition he felt and recorded more of Australia, its magic and mystery, than any other foreign writer. Think of his poem on the kangaroo:

> "Delicate mother Kangaroo
> Sitting up there rabbit-wise, but huge, plump-weighted,
> And lifting her beautiful slender face, oh! so much more
> gently and finely lined than a rabbit's, or than a hare's,
> Lifting her face to nibble at a round white peppermint drop
> which she loves, sensitive mother Kangaroo.
>
> Her sensitive, long, pure-bred face.
> Her full antipodal eyes, so dark,
> So big and quiet and remote, having watched so many
> empty dawns in silent Australia."

"So many empty dawns in silent Australia"! How did he know that, how could he give that feeling of immense age and remoteness—just from feeding peppermint drops to one of the kangaroos, not in the bush, but in the Sydney zoo!

> "Still she watches with eternal, cocked wistfulness!
> How full her eyes are, like the full, fathomless, shining eyes of an Australian black-boy
> Who has been lost so many centuries on the margins of existence!
> She watches with insatiable wistfulness.
> Untold centuries of watching for something to come,
> For a new signal from life, in that silent lost land of the South."

From such visions it seems a long descent to the bungalow at Thirroul where the Lawrences lived. The house was well-built and spacious, but in a state of disorder and dirt from occupation by a family with ten children. Cleanliness was of major importance to Lawrence, as to all puritans, and the long-neglected house was a challenge to his prowess as a charwoman. The place was named Wyewurk, in the dismally facetious manner of suburban democracy, which Lawrence in his novel *Kangaroo* changed to the even more repulsive Torestin—perhaps to work in his joke that it should have been called Toscrubin. But at last, under the labours of the scrubbing-brushes, floors of beautiful jarra-wood began to appear. And as Lawrence and Frieda went into the garden from time to time for a rest they watched the huge blue foam-crested Pacific rollers, so huge and so near that they seemed each time as if they must swirl into the house, and so noisy that they seemed omnipresent.

Thirroul proved a very liveable place, for all food was brought to them in the tradesmen's carts, in one of which they discovered strange and beautiful fish; and the people on the farms were carelessly lavish with milk and butter. Apart from these utilitarian contacts they saw nobody, and Lawrence enjoyed the experience, noting that it was "wonderful to know absolutely nobody, for a vast distance around one." It was the Australian winter, and yet they were able to bathe every day. They took walks along the coast or into the country, where Lawrence delighted in "the pale pure silver" of the gum trees, and in "the extraordinary *delicacy* of the air and the blue sky, the weird bits of creek and marsh, dead trees, sand, and very blue hills." It made him think of the landscape of Puvis de Chavannes, "so apparently monotonous, yet when you look into it, such subtle different distances, in layers, and such exquisite forms."

He loved Australia and its delicate beauty with a strange almost heart-broken intensity of feeling—like a man desperately in love with a beautiful woman he feels instinctively from the first that he must leave, for no real reason, which makes it all the more heart-breaking. Deeply he felt the fascination of the land, was grateful for the "relief in the atmosphere, the relief from tension, from pressure." He had enjoyed intensely, morning after morning, the beauty of the Sicilian dawns with the sun coming up from the Ionian Sea with a splendour as of trumpets; and now he found a more delicate beauty of dawns:

"There was an unspeakable beauty about the mornings, the great sun from the sea, such a big, untamed, proud sun, rising up into a sky of such tender delicacy, blue, so blue, and yet so frail that even blue seems too coarse a colour to describe it, more virgin than humanity can conceive."

Page after page of his novel, *Kangaroo*, and many of his not numerous letters, are filled with evocations of Australia. He was fascinated by it, and only the vulgar conceit of chauvinism could have induced a foreigner to sneer that Lawrence "wasted his time in Australia", instead of hastening direct to the marvels of "touristy Taos". He soon got to like the casualness of the Australian people, and the way they left him alone. If he had really wanted to gratify his "societal self" and fit gradually into another community, this was surely the place to make the attempt. There was little of the class feeling and class hatred he had resented in England. "Class makes a gulf, across which all the best flow is lost", he wrote bitterly, trying perhaps to find excuses for his own aloofness and isolation. He would not admit that the obstacle was in himself, his recurrent belief that the only place for him in any society—class hatred or no class hatred—was on a lonely pinnacle at the top.

He would not yield himself to Australia. He had scarcely begun to be disturbed by its "sustaining magic" and to admit that it would be "a lovely country if one wanted to *withdraw* from the world", when he began perversely pining for the old Europe he had so often and so cantankerously maintained was worn-out, done for, finished, stifling with its monstrous bloodshed and the ghosts of its buried centuries.

"He was not happy, there was no pretending he was. He longed for Europe with hungry longing: Florence, with Giotto's pale tower: or the Pincio at Rome: or the woods in Berkshire—heavens, the English spring with primroses under the bare hazel bushes, and thatched cottages among plum blossom. He felt he would have given anything on earth to be in England. It was May—end of May—almost bluebell time, and the green leaves coming out on the hedges. Or the tall corn under the olives in Sicily. Or London Bridge, with all the traffic on the river. Or Bavaria with gentian and yellow globe flowers, and the Alps still icy. Oh God to be in Europe, lovely, lovely Europe that he had hated so thoroughly and abused so vehemently, saying it was moribund and stale and finished. The fool was himself. He had got out of temper, and so had called Europe moribund, assuming that he himself, of course, was not moribund, but sprightly and chirpy and too vital, as the Americans say, for Europe. Well, if a man wants to make a fool of himself, it is as well to let him."

So there, as so often, he was, loving the place he had abandoned and the place to which he was going, and hating the place where he was—only to develop a passionate nostalgia for it when irrevocably far away. Even the absence of class feeling in Australia, which at one time he had liked and praised, now appeared less desirable.

"This is the most democratic place I have *ever* been in," he wrote to Frieda's sister. "And the more I see of democracy the more I dislike it. It just brings everything down to the mere vulgar level of wages and prices, electric-light and water-closets, and nothing else. You *never* knew anything so nothing, Nichts, Nullus, niente, as the life here. They have good wages, they wear smart boots and the girls all have silk stockings; they fly around on ponies and in buggies—sort of low one-horse traps—and in motor-cars. They are always vaguely and meaninglessly on the go. And it all seems so empty, so *nothing*, it almost makes you sick. They are healthy, and to my thinking almost imbecile. That's what the life in a new country does to you: it makes you so material, so *outward*, that your real inner life and your inner self dies out, and you clatter around like so many mechanical animals. Yet they are very trustful and kind and quite competent in their jobs. There's no need to lock your doors, nobody will come and steal. All the outside life is so *easy*. But there it ends. There's nothing else. The best society in the country are the shopkeepers—nobody is any better than anybody else, and it really *is* democratic. But it all feels so slovenly, slipshod, rootless, and empty, it is like a kind of dream. Yet the weird, unawakened country is wonderful and if one could have a dozen people, perhaps, and a big piece of land of one's own . . ."

And how soon he would have loathed his dozen people and big piece of land in Australia if he had ever got them! But if that was the way he felt about new countries in general and Australia in particular, why on earth did he not return immediately to "lovely, lovely Europe"? Well, it seems that just as he had worked himself almost to that point he received a batch of fourteen letters from England and Europe. He read them "with a sort of loathing" and: "He wished that every mail-boat would go down that was bringing any letter to him, that a flood would rise and cover Europe entirely, that he could have a little operation performed that would remove from him for ever his memory of Europe and everything in it. Never had he felt so filled with spite against everybody he had known in the old life, as now."

So there, as Henry James might have remarked, he so very much was.

6

"Dio mio, I am so ridiculous, wavering. . . ." He had said it himself, but what a tragical waste of nervous energy and emotion! Why attach so much agonised importance to passing moods and express them in terms so vehement? What did it matter to the world whether he did or did not like Australia or repudiate Europe?

Well, he did; but it would be a mistake to suppose that his whole life in Australia was nothing but a series of waverings. Underneath them he nearly always intended to go on to Taos, and he also worked very hard, since he wrote his novel, *Kangaroo*—or nearly all of it —in between the 28th May, when the Lawrences reached Sydney, and the 3rd July, when he scribbled a note: "Have nearly written *Kangaroo*."

It is a strange, fascinating, beautiful, exasperating book thrown together with a carelessness of "form" which goes almost beyond *Aaron's Rod. Au fond, Kangaroo* is a travel book like *Sea and Sardinia*, the adventures of Lawrence and Frieda in Australia. On to this is grafted a long account of the then latest phase of his matrimonial battle, two long and passionately angry chapters on his experiences during the war, and a wholly invented set of social and political experiences. It is said that years afterwards something of the kind did happen in Australia, but in fact the contest between the diggers and the trade unionists was simply the struggle between fascists and communists which Lawrence had seen going on in Italy. The Lawrences knew nobody in New South Wales. Nobody had heard of him there and his arrival passed quite unnoticed. The Australian characters are based wholly on ship's acquaintances and the few people he met during the fortnight at Perth.

What is perplexing is that he, supposedly so much interested in primitive people, barely mentions the aborigines and made not the slightest effort to learn anything about them. True, to see a corrobborree he would have been compelled to make a very long and probably expensive journey into the bush, and would have run the risk of real dangers such as were wholly absent from the "touristy" ceremonies of American Indians. Yet the brief stay in Australia had made a deep impression on him. As the ship which was taking him to San Francisco drew away from the Sydney dock he was greatly moved:

"He felt a deep pang in his heart leaving Australia, that strange country that a man might love so hopelessly . . . farewell Australia, farewell Britain and the great Empire. Farewell! Farewell! The last streamers blowing away, like broken attachments, broken heartstrings."

As a matter of fact the farewell to "the great Empire" was premature, for they touched at Wellington, New Zealand, on the 15th August. New Zealand was Katherine Mansfield's home, and Lawrence sent her a card—his first communication with her since January 1920, when, according to Murry, Lawrence had written her a letter "so monstrously, so inhumanly cruel" that Murry had threatened to thrash him if he ever met Lawrence again! The postcard no doubt was meant as a gesture towards reconciliation—too late, she was dying.

From New Zealand they went on across the Pacific, touching at Raratonga and Tahiti, where they picked up some people who had been making a motion picture. It appears that their champagne-drinking and uninhibited sex behaviour so scandalised Lawrence that he denounced them to their faces as bitterly as if he had been the puritanical missionary in Somerset Maugham's *Rain*. Alas, the rebuke seems to have a sheer waste of moral energy, for the wicked merely laughed.

It was already September when the Lawrences reached San Francisco, where they landed with only twenty dollars—Lawrence having over-spent on the voyage. But nothing could be more misplaced than lamentations over his supposed poverty. As a matter of fact he took a room in one of the best hotels, and telegraphed for money to his New York agent, who had a considerable sum in hand for him. Moreover Mabel Luhan had arranged everything, sending railway tickets with the message "from San Francisco you are my guests." It was done handsomely and in style. With her Indian chauffeur, Tony Luhan, she drove to meet the Lawrences at the main railway station, and brought them by car to Santa Fé, and on by what was then a rather perilous road to Taos. There they found that she had provided them, as she had promised, with a new "*very* pretty adobe house, with furniture made in the village, and Mexican and Navajo rugs, and some lovely pots." Lawrence was greatly pleased. He found the house very comfortable and "in the best of taste", and he liked the view over the desert of "whitish-grey sage-brush" to where three miles away the Indian Pueblo rose up "like a pile of earth-coloured cube-boxes in a heap" with the mountains beyond.

While he was still "dazed and vague" from the long voyage and train journey and feeling "nearly shaken to bits" by the jolting over the trail up from Santa Fé, Lawrence was whirled off on a five days' motor trip over bumpy desert trails to see an Apache fiesta. His heart "kindled with Fenimore Cooper". Lawrence loved this playing at Indians as much as he soon got to love playing cowboys at Taos, even though his prejudices were shocked by the discovery that these Apaches had "a cult of water-hatred" and since they never washed "flesh or rag" they emitted "an unbearable sulphur-human smell".

He was also taken aback to find that for the Indian ceremonies it had been found necessary to post rather truculent native sentries to warn off the intrusive white man.

These were minor drawbacks, and there can be no doubt that despite them and his fatigue he was "thrilled" by the experience. For two days they had driven "across desert and mesa, down canyons and up divides and along arroyos" and at evening came on the Apache encampment—"the points of Indian tents, the tepees, and smoke, and silhouettes of tethered horses and blanketed figures moving." He liked "the drums with their strong-weak, strong-weak pulse" and the curious shuffling and yelling of the dances.

"From the gathering darkness around, men drifting slowly in, each carrying an aspen twig, each joining to cluster close in two rows upon the drum, holding each his aspen twig inwards, their faces all together, mouths all open in the song-shout, and all of them all the time going on the two feet, pàt-pat, pàt-pat, pàt-pat, to the thud-thud of the drum and the strange plangent yell of the chant, edging inch by inch, pàt-pat, pàt-pat, pàt-pat, sideways in a cluster along the track, towards the distant cluster of the challengers from the other kiva, who were sing-shouting and edging onwards, sideways, in the dusk, their faces all together, their leaves all inwards, towards the drum, and their feet going pàt-pat, pàt-pat, pàt-pat, on the dust, with their buttocks stuck out a little, faces all inwards, shouting open-mouthed to the drum, and half laughing, half mocking, half devilment, half fun. *Hie! Hie! Hie! Hie-away-awaya!* The strange yell, song, shout rising so lonely in the dusk, as if pine trees could suddenly, shaggily sing. Almost a pre-animal sound, full of triumph of life, and devilment against other life, and mockery and humorousness, and the pàt-pat, pàt-pat of the rhythm."

Meanwhile, Frieda had remained at Taos artlessly replying to the "many questions" put to her by Mabel Luhan, and "giving the show away completely as usual." But what show was there to give away? Mabel Luhan was naturally curious to know more about this queer guest she had acquired. Long before his arrival she had received a sort of confidential report on him from "a girl who had known them in England", possibly the Esther Andrews who had stayed with them in Cornwall that Christmas when the policeman came. She had said:

"He is one of the most fascinating men I ever met. The first time I ever saw him, he talked for a whole afternoon, almost steadily. He will do this at once, and without the slightest self-consciousness if he feels a sympathy in his listener. He talks as brilliantly as he writes and as frankly. But at the slightest touch of adverse criticism or hostility, Lawrence becomes violent. His vituperation is magnificent. He spares none. He has quarrelled with everyone. He says he has no friends that he has not quarrelled with. Lawrence is a Puritan, really, and his intellectual reaction against it is so violent that he hurls himself against it with all of himself, destroying himself as he does it. And yet he is the gentlest, kindest person in all human relations that anyone could be on this earth. But the inner tumult wears him out. When a mood or an impulse is in him, there is no such thing as repression. The war was a horrible thing to him, came darned near killing him, through the intensity of his emotion about it."

Well, that is a good portrait, though Frieda could certainly have added to it. She herself did not then realise how fragile he was for all his immense energy or the hold which tuberculosis had on his lungs. But she may have told Mabel Luhan how restless he often was, how passionately venomous sometimes in hatred and envy, how exasperating in his endless wrangling. And she may have spoken of William Henry. What she would have found difficult to explain and to make credible was that unappeasable hunger for crude power which often came on him, and which in its latest form had made much of her life miserable in Australia. He had made up his mind that he would crush "the modern woman" in Frieda, and reduce her to a state of complete "submission and obedience" to her godlike lord. He has put it in fictionalised form in *Kangaroo*, which had been written but a few weeks before the arrival at Taos:

"He was a determined little devil, and once he'd got an idea into his head not heaven nor hell nor Harriet would ever batter it out. And now he'd got into his head this idea of being lord and master, and Harriet's acknowledging him as such. He was to be lord and master, and she the humble slave. She was to submit to the mystic man and male in him, with reverence, and even a little awe, like a woman before the altar of the great Hermes. She was to believe in his adventure and deliver herself over to it; she was to believe in his mystic vision of a land beyond this charted world, where new life rose again."

Now of course it is open to anyone to protest that this is taken from a novel and therefore suspect, but the novel is purely autobiographical in these scenes, and there can be no doubt that, just as he described it, Lawrence had gone on "yap-yap-yap" at Frieda with wearisome iteration that she was to submit utterly and be reverent and awe-struck and believe in his godlike mission. But what was her response? With engaging candour and quite unbiased accuracy he put down her side as frankly as his own:

"And she just couldn't. His land beyond the land men knew, where men were more than they are now: she couldn't believe in it. 'Then believe in *me*,' he said desperately. 'I know you too well,' she replied."

Crushing and cogent retort! Gone for ever were the days when she could more than half-believe that he could atone to her for the loss of her children by creating a new and far better world for them. She might still believe in him as a wonderful if maddening husband and a great artist, a life-giver, but she would not and could not believe in him as a messiah, a leader of men, or her lord and master:

"Him, a lord and master! Why he was not really lord of his own bread and butter; next year they might both be starving. And he was not even master of himself, with his ungovernable furies and his uncritical intimacies with people. If he had been naturally a master of men, general of an army, or manager of some great steel works, with thousands of men under him—then, yes, she could have acknowledged the *master* part of the bargain, if not the lord. Whereas, as it was, he was the most forlorn and isolated creature in the world, without even a dog at his command. He was so isolated he was hardly a man at all, among men. He had absolutely nothing but her. Among men he was like some unbelievable creature —an emu, for example. Like an emu in the streets or in a railway carriage."

Every word of that is absolutely true, and it is truly extraordinary that a man should see through his most cherished pretences so accurately and record them against himself so ruthlessly. It is perhaps a more common experience that, knowing his faults and follies or whatever you wish to call them, he was quite incapable of abandoning them until and unless they abandoned him. Yet while he jeers in this pitiless fashion at his own perversity, conceit and obstinacy, he is liable at any moment to turn a complete somersault and see himself as the phoenix, the One and Only, to be worshipped as lord and master:

> "Oh, I bring these heartless, hapless drones,
> Down in a trice on their marrow bones,
> To call me king and lord!"

The moment Lawrence saw Frieda and Mabel Luhan together on his return from the Apaches, his quick intuition instantly told him that Frieda had been blabbing. Frieda was too open and honest to have any defence or ruses against the deft questions of a woman of the world, and few things angered Lawrence more than Frieda's "giving the show away", especially as it looked as if he had been purposely sent out of the way.

"Oh that mine enemy had written a book" was not often on Lawrence's lips—it seldom is with professional authors—but one might say his version of it was: "Oh, let me put mine enemies *in* books." At any rate, he at once proposed to write a novel based on the life and adventures of Mabel Luhan, and to that end began spending every morning at her home in long conversations. Whereupon, of course, Frieda began to get jealous. It was a common enough experience for them—the woman attracted by Lawrence's unique gifts as a writer and a charming personality who came to think (usually after listening to his complaints) that Frieda needed advice on how to look after him. Considering what she had sacrificed for him and what she had to put up with, and that she knew nobody could possibly be to him what she was, this not unnaturally always made her furious. So there would be a battle; Lawrence would be rescued or thwarted—whichever you choose—and would thank her in these terms:

"All women are the same—bossy—absolutely without decency. And it's your business, Frieda, to see that no other woman comes near me."

Meanwhile Taos was seemingly exactly what he had so often longed for in England. It was close to the Rockies—in them, really—though hardly in sight of the Pacific, as he had seemed to expect long before. There were friendly Pueblo Indians to explain their customs and rites for him to report and theorise over. And there was the fun, which he enjoyed immensely, of learning to ride one of Mabel Luhan's horses cowboy-fashion across the desert. Lawrence was very quick to learn—I believe he never had a spill—and sported white riding breeches, a cow-boy hat, a blue shirt and white tie, and a Mexican saddle. Yet this which surely looks like a moment of "fulfilment" was the very time when he was consumed with nostalgia for Australia—"still I haven't extricated all of me out of Australia. In one part of myself I came to love it—really to love it, Australia."

The 30th September, the feast of San Geronimo, is a great day with the Pueblo Indians, who are nominally Roman Catholics but still hold tenaciously to some of the ancient magical rites of animism, perhaps rather more consciously and deliberately than the remote communities of southern Europe which still cling to pre-Christian customs. As with the Apaches, Lawrence was "thrilled" by the San Geronimo dancers, "the men with their fox-skin swaying down from their buttocks, and the women with seed rattles following. Never shall I forget the utter absorption of the dance, so quiet, so steadily, timelessly rhythmic, and silent, with the ceaseless down-tread, always to the earth's centre, the very reverse of the upflow of Dionysiac or Christian ecstasy."

He managed to persuade himself that until he went to New Mexico and saw these dances he had never experienced any "permanent feeling of religion". It would be easy to refute that from his own previous writings, and what thrilled him on this occasion was not so much religion as primitive magic. But though he responded so warmly to these Indian dancers, it is truly a misrepresentation of his thought and feelings to maintain that he wished to project himself and us permanently back into that primeval "mindless" world. He evokes as only he could the emotions he felt at the dances and in listening to an old Indian reciting "in a distinct, plangent recitative voice, male and yet strangely far-off and plaintive, reciting, reciting, reciting like a somnambulist", but he repudiates all thought of identifying himself with either:

"It was not for me, and I knew it. The soul is as old as the oldest day, and has its own hushed echoes, its own far-off tribal understandings sunk and incorporated. We do not need to live the past over again. Our darkest tissues are twisted in this old tribal experience, our warmest blood came out of the old tribal fire. And they vibrate still in answer, our blood, our tissue. But me, the conscious me, I have gone a long road since then. And as I look back, like memory terrible as bloodshed, the dark faces round the fire in the night, and one blood beating in me and them. But I don't want to go back to them, ah, never. I never want to deny them or break with them. But there is no going back. Always onward, still further."

Surely nothing could be more downright and explicit a repudiation of the constantly repeated charge that Lawrence wanted to take us back—back to "the savage", to "the mindless", to "the amoeba".

Apart from these vivid sketches of his new experiences he did not write very much at this time. The last chapter to *Kangaroo* was very soon written, but the project of a new novel in collaboration with Mabel Luhan never got beyond discussion and a few rather incoherent notes. It was probably at this time that he wrote his poem, 'Eagle in New Mexico':

> "Erect, scorched-pallid out of the hair of the cedar,
> Erect, with the god-thrust entering him from below,
> Eagle gloved in feathers
> In scorched white feathers
> In burnt dark feathers
> In feathers still fire-rusted;
> Sickle-overswept, sickle dripping over and above."

Not one of his happiest successes, but it appears that within ten days he had become distressed by the tension between Frieda and Mabel Luhan, and also by uneasiness at his partial material dependence. The great drawback to the place, he wrote, was "living so much under the wing of the *padrona*." Already he was bracing his will-power for a contest with "the will of the American woman", which he denounced so frequently and picturesquely.

At a distance of about seventeen miles from Taos on a mountain-slope known as the Lobo, above the trading post of San Cristobal, Mabel Luhan owned about a hundred and seventy acres of rough land with an adobe shack which served as a shooting box for her son. There were three or four other ranch-houses and shacks. Eventually Mabel Luhan gave Frieda this property, which the Lawrences called Kiowa ranch; and he forced her to accept in return the manuscript of *Sons and Lovers*, which, however, she gave away. To this remote spot Lawrence insisted on moving from what he called "the smart house" at Taos, but as Mabel Luhan's place was required, the Lawrences rented two other adobe cabins from a rancher named Hawk, at del Monte.

Although Lawrence had seemingly not had any lung attack since leaving Ceylon, and was energetic enough in riding and carrying out his usual household tasks, he was certainly not strong enough to undertake all the heavy rough work necessary for staying the winter in a log-hut eight thousand feet up in the Rockies. He could not possibly have looked after Frieda and himself without help during the ten or twelve coldest winter weeks of frost and deep snow. And this he was fortunate enough to find. Two young Danish painters, Merrild and Gótzsche, had arrived in Taos about that time in a very ancient Ford car. Since they were poor and quite unknown they were not considered much of an acquisition by that cultural centre, but Lawrence liked them, and after a short acquaintance proposed that they should inhabit one of the del Monte cabins at his expense, in exchange for which they would help him with the heavy work of felling trees for fuel and so forth.

Under the snow that landscape, which at any time always deeply moved Lawrence, seemed to him of incomparable beauty; but apart from that most important factor, life there was inevitably hard, primitive and monotonous. He did little literary work that can be traced, except for the trifling job of proof-correcting 'The Captain's Doll' and *The Ladybird.* His creative writing seems to have been limited to poems. 'Blue Jay' was certainly written up on the Lobo during the snow period:

"The blue jay with a crest on his head
Comes round the cabin in the snow.
He runs in the snow like a bit of blue metal,
Turning his back on everything.

Every day since the snow is here
The blue jay paces round the cabin, very busy, picking up bits,
Turning his back on us all,
And bobbing his thick dark crest about the snow, as if
darkly saying:
'*I ignore these folk who look out*'."

The poem about the mountain lion was written in January 1923, and is both characteristic and revealing. It appears that the four of them were riding into the entrance of the Lobo canyon when they met a couple of strange Mexicans who had just trapped "a long slim cat, yellow like a lioness." They allowed Lawrence to admire the beautiful dead beast and to lift her face:

> "Her round bright face, bright as frost,
> Her round, fine-fashioned head, with two dead ears;
> And stripes in the brilliant frost of her face, sharp,
> fine dark rays,
> Dark keen fine rays in the brilliant frost of her face.
> Beautiful dead eyes."

And he mourned for the beautiful dead cat like a brother, for in her lithe destructive beauty he saw a symbol of himself, and in the wanton trapping and killing of her, a symbol of his own fate in the world of men. From the dead mountain lion he looked out, far away:

"... to the dim of the desert, like a dream, never real;
To the snow of the Sangre de Cristo mountains, the ice of the mountains of Picoris.
And near across at the opposite steep of snow, green trees motionless standing in snow, like a Christmas toy.

And I think in this empty world there was room for me and a mountain lion.
And I think in the world beyond, how easily we might spare a million or two of humans
And never miss them.
And yet what a gap in the world, the missing white frost-face of that slim yellow mountain lion."

You can see from that how much of an outlaw he felt himself in the world, as well as his habit of identifying himself with animals. It is said that the Taos Indians have a habit of giving some animal name to the pale-faces who come to dwell among them for a longer period than the usual run of tourists, and Lawrence, much to his displeasure, had been nicknamed Red Fox. We are so accustomed to think of the fox as a fleeing something thumped after by horsemen and a lot of yelping dogs that we forget the real savage beauty of the beast—his sleek sunny red pelt and gleaming white teeth, his swift grace as he pounces on a chicken, a sort of animal Robin Hood. Lawrence would have preferred to be a mountain lion or an eagle, or even perhaps a snake, for in some moods he liked to think of himself as a dangerously beautiful adder whom people could admire and touch only at their peril.

Meanwhile Red Fox and the woman who refused to be a squaw and the two young Danes battled their way through the Rocky Mountains winter. There were heavy snowstorms, which for days kept them imprisoned in their shacks, with endless talks and singing of folk songs and sometimes fearful quarrels between Frieda and Lawrence—that black corrosive devil of rage seizing him, and Frieda refusing to yield to it. When the weather was clear the three men sometimes went on walks through the snow, Lawrence inventing a multitude of ingenious excuses to stop and rest because he would not admit that the young men were stronger and faster walkers. One day the two of them stepped out trying to reach a near peak and, looking back, saw Lawrence a forlorn black speck far below them, unable to follow. Then he insisted on giving them lessons in Spanish, but in such a prim school manner and with such old-fashioned phrases and method that Frieda made them wilt with ruthless mockery. His curious prudery remained, for one day when a girl painter had walked the seventeen miles from Taos to see them, he absolutely refused to allow her to sleep in the Lawrences' cabin, and was exceedingly angry because the Danes refused to turn her out of their cabin to walk another seventeen miles back in the frozen snow at night.

A strange and painful story has become attached to the little bitch, Bibbles, of whom Lawrence made a special pet at that time —the heroine of the best of his Whitmanesque animal poems. As was his wont, the poem is a projection of himself into the animal, even down to denouncing in the little dog his own weakness in forming uncritical friendships, and as a severe warning to Frieda. Through Bibbles he tells Frieda that now he does not want sex or "love", particularly not "love" but: "Fidelity! Loyalty! Attachment! All right, my little bitch. You learn loyalty and I'll protect you." From what? Why, from "the great ranch-dogs" which were after her now she had "come sex-alive".

It is quite impossible to say whether Lawrence had seriously applied to himself Frieda's jest about his not being master even of a dog, or whether his taking up with one of the animals was a pure coincidence. But, in spite of all the humour and subtle observation of the 'Bibbles' poem, there is no doubt that Lawrence did intend to be the bitch's lord and master and that she should yield him "utter submission and obedience". And no doubt if a human being desires such an absurd and profitless relationship the place to look for it is among the dogs. Unluckily for the success of the experiment Lawrence attempted to dominate, not just the personality of a little bitch, but the august, mysterious and unalterable mandates of Nature. Bibbles did not want to be protected against her sex life, could not.

The practical Danes, observing this state of affairs, proposed the normal coercion of leash and captivity for a certain time. But these Lawrence utterly rejected. To employ such vulgar methods was destroying the whole value of Bibbles's "Fidelity. Loyalty. Attachment!" which he was convinced she would yield voluntarily to his natural lordship. In other words, he had only to impress on her that he did not wish her to consort with any male dog and that would be enough. *Aenœidum genetrix, hominum divomque voluptas!* On the very first opportunity, this disloyal, detestable, democratic, ungrateful, perverse female gleefully eloped with the first of the "great ranch dogs" who strolled by.

During this absence of Bibbles in the pine-woods Lawrence was in a "gloomy and brooding" mood, and talked dejectedly and at length on the evil effects of mongrelism in man and brute. When Bibbles returned she was angrily whipped by her outraged lord and master, and next morning either from terror of him or love of the ranch-dog once more disappeared into the forest. This time when she returned she did not dare return to him, but went to the cabin of the Danes, fawning and begging to be forgiven and taken in; which of course she was. Suddenly, about noon, Lawrence burst into the shack, pale, trembling with rage. "So there you are, you dirty, false little bitch!" and he knocked her flying off Gótzsche's knee. He rushed after her, upsetting chairs and table, and pursued her into the deep snow, caught her and kicked her, yelling obscene insults at her. In his insane rage he was killing her.

All this had happened so quickly and disconcertingly that the Danes had been too surprised to move. The terrified yelps of pain suddenly galvanised them into action, and Merrild rushed between Lawrence and Bibbles. He was in a state of such uncontrollably murderous rage that if he had been strong enough he would have killed the man as well as the "false dirty bitch". He glared at them in murderous hate, but he had no weapon, and knew he was no match for Merrild's fists, and as the men faced each other poor Bibbles hopped away through the snow; and when she was gone, they broke apart.

After such a scene of antagonism, so close to a real physical fight, Lawrence would normally have loathed his antagonist, and have got rid of him with cold detestation on the first opportunity. But he could not live up there without the Danes, and the alternative was either to go back to Taos and humble himself to Mabel Luhan, or go right away—and where was he to go? He preferred to make it up. His vanity could not endure to apologise or even to refer indirectly to the scene, but he "baked bread and some delicious cake" for the Danes and was "very, very nice".

A few days later, winter and hardship got at Lawrence's lungs, and he was forced to go to bed to rest, assuring the others as usual that it was "only a slight cold" and he would soon be up. Bibbles had been living with the Danes; but one day she came and jumped on Lawrence's bed as she had been used to do of old, and was eventually received back to favour. But what an irony in the whole fantastic episode, for after all in the contest it was the little bitch who won, and had her puppies.

Another, but very different, shock came to him that winter. After the long silence there came two letters from Murry, the first saying that Katherine Mansfield had gone to Gourdjieff's establishment at Fontainebleau, and the second to announce her death. Lawrence had certainly not understood the significance of the first letter, so that the second was a real blow to him:

"Yes, it is something gone out of our lives. Yes, I always knew a bond in my heart. Feel a fear where the bond is broken now. Feel as if old moorings were breaking all. What is going to happen to us all? Perhaps it is good for Katherine not to have seen the next phase. We will unite up again when I come to England. It has been a savage enough pilgrimage these last four years."

It was a very striking phrase, "savage pilgrimage", but surely a great exaggeration to use it, as Catherine Carswell has done, as the symbol of Lawrence's life. The inconveniencies he suffered during the war, even the poverty, about which he developed such enormous rages, were little enough compared with what millions of men endured. And then, his "savage pilgrimage" of four years was wholly voluntary, and consisted in having headquarters for a couple of years at Taormina, the most fashionable resort in Sicily, with pleasure excursions to Malta, Sardinia, Naples, Capri, Amalfi, Rome, Florence, Venice, Bavaria and Austria; in crossing oceans on luxury liners, staying with friends in Ceylon and Perth, living in a large Australian bungalow on the edge of the Pacific, and a "smart new house" in Taos. The Lawrences were ten days at icy-mountainous Picinisco and ten weeks on the Lobo.

If the "savagery" of the pilgrimage is held to lie in Lawrence's poverty, the answer is that the poverty of the 1920s is imaginary. For some reason Lawrence, when writing to the Carswells, always made a poor mouth about his finances and made himself appear much poorer than he was. Here is one example. Just a few weeks after he had made his Federal Income Tax return for 1922, he complained to Catherine Carswell that his "prosperity is only relative, especially with so many relatives in Germany". But quite apart from English earnings of about three hundred pounds and royalties on foreign translations, his American earnings alone for that year amounted to $5,439.00, less 10 per cent agent's commission and $70.00 of Federal income tax. I should say that most people far from calling that a "savage pilgrimage" would consider it a very enviable existence indeed. And if he either lived in complete isolation, or carried his famous capacity for quarrelling with him so that everywhere he was the "rejected guest"—well, he surely had chiefly himself to blame.

7

THROUGH Mabel Luhan the Lawrences had come to know Witter Bynner, an American of private means, and his young friend Willard or "Spud" Johnson, editor of a small Western periodical called *The*

Laughing Horse, to which Lawrence often contributed. When the Lawrences arrived first at Santa Fé, there was no accommodation for them as the hotel had burned down, and it was Bynner who came hospitably to the rescue. Through Bynner's kindness they were accompanied on their first trip to Mexico City by a man who knew the country well, and was able to introduce them; valuable help when first visiting a foreign country. Perhaps it is almost superfluous to note that unflattering "portraits" of both Bynner and Johnson appear in the opening pages of *The Plumed Serpent*, Lawrence's novel of old Mexico. On the 15th March, 1923, the Lawrences descended from their mountain solitude, "a hateful dark snowy day", and by the 19th they were at El Paso, the frontier town on the way to Mexico.

But what of Mabel Luhan, to whom, after all, Lawrence was to some extent indebted for all this Western American travel and new experience? If we are to believe Merrild, he had at this time developed a homicidal loathing for her. Now, Lawrence had never pretended to be a pacifist at any time during the war, and in his wildly exaggerated way often declared that there were people who ought to be killed and that he would like to kill them—like the "one or two million Germans" he wanted to sacrifice to his rage about the war in 1915. In *Kangaroo*, in the chapter, 'A Row in Town', one of the characters exults in his pleasure at having killed two or three men in a riot, and the character who is Lawrence listens in silence, and makes no protest.

It appears that one wintry day on the Lobo, Lawrence entertained the Danes with his views on the importance of killing other people, vehemently asserting that it was "important" for all three of them "to kill some of the beastly disdainful bankers, industrialists, lawyers, war makers and schemers of all kinds." After demurring for a little, Merrild pretended to be convinced, and, to see how far Lawrence would go, suggested that since there is no time like the present this retributive slaughter ought to begin at once. Suspecting nothing, Lawrence at once eagerly concurred; whereupon Merrild asked with whom he proposed to begin.

"He hesitated for a moment, then he said slowly and with emphasis: 'I will kill Mabel first.' "

In spite of this, there was a farewell interview between them before he left Taos, though if he approached it in that frame of mind it can hardly have been very cordial, especially since Mabel Luhan might legitimately feel that he had not altogether fulfilled her expectations. Something physical or mental or both had been wrong with him during much of that first visit, as he himself recognised when he wrote her in January 1924: "If only we'd kept up an honest laugh, then the vileness of 1923 need not have been."

But he wrote that at a moment when he was eager to return to Taos. When he left for Mexico in March 1923, he was quite uncertain whether he should return to Taos ever, and indeed planned to be in England "early in August", perhaps to carry out his promise to "link up again" with Murry. He did make a flying visit to England in the winter of 1923–24, but apart from that remained in Mexico or New Mexico until September 1925.

From the point of view of his work as a literary artist Lawrence was, as so often, instinctively right to found his main book on Mexico and not on New Mexico. There, after all, was the centre of the primitive civilisation in which he had been interested long before he left Europe. New Mexico is scenically fine, but to my judgment less so than parts of Utah, Arizona and California; and can hardly be compared with old Mexico with its snow-capped volcanoes and dramatic variations of climate. Santa Fé is indeed older than any French or English settlement, but gives the impression of a 16th century adobe Spanish town built in 1920, a sensation rather increased than modified by notice boards inscribed "Welcome, Mr. Tourist" and "Thank you, Mr. Tourist." It had evidently long ceased to be even an outpost of Aztec civilisation.

Mexico was the last of Lawrence's "thought-adventures" in travel, the last inspiration for a large-scale book, with the exception of that "epilogue to his travels", *Lady Chatterley's Lover*. It was also the last of his attempts to identify himself with another community, if he was ever serious about that for more than a passing whim. After Mexico he abandoned his search and drifted back to western Europe, chiefly Italy, which was more congenial to him and where he produced much of his best work. The mood in which he entered Mexico is perhaps best illustrated by a fragment of an essay written in the autumn of 1923 when he was wearily journeying through remote parts of Mexico, without Frieda, in the company of Gótzsche. It sums up with lucidity and brevity all the disillusion, all the sense of loss which had been deepening on him since he had begun to realise the implications of the war in 1915. That war brought a whole world to an end, but what end? He answers himself:

"Why, the end of democracy, the end of the ideal of liberty and freedom, the end of the brotherhood of man, the end of the idea of the perfectability of man, the end of the belief in the reign of love, the end of the belief that man desires peace, harmony, tranquillity, love and loving kindness all the while. The end of Christianity, the end of the Church of Jesus. The end of Science, as absolute knowledge. The end of the absolute power of the Word. The end, the end, the end."

Now, ever since Lawrence re-wrote *The Rainbow* at Greatham in 1915, during those mental battles which drove him to the edge of insanity, those ideas had been implicit in his writing—never so baldly and clearly and with such a devastating holocaust of all that men had believed, but surely there. It was that repudiation of what he considered dead idealisms which roused so much antagonism and hatred for him, and not the alleged offences against conventional sex, which were simply a convenient if cowardly way of trying to bring him down.

This, if we make all due allowance for the disturbance of physical health and his unbalanced temperament, gives the clue to his restlessness, his wanderings, his recoil from England which clung to what he considered dead religion, dead ideals, a dead form of society. Hence his search for some other way of life that would supersede what he believed to be a hopelessly outworn way of life. How much of all this was due to purely personal reactions, his own rages and repulsions, has been made clear. But after the second world *debâcle* of 1939, which he always predicted so vehemently, his intuition seems far less fanciful than it did in 1915 or even in 1923. Right or wrong, the essential point here is that he believed this, and held to it fairly continuously.

Lawrence seems to have been dismayed and disappointed by his first experiences of Mexico, but that may have been due to fragile health and the fatigue of the journey. He left El Paso in "an unkempt Pullman" which jogged through "endless deserts" and was charged enormous prices for "doubtful scraps" of food in the restaurant car. Instead of the "nice neat nigger" of the American train they were waited on by "a rather shoddy small-pox-marked Pullman-boy." Mexico had only recently gone through the shattering experience of one more "revolution of the people", only to see yet another looming in the near future. Strange to relate, Lawrence, who from time to time declared that he was interested only in "the revolution of death" and greatly despised bourgeois notions of safety, took a rather gloomy view of the Mexican situation:

"It's got a rattlesnake coiled in its heart, has this democracy of the New World. It's a dangerous animal, once it lifts its head again. Meanwhile, the dove still nests in the coils of the rattlesnake, the stone coiled rattlesnake of Aztec eternity."

Soon after his arrival in Mexico City, Bynner and Johnson took Lawrence to see a bull-fight, which he hated nearly as much as he hated the audience of half-revolutionised, anti-white-man proletarians. No school-marm, corseted with virginal prejudices about kindness to animals, could have achieved his white-heat of revolt and condemnation. He was outraged when Mexican hooligans began throwing each others' hats into the arena, and much more so when they playfully hurled rotten oranges and banana skins at him and his friends. The mob then suddenly abandoned their own cheap seats and invaded the more expensive reserved ones, swirling round Lawrence and his friends and impudently squatting with heavy southern buttocks on their northern feet:

"I really hate common people."

But this was nothing to his disgust when he was forced to watch the age-old ritual sacrifice of the power-giving Bull, symbol of Sex and the Sun, in rites which were derived from far-away Phoenician Iberia and Minoan Crete. Lawrence thought the bull-fighters looked like "eunuchs or women in tight pants, with their rather fat posteriors and their squiffs of pigtails and their clean-shaven faces." The bull's goring a couple of horses finished him. As he rose to leave in passionate disapproval, amid the hoots of the audience, he declared that there was no gallantry or pluck in bull-fighting. It was "just a performance of human beings torturing animals . . . dirty little boys maiming flies . . . bastards . . . thank God a million times that I know poltroonery and dirty-mindedness when I see it."

At Frieda's desire they had for once gone to a first-class hotel to make up a little for her very uncomfortable winter in a snow-bound shack on the frozen Rockies. But it was not a success, for Lawrence thought the other people looked painted and immoral;

so they took refuge in a small Italian hotel. He was invited to fashionable tea-parties, and hated the guests both American and English, partly because they *would* discuss the recent revolution. Then he went to see the frescoes of a (then) modern artist whose own original theory was that "only the ugly is aesthetic". Lawrence thought his paintings "hideous, hideous without mirth or whimsicality", hated their vulgarity and stupidity, their "maniacal ideas of socialism, politics and La Patria—mechanical as a mousetrap." This resulted in an acrid altercation, during which the "artist" asked Lawrence if he knew everything, as foreigners usually know everything about Mexico. Lawrence met the situation admirably:

"I know what I feel, and I want a taxi and I want to go home. I don't want to see any more stupid vulgar pictures."

Lawrence, it must be remembered, was always unhappy in large towns, and to his frayed nerves Mexico City seemed noisier and more disorderly even than Naples. He was uneasily conscious of the smouldering violence and revolutionary threat. Only a few weeks back he had been urging the duty of assassinating bankers, industrialists, lawyers and so forth. But when, as if in answer to his wish, he found himself among a people who to some extent had carried out that programme, he was disgusted. He had the liveliest apprehension that a sort of mopping-up revolution might take place at any moment.

So he announced that he was leaving at once for Europe, or perhaps for England. Then he changed his mind, and thought he might go to Lake Chapala, though Bynner and Johnson amused themselves by plying him with all the horrific stories they could invent of hotel-managers murdered by bandits with machetes, and hacienda-proprietors hideously mangled. This probably decided him to go—he was not going to let a couple of American dude poets imagine they could frighten an Englishman from Nottingham. Besides, if he was to write a novel about Mexico, it had to be based on something a little more interesting than the population of Mexico City. So there was yet another train journey, and at once he came alive and began to live the world. When the train stopped he looked:

". . . at the men who stood in groups, with their hats tilted against the wind and their blankets folded over their shoulders and up to their eyes, against the dust, motionless standing like sombre ghosts, only a glint of eyes showing between the dark sarape and the big hat-brim; while donkey-drivers in a dust-cloud ran frantically, with uplifted arms like demons, uttering short sharp cries to prevent their donkeys from poking in between the coaches of the train. Silent dogs trotted in-and-out under the train, women, their faces wrapped in their blue rebozos, came to offer tortillas folded in a cloth to keep them warm, or pulque in an earthenware mug, or pieces of chicken in red, thick, oily sauce; or oranges or bananas or pitahayas, anything. And when few people bought, because of the dust, the women put their wares under their arm, under the blue rebozo, and covered their faces and motionless watched the train."

The Plumed Serpent must have been started early in May 1923, for there is a jotting by Lawrence giving the 2nd May as the date when he and Frieda moved into the house by Lake Chapala. By mid-May he was already well advanced, and expecting to finish the first draft by the end of June or beginning of July. He worked at the book, as he always did when possible, out-of-doors, "sitting by the lake under a pepper tree". He broke off to take a two-day expedition up the lake, during which they found a "possible" house for a permanent residence, but did not take it because of the new revolutions which were expected, and "why should one work to build a place and make it nice, only to have it destroyed?" And there was yet another excursion, when the Lawrences went with Bynner and Johnson to see the pyramids at Teotihuacan.

And then, suddenly, this important manuscript was abandoned, unfinished, and we find the Lawrences on their way to New York by way of New Orleans! Possibly the departure of Bynner and Johnson, and the growing threat of "more revolution", may have had something to do with this unexpected move, but the real reasons came from Frieda. Much as she enjoyed their nomadic life she had no career as an artist to occupy her and to give a purpose to everything that happened. She was weary temporarily of New Mexican discomforts and old Mexican horrors. At Teotihuacan she had shuddered at the thought of "the old sacrifices, hearts still quivering held to the sun for the sun to drink"; and coming in the twilight on "a huge stone snake, coiling green with great turquoise eyes", she had taken fright and "ran after the others" as fast as she could move. Then, a long time had passed since she had seen her children, her mother and sisters. She said she pined for the placidity of

England, and that she wanted to spend part of the summer near her children, in Devonshire.

But the main reason of course lay in the battle for dominion between Lawrence and herself, he still insisting "hammer, hammer, hammer" on her complete submission and obedience, and Frieda as obstinately refusing. An American like Bynner was highly scandalised by Lawrence's attitude and frequent insulting remarks to her, and encouraged her to independence. "If you and Lawrence quarrel," Bynner said, "why don't you hit first?" If we may trust the evidence of *The Plumed Serpent*, Lawrence's imagination was beginning to soar to fresh levels of exaction. He was playing with the idea of what he would do if he were the leader of the coming revolution, which he decided must involve a revival of the ancient Mexican gods, especially Quetzalcoatl, the Snake-Bird-god, with whom he identified his imaginary leader. In the novel Kate-Frieda succumbs and worships. In real life Frieda insisted she was going to Europe whether Lawrence came or not.

What arguments, what strategy Frieda used to extricate herself from the coils of the Snake-Bird-god are not recorded; but if she imagined Lawrence was going to abandon his novel and his fascinating dreams of god-like authority in order to come along cheerfully with her to Europe, she made a mistake and underestimated his mulish obstinacy. At first he seems to have been so much surprised by her determination that he started off with her. But the journey was long and broken. They went by boat from Vera Cruz to New Orleans, and on by train to New York. As it was very hot they moved out to the New Jersey country, to wait for vacancies on the crowded holiday-season ocean liners.

This gave Lawrence time to work up one of his "Balaam's Ass" repugnances to going to Europe. Frieda managed to book a passage for herself leaving on the 17th August, and already on the 7th he wrote Catherine Carswell: "I'm not coming to Europe after all. Find I just don't want to—not yet. Later." He already had his plan, for he wrote Murry: "America means nothing to me. Yet I'm going right west again—I think to Los Angeles and into the mountains: perhaps to sail the Pacific. I suppose I'm the saddest, at not coming." If he was the saddest, he was also the maddest, for on the quay just before Frieda sailed they had the bitterest and most violent of all their violent, bitter quarrels—so bad that Frieda half-believed all was over between them. But if she had given in at that point, that would have been fatal to her, and she might have fallen into the "submissive obedience" state. There was nothing she could do at that point but either insist on going or become what she had so long fought against. So Lawrence had to let her go, but his obstinacy made him prefer to let her go alone. It remained to be seen which would get lonely first, and he was quite confident that she would return to him wherever he was; and that would be a victory for him.

So he let her sail alone after bitterly reviling her, and drifted West by way of Buffalo and Chicago to Los Angeles. He had chosen Los Angeles because the Danes were there, and he had not had any particular quarrel with them except the near fight over Bibbles on the mountain, and he had decided to forgive them for being in the right. They met him at the railway station in their museum Ford, and drove him to the Miramar Hotel at Santa Monica. It is strange to think of Lawrence in Hollywood, but his presence there was as much overlooked as it had been in Sydney. The Danes were a little perturbed about him. They thought he was "not the same as he had been at del Monte" and that the separation from Frieda made him "restless and in a lonely mood".

This depressed state of mind seems to have affected even his appearance. A photograph taken a few weeks earlier in Mexico shows him gay, laughing, neatly-dressed, distinguished and good-looking. A snap-shot of him on the Santa Monica cliff-walk shows a quite unbelievable metamorphosis into an ugly, dreary, shabby Lawrence looking like a melancholy bum waiting to take his place in a bread-line.

During most of the month of September he hung about Los Angeles in an aimless way. He visited Santa Barbara, and went to see an eclipse of the sun at Lompoc. His opinion of California was: "a queer place—in a way, it has turned its back on the world, and looks into the void Pacific. It is absolutely selfish, very empty, but not false." He was very soon tired of it, and persuaded Götzsche to accompany him to Mexico. The idea was "to look for a place to live in. Perhaps I shall find a little ranch there. Put a peg in the world, a new navel, a new centre."

It is not surprising that this nomad failed to find his centre in Mexico, though he was actually offered six or eight acres of land free on the Gulf of California if he would promise to build on them. What is surprising is the fact that this is the only one of Lawrence's travels which sounds dreary. On every other occasion an expedition into country he did not know made him happy, excited, observant of everything; but on this occasion it was not so. He was so subdued that he did not even quarrel with Gótzsche, though Gótzsche brooding over his odd behaviour came to the equally odd conclusion that Lawrence ought to have some occupation besides writing. He also reported that Lawrence was completely at a loose end without Frieda, and at times seemed insane.

From California they travelled through the provinces of Sonora and Sinaloa, and about the middle of October reached Guadalajara in Jalisco, not very far from the Lake Chapala the Lawrences had left so hurriedly in the summer. Lawrence had found Los Angeles too full of people, too noisy with traffic; Sonora was too much the other way, it was "much wilder, emptier, more hopeless than Chapala. It makes one feel the door is shut on one." The journey really was a hard one, too hard for someone in Lawrence's state of health.

They had gone by train to Guaymas on the Pacific coast, finding it hot and dirty, and then on to Navojoa. From there they visited Minas Nuevas, a Swiss-owned silver-mine, over roads so rough that Lawrence was "bruised wherever I look". They also went to see a "big wild cattle hacienda" and "strange desolate, brutal places, beautiful enough, but weird and brutal." Under "a blazing sun, a vast hot sky", they travelled wearily through "big lonely inhuman hills and mountains", on to a "flat blazing littoral with a few big palms and glimpses of a dark blue sea which is not quite of this earth". Sometimes the train stopped at desolate stations with a few wretched adobe huts, sometimes they had to change trains, and waited as much as a whole day for the next one. At last they came to Mazatlan, which was still more unendurably hot. So on, on, three thousand feet above the sea to Tepic, which was cooler; and then by a shattered Ford omnibus of extreme age over ninety kilometres of road so pot-holed and with jolting so violent they had to hold the seat with one hand and the roof with the other, and arrived with splitting headaches. They rode on mules for nine hours to reach Ixtlan, and six hours more next day to reach the junction of Estlatlan, where they collapsed into the train for Guadalajara.

Lawrence was never careful to choose the right season of the year for travelling in a new country—I suppose he would have thought such a precaution "bourgeois". In this case he experienced the hottest month of a hot country, and the strain of such rough travel on his health must have been very severe. It is astonishing he did not break down, as he did about sixteen months later. This fatigue and the absence of Frieda may account for his seeing chiefly the dreary aspects of this journey, a unique experience for him. Mexico seemed quite a different country. At first he had thought he would not go to Chapala without Frieda, but later took Gótzsche to see the beautiful place he had admired so much. When they arrived there, Lawrence was amazed and chagrined to find that it had changed completely. What could have happened? "Somehow it becomes unreal to me now," he told Gótzsche, "I don't know why."

In spite of this emotional disturbance and spiritual depression and his exhaustion by rough travel he continued to write. Between the extreme dates of 18th August and 22nd November (during which occurred all the travels just described), Lawrence re-wrote the whole of Molly Skinner's Australian novel, *The Boy in the Bush*. It was a curious notion of collaboration—he took her plot, characters, episodes and intimate knowledge, and re-cast them entirely in his own style to please himself. In addition, the note-book he was using at the time (which includes his list of characters for the Australian novel) contains many fragments of essays, some of them used afterwards for periodicals, others abandoned, all interesting.

Meanwhile what had happened to Frieda? Evidently she was not giving in, since more than two months after their angry parting in New York he still had heard nothing of her. He "supposed Germany swallowed her." Not Germany but Hampstead, where she had rented a small flat and was able to see her children. At the same time she was seeing a good deal of Lawrence's English friends and acquaintances, and enjoying her importance as wife of an already celebrated author. These people were all provincials in the sense that they were centred on the narrow literary world of London, knew little of Europe, and nothing at all of the vast world outside Europe. He was far more sensitively aware of changes going on in the world and the relative importance of various parts of it. In fact, they didn't notice it at all. They thought he was "in the wilderness", wasting his time and energy in "out of the way places", and of course their affection for him naturally meant that they wanted him back.

It is perfectly true that Lawrence had begun his literary life as a naïve provincial with a regionalist novel. He had developed with great rapidity, and especially since 1919. It is a curious fact that in this century there are writers with intensely cultivated reputations in their own country who are scarcely known outside and not read at all in other countries. Lawrence had become just the opposite. In England, as he went on producing book after book, entirely to please himself, he was supposed to be a spent force. Meanwhile, quite outside their knowledge, he was fast becoming a successful world writer. Already at that date (1923) he was more widely read in the United States than in England—in March of 1923 he had signed contracts for the American issue or re-issue of seven of his early books as well as all his future work. Translations of his books had appeared or were being undertaken in many foreign languages, without his making the least effort or intrigue to obtain them. In short, he was a world writer, who was more read and more respected outside his country than in it. *Birds, Beasts and Flowers*, then just about to appear, had been wholly written out of England on non-English themes, and was to date his most original contribution to poetry. People whose standard of fame was a favourable review in *The New Statesman* or *The Times Literary Supplement*, could not be expected to understand that Lawrence was winning a vastly wider and more enduring fame among people who had never heard of those periodicals.

Lawrence was naturally much more aware of the real situation than they were. To one of those who wrote urging him to "come home and all will be forgiven," he replied with some acerbity:

"Anyhow, though England may lead the world again, as you say, she's got to find a way first. She's got to pick up a lost trail. And the end of the lost trail is here in Mexico."

Staying at the Hotel Garcia, Guadalajara, Jalisco, in fact, and not in a London club. Nevertheless, in a curious mood between wrath, irritation and sweetness, Lawrence was slowly preparing himself to go to England. Not that he was influenced more than a trifle by these condescending urgings to return to that sole centre of intellect and world influence, but because he needed Frieda and was realising that she was not going "to submit and reverence him", and that if he wanted her he had to go and get her. It was a battle almost wholly of his creating, a curious anachronism in him, as if he had been born into a more primitive state of society where the sexes are at war. The strange, violent and seemingly pointless battle between Anna and Will Brangwen in *The Rainbow* gives some idea of the earlier phases of this struggle—in a chapter significantly called Anna Victrix. But it had been renewed, and had now reached its crisis, to which there were three possible solutions. The lovers could remain permanently apart; she could "submit" and go to him in Mexico; he could swallow his bile and his pride, and go to her in London as he had gone to her eleven years before in Germany.

Writing of this battle between them after his death, Frieda wrote: "I think he was right; I should have gone to meet him in Mexico, he should not have come to Europe; these are the mistakes we make sometimes, irreparable."

She forgets what "submission" on her part that return to Mexico would have involved. At the time, however, her instinct was to force him to come to her; and his slow digestion of that tough and bitter fact was accompanied by strange moods and bitter rages. In some consternation Gótzsche reported from Guadalajara that he was "avoiding L. as much as possible—he is really insane when he is as now. You know his ways and how he bends his head far down, till his beard is resting on his chest and he says (not laughing) 'Hee, hee, hee' every time one talks to him. A cold stream always runs down my spine when he does that. I feel it is something insane about him."

Gótzsche thought that Lawrence realised he was in danger of losing Frieda and that he could not live without her. Evidently, when he dropped his insane tittering, and talked to his Danish friend, he could not help discussing this situation, and worked himself into such agitation that Gótzsche reported (truly enough) that Lawrence was "bodily, emotionally and mentally overworked." Evidently he was trying to face the possibility of the worst, but always with his usual instability and waverings. Only two days before they left Guadalajara on their way back to Europe, Gótzsche reported on him again:

"Lawrence is impossible to understand. He seems to be absolutely nuts at times, and to have a hard time with himself. He overestimates himself. He thinks he can show by his feelings what people think and do. At other times he is so reasonable and so overwhelmingly good that there is no end to it. He is afraid Frieda will avoid him; he says that she can have a house in London and have her children with her, then he can travel alone. 'She will hate it before long,' he says, biting his lower lip and nodding small, quick nods. The fact is that he is afraid she will like that arrangement only too well. Nevertheless, he has a large heart and means well, but his ideas are so impractical that it is doubtful he will get anyone to accept them."

By an interesting coincidence on the very same day that Gótzsche wrote that (10th November, 1923) Lawrence wrote a crazy letter to his German mother-in-law which shows how furiously he resented having to give in, and how willingly he would have renewed the war with Frieda if he saw the slightest chance of succeeding. The letter is full of bellicose Teutonism, which he may have thought would flatter her (though in point of fact she was as much French as German), and is virtually an appeal to her to side with him against her daughter. He tells her that what he wants from woman is strength, "battle-strength" and not love—detestable love!

" 'England is so quiet', writes Frieda. Shame on you that you ask for peace to-day! I don't want peace. I go round the world fighting. Pfui! Pfui! In the grave I find my peace. First let me fight and win through. Yes, yes, mother-in-law, make me an oak-wreath and bring the town music under the window, when the half-hero returns."

A week later the distinguished "half-hero" was in Mexico City on his way to recover the strayed wife who so disgustingly wanted peace and love; and on the 22nd of November he sailed from Vera Cruz for Plymouth. It was not a good time of the year to leave a blazing hot country for the winter damps and fogs and frosts of north-west Europe. By the time they reached the approaches to the Channel the weather had become very bleak, and December was upon them. Exactly four years had passed since he had stood on the deck of the Channel steamer looking back with breaking heart at the snow-streaked cliffs of England sinking slowly out of sight "like a grey coffin". Now in the cold early darkness of a December evening he stood in the prow of his ship peering ahead and remembered that day:

"It is four years since I saw, under a little winter snow, the death-grey coast of Kent go out. After four years down, down on the horizon, with the last sunset still in the west, right down under the eyelid of the shut cold sky, the faintest spark, like a message. It is the Lands End light."

8

As might have been foreseen, this forced return to England achieved only one important purpose—that of a reconciliation between Lawrence and Frieda. For the rest it was a humiliating failure, leaving everybody concerned rather frustrated and bewildered. On the other hand there was one very distinct gain. By leaving Mexico when he did Lawrence avoided political disturbances and riots, the predicted "revolutions", which are much more interesting and endurable in the imagination than in squalid fact. Certainly, to his sensitive temperament, this abrupt tearing himself from Mexico was a shock. He still had to finish *The Plumed Serpent*, and we know how carefully Lawrence's "daemon", his "Balaam's Ass", fostered the artist in him. He still wanted Mexico and New Mexico more than anywhere else because they were what the artist in him most wanted. But then a transition so sudden and unexpected to London had its advantages. He saw England and the English with new instructed eyes, a new amazement:

"England seems to me the one really soft spot, the rotten spot in the empire. If ever men had to think in world terms, they have to think in world terms to-day. And here you get an island no bigger than a back garden, chock-full of people who never realise there is anything outside their back garden, pretending to direct the destinies of the world. It is pathetic and ridiculous. And the 'superiority' is bathetic to lunacy.

"These poor 'superior' gentry, all that is left to them is to blame the Americans. It amazes me, the rancour with which English people speak of Americans. Just because the republican eagle of the west doesn't choose to be a pelican for other peoples' convenience. Why should it?"

Frieda's absurd belief that Lawrence would "fulfil" himself by living in London and playing an active part in *The Adelphi* was doomed to speedy extinction. However much he might yield to her in their love relationship, he realised that she knew nothing about him as an artist. In the case in point *The Adelphi* was largely based on the provincial fallacies Lawrence exposed with such devastating scorn.

The very arrival had been inauspicious. It will be remembered that there had been a violent quarrel on the quay at New York just before Frieda left. She and Murry went down to meet him at the station in London, and he was immediately livid with jealousy when he saw they were on friendly terms. Lawrence's jealousy was as extreme as his egotism, and he could not bear Frieda to have any friends, only passing acquaintances chosen by himself. Within a few days he was ill in bed with the inevitable "cold", suffering a bedroom with Morris wallpaper, tea in old cups, and visitors with English voices. Of course, as ever, he was no sooner in one place than he wanted to be somewhere else. There in London he wished he were back in New Mexico.

In New Mexico! After his quarrels with Mabel Luhan and "all the vileness of 1923"! But a great change had occured in that quarter. She had seen the mistake of taking his tantrums and insults too seriously, and had written him a "making it up" letter to Guadalajara, and, as he always did in such cases, he replied immediately and very amiably. This may have been due to rumours of his permanent separation from Frieda, but as the published correspondence shows, they started a brisk exchange of letters in which Mabel Luhan even promised to be "submissive" (!) and Lawrence exhorted her to "fierce recklessness, based on trust, like the recklessness of Pan; trusting deep down to the springs of nature, the sources; and then the laughter", promising in a negligent parenthesis that "one day I will come and take your submission."

But in Frieda there was not submission, and still the battle flared, rising on one occasion to a violent crisis. It appears that Frieda must have known what he was intending to do with the yet unwritten parts of *The Plumed Serpent*, where his Mexican leader becomes identified with Quetzalcoatl, and that Lawrence identified himself with the Mexican. It may have been that, or perhaps merely a chance shot based on other happenings, which made her accuse him before others of being such a preposterous egoist that he "made a god of himself". Perhaps because it was true this roused him to fury, and he began abusing her in Derbyshire dialect, which he always seemed to think had some special virtue in it. Finding this failed to make any impression on her he began smashing the cups and saucers and tea-pot with a poker, threatening her violently:

"Beware, Frieda! If ever you talk to me like that again, it will not be the tea things I smash, but your head. Oh yes, I'll kill you. So beware!"

And smash came the poker on the head-shaped tea-pot. Futile violence! impressive only to the hushed and frightened onlookers, for Frieda knew and he knew that he would do no such things. The mere fact that he had come to London proved his psychological defeat in the battle of wills. He knew it perfectly well, but he wanted the onlookers to be deceived. When he had finished, Frieda quietly swept up the broken pieces and threw them in the dust-bin. After all, he had to pay for them.

From that point of view, the long journeys from Mexico to New York to Los Angeles back to Mexico to London had been almost pure waste. How much of his hard-earned money had been spent on this capricious travel? It is difficult to estimate, but certainly it was more than he should have spent. But now that he was in London and in contact with English friends he had not seen for years, there rose before him once more the phantom of Rananim, the dream of the "colony of friends" he was to rule. Why should they not in Laurentian phraseology "make a life together" in the Taos which had been re-opened to him by the temporary truce with Mabel Luhan? He had written her in rather canting terms that "it would be good if we could make a bit of a life in Taos." He does not seem to have asked himself how much Mabel Luhan would have liked the very heterogeneous set of disciples he proposed to import from London. Yet so dear to his heart was the scheme that he not only obliterated all "the vileness of 1923" but praised her poetry and Tony Luhan's prose. He who had sneered at Gabriele d'Annunzio and Somerset Maugham!

Lawrence, after some preliminary soundings, decided that he would give a dinner to his threatened victims, both to celebrate his prosperity and give a start to this latest revival of Rananim. For this he chose the Café Royal. Much undeserved praise has been lavished on Lawrence as a cook, when in fact all he knew was English cottage cookery with a few German and Italian *plats*. He was ignorant of good French cookery and knew nothing of wines —he was quite capable of duplicating Thackeray's atrocity of ordering a bouillabaisse in Paris and drinking a red wine with it.

The project started under evil auspices. When Lawrence and Koteliansky went to order the meal at the Café Royal, the manager looked upon them with suspicion, demanded a deposit and refused to accept Lawrence's cheque. The guests were certainly all more or less admirers of Lawrence's genius and more or less devoted to him personally. They were: Mary Cannan, Dorothy Brett, Catherine and Donald Carswell, Murry, Gertler and Koteliansky. He had known them all for years, and most of them had stood loyally by him in times of persecution. What in his egotism he failed to consider was that their admiring him did not mean that they liked each other or could live harmoniously together.

At the beginning of this ill-advised meal certain antagonisms were perceptible. Some even of the guests were unknown to each other, and Lawrence himself had apparently not seen Brett since 1915. So the celebration opened in shyness and taciturnity. With the idea of breaking down this British reserve Lawrence plied them with wine, and in doing so drank a good deal himself. But it is not wine that makes good fellowship, but good fellowship which gives value to wine. From bordeaux they went on to port, a wine which Lawrence could not digest. It went to his head, and he began talking Spanish. Koteliansky made an absurd speech, breaking glasses, and declaring: "Lawrence is a great man—nobody here realises how great he is—especially no woman here or anywhere can possibly realise the greatness of Lawrence." By this time the hero of the hour was beginning to realise that in his nervous anxiety to make things go he had drunk too much wine, and was looking "pale and frightfully ill." Instead of breaking off the meeting with an apology, he obstinately persisted in trying to carry out the real purpose of the gathering. He made a discourse about himself and his struggle with the world, and wound up by asking which of them would return with him to New Mexico "to make a bit of a life of it." One by one all save Mary Cannan said they would go, and not one of them really meant it except Dorothy Brett. Murry emotionally kissed Lawrence, who put an arm round his neck saying: "Don't betray me." To which Murry replied: "I love you, Lorenzo, but I won't promise not to betray you." And then a minute or so later Murry's messiah fell forward and was sick on the tablecloth.

From all this Frieda sat coldly aloof, and allowed Brett and

Catherine Carswell to contend in serving the incapacitated master. Murry and Koteliansky then devoted themselves and carried his unconscious form to a taxi, and put him to bed in Hampstead. Lawrence's comment on the episode next day as recorded by Catherine Carswell was this:

"Well, Catherine, I made a fool of myself last night. We must all of us fall at times. It does no harm so long as we first admit and then forget it."

After this disastrous and somewhat humiliating little affair, Lawrence was glad to escape from England to Paris and Baden-Baden. And now a fresh and quite unexpected worry began to menace him. All his letters at this time contain references to his American publisher, "the miserable Seltzer", who was failing to answer letters and telegrams, and paying no money into Lawrence's bank. The fact was that the loyal Seltzer had got into financial difficulties through publishing too many Montparnasse Americans, and was unable to pay Lawrence the royalties his books had earned. But this did not cripple Lawrence, though it made an excellent point against those he feared might borrow money. His own notes show that after the expensive journey back to Taos, buying horses, and the expenditure of about five hundred dollars on repairing Kiowa ranch, his bank balance in October 1924 amounted to three hundred and three pounds in England and $2,285.00 in America.

It was on the 5th March, 1924, that the Lawrences once more set sail (by the *Aquitania* this time) for America, accompanied by the one recruit to Rananim, Dorothy Brett, amiably described by Lawrence in a letter to his mother-in-law as "a little simple but harmless." In her defence let me hasten to say that in Taos the Indians said of her: "Señorita with the dagger very dangerous"; for she pluckily carried a dagger to protect herself. She is the daughter of an English peer, Viscount Esher, and hence always unctuously referred to by Lawrence in his letters as: "Hon. Dorothy Brett", as if she were a member of Congress and not an English lady. Owing to her deafness she carried an ear-trumpet.

Among the others Murry alone still protested that he would soon follow them, and possibly intended to do so. Lawrence had already written to Mabel Luhan: "I rather hope Murry won't come to Taos. Don't trust him very well." But Lawrence was really asking a great deal, for *The Adelphi* at that time was a success, and could hardly have been edited from the Lobo. Why should Murry go to New Mexico and do the chores on a greatly reduced income? Moreover, the two friends were differing once more about the things that really matter, Lawrence maintaining that Life is a form of Death and Murry, with equal originality, that Death is a form of Life.

At New York the three of them—Lawrence, Frieda, Brett—were met on the dock by Seltzer, who, Lawrence thought, "looked very diminished"—owing money. They "struggled up to 100th Street, buried in luggage, in a taxi, in half a blizzard, New York looking vile." The Seltzers did their best, taking them to the theatre and to supper afterwards at the Waldorf. This, unfortunately, did not turn out very well, since Lawrence thundered against the wickedness of people who have enough money to sup at the Waldorf. What would he have said if Seltzer had taken him to a fifty-cent cafeteria?

They moved on to Chicago, meeting the editress of *Poetry* and a number of writers, and then to Taos, where they spent about six weeks. The Lawrences occupied one of Mabel Luhan's two-storeyed houses and Brett lived in a studio close at hand. Their time was occupied in cantering about on horses, being patronised by the Indians, and working up to another quarrel with Mabel Luhan. They also made excursions and bathed at the Ranchos Hot Springs, where Brett thought Lawrence looked "Wicked and Pan-like" with his "eyes gleaming wickedly" as the water dripped from his hair and beard.

What would have happened if Lawrence had brought his Café Royal ark-full of immigrants? Fortunately, although Mabel Luhan thought Brett "a holy Russian idiot" and was wildly exasperated by her Georgian habit of calling everything "lit-tle", they were both ladies and could come to terms of understanding. Lawrence, one feels, did little or nothing to smooth over these complicated adjustments, and he evidently failed to realise the elementary fact that when a woman offers "submission" she means she expects you to do exactly what she wants.

Thus, one cheerful morning, Mabel Luhan innocently remarked that she felt wonderful. Instead of smiling and saying: "Fine!", Lawrence frowned, and made this gracious observation:

"You think it's good health, but it isn't. You think it's *good*, but it isn't. It's just sheer unrestrained ego, that's what it is. It's the destroyer. It's the thing that causes all the trouble."

Poor fellow, with his scarred lungs and nerves frayed by past poverty and suffering, what would he not have given for the abounding health he pretended to despise.

Frieda writes airily of this period: "We stayed with Mabel Luhan, but somehow we didn't get on." Yet they could not have complained that she was unappreciative or ungenerous, for it was now that she offered Lawrence her hundred and seventy acres of land on the Lobo; and when he refused insisted on giving it to Frieda. (I should very much like to hear of any American author being given even half an acre of British territory.) This, he had been saying for years, was what he wanted—a little farm in the Rocky Mountains; and the handsome gift was a challenge.

As a matter of fact, at first he was delighted. Seeing that the broken-down adobe shacks needed to be re-built, Lawrence after a wobble of indecision went heartily to work. Indians were brought in to help, and an irrigation ditch was begun, to bring water from the Gallina Canyon about a mile away. Disregarding his health Lawrence overworked himself with hard manual labour, but that never came between him and the world's beauty. The spirit of place so often meant more to Lawrence than any person, and this was especially true of his Kiowa Ranch. How much it meant to him, how deeply he loved it, may be guessed from what he wrote about it at various times. At the period when he was working at the navvying task of the irrigation ditch his poetic sense was at its highest.

"All those mornings when I went with a hoe along the ditch to the Canyon, at the ranch, and stood, in the fierce proud silence of the Rockies, on their foot-hills, to look far over the desert to the blue mountains away in Arizona, blue as chalcedony, with the sage-brush desert sweeping grey-blue in between, dotted with tiny cube-crystals of houses, the vast amphitheatre of lofty, indomitable desert, sweeping round to the ponderous Sangre de Cristo mountains on the east, and coming up flush at the pine-dotted foot-hills of the Rockies! What splendour! Only the tawny eagle could really sail out into the splendour of it all. It had a splendid silent terror, and a vast far-and-wide significance which made it way beyond mere aesthetic appreciation. Never is the light more pure and over-weening than there, arching with a royalty almost cruel over the hollow uptilted world. Those that have spent morning after morning alone there pitched among the pines above the great proud world of desert will know almost unbearably how beautiful it is, how clear and unquestioned is the might of the day. Just day itself is tremendous there. It is easy to understand that the Aztecs gave hearts of men to the sun. For the sun is not merely hot or scorching, not at all. It is of a brilliant and unchallengeable purity and haughty serenity which would make one sacrifice the heart to it."

Experiences such as this, and their singularly moving expression in language not altogether faultless but of peculiar intensity, give us Lawrence in his greatness and uniqueness. There is nothing petty or absurd about such feelings which certainly have the "religious" quality he claimed for himself. They are the greatest possible contrast to his bickerings and revenges by pen-caricature. A contrast, also, to his theorising of the moment hinted by the reference to the Aztecs and their death-ritual; for there are indications that his megalomania did make him think of himself as a sort of anti-Christian messiah, a new incarnation of Quetzalcoatl able to change the whole world of man. Such was his longing for power! Yet his true power as a great artist is most revealed when he forgets himself and such overweening ambitions, and lives and writes "breast to breast with the Cosmos". He has written wonderfully of strange emotions, the tortured relationships of over-strung people, the light and darkness of sexual desire; and satirical portraits which for hatred, vindictiveness and cruelty are hard to match in literature. But when he could occupy himself with simple manual labour, in solitude, in the presence of great natural beauty, another self seemed to emerge, and he felt a bliss and exaltation unknown or almost unknown to other men.

The ranch in the Rockies was not the only place where he experienced such a spiritual uplifting. It was evoked even more intensely by England, Sicily and Australia, but he delighted to identify himself with a scene so grandiose and so far from the ordinary experience of men. Yet in his complex and tortured personality there remained the English working-man. He is revealed in the Lawrence who liked manual labour and tinkering about the house, as he had seen his father do. There are still many relics of him at Kiowa Ranch, but none more touching than the little English garden between the adobe houses and the alfalfa field, shaded by the huge centuries-old pine he revered. It is just such a garden as you may see by any old-fashioned English cottage, even to the flowering currant. It is so unexpected on the lonely mountain slope, eight thousand feet up, twice as high as the highest point in England; and its cottage vegetables and flowers make such a contrast with the vivid alien colours of the Rocky Mountains wild flowers—the Indian Paint-Brush, the scarlet lobelia, the wild lupins and parti-coloured columbines and the miscalled blue-bell. And over it towers that enormous pine tree, older and vaster it seems than any European pine, that "great pillar of pale, flakey-ribbed copper" which rises there "in callous indifference" with the wind "hissing in the needles, like a vast nest of serpents." He was thinking of it when, having left the ranch for ever but surely with deep regret, he wrote from the Italian Riviera: "Perhaps when I have a *Weh* at all, my Heimweh is for the tree in front of the house, the overshadowing tree whose green top one never looks at."

The absurdity of saying that he "hated America"! Industrial America, yes, but he hated industrialism everywhere, and no intelligent person can be conditioned to an alien nationalism. But to realise what that mountain-side and his ownership of those American acres meant to him, read the last fifteen pages of *St. Mawr*, the last essay of *Mornings in Mexico*, and the essays called 'New Mexico', 'Pan in America' and 'Taos'. It was to him an ecstasy, at once fierce and delicious, seductive and appalling. There were times when his active imagination conjured up fears of solitude and of ghosts, fears of Indians and even of the grizzlies, which no longer exist there. And, lamentably enough, at the very time when part of him was living in this pure exaltation, another part was sad and acrid with vindictive hate.

It is strange. There in New Mexico he had come as near to his Rananim as seems humanly possible, busy with building, carpentring, hoeing and irrigating, riding horses, milking the cow, baking and scrubbing, writing and painting. You would suppose that such a life would lead to what the ancients called "Ataraxia", an indifference to poor humanity and its faults and troubles. But, as Aldous Huxley has pointed out, one result of living as "a bit of a hermit" in mountain solitudes is that a man tends to become "sort of *ex cathedra*"—which in Lawrence's case too often meant being peculiarly censorious and venomous.

That hatred comes out with extraordinary intensity in almost the whole of *St. Mawr*, which ends up in such a different way with the passionate evocation of the mountain. Brett has related how Lawrence sat at table, neglecting his food, to read out parts of *St. Mawr* with his eyes "twinkling with amusement" and so much laughter that from time to time he had to stop. The great red stallion, *St. Mawr*, is a most obvious symbol of Lawrence, and in the story it deliberately falls back crushing its rider and brutally kicking another man in the face. This was read with such "keen joy and pleasure" that Frieda was horrified by the venomous cruelty, and said so. But he paid no attention to her, and went on to describe the state of the mangled rider "with great relish and giggling".

All this physical exertion at such a height and under so powerful a sun, added to the nervous excitement of writing and the paroxysms of hatred which swept over him at times, and the constant irritation of his false relationship with Brett and Mabel Luhan, had to be paid for. It was not very long after the day when he had read out those vindictive passages from *St. Mawr* that he turned aside to spit as he often did, and there came "a splash of bright red blood." Though he took to his bed he would not admit that it was due to tuberculosis, and when Frieda went to him and asked when he would see the doctor, he flew into a paroxysm of rage.

"What do you *mean?* Why have you sent for the doctor? How *dare* you!"

And in his pathetically impotent raging against the disease which gripped him he threw at Frieda's head the iron ring he used as an egg-cup, raving on:

"You *know* I dislike doctors. You *know* I wouldn't have him or you wouldn't have sent for him behind my back. I *won't* see him, I *won't*. I'll go out and hide in the sage brush until he goes. I'll teach you."

Of course, he simply could not endure the inferiority of being a sick person, could not bear to be told yet again by a doctor that he had tuberculosis, and must lie still and rest and be peaceful. From the report telephoned down the doctor had feared another attack of pneumonia, which if true meant that Lawrence must be taken to hospital. He therefore sent Willard Johnson on ahead to help carry him to the car, and arrived himself with plenty of blankets to wrap up the patient for the journey back to Taos. With the doctor actually there Lawrence submitted meekly enough to examination. As there was no condition of pneumonia, he was given the usual advice, to lie quite still for the bleeding lung to heal. But as soon as the doctor had left, Lawrence insisted on treating himself with an old-fashioned poultice such as his mother had put on him in his childhood, and then told Frieda what she was to say to the others, which was this untruth:

"It's all right. Nothing wrong; the lungs are strong. It is just a touch of bronchial trouble—the tubes are sore."

Nobody can say he was wrong to do this. Even from a medical point of view it might have been of psychological benefit provided he had taken the necessary physical precautions. His comparative neglect of them may have been due to ignorance, but far more to an instinctive belief that better a short life than the quarter-life of a permanent invalid prolonged to seventy. The inevitable feeling of depression and hopelessness which dragged him down at these periods of physical suffering were always attributed by him to some other cause. He wrote to Murry:

"Did I tell you my father died on September 10th, the day before my birthday? The autumn always gets me badly, as it breaks into colours. I want to go south, where there is no autumn, where the cold doesn't crouch over one like a snow-leopard waiting to pounce. The heart of the North is dead, and the fingers of cold are corpse fingers. There is no more hope northwards, and the salt of its inspiration is the tingling of the viaticum on the tongue."

9

THESE periodic attacks on his lungs invariably made Lawrence restless, especially since he always blamed them and his subsequent depression on the place he was in. Although the arrangements for living up on the ranch were much better and more comfortable, he did not feel inclined to spend another winter there—especially without the Danes to help. And there was still that unfinished *Plumed Serpent* tugging him back to Mexico. Though I seem always to be recording some new move, I do not believe Lawrence was unduly restless. As a guide I made for myself a careful (and I think complete) list of all his journeys from Croydon on (omitting mere weekends and short excursions) and they were far fewer than I had expected. True, he enjoyed a freedom of movement about the world which is now denied to most people, but he made an incomparable use of it. In his lifetime there were tens of thousands of wealthier English people who rushed about the world far more than he did, with absolutely no result except boring themselves and other people and wasting opportunities.

Even that spring and summer at Kiowa, with all their intense activity and his illness, were interrupted by at least one important excursion which must be described. In August of 1924 Mabel and Tony Luhan drove the Lawrences across the desert to see the Snake Dance of the Hopi Indians, a very famous Indian ceremony which annually attracted as many as three thousand white spectators. During this animistic ritual some of the Indians carry live rattlesnakes in their mouths, and eventually two so-called "priests" rush out carrying them into the desert and set them free, either as ritual offerings or as sacred messengers to the gods. Lawrence has left two, almost contradictory, accounts of this journey and the interesting magical practices. The first was written for Willard Johnson's *Laughing Horse*, and is Lawrence in a laughing satirical mood "debunking" the whole affair and the tourists who crowded to see it:

"Just a show! The south-west is the great playground of the white American. The desert isn't good for anything else. But it does make a fine national playground. And the Indian, with his long hair and his bits of pottery and blankets and clumsy home-made trinkets, he's a wonderful live toy to play with. More fun than keeping rabbits, and just as harmless. Wonderful, really, hopping around with a snake in his mouth. Lots of fun! Oh, the wild west is lots of fun: the Land of Enchantment. Like being right inside the circus-ring: lots of sand and painted savages jabbering, and all that. Come on, boys! Lots of fun!"

This cheerful irreverence is kept up for pages, and though it can probably only be fully enjoyed by those who have seen the south-west, anyone can see that it would be disagreeable to serious Taosists. All very well for Lawrence to titter his derision of decadent Europe and all its tiresome old culture, but not so good when he turned it on them. According to that gospel, living in New Mexico and being matey with Indians solved most personal problems, if not the problem of the Cosmos—that and bathing in the radio-active

Ranchos Hot Springs. Now it is impossible to say whether Lawrence repented of his tar-and-feather offence, or whether—as is more likely—it was just a mood of irritation with the Luhans, a bit of spite. At all events he undoubtedly did change his mind, and wrote a far more sympathetic essay containing passages which are so solemn and appreciative as to appear a little over-cooked:

"Man, little man, with his consciousness and his will, must both submit to the great origin-powers of his life, and conquer them. Conquered by man who has overcome his fears, the snakes must go back into the earth with his message of tenderness, of request, and of power. They go back as rays of love to the dark heart of the first of suns. But they go back also as arrows shot clean by man's sapience and courage, into the resistant, malevolent heart of the earth's oldest, stubborn core. In the core of the first of suns, whence man draws his vitality, lies poison as bitter as the rattle-snake's. This poison man must overcome, he must be master of its issue. . . ."

And so forth. Frankly, to me it rings false, and is one of the very few occasions when Lawrence wrote in betrayal of his integrity. I think he did so when he wrote the very worked-up "poetic" piece about Garsington to please Ottoline Morrell, and I think he did so here, for a similar reason.

It was on the 11th October, 1924, that the Lawrences came down from their mountain perch, and set out for Mexico City, taking with them "the Brett". Because of the anarchic state of the country and of rumoured bandits, the train carried a truckload of the same disguised as soldiers, with others on the roof. When the Mexican Indians boarded the train, Brett (who may possibly have read the works of D. H. Lawrence) noted that "a wild pride comes from them; their glistening brown arms and neck in their low-cut bodices, gleam proudly."

Evidently Lawrence was more than usually out of health and spirits, for he found Mexico City peculiarly depressing on this occasion. The capital struck him as "shabby and depressed—no business doing—no money". (A strange point of view from one who wrote: "O start a revolution, somebody, not to get money but to lose it all for ever!") Frieda caught a cold and he was invited to an evening with the P.E.N. Club. "We've both had terrible colds —Mexico City not worth coming for—chilly, reeking with influenza and bad spirits." There was a meeting with Somerset Maugham, which went off rather poorly as such meetings of the famous often do. Lawrence complained grievously: "Everybody in this damned city coughing and sneezing: it's been very chilly: snow low down on Popocatepetl. And the town uneasy and depressed: as if the bottom had fallen out of the barrel. Don't like it."

A picturesque way out of this difficulty was found for the Lawrences by the British vice-consul, whose brother was a priest at Oaxaca—"a little town in the south of Mexico—about five thousand feet up—with a perfect climate: sun and roses." Accordingly they moved down there with Brett, and Lawrence began to work steadily and rapidly on the last part of *The Plumed Serpent*. He must have completed the novel and also have written the first four sketches of *Mornings in Mexico* between the 18th November, 1924, and the end of January 1925. The very last entry in the journal, begun five years earlier in Capri, runs thus: "Nov. 17th, 1924. Balance in National Chase bank $2004.00 to Oct. 31st. Move into Richards' house to-morrow."

This Richards was the English priest, and the house he found for them was a "rather crumbly adobe house built round two sides of a garden *patio*", with orange and banana trees, two green parrots and a little dog called Corasmin. The place was unfurnished, but furniture was to be borrowed, and they soon had it pleasantly arranged. Lawrence and Frieda went marketing for local pottery and more of the serapes—the brightly coloured blankets—which they had bought the year before in Chapala. These they hunted out from "a babel and a hubbub of unwashed wild people—heaps of roses and hibiscus flowers, blankets, very nice wild pottery, calves, birds, vegetables, and awful things to eat—including squashed wild locust-beetles."

Brett was not living with them. In spite of her status as the one sincere adherent to Rananim, she had been told to go to a hotel by the master, and was not even allowed to buy herself the picturesque trifles she craved for. These things, Lawrence told her, were not meant for her but for the Indians. (Why then did he buy them?) She was allowed a pair of *huaraches*, Mexican sandals, after careful sniffing had proved that they had not been tanned by the popular Mexican method of steeping in human excrement.

In a southern community the market is usually the liveliest, most picturesque and humanly interesting scene. Every Saturday the Indians came to the Oaxaca market from the outlying country, "white dots of men threading down the trail over the bare humps of the plain, following the dark twinkling movement of asses, the dark nodding of the woman's head as she rides beside the baskets." The donkeys carried tomatoes and gourds, charcoal and wood-faggots and "twin great nets of bubble jars". Among the quick-trotting donkeys moved slow heavy ox-carts. The market itself was a "huge roofed-in place" with a fountain in the centre, surrounded by flowers, "red, white, pink roses in heaps, many-coloured little carnations, poppies, bits of larkspur, lemon and orange marigolds, buds of madonna lilies, pansies, a few forget-me-nots"—only the flowers from the cool hill places, not the too common tropical flowers.

There were lines of stalls, some with "brilliant vegetables", others with bread, cheese, butter, eggs, chickens, turkeys, meat. In another part were the coloured blankets and native clothes and huaraches, and over all came the noise of the Indians talking, "as if all the ghosts in the world were talking to one another—a noise something like rain, or banana leaves in a wind, the queer hissing murmurs of the Zapotec *idioma*, among the sounds of Spanish, the quiet aside-voices of the Mixtecas." Through it all moved Lawrence with his light quick step, noticing everything, remembering everything to the least detail.

One thing about this market he disliked very much. Under the slow but ruthless attack of tuberculosis his face had changed entirely from that of the young man with the Philip IV chin, and had taken on that drawn mask-like look of dignified suffering often to be seen in such patients. That look added to his beard made inevitable the derisive whisper of "Cristo! Cristo!" which followed him everywhere in Mexico. This was especially annoying when in the imagination he was evoking and to some extent identifying himself with Quetzalcoatl. But there were other and more serious inconveniences about residence in Oaxaca:

"Everything is so shaky and really so confused. The Indians are queer little savages, and awful agitators pump bits of socialism over them and make everything just a mess. It's really a sort of chaos. And I suppose American intervention will become inevitable. You know, socialism is a dud. It makes just a mush of people: and especially of savages. Socialism here is a farce of farces: except very dangerous."

And though his vivid imagination may have exaggerated them, there were dangers in the situation. The town of Oaxaca had been isolated for months, and this might happen again at any time if through violence the slender thread of railway were cut. When he had been in Mexico City Lawrence had disliked it so much that his one wish was "to get away into the country and be by myself", but once there he was appalled by the thought that in the event of another "revolution" he might not be able to get away—"Fancy being shut up here for years! How awful!" He heard rumours of mysterious and incurable diseases said to be infecting the remote mountain population. White residents hinted that it was dangerous for him and the two women to go beyond the town limits, as they might be murdered.

He did not allow himself to be intimidated, but visited the ancient ruins at Mitla, and went with his native servant, Rosalino, to look at some of the mountain villages, where the Indians were so frightened by his white face and red beard that they fled in terror, as from some weird foreign demon. There were irrational fears in the Mexico Lawrence discovered for himself. Wonderful as it all sounds in the vivid prose descriptions and poetic incantations of *The Plumed Serpent*, the prosaic reality was less attractive. The sensation that everywhere about you is squalid fear is depressing, and almost from the beginning of his residence in Oaxaca Lawrence seems to have felt more and more repelled by what he called "the vibration of this rather malevolent continent."

The revolutionary spirit even caused a slight domestic upheaval. Frieda, who was slow to entertain suspicion or resentment, could gradually work herself into what Lawrence called "states", when she became furiously jealous. Apparently all through this Mexican journey she had been slowly blowing up the fires of her wrath against Brett. In Frieda's view there was altogether too much loyalty in Brett, who invariably took Lawrence's side in every difference of opinion, and who went off with him every day—he to write, she to paint, leaving Frieda to play with Corasmin and the parrots. To Frieda Brett's adoration of Lawrence was just "a silly old habit", and she expressed her sentiment freely:

"Brett, I detest your adoration for Lawrence. Only one thing I would detest more, and that is if you adored me."

And accordingly some time towards the end of January Frieda, who from the beginning had insisted that Brett must live at the hotel and not with them, began hammering at Lawrence that she did not want Brett to be "a part of our life any more." At first he flew into a rage, and then, as usual, did as Frieda wished; and Brett went back to Mexico City. Perhaps by way of reassuring Frieda as to her intentions, Brett in one of her letters made some mention of an attentive Captain she had met. In reply she received a long, angry, rambling, didactic letter in the following terms:

"I know your Captain. There is a kind of little warm flame that shakes with life in his blue eyes; and that is more worth having than all the high-flown stuff. And he is quite right to leave his door open. Why do you jeer? You're not superior to sex, and you never will be. Only too often you are inferior to it. You like the excitation of sex in the eye, sex in the head. It is an evil and destructive thing. Know from your Captain that a bit of warm flame of life is worth all the spiritualness and delicacy and Christlikeness on this miserable globe. No, Brett, I do *not* want your friendship. Your 'friendship' for me betrays the essential man and male that I am, and makes me ill. Yes, you make me ill, by dragging at one half at the expense of the other half. And I am so much better now that you have gone. I refuse any more of this 'delicate friendship' business, because it damages one's wholeness."

This from the man who had insisted so emphatically to Katherine Mansfield his belief in friendship, "friendship permanent as marriage" between man and man, woman and woman, man and woman; and this the reward of the fidelity and loyalty he claimed to value above everything, in one whose fidelity and loyalty to him cannot be questioned. And then to give her the brush-off and send her away alone in a Mexico seething with revolution!

So, Lawrence and Frieda were left alone in the old Oaxaca house with its picturesque *patio* and Rosalino and Corasmin, the dog, and the two parrots. But if Lawrence was unfair when he accused Brett of making him ill, he was, when he wrote that letter, about to learn something of the death-dealing powers he had been evoking so seriously in his *Plumed Serpent* hymns. Now he was to find out what terrors and scourges might be wielded by his Itzpapalotls,

Huitzilopochtlis and Quetzalcoatls, and how perfectly ready they were to accept *him* as a human sacrifice.

All the bedrooms at the Oaxaca hotel were fitted with mosquito nets, but in his own house there Lawrence personally refused to have one. Mosquito curtains were unnecessary, a modern fad. To keep mosquitoes off all you need to do is to pull the sheet over your nose. Most unluckily Lawrence one night uncovered his rather bulbous nose and discovered in the morning that it was covered with mosquito bites.

Oaxaca was in the malaria region. Lawrence, it will be remembered, had been accustomed to deny the validity of science ("all scientists are liars") but I do not know if he went so far as to deny that malaria is transmitted by the bite of infected anopheles mosquitoes—certainly one letter of his seems to imply that he thought malaria was "caused by bad air". Nor do I know which god of the terrifying Mexican pantheon is supposed to wield malaria as part of his celestial punishing equipment. But certain it is that even as Lawrence wrote that harsh letter to Brett he was sickening for the illness. Moreover, in tropical lands where sanitation is not studied, lettuces and all green salads are apt to carry infections which cause serious disturbances inside. At the very moment that Lawrence went down with a bad attack of malaria he was also smitten by the Mexican god of diarrhœa and dysentery. And this double attack on his life centres soon extended to his tubercular lungs.

It was a combination of diseases which must surely have killed anyone who did not come of a tough stock and possess great reserves of vitality. The native doctor who had been attending him at first, seeing him so ill, was very much afraid that this Cristo-looking foreigner would die on his hands and he be held responsible by some distant but odious and powerful authority. An English soldier-missionary brought him soup and prayed over him, and the few English and American residents did all in their power to help.

One night of stifling heat broke into fierce stabs of lightning and crashes of near thunder. In the early Taos days Tony Luhan in a thunder-storm had said: "The white people say that the thunder comes from clouds hitting each other, but the Indians know better." At this Lawrence had "giggled nervously", but this Mexican storm was nothing to laugh at since it was the forerunner of an earthquake. In the brief pauses between the rolling thunder Lawrence heard outside the dismal howling of dogs and confused noises of frightened horses. With a sudden awful crash the earthquake-god smote the shuddering town. In the darkness Lawrence, and Frieda in the next room, could hear and feel the ceiling beams thudding up and down in their sockets on the shaking walls, with a noise like the stamping of many horse-hoofs. Frieda, crouching in terror under her bed, called to him to do the same; but he was too weak with illness to move.

This series of calamities at Oaxaca made a crisis in Lawrence's later life. It ended his life as a world-wanderer, and henceforth set limits to all his physical activities. He had always lived a threatened man, but one of great courage and hope. Now, however much he might try to conceal it from others and even from himself, he must have known that he was a doomed man who could not hope for much more life.

He had been so over-confident of his own rightness and powers. Sooner than others he had guessed the inevitable collapse of the old European order, and he had been so sure that he knew the way out, that "the end of the lost trail is here in Mexico", that the "conscious" life had to be somehow made submissive to "dark unconscious" impulses. When he played, but with a good deal of seriousness, with the notion of reviving the Mexican gods, he thought of them really as symbols of old-forgotten unconscious impulses and powers. But now the quest had failed, the dark gods of the death-ritual had turned upon him, smiting him with malaria and dysentery, with thunder and earthquake and terror.

It was an evil time for him, and in his distress his thoughts rushed back to England. He would "go home" at once, or at any rate as soon as he was well enough to reach Vera Cruz and get a ship:

"Something in the hard, fierce, finite sun of Mexico, in the dry terrible land, and in the black staring eyes of the suspicious natives, had made the ordinary day lose its reality to him. It had cracked like some great bubble, and to his uneasiness and terror, he had seemed to see through the fissures the deeper blue of that other Greater Day where moved the other sun shaking its dark blue wings. Perhaps it was the malaria: perhaps it was his own inevitable development: perhaps it was the presence of those handsome, dangerous, wide-eyed men left over from the ages before the flood in Mexico. He was ill, and he felt as if at the very middle of him, beneath his navel, some membrane were torn, some membrane which had connected him with the world and its day. . . . He wanted to go home. It did not matter that England was small and tight and over-furnished, if the Greater Day were round about. He wanted to go home, away from these big wild countries where men were dying back into the Greater Day, home where he dare face the sun behind the sun, and come into his own in the Greater Day. But he was as yet too ill to go. He lay in the nausea of the tropics, and let the days pass over him. The door of his room stood open on to the *patio* where green banana trees and high strange-sapped flowering shrubs rose from the water-sprinkled earth towards that strange cage of blue which was the sky over the shadow-heavy, perfume-soggy air on the closed-in courtyard. . . ."

It was hard enough to bring him out alive from the death-trap he had entered so blithely and wilfully. They moved him from the house to the Oaxaca hotel, where he could have better service and attention. And day after day had passed over before he was not too weak to attempt the two hundred and forty miles of slow twisting railway travel which must be traversed before he could reach even Mexico City. His weakness was so great that even that journey had to be broken half-way.

They were alone together in a little wayside railway hotel in the intense tropical heat, and as she looked at him Frieda's courage and strength, which she had kept intact until that moment, suddenly crumbled as she realised the truth. All night long she "cried like a maniac" and said to herself over and over again, miserably, hysterically: "He will never be quite well again, he is ill, he is doomed. All my love, all my strength will never make him whole again."

Under the imminent threat of death and parting, isolated in disaster, the old passion and tenderness between them burned through all the ashes of foolish conflict. Lawrence had believed he must die and that Frieda would bury him in the "ugly cemetery" at Oaxaca. She had tried to laugh it away. But in the mood of that night death had seemed certain to him, almost certain, and her heart had nearly broken when he said: "But if I die, nothing has mattered but you, nothing at all."

10

No, "going home" was not so easy for him as it had seemed in the first relief of his survival of the death crisis of his illness. It had been hard to reach even Mexico City, and it did not prove very easy to escape from Mexico itself. True, the hotel in the capital was much more comfortable and there were friends to visit him, but there were also the detested doctors who, he complained, made him endure "all sorts of examinations, blood tests, etc."

Coming abruptly into his bedroom one day Frieda found one of the doctors with Lawrence. He turned to her and said point-blank: "Mr. Lawrence has tuberculosis." At these words Lawrence looked at her with "unforgettable eyes", and again she tried to comfort him. She must have known this before, although, as had happened with the blood-spitting on the ranch, he tried always to convince her and the others that he had not got consumption "really, only the bronchials are sore". And in a way he had convinced her. But now on top of her own forebodings she was formally warned by the doctor that Lawrence was doomed. These doctors in Mexico City may have realised from talking to her that Lawrence had succeeded in hiding his true condition from her. Not only did one of them make that categorical assertion in Lawrence's presence, so that he could never again deny it, but they collectively met Frieda and told her plainly:

"Take him to the ranch; it's his only chance. He has T.B. in the third degree. A year or two at most."

Well, he lived longer than they expected, but it was only for five years, instead of the two predicted. What was almost miraculous is that he continued to write and often at his best up until the end. But even before he fell so ill at Oaxaca he seemed to feel that he was coming to an end of the long books which demand such concentrated energy. "I feel it will be a long time before I do another novel," he admitted later.

In that weary spring of 1925 the doctor said he was too ill even to risk the sea voyage to England, and certainly not able to survive another northern winter; so there was nothing for it but to try the ranch. It was a wreck of the old Lawrence who set out by Pullman, only to be held up at the frontier and "tortured by immigration officials, who made all the difficulties in the ugliest fashion" to stop his entering the United States. A foreigner in his state of health was not to be allowed in, and only the intervention of the U.S. Embassy at Mexico City enabled them to get through. At last they got him back to his mountain-side, and strength gradually returned. Mabel Luhan was away, and Brett was sent down to del Monte, where she received this peevish note from him:

"It's no good our trying to get on together—it won't happen. Myself—I have lost all desire for intense or intimate friendships. Acquaintance is enough. It will be best when we go our separate ways. A life in common is an illusion, when the instinct is always to divide, to separate individuals and set them one against the other. And this seems to be the ruling instinct, unacknowledged. Unite with the one against the other, and it's no good."

That was once more a repudiation of much that he had preached for years—it is the familiar self-repudiation. But when he reached the ranch he was too weary to endure the strife he insisted on making a part of every friendship. Of course, that letter to Brett did not mean that they were never to meet again. Indeed, since his letters at the epoch are few and what he wrote not very useful as biography, we should know very little about that summer but for Brett's notes.

As Lawrence gradually recovered strength and energy, the terror and wretchedness of those last weeks in Mexico gradually faded until it was as if they had never been. Once more he began to enjoy the sensations of living with his own peculiar intensity. When he first reached the ranch that spring he was so weak that he could just manage to climb laboriously into the saddle. A few weeks later he could leap into it as lightly as a cat, and what is more had taken on all his old chores. There were the horses, and the cow Susan about whom he fashioned so many stories. It was Lawrence who milked her morning and evening, and as she liked to run away and hide in the shrubs, she often had to be found and pursued, on foot or on horseback. He would look for her through the opera glasses given him by Frieda's mother, and curse Susan's obstinacy and perversity as he had cursed his nanny-goat ("you, *crapa*!") in Sicily.

Once again he was able to knead and to bake bread in the outdoor oven. He worked once more on clearing the irrigation ditch and watering the field and garden—he liked to feel the cold mountain water running over his bare feet as he worked. He chopped wood and built a shelter for the cow. One day he shot a porcupine and then was filled with agonies of remorse, as when he threw the "clumsy log" at the snake; and wrote a long and most interesting essay about it. On another occasion he spent hours picking the porcupine quills from the swollen nose of a strange dog. Of course it wanted to stay for ever, and when, trying to get rid of it, he threatened it with a switch, he accidentally hit its wounded nose and it fled yelping with agony—and Lawrence was left pale and trembling with shame and remorse. And once more he became absorbed in the beauty of the land, as he watched:

". . . the vast eagle-like wheeling of the daylight, that turned as the eagles which lived in the near rocks turned overhead in the blue, turning their luminous, dark-edged patterned bellies and underwings upon the pure air, like winged orbs. So the daylight made the vast turn upon the desert, brushing the farthest outwatching mountains."

Once more, day after day, he looked over the desert to the canyon of the Rio Grande, saw "the little brown adobe houses" of the distant villages, sometimes "far-off rocks, thirty miles away" and "the puckered folds of mesa-sides" and then the sun setting in a blaze "above the shallow cauldron of simmering darkness, when "the round mountain of Colorado would lump up into uncanny significance, northward."

"Ah," he exclaims, looking at it, "it was beauty, beauty absolute!" But as that summer of 1925 passed slowly over him his delight in that "beauty absolute" must have been more and more shaded with pain and regret. It was not because his sudden tenderness for Frieda seemed to have died down, and given place to the old wrangles and stresses. He was used to such strife, and indeed seemed to think it an essential part of married life. No, his sadness did not come from these contentions, nor even from the fact that he lived as one reprieved but for a short time from death. However much he put it aside then, and later wrote confidently of returning to the ranch from Europe, he must have realised that this was almost certainly his last period at Kiowa.

There is a very simple explanation of why he left his beloved ranch in the autumn of 1925 and never returned. It was no "hatred of America", but simply the fact that in his state of health re-entry to the U.S. was impossible, especially since he had already been held up once. The intervention of a sympathetic American Embassy had got him through on the plea of saving his life, but the visa could only be for six months, and he must have known that the laws would forbid his being granted another. So as each day dropped away and he looked at that immense panorama of desert and mountain in the sunset glow, he must have had the sadness of knowing that he was looking at them for the last time.

The visa was due to expire at the end of September 1925, and just before it became invalid the Lawrences sailed from New York for Southampton—now after nearly six years he was really completing his circling of the globe. But of course "home" in the reality of approaching winter turned out to be hardly the refuge he had imagined on his sick-bed in Oaxaca—even if we did not make allowance for his inevitable changeableness. In October he wrote from London:

"I feel queer and foreign here but look on with wonder instead of exasperation, this time. It's like being inside an aquarium, the people all fishes swimming on end. No doubt about it, England is the most fantastic Alice-in-Wonderland country."

His attempts to link up with some of these queer fish from his past were not altogether successful. By a clumsy attempt to repay a five-pound note given long before to buy Frieda a coat, Lawrence managed to hurt one of his most loyal and unselfish admirers, Catherine Carswell. Oddly enough, though he could easily afford it, she somehow still had the impression that he was as hard up as in the bitter days of "precarious borrowing" during the war. But though his royalties did decline between 1925 and 1928, and he had spent a disproportionate amount of his income on travelling, his income for 1925 must have been about one thousand pounds.

From Oaxaca in November and December of 1924, he had written very harshly to Murry, who had been told that one of his letters was "a little yellow cry" from his liver, and that he "rotted his manhood at the roots" with introspective sentiment. The second letter had been still more violent and insulting. Still, Murry by now knew well enough that Lawrence wrote vehement insults to his friends one day, and forgot them the next. The two agreed to meet once more, and to show his repentance Lawrence, instead of apologising, brought "a nice bag of fruit". Alas, the two friends seemed doomed to disappoint each other. Lawrence found it impossible to take Murry seriously as a writer, and deplored what he considered his sentimental Christianism. "Must you really write about Jesus?" Lawrence asked truculently, adding: "Jesus becomes more unsympatisch to me the longer I live."

More interesting from its light on Lawrence's own writing is the note: "Been motoring all over my well-known Derbyshire." Although this motor trip was apparently repeated, this one in the autumn of 1925 almost certainly is that described as taken by Constance in *Lady Chatterley's Lover*. It is very characteristic of Lawrence that the core of that book, the meditation which gradually unfolded into one of the most heatedly discussed erotic novels of the century, was based on an excursion which revived in full fury his passionate hatred of the ugliness and meanness of Industrialism. They hurt him all the more since for so long he had been living in places which, whatever their drawbacks, were not ugly. "The horrors of my childhood came over me like a smothering flood," he told Catherine Carswell on his return from this expedition. And this is what he had seen and felt as he revisited "home" after his wandering years.

"The car ploughed uphill through the long squalid straggle of Tevershall, the blackened brick dwellings, the black slate roofs glistening their sharp edges, the mud black with coal-dust, the pavements wet and black. It was as if dismalness had soaked through and through everything. The utter negation of natural beauty, the utter negation of the gladness of life, the utter absence of the instinct for shapely beauty which every bird and beast has, the utter death of the human intuitive faculty was appalling. The stacks of soap in the grocers' shops, the rhubarb and lemons in the greengrocers! the awful hats in the milliners! all went by, ugly, ugly, ugly, followed by the plaster-and-gilt horror of the cinema with its wet picture announcements: *A Woman's Love!* and the new big Primitive chapel, primitive enough in its stark brick and big panes of greenish and raspberry glass in the windows. The Wesleyan chapel, higher up, was of blackened brick and stood behind iron railings and blackened shrubs. The Congregational chapel, which thought itself superior, was built of rusticated sandstone and had a steeple, but not a very high one. Just beyond were the new school buildings, expensive pink brick, and gravelled playground inside iron railings, all very imposing, and mixing the suggestion of a chapel and a prison. Standard Five girls were having a singing lesson, just finishing the la-me-do-la exercises and beginning a "sweet children's song". Anything more unlike song, spontaneous song, would be impossible to imagine. a strange bawling yell that followed the outlines of a tune. It was not like savages: savages have subtle rhythms. It was not like animals: animals *mean* something when they yell. It was like nothing on earth, and it was called singing. . . . What could possibly become of such a people, a people in whom the living intuitive faculty was dead as nails, and only queer mechanical yells and uncanny will-power remained."

Nor was this the full extent of his appalled horror at the spectacle of "home". When he saw "the great lorries full of steel-workers from Sheffield, weird, distorted, smallish beings like men, off for an excursion to Matlock", why then his "bowels fainted". He thought to himself: "Ah, what has man done to men? What have the leaders of men been doing to their fellow-men? They have reduced them to less than humanness; and now there can be no fellowship any more! It is just a nightmare!"

This is the vision which impelled him to write *Lady Chatterley's Lover*, in which he imagined a world where "a new phallic tenderness" between man and woman would render such mutilatings and desolation impossible. With eyes and memory still thronged with visions of the world's infinite beauty, he saw with startled horror the squalid drabness of the "home" in which he had grown up. He recoiled from the sight with fear, repugnance, blind hatred, such as he had felt in his boyhood when he gazed in agonies of self-conscious misery from the window of the public library and felt the panic urge to fly from the industrial monster. In his strange unpractical conceit he had come to believe later that he could by mere words bring to birth a new world. But what did he want? his readers asked themselves. Indeed the question is not to be answered, for he wavered so much he never knew himself.

His "practical" politics never got much beyond the point of: Get out of that throne, I want it. Power for power's sake, the meanest of ambitions after money for money's sake. He was a democrat among aristocrats, an aristocrat among democrats. He saw himself as a leader of humanity, with inferiors but no superior. Is there any conceit so colossal as proletarian conceit? At one moment he would boast himself, in uncouth dialect, a collier's son, and the next proclaim himself a mouthpiece of the gods—equal to the gods, himself a god. He achieved a most strange mixture of his mother's back-street Victorian morality and intellectualised emancipation. The sexual habits and behaviour of everyone else were wrong, and he alone right. Having run away with a married woman he gravely dogmatised on the irrevocable sanctity of marriage.

In all his self-contradictions, he never wavered in the belief that industrialism as practised meant the enslavement and degradation of mankind. Here he was clearly Ruskin's pupil. It was not a question of "changing the system", substituting a new administration and distribution. Industrialism, machines and machine-minders were the evil, and must be totally abolished. He had really believed at times that he could do this by himself:

> "See if I don't bring you down and all your high opinion
> And all your ponderous roofed-in erection of right and wrong.
> Your particular heavens,
> With a smash.
>
> See if your skies aren't falling!
> And my head, at least, is thick enough to stand it, the smash.
>
> See if I don't move under a dark and nude, vast heaven
> When your world is in ruins, under your fallen skies.
> Caryatids, pale-faces.
> See if I am not Lord of the dark and moving hosts
> Before I die."

So he refused to accept the defeat of Oaxaca, and, after shuddering once more over the horrors of "home", slipped off to Frieda at Baden-Baden. Following a few unpleasant days in Switzerland they took a villa at Spotorno on the Italian Riviera. There Lawrence began work again, not on *Lady Chatterley*, which he held in reserve, but on short novels, *The Virgin and the Gipsy* and *Glad Ghosts*, which return to European and English themes as if his long wanderings had never been. The former especially is more in his 1912 manner than 1926.

But on the whole he was ready to enjoy a rest from his many

literary labours and to enjoy, instead of fretting over, one of those inevitable periods of lying fallow which come to every artist. "To kill yourself like Keats, for what you've got to say, is to mix the egg-shell in with the omlette", he wrote Murry. "In short, shut up. Throw the Adelphi to the devil. I don't care a straw who publishes me, and who doesn't, nor where nor how, nor when nor why. I'll contrive, if I can, to get enough money to live on. But I don't take myself seriously except between eight and ten a.m., and at the stroke of midnight. No, no! I'm forty, and I want, in a good sense, to enjoy my life."

Not taking himself seriously was an innovation like his sudden conversion to hedonism, "in a good sense". Of course it may have been merely a jeer at Murry's industry, but it is a fact that at this time he was much occupied with the revival of an old project to buy "a lugger" or some such melodramatic craft, hire a captain and two men to navigate the mysterious object, and thus explore the Mediterranean. He still wanted to know the beauties of the world, but knew that if he was to do so without sudden disaster he must travel easily and without fatigue. Since his return he had linked up with the Brewsters again, and offered to put up one hundred pounds towards the expenses of a boat if they would join him.

All these cheerful plans for "enjoying life" were doomed to frustration. As winter settled down there came on him the lamentably inevitable "sore chest" and he was soon writing disconsolately:

"I'm in bed these six days with 'flu—don't see daylight yet. It gave me bronchial haemorrhage like at the ranch, only worse."

After all their experience of Italian winters, they had been foolish enough to rent a flimsy summer villa with no proper means of heating. And this lung condition was aggravated, if indeed it had not been brought on, by another fierce battle in the long struggle between himself and Frieda. She shall tell the story:

"My daughter Barbara, now grown up, was coming to stay with me. She was coming for the first time. I was beside myself with joy to have her. I had not waited in vain for so many years and longed for these children. But Lawrence did not share my joy. One day at our evening meal came the outburst: 'Don't you imagine your mother loves you,' he said to Barby, 'she doesn't love anybody, look at her false face.' And he flung half a glass of red wine in my face. Barby, who besides my mother and myself was the only one not to be scared of him, sprang up: 'My mother is too good for you,' she blazed at him, 'much too good; it's like pearls thrown to swine.' Then we both began to cry."

Then Frieda's other daughter, Else, arrived, and to counter them this jealous creature brought in his sister Ada and a friend, and whined to them of Frieda's unkindness to him—which led to bitter female rows. Ada said to Frieda with an amiability worthy of her brother: "I hate you from the bottom of my heart." One night after Frieda had reconciled herself with Lawrence, Ada persuaded him to lock his door against his wife.

"Chapter of dismalnesses!" was Lawrence's report on the situation to Brett, who had followed him from New Mexico and was now staying with the Brewsters on Capri. So long and dismal was the chapter that Lawrence became dissatisfied with his own handiwork and went off to the Brewsters, leaving Frieda and her daughters at Spotorno. Evidently he was still under the spell of his motor trip through the Midlands, for he discoursed to Brett and the others of his early life, painting for them "a vivid and very terrible picture" in which the whole Lawrence family suffered "a lack of the bare necessities of life." In a like mood of acute self-pity he bewailed to Brett the atrocious behaviour of Frieda:

"We sit down," says Brett, who affects the historic present, "with our backs against some rocks, under the trees. The sea is a deep ultramarine blue, the olive trees a waving mist of silvery green. We watch the sea and the olive trees for a while in silence, then you slowly begin telling me the events that led to you coming here. You sigh wearily.

" 'I'm so tired of it all, Brett,' you say. 'Oh, so tired.'

" 'I know,' I say, 'It's terrible.' "

The Bay of Naples seems to stimulate the sadness of English poets, for at that moment they were looking on much the same scene as that which caused Shelley to mourn that he could lie down like a tired child and weep away his life of care. But in Lawrence's case (as possibly in Shelley's) his wife was for a time seriously estranged. Frieda could not forgive him for that locked door, nor for the prolonged silly jealousy of her children which had embittered her life for so many years. After the battle of Mexico she knew he would have to come back to her. Sure enough, after a period of what he thought was punishing her with sulks and silence, he could hold out no longer, and sent her a propitiatory offering. It was one of his own paintings, depicting the whale of Scripture just about to swallow Jonah, with the inscription: "Who is going to swallow whom?" This was not quite so tactful as it looks, for painting was associated by Frieda with what she considered the intrusive Brett, and at Spotorno Lawrence had been very rude about Frieda's "rotten pictures". "I was still angry," she says; and presumably wrote "the cruel hard letter" which is said to have upset him so much.

It was surely a felicitous irony which made two of the deserted children act as reconcilers and argue Frieda into taking him back. "Now, Mrs. L.," they said. "Be reasonable, you've married him, now you must stick to him." So in due course he was informed that he might return to Spotorno; which left him with the problem of Brett. She was the one convert to Rananim who had never shown resentment but had always given cheerful submission. She had never contradicted the master even when offered a reward to do so. She always took his side in a wrangle, even if by chance he happened to be right. She had followed him five thousand miles from London to Taos, from Taos to Oaxaca and back, and five thousand more miles from Taos to Capri. Now she was told to put her name on the quota of English immigrants to the United States, and to remain at Taos.

Naturally she was reluctant to do this, for what she liked was Lawrence's company, not the solitary occupancy of the little shack in the Rockies. She made every effort to avoid her fate, in spite of such cheerful and specious exhortations as these:

"Cheer up, Brett, why can't you learn to accept? There is nothing to fuss about." And: "Every rose has its thorn, Brett. You know I don't believe in love or friendship." And: "Cut out the ecstasy, Brett, cut it out. Think of the Beyond."

Devilish consoling at such moments, to think of "the Beyond". But he was inexorable, and her last sight of him was from the deck of the boat taking her to Naples. As she watched him, "a small figure, waving the blue and green scarf" she had given him, something seemed to tell her she would never see him again.

Although he was dying to be back with Frieda, Lawrence did not return with any unseemly haste or lack of dignity. Accompanied by two elderly maiden ladies of impeccable morality he travelled "slowly north, staying in Rome, Perugia, Assisi, Florence and

Ravenna." And so back to Spotorno, where Frieda and the two girls met him "all dressed up festively" in their best clothes. "Then," says Frieda Victrix, "we all four had peace."

11

THAT ugly scene of the wine-throwing at Spotorno is the last recorded when Lawrence's "dark self" got the better of him and betrayed him into words and actions which cannot but alienate sympathy. For the years of life yet remaining to him he was, in spite of ever-increasing physical suffering and weakness, more like the pre-war Lawrence described by David Garnett. Of course he was a satirist, sometimes a vindictive and venomous one, and often perversely at loggerheads with himself, his friends or the world in general.

Now that he was more or less permanently back in the Europe he had rejected so contemptuously he found to his surprise that he liked it. He went so far as to say in print that he had been a fool to say that Europe was finished for him—"It wasn't Europe at all, it was myself, keeping a stranglehold on myself." He even found it a relief to his nervous tension to be by the Mediterranean, and "gradually let the tight coils inside oneself come slack." For years now he had lived in that state of being "physically and mentally and morally overworked", harrying and driving himself with ruthless self-discipline.

He had been happy in the past in Italy and had written much of his best work there. And now he found the house which remained the Lawrences' headquarters until the end of 1928. This was a large Tuscan farm-villa, the Villa Mirenda, at Scandicci, a hamlet lying among beautiful hills of pine and olive only about seven miles from Florence. The villa itself was in the midst of vineyards, and the lower floor was filled with apparatus for making and storing wine. Italian wines are often so delicate that a short journey injures them, so that Italian œnophiles of a happier epoch built such country houses as the Mirenda (or Fête Champêtre) to enjoy the wines at their best. It was an appropriately Bacchic dwelling for a poet, though the upper floor on which the Lawrences lived was less splendid than the handsome exterior led one to expect. There was a sequence of rooms built on the four sides of a square, all communicating in the old Italian style, so that if the doors were left open you could, if you chose, walk round the apartment for ever. At the top was a glassed-in look-out, with wonderful views over the surrounding country and down to Florence with its great dome, in the valley of the Arno.

Here Lawrence spent the spring and summer of 1926, in what for him was comparative idleness. He revised and typed out Frieda's German translation of his play, *David*, but lived "very quietly", going about in shirt and trousers and sandals, taking picnics out to the stream, and feeling much better in health in the summer days "all hot and relaxed." Tuscany continued what Liguria had begun for him—the relaxation of his own inner tension which had been tightened almost to insanity by American nervousness and lack of repose. For a time Lawrence was able to discard his own highly exacting puritanism, lived life as the days brought it without all that self-conscious conceit about being "responsible" for the universe. He jibbed at the publishers' hints for another novel, and declared he was going to write just "bits of things". Further urgings brought this from him: "I'm not going to lay myself waste again in such a hurry. Let the public read the old novels." And to a friend he wrote:

"In the real summer, I always lose interest in literature and in publications. The *cicadas* rattle away all day in the trees, the girls sing, cutting the corn with the sickles, the sheaves of wheat lie all the afternoon like people dead asleep in the heat. I don't work, except at an occasional scrap of an article. I don't feel much like doing a book of any sort. Why do any more books? There are so many, and such a small demand for what there are. So why add to the burden, and waste one's vitality over it? Because it costs one a lot of blood."

It looks as if for a time he had taken the warnings of doctors seriously. At any rate for that summer he lived as he ought to have lived for years if he wished to prolong his life and to escape the irritations which maddened him when he overworked. Certainly, he was particularly charming in 1926, and one can now see why. He lived quietly in a genial climate near the Florence he loved, seeing enough acquaintances to keep him from loneliness but not so many as to disturb him, amusing himself with his painting and the tasks he enjoyed, and above all not tearing himself to pieces with the strain and effort of some large-scale piece of creative writing.

Apart from the indispensable "business" letters, he wrote chiefly to Brett (about the ranch) and to Rolf Gardiner about his youth organisation. "I believe we are mutually a bit scared," Lawrence wrote Gardiner, "I of weird movements, and you of me." It was an evil moment when under nordic pressure Lawrence began penning such nonsense as "the Latins have a sort of inner helplessness and lack of courage in them" and "one must look for real guts and self-responsibility to the Northern peoples." Why couldn't the self-responsible northern people with their guts leave him alone? Here is what he really felt about the people of the Mediterranean:

"For centuries upon centuries man has been patiently modelling the surface of the Mediterranean countries, gently rounding the hills, and graduating the big slopes and the little slopes into the almost invisible levels of terraces. Thousands of square miles of Italy have been lifted in human hands, piled and laid back in tiny little flats, held up by the drystone walls, whose stones came from the lifted earth. It is a sculpture of all the landscape. And it is the achieving of the peculiar Italian beauty which is so exquisitely natural, because man feeling his way sensitively to the fruitfulness of the earth, has moulded the earth to his necessity without violating it."

In spite of the late summer heats of Tuscany which seem always to come sooner or later, Lawrence might have done well to remain quietly with such thoughts among the "rattle of cicadas" until autumn brought the grape-harvest. But he could not long remain still and peaceful, and that year the Lawrences made quite extensive journeys—to the Schwiegermutter in Baden-Baden, to London, where Frieda stayed near her children while Lawrence visited friends in Inverness-shire and then accompanied his sisters to the Lincolnshire coast. This part of England had given him his first glimpse of the sea, and still pleased him:

"I feel very well here," he wrote Brett, "but I don't write a line, and don't know when I shall begin again. I shall have to do something or other, soon."

This looks as if he was beginning to worry about being idle, and felt short of money. As a matter of fact, although he liked to give the impression that he lived as "precariously" on his literary earnings as on loans in war time, Achsah Brewster has innocently revealed what none of the rest of us knew—that he had investments in America. When the great slump of October 1928 came, Lawrence refused to allow Frieda to read the Wall Street stock-market quotations to him. Achsah Brewster thought this was because of his complete indifference to money. I do not think he was such a fool—he merely wanted to be spared the exasperation of learning how much he had lost. But it was a salutary answer to his exhortation about making a revolution to lose all the money.

His talk that summer was very lively and fascinating, and he had already thought of doing one of his slow-moving books, the essays published after his death as *Etruscan Places.* He prepared these subjects more carefully from the point of view of academic information than is usually supposed. He looked over a number of illustrated books on Etruscan subjects from the London Library, and carried about with him Pericle Ducati's *Etruria Antica,* then supposed to be the best Italian work on the subject. Of course he still retained all his old habits of perverse and casuistical argument, so happily taken off by Aldous Huxley in *Two or Three Graces,* which was published in this year, 1926. The character of Kingham presents a perfect picture of Lawrence at such times:

" 'I think there's something really devilish about the women of this generation,' he said to me, in his intense emphatic way, some two or three days later. 'Something devilish,' he repeated, 'really devilish.' It was a trick of his, in writing as well as in speech, to get hold of a word and, if he liked the sound of it, work it to death.

"I laughed. 'Oh, come,' I protested. 'Do you find Catherine, for example, so specially diabolic?'

" 'She isn't of this generation,' Kingham answered. 'Spiritually, she doesn't belong to it.'

"I laughed again; it was always difficult arguing with Kingham. You might think you had him cornered, you raised your logical cudgel to smash him. But while you were bringing it down, he darted out from beneath the stroke through some little trap-door of his own discovery, clean out of the argument. It was impossible to prove him in the wrong, for the simple reason that he never remained long enough in any one intellectual position to be proved anything."

This is a perfect exposition of Lawrence's methods of evading an argument. When it was a question of fact he abandoned the trap-door for a direct action of brow-beating, attempting to over-whelm his antagonist by sheer force of rage and assertiveness. Thus Petrarch, according to his biographers, was a clerk in holy orders who at most may be credited with two natural children. To prove some "point" in a discussion Lawrence asserted that he was a married man with *twelve* children, despite the protests of those present. He even went to the length of printing his assertion, with the "*twelve*" in italics, just to make clear that he was not abandoning his position because of a few reference books.

I do not know if Lawrence ever read that portrait of himself as 'Kingham', but he assuredly bore Huxley no ill-will for it; though two years later he took serious exception to the more flattering if less accurate portrait of himself as 'Rampion' in *Point Counter Point*. At all events, their acquaintance of 1915 was renewed in the autumn of 1926, and the two writers became as near friends as was possible without the risk of explosions. It was a happy alliance, since Huxley's very different type of mind was a complete foil to Lawrence's. Huxley's unaffected recognition of Lawrence as one who had in him "something different" from the other eminent contemporaries he knew, as one "superior in kind, not degree," was very important to Lawrence. It was recognition of a kind which had been persistently denied him.

Of course, Lawrence was never able to reveal himself at his best except to those who were able to feel and to respect this "something different" in him. He could only give himself when he felt this unspoken recognition, and when it was absent he could do nothing —hence Galsworthy's impression of him as "dead" when in fact he was the most vividly alive man of his time. His rage when he thought his confidence had been betrayed, as he often too sensitively imagined, always led to outbursts of denunciation. He needed cool handling and not too close an intimacy. Unluckily it was nearly always over-sensitive and emotional persons like himself who were most drawn to him, whom he was as bound to hurt as they to hurt him.

Had the return to Europe suddenly rid him of his power-complex? Certainly we hear no more of his exacting "utter submission and obedience" from Frieda, any more than we hear of his identifying himself with Quetzalcoatl. But he was undoubtedly attracted by

Rolf Gardiner's ideas of leadership and also by Frederick Carter's mystical theories. Moreover from time to time Lawrence continued to pour out his hatred of the British and American upper and middle classes—who, naturally, provided all his personal friends and admirers.

This visit to England in the summer of 1926 was the last occasion when Lawrence saw his native land. Partly he was kept away by his illness, which made all winter visits dangerous, but mostly by the attacks launched upon him by the British press and British officials for such of his later work as *Lady Chatterley's Lover*, *Pansies*, and for the public exhibition of his pictures. It might be supposed that after his illness and suffering in Mexico in 1925 he would have passed the maximum of creative energy. As a matter of fact, his long rest seemed to renew his powers. In addition to the work just mentioned, the last fifty months of his life produced *Etruscan Places*; a re-written *Collected Poems*; *The Man who Died*; *Apocalypse*; long and short stories; polemical pamphlets, essays and verse squibs arising out of the attacks on him; his very fine *Last Poems*; and, most unexpectedly, a career of considerable success as a free-lance contributor to newspapers.

If you consider that *Lady Chatterley's Lover* is quite a long book, and that in his scrupulous way he wrote the whole of it three times; that he was often so seriously ill that even he had to stop writing; this is a wonderful achievement for a man who was slowly dying. All the more so since he wrote many more letters than during his travels beyond Europe, and that until quite near his death they are still often most original and entertaining. Significantly, his return to Europe coincided with his decline of interest in the theme of personal power over men and still more of that absorption in death and the death-ritual and life-in-death experiences which culminated in *The Plumed Serpent*. He seemed now to swing back to the themes and the ambiance of his earlier books. *The Virgin and the Gipsy*, written at Spotorno in 1925–26 is much nearer to his work of 1912–14 than to the later period. He had never abandoned the theme of sex as a motive force in human conduct—few novelists do. But now he returned to it as a dominant theme, abandoning his long-cherished belief in the battle of the sexes and the need for woman to submit, and putting forth instead a more poetic and purely physical theory of what he called "phallic tenderness".

As I have already pointed out, the starting point of *Lady Chatterley's Lover* is not from the characters of 'Constance', 'Clifford' and 'Mellors', but from Lawrence's own recoil from the ugliness of "his" Midlands. What was the remedy, where the way out? How had he found his own way out? Through his love for Frieda. Therefore, by a most singular but very characteristic process, which can scarcely be called reasoning, he leaped to the conclusion that salvation was to be achieved through "phallic tenderness". Curious as this sounds, it is the true explanation of a book which puzzled and offended many, and has been read with feelings and from a point of view which Lawrence held in the utmost repugnance.

In any case it is clear that the book was begun at Scandicci in October of 1926, very soon after the Lawrences returned from England. I find that I stayed with them there for a few days, from the 6th October onwards, and thus had the good fortune to be with him at a time when he was at his freshest and most charming after his long rest from hard work, and before his nerves became frayed again by the exacting task of writing this book and all the opposition that came from its publication. In fact, he was so easy and cheerful that I even wonder if, in the early half of the month, he had yet decided to do the book. Certainly, on the 9th he wrote his agent that he intended "just to do short stories and smaller things" and said of the Mirenda that it was "nice to sit in the big empty rooms and be peaceful."

I was fortunate to be with him when he was in a mood "to sit and be perfectly content doing nothing." Not very long afterwards I wrote down my recollections of one such afternoon spent with him at Scandicci. As records of his evil moods are so much more common than of his good moods, that will perhaps serve as my apology for quoting it here. The women had gone into Florence, and he and I sat on deck-chairs under the chestnut trees beside the villa.

"The October afternoon was very warm and golden, and we talked about this and that, and occasionally a ripe chestnut slipped out of its bulging spiky burr and plopped in the grass. Our real interest was not in talking, but in the children of the *contadini*. Every now and then, a shy little barefoot child would come stealing through the bushes with a bunch of grapes. Lawrence would say: 'Look! There's another. Pretend not to see.' The child would come very stealthily forward over the grass, like a little animal, and then stop and gaze at him. Finally, Lawrence would look up, and say with a pretence of surprise, 'Che vuoi?' 'Niente, Signor Lorenzo.' 'Vieni qui.' Then the child would come up very shyly, and present the grapes. 'Ma, cosa hai li?' 'Uva, Signor Lorenzo.' 'Per me?' 'Sissignore.' 'Come ti chiami?' And then was a grand scene, trying to make out the child's name. We were terribly puzzled by 'stasio', until we decided it must be 'Anastasio'.' But every time, Lawrence, ill as he was, went into the house to get the child a piece of chocolate, or some sugar when the chocolate was gone. And each time he apologised to me for the seeming generosity (for at Vendemmia grapes are worth nothing, and chocolate and sugar are always luxuries) by telling me how poor the peasants were, and how the children ought to have sugar for the sake of their health."

12

THE first of the three existing versions of *Lady Chatterley's Lover* was completed by February 1927. In addition to this, Lawrence had begun working enthusiastically on a new series of paintings. It was on the 9th February, 1927, that he wrote to Brett:

"I've nearly done my novel. Shall let it lie and settle down a bit before I think of having it typed. And I challenge you to a pictorial combat. I'm just finishing a nice big canvas, Eve dodging back into Paradise, between Adam and the Angel at the gate, who are having a fight about it."

On the 28th of the same month he sent his agent the manuscript of his now famous attack on Galsworthy; and by the 11th March he records having finished a new story, 'The Lovely Lady'. The first result of this return to the régime of overwork was an attack of " 'flu" towards the end of February and another early in March. He reported rather too optimistically: "I've had digs of 'flu—not bad but beastly—this last fortnight. Hope it's about over."

Over Christmas, of course, all work of a literary and pictorial kind had been put aside in order to give the peasants and their children the kind of German-English celebration which is almost unknown in Latin countries. Being in Italy, they were not so foolish as to buy a Christmas tree. When Frieda innocently suggested to their peasant friend, Pietro, they should buy them one in the market at Florence, he was shocked and pained. Buy a little pine tree? Madonna mia, no! It will be quite easy, Pietro said. "I'll get one for the Signora from the priest's pine-wood."

Once the tree had been obtained, no matter how, the Lawrences with Pietro's help set to work covering the pine-cones with gold and silver paper, and hanging the branches with coloured toys and candles. All the children and adults of the hamlet were invited, twenty-seven in all, and entertained with sweet wine and biscuits for the women, wine and Toscana cigars for the men. As for the children—they were wild with delight and pleasure. Never before had any of them seen a Christmas tree, never had one of them owned a toy. No wonder then that the wild little things handled their cheap wooden presents with awe, and that it was almost impossible to persuade them to go home.

Only those who knew Lawrence will know how much he delighted in giving such a treat, and how competently he could take charge of such a complex of human beings, and send them all, children and parents, happily home. At such times you could really think of him as the offspring of some ancient god, no Snake-bird eater of hearts, but a child of Iacchus or of some Latin small divinity of Olive and Vine and Wheat, not too grand and aloof to rejoice with common men and share their lot, even to their mortality.

In January of 1927 Earl Brewster suddenly arrived back from India, and spent a couple of days with them, talking eagerly of his experiences to two sympathetic listeners. Unlike most brilliant talkers, Lawrence would always be silent and listen when he thought some genuine experience was being honestly related. The Brewsters and the Huxleys were probably his closest friends during his last years, partly because they were financially respectable, but also because they did not intrude their views on him or exasperate him with scenes and wranglings, but enjoyed his moods of gaiety and wit, and passed lightly over his serious faults.

In March Frieda departed on one of her trips to Germany, and Lawrence chose to spend the time with the Brewsters. He stayed for a time with the family at Ravello, and then went with Brewster alone to visit the Etruscan sites of Cervetri, Tarquinia, Vulci and Volterra. This was the last of Lawrence's "thought-adventure" travels, and how reduced in scale from the days when he launched boldly into the vastness of Australia or Mexico! The essays he wrote about the tour form the last of his travel-books. It is true that *Etruscan Places* is not complete, in the sense that he had meant to visit other sites, though as time went by he could not summon up strength for the journeys. As a matter of fact, in the book as it now exists he has said practically all he had to say about the Etruscans. And he came to realise that, although George Dennis wrote a century ago, it is still not possible for an amateur to equal —let alone excel—such an English classic as *Cities and Cemeteries of Etruria.*

Yet this is another book which enables a sympathetic reader to understand and to follow in detail what Lawrence's life was. Perhaps it does contain some rather doubtfully valid holding forth about the Etruscans, but for the rest its pages give us a picture of Lawrence as he was in those last years. It is typical of him that he was as much interested in the Tarquinia of the day as in the painted tombs more than two thousand years old he had come to see. He was as much interested by Luigi, the Maremma herdsman, and the young German archæologist who hated archæology, as by Larth Tarchu and the Tomba della Caccia e della Pesca. Take, for instance, his sketch of the wild shy Luigi:

"The boy is getting over his shyness, now he is warmed up to driving, and proves outspoken and straightforward. I said to him: 'What a good thing the road is dry.' 'If it had been fifteen days ago,' he said, 'you couldn't have passed.' But in the later afternoon when we were returning by the same road, and I said: 'In bad wet weather we should have to come through here on horseback,' he replied; 'Even with the *carretto* you can get through.' 'Always?' said I. 'Always!' said he. And that was how he was. Possibility or impossibility was just a frame of mind with him."

Well, that was very much how they were with Lawrence, so that it was impossible to predict how he might respond to anything or anybody. But in the case of Luigi, Lawrence overlooked first the Italian habit of saying always what it is supposed will please the insane foreigner, and second, by this time Luigi had formed a plan that Lawrence was to buy a large house in the foot-hills beyond Maremma, where they would ride on horses, and go shooting wild boar "even out of season, for there is no one to catch you."

Amusingly, Lawrence was tempted by what would ordinarily have been to him an uncongenial way of life, as he always was tempted by anything which seemed to offer a taste of the unfamiliar. Luigi's hope was that through the rich, "immensely rich", English lord who had fallen in love with him he might escape from servitude to the Tarquinia baker, back, back to the freedom of the wild Maremma he loved. It is so often the Italian's dream, and it was nice of Lawrence to share it.

At Volterra, during that tour, Brewster pointed out to Lawrence an Easter egg in a shop window, which showed a little cockerel escaping from the broken shell. Brewster remarked that it suggested a title: "The Escaped Cock—a story of the Resurrection." And it seems that from this hint came the story more usually known as *The Man Who Died*; on which Lawrence began work as soon as he got back to Scandicci.

Nothing could stop him from again over-working mentally and physically, for it seems that at this period he wrote the second version of *Lady Chatterley's Lover*, in spite of the fact that he had promised he would write nothing "until July". Frieda brought him back a cold from Germany and he seems to have had an attack of malaria—and notwithstanding he wrote the second *Lady Chatterley* and *The Man Who Died* and *Etruscan Places* and painted and went off in the heat to visit the Huxleys at Forte dei Marmi: "beastly, as a place: flat, dead sea, jellyfishy and millions of villas, but the Huxleys were very nice with us, and they have such a nice little lad."

Alas, he had forgotten the warning of the Mexican and American doctors, and once more was overworking himself in every way and tearing his nerves to shreds. Compared with his gaiety and repose of a year before his furious outburst to the Brewsters about two stupid, insignificant American girls is worth quoting, if only to show how the effort of creative writing once more was stirring in him moods of excessive and almost insane irritation:

"Really, *nothing* is worse than these Americans. They've cut out *everything* except personal conceit and clothes. I was in the Uffizi —Ufizzi—Uffizzi—with them yesterday—'My, look what awful hands she's got!' is all that comes out of B. for Lippo Lippi—they've never even *heard* of Botticelli—call him Bo 'acelli, with the stopped breath instead of the "t"—they don't know what the Renaissance was. Standing in the Piazza Signoria I say—There! that's Michaelangelo *David*—and they reply: which one is it then?—that one at the end?—meaning the Bandinelli. Then B. discovers that—'that guy's got a stone in his hand, I guess he's the nut.' It's partly affectation, but it's such a complete one that it's effectual. They simply *can't see* anything: you might as well ask a dog to look at a picture or a statue. They're stone blind, culturally. All they can do is to call a man "that guy" or a woman "that skirt". M. would *like* to be able to see; but it's too late: the American cataract has closed over her vision, she's blind. But it's a process of atavism so rapid and so appalling, I could kill them dead. It's pure atavism. They've negated and negated and negated till there's *nothing*—and they themselves are empty vessels with a squirming mass of nerves. God! how loathsome! It's horrible. And it's largely the result of an affectation of "freedom" from old standards, become a fixed habit and a loathsome disease. Because there's the elements of a nice woman in each of them. . . . And I feel I'd rather go and live in a hyena house than go to live in America."

A robust man could hardly have made the incessant demands on strength and energy that Lawrence once more was making, without having to pay for them. In Tuscany that summer of 1927 was very hot, and, instead of resting and taking life easily, Lawrence persisted in working and going about as if he were a healthy man in the prime of his strength. One blazing afternoon in July he went into the Mirenda garden, where he picked a large basket of fine peaches, which he brought into the house and showed proudly to Frieda. He went to his own room, and a minute or two later she heard him call her "in a strange gurgling voice", and found him lying on his bed looking at her "with shocked eyes, while a slow stream of blood came from his mouth."

It was of course a lung hæmorrhage brought on by over-exertion in the heat, and by far the worst he had yet suffered. A distracted message to Florence brought our friend, Orioli, accompanied by the Italian specialist, Dr. Giglioli. For days Lawrence lay in extreme danger and weakness, in heat so intense that even iced milk curdled in a few hours. Once more his toughness and vitality slowly triumphed, and when he was well enough to travel Frieda took him —feeling "shaky, shaky"—to Karnten in Austria. Even now he persisted in keeping up the old bluff that he did not have tuberculosis, and wrote that the attack was "due, radically, to chagrin", but what chagrin? To Brewster he was honest enough to confess that "the cough is a nuisance, and I wish I could get a new breathing apparatus." He was taken to Baden-Baden, where he even consented to see, though not apparently to obey, a German lung specialist, "a mild man like mashed potatoes".

As usually happened when Lawrence had a hæmorrhage, he took a dislike to the place where it struck him, and though he returned to the Villa Mirenda in October of 1927, he was now anxious to escape. "I'd like to clear out of Italy for good," he wrote. And absurdly thought he would be happier in Devonshire—"time to go home, I feel." Then he changed his mind. If he could collect the money he thought he would like to take a long sea voyage. He had heard that the Messageries Maritimes would take you round the world for as little as one hundred and twenty pounds, that they might "drop off at San Francisco and see Taos again". But whatever he did and wherever he went, after that terrible stroke from his lungs Italy had become "stupid", had "sort of gone dead."

Now, in that strait of illness, he cheered himself by painting a pleasantly wanton picture of "fauns and nymphs"—and why not? He worked, and worked perhaps too hard, at re-arranging and re-writing his *Poems* for the collected edition of 1928, described by him as "dabbing at poems". Indefatigable hero of the pen, he wrote his third version of *Lady Chatterley's Lover*. And at Christmas once more gave the peasants' children their tree. Before the end of January he was out of "stupid" Italy and high up in the snows of Diablerets with the Huxleys.

Meanwhile, after going through agonies of indecision and wavering, Lawrence was coming to believe that he ought to publish *Lady Chatterley's Lover*. His remark to Frieda: "It will bring me only abuse and hatred again", shows that he was to some extent prepared for what happened, though no sane person could possibly have foreseen the morbid degeneracy of British sex-hatred and its hysterical expression in the periodical press, backed by the curiously vindictive action of British officials.

After much discussion Lawrence thought that he would issue one thousand complete copies through Orioli, and allow the ordinary publishers to make any cuts demanded by the quaint customs of the country. Typed copies would be supplied to Secker in England and to Knopf in New York. Knopf, it appears, liked the book very much, and was hopeful that his advisers could prepare, without too much mutilation, a version which could be steered through the anti-sex lobby. Secker was more realistic, and at once pointed out that effective expurgation would destroy the poetry of the book and most of his meaning. He was right. The miserable version publicly issued in 1932 is perfectly inadequate, a sort of *Hamlet* not only without the Prince of Denmark but without the whole royal family and Ophelia.

Why, in his state of health, with so short an expectation of life, with his sensitiveness, with his extreme horror of rebuff and insult, did Lawrence ever issue that book? It is a question. I have heard numerous motives alleged, some on a low level, others much higher. It is true, I think, that his reputation rather declined than advanced between 1925 and 1928, and that he may have felt the necessity of doing something startling to regain public attention. With James Joyce so successfully defying convention with *Ulysses* and being flattered on all sides, Lawrence may have thought he would be cowardly not to express his own completely different view of life and sex. It is true, also, that while Lawrence was still earning enough for his needs, he hoped that an extra thousand pounds might give him the funds to carry out his project of Mediterranean travel. When Norman Douglas questioned him about his motives for publication, Lawrence replied "to put some spirit and guts into the younger writers". I never knew anyone who cared less about "the younger writers", and I simply don't believe it was a motive with him.

The main reason, surely, was that *Lady Chatterley's Lover* was the expression of his latest phase of thought. Why, after all, should he hide it? If it led to a fight, as it obviously would, well, he enjoyed fighting. Life, he had once declared, was not serenity or enjoyment, but "ninety per cent smash, smash, smash." He was not interested in such a primitive activity as to wish to "*épater les bourgeois*", as witness this emphatic rejection of André Gide's *Les Faux Monnayeurs*:

"Interesting as revelation of the modern state of mind—but it's done to shock and surprise, *pour épater*—and *fanfarons de vice*!—not real."

Between the writing of *The Plumed Serpent* and that of *Lady Chatterley's Lover*, there seems to have been a change in Lawrence's views of life and sex, which was rather more lasting than his usual chopping and changing. Of course, his peculiar prejudices did not disappear, but there was a definite alteration. His early writings on sex which were viewed with alarm by such disinterested defenders of female chastity as Ford Madox Hueffer and Robert Lynd owed their dangerous quality to their sincerity—they were thought to be indecent because they were well-written. Then came a change, before the war, due most probably to some acquaintance with the contemporary literature of Germany. During this period, Lawrence tended to see sex relations as a battle, a contest of Love and Hate.

Of course, there are numerous examples of human lovers who, like cats, have to have a row before they make love; but it has long been clear that Lawrence was an outstanding example of what he was always denouncing in others, namely "sex in the head", which he built up into a philosophy of salvation. In war somebody usually has the illusion of victory, and it will surprise nobody to learn that in the Battle of Sex Lawrence agreed with the Germans that Man should be the victor and Woman the victim. He reckoned without his Brünhilde, who put up as sporting and successful a defence as any friend of the ring could hope to witness. With his very pleasing gift of being able to see when he made a fool of himself, Lawrence conceded her repeated victories. But, a glutton for punishment, he always came up again, until she convinced him in Mexico and Spotorno that he was completely outclassed.

Well, if he couldn't rule his wife, he still might rule the world—into all of which we have looked only too often. Yet, still, after all that had gone on, back in the comparative sanity of Europe, Lawrence had played with the idea of leadership, only at last to reject it. To Rolf Gardiner he wrote sadly:

"I'm afraid the whole business of leaders and followers is somehow wrong, now. When leadership has died, then it will be born again, perhaps, new and changed, and based on reciprocity of tenderness. The reciprocity of power is obsolete. When you get down to the basis of life, to the depth of the warm creative stir, there is no power. Yes, one can ignore Fascism in Italy for a time. But after a while, the sense of false power against life is very depressing."

Depressing isn't the word—how would you like to be ordered to eat your "own national potatoes" twice daily and to praise them to "all foreigners" merely because there is a glut? Just what Lawrence meant by "reciprocity of tenderness" in this connection I shall not attempt to divine, but there the new word was, "tenderness!" usually "phallic tenderness", for the sake of which the aristocratic Connie was to desert her titled and intellectual husband for the tenderly phallic gamekeeper. Impossible to deny that it all inhabits that short step between the sublime and the ridiculous.

There was nothing new for him in the story of the upper-class woman leaving her husband for the lower-class man. It was his own triumph, of which he was inordinately and class-consciously proud. Lawrence had never grown weary of telling us of the aristocratic women who had "found fulfilment" with gamekeepers, grooms, gipsies, colliers, Indians and Mexicans. But this last book was to clear up one ambiguity. Beyond the possibility of doubt he would show that the essential basis of marriage rests on the physical sex relationship, which is *not* "ugly" and "unpleasant" and "unnecessary" and all the canting rest of it. He would write a poem of physical sex (it had been done before) and in doing so rehabilitate the ancient Saxon words which through the sad centuries have become so laden with the defiled and hideous repressions of priest-harried generations. A 15th century glossary in the British Museum Library carries the innocent entry: "Coynt, a woman's thynnge". Can such serene innocence be recaptured in an age of newspapers? So Lawrence apparently hoped. An American critic, Horace Gregory, has credited him with such intentions:

"Not since the writing of *Sons and Lovers* had Lawrence been so confident that he was writing something important, something that would drive the enemy into a far corner. Just as the earlier book was to represent the case history of thousands of inarticulate young men, so Lady C. was to state a cause for millions who sought a solution of the world's problems through normal sex. The book was to say all the inarticulate daren't say, and good old English four-letter words were to come into their own. These were to walk across the printed page as nakedly as Mellors and his lady. The English novel was to be no longer whipped into decorum, hiding its shame behind chiffon and lace, broadcloth, tweed, linen and serge."

It is a mistake to approach Lawrence simply as an English novelist. True, like most genuine artists, he adopted the forms and idiom popular in his time, but he cared very little for "the art and craft of fiction" which, as he liked to point out, were almost faultlessly practised by a lot of rather uninteresting writers. He used loose novel forms as he used loose poetic forms to hold his life experiences and his preachings. In so much of all this he was in his work making use of ideas current in Germany during the 19th century. Thus, long before Lawrence was born, Richard Wagner had written down the essence of Lawrence's beliefs and teaching in sentences such as these:

"Art is an immediate vital act, the expression of man. . . . The first and truest fount of Art reveals itself in the impulse that urges from Life into the work of art; for it is the impulse to bring the unconscious, instinctive principle of Life to understanding and acknowledgement as Necessity."

Art, Wagner goes on to say, is "an inbred craving of the natural, genuine, and uncorrupted man". It is not a product of the mind alone, "which brings forth Science", but of "the deeper impulses of the Unconscious." All great creations, according to Wagner—and to Lawrence—come from the Unconscious, and the "conscious mind merely exploits and breaks up direct impulses." After denouncing, just as Lawrence afterwards denounced, "luxury, fashion and the whole art-traffic of our shameless age," Wagner claims in the jargon of 19th century liberalism that "the impulse of the Unconscious comes only from the People."

Whether Lawrence had read Wagner's *Art-Work of the Future* or merely picked up the ideas at second-hand cannot be determined, but everyone acquainted with Lawrence's work and life must see how he clung to them through all his many changes, waverings and self-contradictions. Nowhere are these essentially Wagnerian theories worked out more thoroughly by Lawrence than in *Lady Chatterley's Lover*. Of course he went beyond and repudiated Wagner by abandoning the "decent" attitude to sex—but that, after all, was a modification of German thought introduced by Freud. Prudery and property were no longer to be the basis of society, but rather challenged and derided as humbug.

In deciding to publish a book so startling to the uninstructed Lawrence probably knew that the offal and dust-cart shootings of periodical "criticism" would be dumped on him. He probably did not anticipate that he would start a paper war which would last for the rest of his life, as well as bring him into sharp conflict once more with his old enemy the cultured English policeman who decides what is and is not literature. Reluctantly Secker and Knopf had come to the conclusion that the book was a little ahead of the times, and were unwilling to risk the damage to their businesses which might be visited on them by the frenzies of the inhibited. Lawrence, on the other hand, was an economic light horseman on the safe side of the Pas de Calais. After all, it was his book and his battle; so they wished him good luck and left him to it.

He was far from taking the matter in any frivolous or too light-hearted way. It was, he announced, "a great occasion" when, having lunched in Florence with Orioli, they "took the MS. of the novel to the printer." Norman Douglas may have been there too. At any rate Lawrence notes in the same letter: "Saw Douglas to-day—but nothing new about him, still thinking of Jerusalem and preferring Chianti." There was a certain amount of comedy for anyone but the exasperated author in the business of trying to print an English book in Italy. None of the compositors, not even the master-printer Franceschini, knew a word of English; and according to Lawrence some of them could not even read or write. It is not surprising then that the production of proofs was, for the epoch, very slow—about half the time now needed by the skilled British. Misprints were also numerous and maddening:

"I've corrected forty-one pages of proofs," he wrote to Aldous Huxley, "and it was *almost* Maria's typing over again. Dear Maria, all those little mistakes you made, and I followed like Wenceslas's page so patiently in your footsteps: now it's a Florentine printer. He writes dind't, did'nt, dnid't, dind't, din'dt, didn't like a Bach fugue."

His intention had been to leave the Villa Mirenda at the end of his lease in April, for with his usual revulsion of feeling the long-beloved Italy was now distinctly out of favour. That hæmorrhage probably came to his mind every time he entered his bedroom. At all events, he decided that Italy was bad for him, poisoned him. Of course, life under Fascism gradually became oppressive even to the foreigner, and it was always a mystery to me how Lawrence could stand it for so long. Well, in April, he had got to the point of removing his pictures from the walls and beginning to pack, when Frieda, who wished to stay on, "looked so gloomy" that he relented, re-hung the pictures, "and paid six months rent—not worth getting into a state about."

This year 1928 was one of public storm and stress for him. The story suggested to him by Brewster in Volterra on their *Etruscan Places* tour was written and eventually published under the title of 'The Escaped Cock' in *The Forum*. This led to a six-months wrangle of letter-writers in the correspondence columns, but to no attempt at suppression. One gets the impression that at this time America was less illiberal to independent writers than England, perhaps because of the fight on their behalf waged so successfully by the well-known attorney, Morris Ernst. No such legal champion arose in England or was likely to arise. Apparently no English periodical dared publish 'The Escaped Cock', which was not published in England until after Lawrence's death, when (1931) they risked an expanded version under the modest title of 'The Man Who Died.'

The six months rent for the Villa Mirenda was wasted, for the Lawrences spent there hardly more than one month of the six. He again became very restless, and decided that he would go to Switzerland to join the Brewsters, with whom indeed the Lawrences spent most of the next few months. As if 'The Escaped Cock' and *Lady Chatterley's Lover* were not sufficient for excitement, he made all secure by agreeing to an exhibition of his recent pictures at Dorothy Warren's Art Gallery. This exhibition, originally planned for October of 1928, was for various reasons postponed until June–July of the next year. He had made the decisions which in the last twenty months of his life involved him in such a tumult of outraged spinsters.

13

LAWRENCE'S aversion from Italy, now that he had taken a dislike to the place, caused him at last to pay some attention to the friends who had been long urging that in his state of health he ought to avoid the torrid summer heats and damp winter fogs of Tuscany, and should spend those seasons of the year in the high dry air of Switzerland which had been proved so beneficial to consumptives. It is possible that his early and irrational dislike for Switzerland may have been based on the fact that it was associated with the disease which for so long sapped his strength, and whose existence in himself he had persisted in denying. Now, when it was too late, he consented to go.

Lawrence's thrift and horror of waste made him worry at the thought of the Villa Mirenda standing unused for several months —and he offered it free to the Brewsters. They, very wisely, preferred his company to his villa. They came to lunch and found Lawrence dressed, as he nearly always was during the warm months of those years, in a bright blue Bavarian jacket with white buttons, which brought out more than ever the blueness of his eyes. The Brewsters, who were painters, were greatly interested by the pictures of Lawrence's which hung on the walls, and Achsah Brewster especially enjoyed "their sensitive colour, ease of technique, spontaneity and expressiveness."

It was over this cheerful luncheon that the Brewsters decided to come to Switzerland also; and a few days later they started off on one of those journeys Lawrence always enjoyed so much, with no more precise objective than "the French Alps". Evidently they intended to wander for a little as the whim took them, staying where they pleased for as long as they pleased, even settle for months if they wanted—in short do the pleasant things people are now not allowed to do. Lawrence was in high spirits, and as the train gradually emptied of passengers, got Frieda and the Brewsters singing folk songs and kept them "in a state of exhilaration" until they reached Turin.

With Lawrence still in holiday mood, they sauntered on to Chambéry and Aix-les-Bains. "How happy we felt!" The Brewsters, faithful to vegetarianism and Buddha, ate only salads, for which they were unmercifully quizzed by Lawrence, who savoured with extra relish his brook trout and grilled chicken. Alas, there came a shadow over their happiness—there always does. They had motored far into the mountains and had found the ideally lovely village and the ideally quiet hotel, only to be asked to leave next morning because of Lawrence's cough: consumptives were not allowed. "I thought from the beginning that there was something *mingy* about that inn-keeper," was Lawrence's comment.

So they gave up the thought of further wandering, and took refuge in a hotel near Vevey where they were all known and welcomed. With rest and good nursing Lawrence's cough returned to its ordinary state, and Frieda felt he was well enough for her to spend a few days with her mother. But he wanted her back, and if anyone still thinks that Lawrence did not love his wife he should consider these notes made by Achsah Brewster at the time:

"On the day for Frieda's return from Baden-Baden Lawrence consulted the time-table and decided she would arrive by ten in the morning. As no Frieda appeared he met the twelve o'clock express, with the same result. He ate his lunch hurriedly and rushed back for the two-twenty local, but returned shortly looking disconsolate. 'She's probably lost her passport and been held up, or her purse.' I know not how many trains he met, certainly the ten o'clock train, which held no Frieda. We tried to cheer him up, but in vain. He always looked forward so eagerly to her return."

Later in the year, in July, Lawrence and Frieda left the hotel and rented a small chalet at Gsteig-bei-Gstaad, and the Brewsters moved to the hotel in the village below. Perhaps it was a little high, perhaps he over-exerted himself, but he was almost at once laid low by a new lung hæmorrhage. As he slowly recovered, he busied himself with painting; and, with some mockery of himself, started on his successful career as a free-lance journalist. Several of the essays which go to form *Assorted Articles* were written on that mountain-perch of Gsteig.

Meanwhile, Orioli and Franceschini toiling away in Florence (or perhaps we should say that Orioli was in Florence and Franceschini and his analphabets did the toiling) had managed after immense difficulties to produce an unexpectedly handsome edition of *Lady C.*, and Orioli had sent out all the ordered copies by the end of July. As he had only one assistant, and it was summer, the probability is that only a few were sent out daily throughout the month—my own recollection is that my copy reached me about the third week in July.

Since the book had not been printed and published in England and the author was domiciled abroad, the attack was not developed on the lines of that on *The Rainbow*. The object of the pure in heart being to cause financial trouble and insult, the usual legal pi-jaw was abandoned as unnecessary in this case, and guerilla warfare gradually developed from Customs and Postal officials (who can always be trusted to recognise dirt when they see it) and from policemen under the gallant Joynson-Hicks. The muddy-pated rascals were slow, very slow; and as a matter of fact it was the frightened booksellers who began returning copies, to the number of one hundred and fourteen. How was this defection to be dealt with? Very easily. The copies were collected by Enid Hilton, and re-distributed by her and myself.

By the 15th August, 1928, all the original English subscribers had received their copies, but Lawrence was a little disquieted, and noted: "There are rumours of suppression in England, and rumours of ban in America." The weakest link in Lawrence's armour was the fact that he could not secure international copyright, and hence could not be protected from piracy. Meanwhile, the officials were beginning to confiscate copies in England and America to take home to their wives, and pirated editions sold with a rapidity Lawrence had never before experienced.

He let these trifles trouble him too much, and another, fortunately slight, hæmorrhage of the lungs measured the extent of his agitation. Interestingly, his letters are reticent about the confiscations of *Lady C.*, much as they always tried to conceal his lung disorders. Not very many—in fact, very few—of his friends stood by him at this crisis; and I am glad to be able to say that Huxley and David Garnett were among them. But it was a very small band.

In September the Lawrences moved to Baden-Baden to see the Schwiegermutter, and the Brewsters went with them, grieving to see how he was more and more dominated by physical weakness, how quickly he grew weary, for all his energy and life. During a drive they took, Lawrence broke a long silence to say that his father and another man (discreetly referred to as "X", but obviously Norman Douglas) were the only people he had known who always followed joy. "Nothing else but the joy of life had concerned them. X would not admit suffering, disease, poverty or ugliness. For X the war did not exist. He turned his back upon it. When Frieda and Lawrence were desperately poor he simply did not notice it or them." From this well-deserved praise of Norman Douglas, Lawrence more surprisingly went on to praise the gruffer hedonism of his father, linking the two as "blithe spirits true to themselves" who had "kept themselves unbroken", while the rest of us (obviously meaning himself) "have cared too much and let ourselves be shattered by the depth of our affections." Though it came too late, a breath of pure sanity played about Lawrence's brow at that moment.

But what a volte-face! How often and how furiously he had denounced Douglas's hedonism and even the democratic Bynner merely for amusing himself with Chinese poems and Mexican manners. Lawrence had always been harassed by what the Friends call "a concern" for what didn't concern him. He felt responsible for a world he had not created, an obligation to order other men's lives. He had constantly nagged at otherwise cheerful people to "live from the unconscious", without apparently ever asking himself how you can consciously be unconscious.

Even *Lady Chatterley's Lover*, so desperate an attempt of his conscious mind to fly from his unconscious puritanism, is lowered by the fact that it was written less for delight in a passionate love affair and joy of a woman's body than as a kind of erotic lesson, a sermon on sex. Clearly, it was a case of "sex in the head", from every point of view (such as he was always denouncing in others), since there is every reason to suppose that when he wrote the book he was already virtually if not completely impotent. Yet, in his own way, who had enjoyed life more? Who had known more positive happiness, in spite of his myriad inventions for tormenting himself? Here is the endless paradox of Lawrence, that *varium et mutabile* of his spirit which elude our definition and generalisations, but leave always the sense of his strangeness, his uniqueness—a poisoned rose, gold in dung, Balaam's Ass, a Wundertier, a typically English "half-angel-half-idiot". He was, as he said himself:

"a thing of kisses and strife
a lit-up column of rain
a calling column of blood
a rose tree bronzey with thorns
a mixture of yea and nay
a rainbow of love and hate
a wind that blows back and forth
a creature of conflict like a cataract."

Alas, poor Lawrence! In that autumn of 1928 he was not much of a cataract, as he grew ever frailer and weaker, and his "recoveries" slighter and more delusive. In a melancholy mood he wrote to Mabel Luhan from Switzerland, so weary he hardly bothered to hide the truth any more: "Here I just dibble at tiny pictures, and potter about among the trees. A few bad years for everybody. But let's hope we'll get steady on our legs and manage with a bit of real equilibrium afterwards. *Poveri noi*!"

The weather was cold and seldom sunny in Baden-Baden, and the party seem all to have lived like invalids, drinking the waters and listening to the music at the Kursaal. After dinner Lawrence played patience with his Schwiegermutter. His frayed nerves showed in outbursts against the harmless Kursaal crowd, whose faces, he thought, "were blasted, their souls damned." He was taken to see a motion picture and was so "nauseated by its falsity" that he hurried from the theatre to avoid, he explained, "being violently sick."

His letters at the time showed this horror of crowds; and, as I had been lent, for the months of October and November, the remote and beautiful Vigie on the island of Port-Cros, I suggested that the Lawrences might find it restful to spend a few weeks there. One of Lawrence's letters implies that he thought we might stay the whole winter, but my kind French friends offered no more than those two months. It was an error, of course, for he had never really wanted anything so completely remote. But I arranged to come up by ship from Naples to Marseille, meeting another friend at Toulon, and the Lawrences at Toulon or les Salins d'Hyères. As I might have expected, they failed to keep their rendezvous, Frieda being engaged in dismantling the Villa Mirenda and in other engagements. I now regret very much the money I spent in sending telegrams from Port-Cros with prepaid answers to Lawrence (whose reply always was "Waiting for Frieda"), only to find his letters to other people reporting blandly that there was "no sign" of me!

Lawrence would not come to the island without Frieda, and he waited for her at Le Lavandou with his sister, and, part of the time, with the Huxleys. As Frieda's dismantling of the villa took a very long time, the Lawrences did not reach Port-Cros until about two weeks after the original rendezvous.

A "Vigie" is a small fort and look-out (this one dated only from Napoleon III), which in this case had been restored and made unexpectedly comfortable. The whole island of Port-Cros was and still is scheduled as a national monument, and is the most unspoiled of all the smaller Mediterranean islands. Besides the Vigie, an island as large as Capri contains only a tiny fishing village, a hotel, and one inhabited house—at this time of writing wrecked by heroic shell fire. Otherwise. the island is given up to magnificent Mediterranean pines, scented lavenders, rosemaries, cistus, and dozens of other scented plants, with rare wild flowers and fungi which have vanished from the mainland. The view from the walls of the Vigie extended from the snow-peaks of the Alps, eighty miles east, to the twinkle of Toulon's lights after dark, thirty or forty miles west. The colours on the other islands and the mountains of the mainland changed from hour to hour in a sequence of beauty, and nowhere else are dawns and sunsets more lovely, nor the silence and solitude so unbroken.

Poor Lawrence! He was far too ill to enjoy a place more delicately beautiful and undisturbed even than his New Mexican ranch, for this was the Mediterranean beauty he had thrilled to at Taormina, but fresher and more pristine. It was a bitter heart-break to realise that it had come to him too late, and to find that he had to spend his days in bed or in a deck chair, so weak that he could pass the drawbridge only for a few yards, and was almost too weak to climb to the glassed-in look-out. Most unfortunately, Frieda came back with one of her usual heavy colds, which Lawrence instantly caught, and this ended up in a hæmorrhage after he had read the reviews of *Lady Chatterley's Lover* which reached him there. Night after night, I listened to his deep hollow cough, and realised that I had taken on a responsibility I had never dreamed of. How get a doctor up there, with a gap of ten miles of mistral-tossed sea? How get him safely away? Only then did I realise how frail and ill he was, how bitterly he suffered, what frightening envy and hatred of ordinary healthy humanity sometimes possessed him, how his old wit had become bitter malice, how lonely he was, how utterly he depended on Frieda, how insanely jealous of her he had become.

Well, there were good times too, as of old, when he was his charming self, amusing us with his stories or making us laugh at his parodies and imitations. For a time Frieda felt she could relax her nursing vigilance so far as to indulge in the luxury of a washing-day, and the rest of us could not avoid noticing that the wife of the erotic genius was condemned to underclothes of an austerity combining the extreme decorum of the nun with the cheerlessness of the charlady.

He was far too ill to write anything except trifles, and seized on any event as a theme for one of his *Pansies*—from the arrival of Huxley's *Point Counter Point* to a new French book on *Attila*.

It was up there at the Vigie that he received a large envelope of British press cuttings about *Lady Chatterley's Lover*. Why the book was ever sent out for review or why Lawrence's agent in England ever sent him the vile journalistic trash, I have never been able to understand. I have never read such disgusting abuse and vulgarity, such hypocrisy. Here are some of the phrases: "Most evil outpouring—sewers of French pornography—beastliness—muddy-minded pervert—diseased mind—literary cesspool—shameful inspiration—this bearded satyr—book snapped up by degenerate booksellers and British decadents—the foulest book in English literature—poisoned genius." And so forth. *John Bull,* whose editor Bottomley was undergoing or was about to undergo a sentence of seven years' penal servitude for a series of frauds, hoped that Lawrence would be "ostracised by all except the most degenerate coteries", and, funnily enough in the circumstances, regretted that "there is no law at present under which he may be ostracised more completely and for a good stiff spell." Strange that such brutality and malice may find utterance with impunity, and that no law exists to protect artists from the insults of such *canaille.*

What astonished me at the time was that Lawrence was seriously disturbed by utterances which the rest of us received with complete contempt. Perhaps he disliked the thought that his sisters might read them. On top of this came the copy of Huxley's *Point Counter Point.* Now it so happened that all the rest of us were warm admirers and perhaps injudiciously loud in our rejoicings that this book was a Book of the Month in America. We never for a moment supposed that Lawrence would not rejoice in his friend's deserved success. But naturally he must have compared the reception given to Huxley's book with the atrocious insults to his own. The letter he wrote Huxley tries to be just and friendly, but envy lurks in every sentence. He bade me mark his words, within a year Huxley would be in a lunatic asylum. And when, most injudiciously, Frieda let him know that she had read and liked the novel I was writing—well, who will be surprised that I was sent to keep company with the more important offender?

Getting Lawrence back safely to the mainland was not easy. We managed to coax him down to the port safely, and to fortify him with lunch at the hotel before starting. Unluckily, a heavy mistral was rising, and we spent a couple of hours in a small open launch in a sea rising as rapidly as only the Mediterranean can. We shipped a good deal of water, but there was no real danger until the engine broke down, and we began drifting out to sea as we wallowed helplessly in the heavy swell. But within ten minutes the engine was mended, and we managed to get him safely at last to a hotel in Toulon. When we said good-bye he clasped my hand and uttered one of those gnomic epigrams which always embarrassed me. "Possess your soul in patience," he said; though why, I have not the slightest idea.

14

THE winter of 1928–29 was a very cold one, and the Lawrences spent it at Bandol, which is unhappily rather exposed to mistral. Bandol is a little town of two or three thousand inhabitants, close to Toulon, and much more suitable (except for its position) for an invalid than the remote Vigie of Port-Cros. But it was at Bandol that he wrote his last prose work, *Apocalypse*, and the *Last Poems*. At first, he went on jotting down his *Pansies*, making a translation of Lasca's *Story of Dr. Manente* for Orioli, and writing articles for the newspapers. Since he had re-become a sewer and a muddy-minded pervert his newspaper articles were naturally in demand.

His notoriety brought back correspondents from whom he had not heard for years. Ottoline Morrell wrote in a mood of sadness, grieved at being taxed out of her home at Garsington. In return she received a letter-sermon, but went on "coughing over *Lady C.*" Murry wrote to make an enquiry about the original edition of *The Rainbow*, and a chance remark to the effect that "we have missed it, you and I" brought this characteristic *Pansy*:

> "A man wrote to me: We missed it, you and I,
> We were meant to mean a good deal to one another;
> but we missed it.
> And I could only reply:
> A miss is as good as a mile
> mister."

More and more Lawrence was able to live only within the very narrow limits and quiet routine of an invalid's existence. A small French hotel by the Mediterranean was probably as good a winter resting place as could be found, since he still refused even to consider a sanatorium. Frieda, being relieved from all household duties, could give all her energies to the special kind of unobtrusive nursing which was all he would allow and which no one but she could give. Bandol, Lawrence noted without illusion, was "a dull little place," where his chief enjoyment was the lovely winter sunrises over the sea. He found it peaceful and comfortable enough, until the severe winter seemed to him to turn everything "black and cold."

If the place was dull, excitement came from the outside. The announcement of his coming picture-show had attracted the attention of P. R. Stephensen, the Australian printer who had founded the Fanfrolico Press. He came to Bandol to see Lawrence, explaining that he intended to start "a new press—with no Lindsay stuff in it", to be called The Mandrake and to start with a volume of reproductions of the Lawrence paintings. Evidently Lawrence had been sceptical of the success, but he yielded to Stephensen's arguments and wrote the very entertaining 'Introduction'. As it turned out, the book was a complete success when it was issued some six months later. Lawrence reported: "I hear they have already orders for about three hundred copies at ten guineas, and ten vellum copies at fifty guineas are all ordered. World of crazes! But I ought to make about five hundred pounds out of the book—not bad." But for this he had to some extent to thank the action of the Home Secretary and the London police, which had advertised Lawrence so widely and brought the sympathy of all decent people to his side.

In January 1929 there occurred an unusual if not unprecedented event in English literature. A sealed postal packet from abroad, registered and written by an English author of international fame, was seized by British officials, opened and detained. There were in fact two such packets, both from D. H. Lawrence at Bandol. The first, sent off on the 7th January, contained the manuscript of *Pansies;* the second, despatched a week later, held the 'Introduction' to his book of paintings. The excuse made for this behaviour was that they were "looking for pornography," as of course was very natural. In the end they had to return both MSS, having failed to discover anything whatever in the 'Introduction', and in *Pansies* merely a few lines—"piffling", as Lawrence contemptuously noticed. Questions were asked in the House of Commons by Labour members, led by Ellen Wilkinson, and elicited nothing beyond the curious admission that the Home Secretary does not—or perhaps it would be fairer to say, did not then—"seek literary advice when deciding if matter was obscene." It was a contention of the government that a book could be censored before publication merely because the Home Secretary thought it should be censored, for Lawrence was forbidden to print the few "piffling" cuts made in *Pansies.* Little or no protest against this interference with intellectual liberty was made either by the university professors or by known writers.

Here again Lawrence would seem to have been justified in his reflection that "the law is a dreary thing, and its judgments have nothing to do with life." But if the object of the authorities had been to prevent the circulation of Lawrence's books they went the wrong way to work, for it is a fact—whether regrettable or not is a matter of opinion—that readers of the English language will always pay for a book they believe to be obscene. The reader will remember that Lawrence's *Love Poems*, lacking such a recommendation, sold but a hundred copies. P. R. Stephensen received from Lawrence the small bits and pieces cut from fourteen of these very short pieces (there were well over two hundred in the first collection) and published for subscribers an edition of five hundred copies, with fifty on vellum, and lent the plates for a Continental edition. The subscribers' edition sold out at once, and Stephensen was able to pay Lawrence another five hundred pounds in royalties.

Yet another official attempt was made to suppress Lawrence. After a long delay the exhibition of his pictures was opened at the Warren Galleries, London, to coincide with the publication of Stephensen's volume of coloured reproductions. Harsh things have been said against these pictures, not only by those who think a nude obscene when it is not painted as a still life but by many of the too numerous "experts" who publish their views on art. The fact that Augustus John was willing to stand by the pictures as pictures surely tips the balance wholly in Lawrence's favour.

In any case, the exhibition was a great success, probably a unique success for a one-man show by a painter who had never before exhibited. Between the 14th June and the 5th July more than twelve thousand people paid to see the pictures. Naturally such an undeniable success was especially annoying to Lawrence's enemies, and some peculiarly vile and mendacious attacks were published. The Home Secretary, who "did not seek literary advice" when deciding upon matters of obscenity, evidently did not extend his ban to the more loathsome journals which supported his party. At his order, the tramp of hob-nailed boots echoed through the Warren Galleries; and thirteen of Lawrence's pictures were removed, along with four copies of Stephensen's reproductions, and a volume of drawings by William Blake. Hearing that William Blake had been dead for a century, the prosecution withdrew the charge against him.

The persons held responsible for the exhibition, Philip Trotter and his wife, were duly summoned to appear before a magistrate called Mead "to show cause" why these pictures and books should not be destroyed. The court proceedings on the 9th August, 1929, appear to have been more than usually grotesque. The man Muskett, who had formerly exploded in the case of *The Rainbow*, reappeared to describe Lawrence's pictures as "gross, coarse, hideous, unlovely and obscene." That was his opinion, though what Muskett had ever learned about art nobody could discover. In rebuttal of this unsupported opinion, the defence proposed to cite the opinions of people who did know about art—namely, William Orpen, Augustus John, Agnew and several others. They were refused a hearing, in these ineffable words:

"It is utterly immaterial whether they are works of art. That is a collateral question which I have not to decide. The most splendidly painted picture in the universe might be obscene."

Good God! But in that case why did Mead allow the prosecution to bring in the irrelevant aesthetic issue by saying they were "coarse, hideous, unlovely"? Of course, the fact is that it was not a trial at all, but a foregone conclusion. *Lady Chatterley's Lover* was suppressed on the ground that it made the nude too alluring; the pictures on the ground that they made the nude "coarse and unlovely".

Lawrence, with his "battle, battle, battle", was naturally busily engaged in smiting his enemies; and we have all been amused by his satirical verve in such polemical pamphlets as 'Pornography and Obscenity', 'My Skirmish With Jolly Roger', and 'Apropos of *Lady Chatterley's Lover*'. His *Nettles* and additional *Pansies* seem less happy, though some of them are amusing. Taking the hint from his friend, Rhys Davies, Lawrence produced this quatrain:

> "Lately I saw a sight most quaint:
> London's lily-white policemen faint

in virgin outrage as they viewed
the nudity of a Lawrence nude."

And this was very much to the point:

"Oh what a pity, Oh! don't you agree
that fig-trees aren't found in the land of the free!

Fig-trees don't grow in my native land;
there's never a fig-leaf near at hand

when you want one; so I did without;
and that is what the row's about.

Virginal, pure policemen came
and hid their faces for very shame,

while they carried the shameless things away
to gaol, to be hid from the light of day.

And Mr. Mead, that old, old lily
said: "Gross! coarse! hideous!"—and I, like a silly

thought he meant the faces of the police-court officials,
and how right he was. . . ."

The whole series of these repressive episodes was an unhappy reminder of the survival of obtuse Philistinism, and a curious example of the authority of a State being used to support the religious prejudices of the minister of the interior. The natural question to ask here is what was the practical result of the battle which Lawrence waged with so prodigal an expenditure of his last few months of life? When we discover that *Pansies*, *More Pansies* and *Nettles* contain about five hundred items, it is impossible not to wish all this energy had been devoted to finer work. Writing of Lawrence's battle, Horace Gregory has said: "No novelist (or poet) living to-day finds it necessary to continue the half-century fight for sexual liberation in English writing." This may be true of America, though I doubt it; but it is not true of England.

Freedom has been won for medical and psychological specialists and writers who can show some sort of scientific approach, but this is scarcely true of the artist and poet. Since the battle of *Lady C.*

Montalk was sentenced in London to six months' imprisonment for attempting to print translations of Verlaine. While this book was being written an Australian novelist was given a suspended prison sentence, but the press agitation against an English novel failed. The really discouraging symptoms now appear not among officials but in the universities, where the question asked about a new writer is not: Has he genius? but Is he respectable? As long as this church-warden school of criticism maintains itself, one cannot help feeling that Lawrence won a battle and lost a war.

Persons were found willing to exploit Lawrence's inability to secure copyright by issuing pirated editions of *Lady Chatterley's Lover*. In an attempt to deal with this by issuing an authorised edition so cheaply as to undersell the pirates, Lawrence in March of 1929 had travelled to Paris, where he became involved in negotiations touching not only *Lady C.* but the piracy of his story 'Sun', the issue of *The Escaped Cock* in book form by The Black Sun Press, and problems connected with his publications in America.

It was a misfortune that he had no confidential friend to whom he could entrust such business, which always irritated and depressed him, especially since Paris at that treacherous time of the year brought on an inevitable but very ominous attack of "'flu". He was so ill that the rumour went round that he was dying. He rallied, however, and for some reason decided to take the long journey to Mallorca instead of returning to Bandol. He was now so frail that every journey of any length had to be broken to rest, as in this case he accordingly did at Toulouse and Barcelona. He was much occupied by longings to return to Taos, where Brett and Mabel Luhan waited for him; but even if by some miracle he could have got a visa, he was now too ill to make so long and tiring a journey. The world's glamour was fading for him, and when he arrived tired out at Mallorca he found that "he didn't care for it." Rest, quiet, good food brought him back once more to life and enjoyment of the world's beauty. It is like reading Lawrence of the vigorous years to come on a passage such as this:

"Yesterday we motored to Valdemosa, where Chopin was so happy and George Sand hated it.—It was lovely looking out from the monastery, into the dimness of the plain below, and the great loose roses of the monastery gardens so brilliant and spreading themselves out—then inside the cloisters so white and silent. We picnicked on the north coast above the sea, mountainous, and the bluest, bluest sea I ever saw—not hard like peacocks and jewels, but soft like blue feathers of the tit—really very lovely—and no people—olives and a few goats—and the big blueness shimmering to far off north, lovely. Then we went on to Soller, and the smell of orange-blossom so strong and sweet in all the air, one felt like a bee.—Coming back over the mountains we stopped in an old Moorish garden, with round shadowy pools under palm trees, and big bright roses in the sun, and the yellow jasmine had shed so many flowers the ground was brilliant yellow—and nightingales singing powerfully, ringing in the curious stillness. There is a queer stillness where the Moors have been, like ghosts—a bit *morne*, yet lovely for the time—like a pause in life."

Like a pause in life—it was no more, for only a week or two later Lawrence was complaining that "the bronchials have been acting up and making me swear." Evidently his agent must have mentioned the Paris rumour, for Lawrence in writing hopes that he is "not going to die just yet". Almost certainly it would have been best for him to stay quietly in Mallorca, but as usual he took a dislike to the place where he was ill, especially since there was a recurrence of the malaria. In June we find him staying close to the Huxleys at Forte dei Marmi (near Pisa), while Frieda went to her mother. There Lawrence again fell ill and was moved by car from his pension to Orioli's flat in Florence. This time the illness was one of those stomach disorders such as he had suffered in Oaxaca, a "disturbance" as the Italians call it with careful understatement; and of course the lungs came in too. His state was much aggravated by hearing of the prosecution of his pictures, and Orioli became seriously alarmed by Lawrence's condition of weakness. He lay with head and arms hanging limply over the side of the bed, looking, as Orioli afterwards declared, like an old picture of the descent from the Cross.

Fearing Lawrence might be dying, Orioli telegraphed to Frieda, and as soon as he knew she was coming Lawrence rallied at once. After her telegram came to say that she was starting immediately, Orioli said casually: "What will Frieda say when she arrives?" Lawrence pointed to a bowl of very fine peaches which had been brought him, and said: "She'll say 'what lovely peaches!' and eat the lot." And so she did.

When he was able to travel again Frieda took him to Germany.

where the great event for them was the celebration for Frieda's fiftieth birthday. They ate trout and duck and drank Bowle, but as five of the nine persons present were over seventy the feast cannot have been very hilarious. "It was quite nice," Lawrence reported a little satirically, "but the Germans themselves are very depressed, and they leave me hollow. There are lovely roses on the table, and I dread the effect on Frieda of four large boxes of chocolates." He was unhappy among these large healthy Germans, for he was being treated by one specialist for deafness, and was receiving treatment from yet another lung-specialist, whose diagnosis and advice Lawrence as usual reported in a garbled version to suit himself. But it was there in Baden-Baden that he gave up the long struggle and admitted to himself at last that he was dying. Then it was that he began writing his last poems on the theme of death:

"Not every man has gentians in his house
in soft September, at slow, sad Michaelmas.

Bavarian gentians, big and dark, only dark,
darkening the day-time torch-like with the smoking blueness
    of Pluto's gloom,
ribbed and torch-like, with their blaze of darkness spread blue
down flattening into points, flattened under the sweep of
    white day,
torch-flower of the blue-smoking darkness, Pluto's dark-blue
    daze,
black lamps from the halls of Dis, burning dark blue,
giving off darkness, blue darkness, as Demeter's pale lamps
    give off light,
lead me then, lead me the way.

Reach me a gentian, give me a torch
let me guide myself with the blue, forked torch of this flower
down the darker and darker stairs, where blue is darkened on
    blueness,
even where Persephone goes, just now, from the frosted
    September
to the sightless realm where darkness is awake upon the dark
and Persephone herself is but a voice

or a darkness invisible enfolded in the deeper dark
of the arms Plutonic, and pierced with the passion of
dense gloom,
among the splendour of torches of darkness, shedding
darkness on the lost bride and her gloom."

15

THERE could be no doubt, the Lawrence who came down from the north to the Mediterranean in September 1929 was a dying man. He knew it himself, Frieda and his friends felt it. By now, he was far too ill to think of looking for a new place, so inevitably returned to the familiar Bandol, where the Lawrences rented the Villa Beau Soleil. It was a strange perch for the puritanical Lawrence—a "love-nest" built and furnished for some forgotten amour, with "heliotrope-tinted walls and gold-framed mirrors", central heating and elaborate plumbing. Not all the Mexican serapes and Etruscan embroideries could quench this Vie Parisienne *décor*.

But there were compensations, if only that of being able to keep warm in the winter. And the villa had a fine outlook across the Mediterranean, which inspired some of Lawrence's 'Last Poems':

"This sea will never die, neither will it ever grow old
nor cease to be blue, nor in the dawn
cease to lift up its hills
and let the slim black ship of Dionysos come sailing in
with grape-vines up the mast, and dolphins leaping."

Now he slept alone, with curtains fully drawn back so that in his hours of insomnia he could look at the night-sky and the stars and watch the cyclamen-coloured dawn. Frieda now was not allowed to enter his room until he had recovered from the worst bout of morning coughing. "Come when the sun rises," he said to her. And each morning when she entered she felt his gratitude that he had been granted another day to look upon the beauty of the Mediterranean world. Childishly, with a rebirth of her old faith in his almost magical power she pleaded with him to get well. "Everything flourishes," she said desperately. "Plants and cats and goldfish. Why can't you?" And looking from them to her he answered pathetically: "I want to, I want to, I wish I could." With deeper pathos and sense of frustration, he asked in bitter wonder: "Why, oh why did we quarrel so much?" And she tried to comfort him and share the blame by saying: "Such as we were, violent creatures, how could we help it?"

Friends came to be near him. Every day Earl Brewster massaged him with olive oil, and Frieda grieved despairingly to see him "once so strong, straight and quick", now "so thin, so thin." Even she lost her power over him, compared with the days when the mere knowledge that she was coming changed him from a sick man on a bed to one sitting up dressed and almost normal by the time she reached him. Now he said to her in deep sadness: "I could always trust your instinct to know the right thing for me, but now you don't seem to know any more."

Sometimes he dragged himself from his bed and let them take him on short motor trips, but now everything always ended in weariness:

"And if to-night my soul may find her peace
in sleep, and sink in good oblivion,
and in the morning wake like a new-opened flower
then I have been dipped again in God, and new-created.

And if, as weeks go round, in the dark of the moon
my spirit darkens and goes out, and soft strange gloom
pervades my movements, and my thoughts and words
then I shall know that I am walking still
with God, we are close together now the moon's in shadow.

And if, as autumn deepens and darkens
I feel the pain of falling leaves, and stems that break in storms
and trouble and dissolution and distress
and then the softness of deep shadows folding, folding,
around my soul and spirit, around my lips
so sweet, like a swoon, or more like the drowse of a
    low, sad song
singing darker than the nightingale, on, on to the solstice
and the silence of short days, the silence of the year,
    the shadow

then I shall know that my life is moving still
with the dark earth, and drenched
with the deep oblivion of earth's lapse and renewal.

And if, in the changing phases of man's life
I fall in sickness and misery
my wrists seem broken and my heart seems dead
and strength is gone, and my life
is only the leavings of a life:

and still, among it all, snatches of lovely oblivion, and
snatches of renewal,
odd, wintry flowers upon the withered stem, yet new,
strange flowers
such as my life has not brought forth before, new
blossoms to me.

then I must know that still
I am in the hands of the unknown God,
he is breaking me down to his new oblivion
to send me forth on a new morning, a new man."

Through those days and nights of suffering his courage did not falter. "Never in all that illness and suffering," says Frieda, "did he let the days sink to a dreary or dull or sordid level. Those last months had the glamour of a rosy sunset." He kept up his letters, and even planned a little magazine to carry on a battle of lampoons against the dullards in London. He re-read the Bible in Moffat's translation, and produced his essay, 'Apocalypse.' Remembering that for him religion was always subjective, a projection of the human soul, we can link that up with such poems as 'The Hand of God', 'Pax,' 'Lord's Prayer,' and his remark to Brewster that he had probably been mistaken in "dropping the symbol of God".

"All that matters is to be at one with the living God
to be a creature in the house of the God of Life."

But what did he mean by his "God of Life"? Hardly the orthodox Christian God, for at this time he was reading Gilbert Murray's

Five Stages of Greek Religion, and trying to pierce through the foggy pieties of *Revelations* to the ancient Babylonian and Egyptian symbolism it misrepresents. But naturally his thoughts were much on death, sometimes with a touch of bitterness against his persecutors:

> "I have been defeated and dragged down by pain
> and worsted by the evil world-soul of to-day.
> But still I know that life is for delight
> and for bliss
> as now when the tiny wavelets of the sea
> tip the morning light on edge, and spill it with delight
> to show how inexhaustible it is."

Once more he felt moved to utter a protest against industrialism, "the mechanising of man's body and spirit":

> ". . . men that sit in machines
> among spinning wheels, in an apotheosis of wheels
> sit in the grey mist of movement which moves not
> and going which goes not
> and being which is not:
> that is, they sit and are evil, in evil,
> grey evil, which has no path, and shows neither light
>   nor dark
> and has no home, no home anywhere."

And again he was troubled by thoughts of "the evil world soul" which had become so hideously triumphant. But now all other themes faded from him, his dreams of the ancient gods, imaginings of Cretans and men of Tiryns who sailed the Mediterranean forty-centuries ago, his delight in morning and evening, in sun and moon, gentian and geranium and mignonette, his grief at the greyness of the evil world of mechanical living—all faded in the vision of death, for which he prepared and comforted himself with the ancient Egyptian symbolism of the 'Ship of Death':

> "And it is time to go, to bid farewell
> to one's own self, and find an exit
> from the fallen self."

That was putting into terms of poetry what he wrote to Brett at the beginning of 1930: "I am lying in bed, quite ill, cut off from work and everything, trying to get my bronchials healed a bit—very bad this winter." At one time seven of his friends were staying at the hotel Beau Rivage to be near him, and not long after Christmas his sister Ada arrived. It was a difficult meeting. She could not fail to see that he was dying, and it was not humanly possible for her to hide her distress, as he wanted her to do. Finding speech difficult he wrote her:

"I felt awfully unhappy after you had left this afternoon—chiefly because you seem miserable, and I don't know what to say or do. But don't be miserable—or if you must be, at least realise that it's because of a change that is happening inside us, a change in feeling, a whole change in what we find worth while and not worth while. The things that seemed to make up one's life die into insignificance, and the whole state is wretched. I've been through it these last three years—and suffered, I can tell you."

And then he went on trying to deceive her or himself or both by writing optimistically of the "new state" towards which they were tending through suffering, when they would win "a new sort of happiness", within a very few years, and be quite free of the old life—"patience, and we'll begin another, somewhere in the sun." So he wrote her, pretending impossibilities, but in the note-book which held his most secret thoughts he was writing:

> "My soul has had a long, hard day
> she is tired,
> she is seeking her oblivion."

Old friends in England begged him to see and to follow the advice of Dr. Morland, a young English physician who was making a reputation as a specialist in the treatment of tuberculosis. He came out from England to examine Lawrence, and recommended that he should be moved at once to the Sanatorium Ad Astra, at Vence, which is above Cannes. For Lawrence the advice could be only a confirmation of approaching death. He who had recoiled in such an agony of horror from conscription could not but feel that submission to the rules and routine of even the gentlest hospital was the defeat of his life-impulse. Why did he go? Perhaps he was too weary to resist, perhaps he wanted to spare Frieda further nursing.

It was a weary journey by car and train and then car again, for no one apparently thought of hiring a motor-ambulance. He told the sanatorium doctors that he believed he had had bronchitis when he was two weeks old, and that tardy admission looks like abandonment of hope. But friends were still near him, sending fruit and hyacinths and cyclamens. H. G. Wells came to visit him and the Aga Khan, and the American sculptor Jo Davidson modelled a rather too idealised head.

Lawrence was miserable, and with all the suffering of other patients about him his sensitive spirit rebelled. "This place no good" are the last words of his last letter. Still, he put up with it for a month, and then unable to endure it any longer begged to be taken away. On the 1st of March Frieda had him moved to a villa close at hand.

The short taxi journey exhausted him; and he asked Frieda to sleep on a couch beside him, so that he could see her when he woke. On the next day, a Sunday, he took a little food and she read to him from the *Life of Columbus* he had been reading at the sanatorium. He kept saying: "Don't leave me. Don't go away." About five he seemed to be in great pain, and said: "I must have a temperature, I am delirious. Give me the thermometer." Frieda could now hold back her tears no longer, but in a quick compelling voice he told her not to cry. He asked for morphia, and Huxley hurried away to find the doctor.

His mind wandered: "Hold me, hold me. I don't know where I am. I don't know where my hands are. Where am I?" When the injection of morphia was given, he relaxed, saying: "I am better now. If I could only sweat, I would be better. I am better now." To soothe him Frieda sat by the bed holding his ankle, unconsciously answering his last Prayer:

> "Give me the moon at my feet,
> Put my feet upon the crescent, like a Lord!
> O let my ankles be bathed in moonlight, that I may go
> sure and moon-shod, cool and bright-footed
> towards my goal."

At ten o'clock that night he died.

16

TEN of his friends managed to reach Vence in time to go with him to the grave. His coffin, covered with freezias, violets, mimosa and primroses, was buried without ritual and without commemorative speeches, but as it was lowered Frieda said quietly: "Good-bye, Lorenzo."

On the wall at the head of his grave she had them put his emblem of the phoenix, in a mosaic made from coloured pebbles taken from the Bandol beach. A year or two later Lawrence's body was exhumed and taken for re-burial to Taos, where it lies in a memorial chapel on the slope of the Rockies just behind his ranch and almost shadowed by the great pine tree. It is "a peaceful oblivious place" such as he desired, where in the hot months the bees hum in the many flowers, a jay calls harshly, the wind hisses softly through the pine-needles, and in the afternoons there come the crash and roar of thunder. In winter it is covered with silent snow, with sometimes the scream of an eagle, and in the hard frost under the near sparkling stars the distant howling of coyotes.

After his death Lawrence's books were taken over by his first publisher, William Heinemann, who also published his *Letters*, his posthumous books and the vast miscellany of unpublished or uncollected work entitled *Phoenix*. The uniform edition of all his works was kept in print until war conditions made it impossible, but they are being re-issued as fast as material difficulties admit. Much the same is happening in the many foreign countries where Lawrence has become a standard author, and in Italy a new complete edition is under way.

A very great deal has been written about him. A recent bibliography lists over six hundred items of books, essays and articles on D. H. Lawrence. In the years immediately following his death more books of personal reminiscence were published about him than about any other English author since Lord Byron. It is strange that the peer and the plebeian, coming from the same part of England, should have been alike in suffering the vindictive persecution of their countrymen and in winning a literary fame far greater outside their own country than in it. Those of us who knew and remember

Lawrence still feel his influence as a living thing. As he wrote in the last year of his life:

"What man most passionately wants is his living wholeness and his living unison, not his own isolate salvation of his 'soul'. Man wants his physical fulfilment first and foremost, since now, once and once only, he is in the flesh and potent. For man, the vast marvel is to be alive. Whatever the unborn and the dead may know, they cannot know the beauty, the marvel of being alive in the flesh. The dead may look after the afterwards. But the magnificent here and now of life in the flesh is ours, and ours only for a time. We ought to dance with rapture that we should be alive and in the flesh, and part of the living, incarnate cosmos. I am part of the sun as my eye is part of me. That I am part of the earth my feet know perfectly, and my blood is part of the sea. My soul knows that I am part of the human race, my soul is an organic part of the great human soul, as my spirit is part of my nation."

THE END

SOURCES

FROM 1914 onwards I have the advantage or disadvantage of personal acquaintanceship with Lawrence, but as my object was to write a general biography and not merely an account of my relations with him I have held personal recollections severely in check. In the year or two following his death I had the advantage of many talks about him with Frieda Lawrence, and with such close friends as the late G. Orioli. While writing this book I received the help of personal communications from Frieda Lawrence, Rachel Annand Taylor, Aldous Huxley, Michael Arlen and John Middleton Murry. I have kept wholly to first-hand biographical material by writers who knew Lawrence, except for brief quotations from Horace Gregory's *Pilgrim of the Apocalypse* and Stephen Potter's *D. H. Lawrence.*

In the following list the word '(Letters)' after a title only means that the book contains letters by Lawrence not included in the Huxley edition. Unfortunately he had the habit of sending out his letters too frequently with no more accurate date than "Tuesday" or "Thursday". Precise dating of a letter by internal evidence is a difficult business, so that many of these letters are misdated and misplaced.

D. H. Lawrence. *Letters* (Ed. Aldous Huxley)
The White Peacock
Sons and Lovers
The Trespasser
Twilight in Italy
Women in Love
The Rainbow
Aaron's Rod
Sea and Sardinia
Kangaroo
The Plumed Serpent
Mornings in Mexico
Etruscan Places
Collected Poems
Pansies

Nettles
Last Poems and More Pansies
Collected Tales
Assorted Articles
Introduction to *Memoirs of Maurice Magnus*
Reflections on the Death of a Porcupine
Apocalypse
Phoenix
Letters to Bertrand Russell (Ed. Harry T. Moore)

E.T. (Jessie Chambers). *D. H. Lawrence* (Letters)
Ada Clarke (née Lawrence) and Stuart Gelder. *Young Lorenzo* (Letters)
Helen Corke. *Lawrence and Apocalypse*
David Garnett. Introduction to *Love Among the Haystacks*
John Middleton Murry. *Reminiscences of D. H. Lawrence*
Son of Woman
Catherine Carswell. *The Savage Pilgrimage*
Frieda Lawrence. *Not I But The Wind* (Letters)
Earl and Achsah Brewster. *Reminiscences of D. H. Lawrence* (Letters)
Dorothy Brett. *Lawrence and Brett*
Mabel Dodge Luhan. *Lorenzo in Taos* (Letters)
Frederick Carter. *D. H. Lawrence and the Body Mystical*
Knud Merrild. *A Poet and Two Painters* (Letters)
Richard Aldington. Introduction to *Apocalypse*
Norman Douglas. *Experiments* (contains Magnus pamphlet)
Looking Back
Ford Madox Ford (also Hueffer). *Mightier than the Sword*
Katherine Mansfield. *Letters*
Edward D. McDonald. *A Bibliography of the Writings of D. H. Lawrence*
The Writings of D. H. Lawrence 1925–1930
Lawrence Clark Powell. *The Manuscripts of D. H. Lawrence*
E. W. Tedlock, jr. *The Frieda Lawrence Collection of D. H. Lawrence Manuscripts*
Cecil Gray. *Peter Warlock*

The Studies of Lawrence, by Douglas Goldring and Rebecca West, contain some first-hand biographical material.

ACKNOWLEDGMENTS

THE author and his publisher wish to thank the writers and publishers in question for permission to include in the text of this volume quotations from the following works:

THE HON[BLE] DOROTHY BRETT'S *Lawrence and Brett.* (Secker & Warburg.)

E. & A. BREWSTER'S *D. H. Lawrence: Reminiscences and Correspondence.* (Secker & Warburg.)

CATHERINE CARSWELL'S *Savage Pilgrimage.* (Harcourt Brace.)

ADA CLARKE'S AND STUART GELDER'S *The Early Life of D. H. Lawrence.* (Secker & Warburg.)

NORMAN DOUGLAS' *Looking Back* and *Experiments.* (Chatto & Windus.)

E. T. (JESSIE CHAMBERS') *D. H. Lawrence: A Personal Record.* (Jonathan Cape.)

DAVID GARNETT'S Introduction to *Love Among the Haystacks.* (William Heinemann.)

ALDOUS HUXLEY'S *The Letters of D. H. Lawrence.* (William Heinemann.)

FRIEDA LAWRENCE'S *Not I But The Wind.* (William Heinemann.)

MABEL LUHAN'S *Lorenzo in Taos.* (Secker & Warburg.)

MAURICE MAGNUS' *Memoirs of the Foreign Legion.* (Secker & Warburg.)

KATHERINE MANSFIELD'S *Letters.* (Constable.) By permission of Society of Authors.

KNUT MERRILD'S *A Poet and Two Painters.* (Routledge & Kegan Paul.)

JOHN MIDDLETON MURRY'S *Reminiscences of D. H. Lawrence* and *Son of Woman.* (Jonathan Cape.)

INDEX